# Mothers, Infants and Young Children of September 11, 2001

The group of chapters presented in this volume represents ten years of involvement of a group of eight core therapists, working originally with approximately forty families who suffered the loss of husbands and fathers on September 11, 2001. The project focuses on the families of women who were pregnant and widowed in the disaster, or of women who were widowed with an infant born in the previous year.

This book maps the support and services provided without cost to the families by the primary prevention project – the 'September 11, 2001 Mothers, Infants and Young Children Project' – organized by a highly trained group of therapists specializing in adult, child, mother-infant and family treatment, as well as in nonverbal communication. These therapists are Beatrice Beebe, Phyllis Cohen, Anni Bergman, Sally Moskowitz, K. Mark Sossin, Rita Reiswig, Suzi Tortora and Donna Demetri Friedman. The demands of the crisis led these therapists to expand on their psychoanalytic training, fostering new approaches to meeting the needs of these families. They sought out these families, offering support groups for mothers and their infants and young children in the mothers' own neighborhoods. They also brought the families to mother-child videotaped play sessions at the New York State Psychiatric Institute at Columbia University, followed by video feedback and consultation sessions.

In 2011, marking the 10th anniversary of the World Trade Center tragedy, the Project continues to provide services without cost for these mothers who lost their husbands, for their infants who are now approximately ten years old, and for the siblings of these children.

This book was originally published as a special issue of the *Journal of Infant, Child, and Adolescent Psychotherapy*.

**Beatrice Beebe** is a psychologist, psychoanalyst, mother-infant therapist, and researcher in mother-infant communication at the New York State Psychiatric Institute at Columbia University, USA. She teaches at several psychoanalytic institutes in New York City.

**Phyllis Cohen** is a psychologist, psychoanalyst, child and adolescent therapist, and couples therapist. She teaches child, adolescent and couples therapy at several psychoanalytic institutes and at New York University, USA.

**K. Mark Sossin** is a psychologist, psychoanalyst, and Professor of Psychology at Pace University, USA. His ongoing research focuses on infant-parent interaction, transmission of stress, autism, nonverbal/movement behavior, and early childhood affective development.

**Sara Markese** is a clinical psychologist specializing in the treatment of trauma in early childhood and practices in Fairfax, Virginia, USA. She is a former Postdoctoral Fellow, and current research collaborator with Dr. Beebe, in the Department of Child and Adolescent Psychiatry at the New York State Psychiatric Institute at Columbia University.

# Mothers, Infants and Young Children of September 11, 2001

## A Primary Prevention Project

*Edited by*
**Beatrice Beebe, Phyllis Cohen, K. Mark Sossin and Sara Markese**
*with*
**Anni Bergman, Sally Moskowitz, Rita Reiswig, Suzi Tortora, Donna Demetri Friedman, Joseph Jaffe, Andrea Remez, Adrianne Lange and Marsha Kaitz**

Routledge
Taylor & Francis Group
LONDON AND NEW YORK

First published 2012
by Routledge
2 Park Square, Milton Park, Abingdon, Oxon, OX14 4RN

Simultaneously published in the USA and Canada
by Routledge
711 Third Avenue, New York, NY 10017

*Routledge is an imprint of the Taylor & Francis Group, an informa business*



This book is a reproduction of the *Journal of Infant, Child, and Adolescent Psychotherapy*, volume 10, issues 2-3. The Publisher requests to those authors who may be citing this book to state, also, the bibliographical details of the special issue on which the book was based.



*British Library Cataloguing in Publication Data*
A catalogue record for this book is available from the British Library

ISBN13: 978-0-415-50054-8 (hbk)
ISBN13: 978-0-415-50779-0 (pbk)

Typeset in Times New Roman
by Taylor & Francis Books

**Publisher's Note**
The publisher would like to make readers aware that the chapters in this book may be referred to as articles as they are identical to the articles published in the special issue. The publisher accepts responsibility for any inconsistencies that may have arisen in the course of preparing this volume for print.

# Contents

# Notes on Contributors

## THERAPIST BIOGRAPHIES

**Beatrice Beebe, Ph.D.,** Director of the Project, is a psychologist, psychoanalyst, mother-infant therapist, and researcher in mother-infant communication. She is a Clinical Professor of Medical Psychology, Department of Child and Adolescent Psychiatry, College of Physicians & Surgeons, Columbia University, New York State Psychiatric Institute, and co-directs the Communication Sciences Lab with Dr. Joseph Jaffe. She teaches at several psychoanalytic institutes in New York City, including the N.Y.U. Postdoctoral Program in Psychotherapy and Psychoanalysis, the Institute for the Study of Intersubjectivity, and the Columbia Psychoanalytic Center. She also teaches at the Columbia Parent-Infant Program and at *The Anni Bergman Parent Infant Training Program*. She has developed a video feedback consultation process for mothers and infants. She has published four books: Jaffe, Beebe, Feldstein, Crown and Jasnow, *Rhythms of Dialogue in Infancy* (2001, Monographs of the Society for Research in Child Development); Beebe and Lachmann, *Infant Research and Adult Treatment* (2002, Analytic Press); Beebe, Knoblauch, Rustin and Sorter, *Forms of Intersubjectivity in Infant Research and Adult Treatment* (2005, Other Press); and Beebe, Jaffe, Markese, Buck, Chen, Cohen, Bahrick, Andrews and Feldstein, *The Origins of 12-Month Attachment: A Microanalysis of 4-Month Mother-Infant Interaction* (2010, *Journal of Attachment and Human Development*).

**Phyllis Cohen, Ph.D.,** co-director, is a psychologist, psychoanalyst, child and adolescent therapist, and couples therapist. She teaches child, adolescent and couples therapy at several psychoanalytic institutes and at New York University. She is the founder and director of the New York Institute for Psychotherapy Training in Infancy, Childhood and Adolescence (NYIPT), where she teaches and supervises. She is on the executive committee of the Project in Family Systems and Psychoanalysis at NYU Postdoctoral Program in Psychoanalysis and Psychotherapy. She heads a committee on the interface of child and family therapy in Section VIII, Psychoanalysis and Family Therapy, Division 39, American Psychological Association. She has published many papers on infant, child, adolescent and family therapy.

**Anni Bergman, Ph.D.** is a clinical psychologist. She is an adult and child psychoanalyst, a mother-infant therapist and a mother-toddler therapist. She teaches at several psychoanalytic institutes in New York City, and she is a training analyst at the Institute for Psychoanalytic Training and Research (IPTAR) and the Freudian Society. She developed a program to teach therapists mother-infant and mother-toddler therapy, *The Anni Bergman Parent Infant Training Program* (of New York Freudian Society and Institute for Psychoanalytic Training and Research). She was a pioneer in research and treatment with mothers and infants, and mothers and toddlers. She is the co-author of Mahler, Pine, and Bergman, *The Psychological Birth of the Human Infant* (1975, Basic Books). She also authored Bergman, *Ours, Yours, Mine: Mutuality and the Emergence of a Separate Self* (1999, Jason Aronson Publishers).

**Sally Moskowitz, Ph.D.** is a clinical psychologist, adult psychoanalyst, and child, adolescent, and parent-infant therapist. She is a training analyst, supervisor, and on the faculty of the Institute for Psychoanalytic Training and Research Adult Program in Psychoanalysis, and Child and Adolescent Program. She is a co-director, with Anni Bergman and Rita Reiswig, of *The Anni Bergman Parent Infant Program* of The New York Freudian Society and IPTAR. She is a consultant on infant development and parent-infant relationships at Bushwick Impact, a community-based family center in Brooklyn. She is a graduate of The New York University Postdoctoral Program in Psychoanalysis, a graduate of IPTAR, and a member of The New York Freudian Society.

**K. Mark Sossin, Ph.D.** is a Professor of Psychology, Pace University, teaching in an APA accredited combined program in School and Clinical psychology. He is a clinical psychologist, an adult, child, and adolescent psychoanalyst, a couples and infant-parent psychotherapist, and a specialist in early childhood assessment. He is a training analyst, New York Freudian Society, where he is on the faculties of the Child/Adolescent Psychoanalytic Training Program and *The Anni Bergman Parent Infant Training Program.* He is a member of the clinical faculty and supervisor at the Derner Institute of Advanced Psychological Studies, Adelphi University Postgraduate Programs. He is trained as a Kestenberg movement analyst. He is the author and co-author of books and papers on nonverbal behavior, early development, trauma and therapy, including *The Meaning of Movement: Clinical and Developmental Applications of the Kestenberg Movement Profile* (Brunner-Routledge, 1999). At Pace University, he is director of the Parent-Infant/Toddler Research Nursery and serves as vice-president of Child Development Research.

**Rita Reiswig, M.S., L.P.** is a child and adult psychoanalyst and a mother-infant therapist. She directs with Anni Bergman and Sally Moskowitz *The Anni Bergman Parent Infant Training Program* (of New York Freudian Society and Institute for Psychoanalytic Training and Research). She is on the faculty of the New York Freudian Society and the Institute for Psychoanalytic Training and Research. She is a training and supervising psychoanalyst at the New York Freudian Society.

**Suzi Tortora, Ed.D, BC–DMT, CMA,** is a certified and licensed dance/movement psychotherapist and nonverbal communication analyst for infants, children and their families. She specializes in dyadic nonverbal communication video analysis. She is trained as a Laban movement analyst and a Kestenberg movement analyst. She is on the faculty of the postgraduate Institute for Infants, Children & Families of the Jewish Board of Family and Children's Services; the masters dance therapy program at Pratt Institute; and the New School for General Studies. She is a Board Member of the New York Zero to Three Network. Dr. Tortora is the author of *The Dancing Dialogue: Using the Communicative Power of Movement with Young Children* and several chapters and articles on the use of nonverbal communication and video analysis in parent, infant and child psychotherapy.

**Donna Demetri Friedman, LCSW, Ph.D.** is a Doctor of Social Work. She is an adult, child, and mother-infant therapist. She is the deputy executive director of the Riverdale Mental Health Association, an outpatient mental health clinic. She obtained a Masters in clinical social work and psychology, both from NYU. She completed her Ph.D. working with Dr. Beebe. She teaches attachment theory, child development, and clinical practice with individuals and groups at New York University. Dr. Friedman has published several articles and has co-edited a special issue on attachment for *The Journal of Clinical Social Work*. She is currently co-editing a book entitled, *Attachment-based Clinical Social Work with Children and Adolescents*. Dr. Friedman was given the Outstanding Alumna Award for her work in infant mental health in 2009 from NYU.

## IN ADDITION, FIVE OTHER PEOPLE CONTRIBUTED TO THIS BOOK. THEY ARE AS FOLLOWS:

**Joseph Jaffe, M.D.** is Professor of Clinical Psychiatry (in Neurosurgery), College of Physicians and Surgeons, Columbia University, and head of the Communication Sciences Lab, Department of Child and Adolescent Psychiatry, New York State Psychiatric Institute. His interests include neuroscience and theoretical biology. With Stanley Feldstein he is author of *Rhythms of Dialogue* (Academic Press, 1970); with Clay Dahlberg, he is author of *Stroke: A Doctor's Personal Story of His Recovery* (Norton, 1977); with Beebe, Feldstein, Crown, and Jasnow, author of *Rhythms of Dialogue in Infancy* (Blackwell, 2001). For many years, Dr. Jaffe led a research group on nonverbal aspects of communication that has contained as members Beatrice Beebe and Daniel Stern, whose landmark book *The Interpersonal World of the Infant* (1985) consolidated a revolution in psychoanalytic developmental psychology.

**Sara Markese, Ph.D.** is a clinical psychologist specializing in the treatment of trauma in early childhood. She is a former postdoctoral fellow and current research collaborator in the Communication Sciences Lab with Dr. Beebe, Department of Child and Adolescent Psychiatry, New York State Psychiatric Institute. She has published on the treatment of early childhood trauma, and she is co-author with Dr. Beebe on half a dozen basic research articles.

**Marsha Kaitz, Ph.D.** heads the Laboratory for the Study of Parenting and Early Development in the Department of Psychology, Hebrew University, Jerusalem, Israel. Professor Kaitz's research interests include parent-child interactions in normal and pathological populations; regulation processes throughout childhood; the intergenerational transmission of trauma and anxiety, and the influence of acute and chronic exposure to terror on the antenatal health of women and fetal development. Professor Kaitz also heads a Jerusalem-based home-visiting project for distressed mothers of young infants and has been instrumental in establishing branches of the project throughout Israel and Australia.

**Adrianne Lange, M.A.** is a doctoral candidate in the City University of New York's Clinical Psychology Program. For several years she helped to administer the Project for Mothers, Infants and Young Children of September 11, 2001. Her research and clinical interests are in interpersonal communication, particularly nonverbal communication. She is interested in integrating neuroscience and psychoanalysis. She is also a freelance painter and sculptor.

**Andrea Remez, Ph.D.** is a clinical psychologist as well as a psychoanalyst, couples therapist, EMDR therapist, and mother-infant therapist. She is supervisor and instructor at the National Institute for the Psychotherapies.

# Foreword

**Beatrice Beebe, Phyllis Cohen, K. Mark Sossin, Anni Bergman, Sally Moskowitz, Rita Reiswig, Suzi Tortora and Donna Demetri Friedman**

In this book we describe the Project for Mothers, Infants, and Young Children of September 11, 2001. The group of chapters presented here represents 10 years of involvement of a core group of eight therapists working with families of women who were pregnant and widowed in the disaster, or of women who were widowed with an infant born in the previous year. These therapists are Beatrice Beebe, Phyllis Cohen, Anni Bergman, Sally Moskowitz, K. Mark Sossin, Rita Reiswig, Suzi Tortora, and Donna Demetri Friedman.

This book was originally published as a special issue of the *Journal of Infant, Child and Adolescent Psychotherapy.* We wanted to re-print the journal issue as a book in order to reach a wider audience, for the degree to which this trauma continues to impact these families is not generally well understood. Explication of our work may inform future efforts at prevention following traumatic loss.

This Project was a team effort. Prior to September 11, 2001, most of us knew each other in various ways, but we had never worked together as a group. With diverse backgrounds, each therapist brought something unique to the group, including clinical and research expertise in body movement and nonverbal communication, as well as expertise in adult, child, mother-infant, group, family and couples therapy. By meeting together for an evening every other week over the past decade, we developed our program collaboratively, made all our decisions together, learned from each other, and evolved a strong, creative, and mutually supportive group process.

Each of us had a background as an individual therapist. However, we evolved a team approach in response to the needs of the families. We worked in teams of two to three therapists in our support groups for mothers and children, and in teams of at least three therapists in our filming consultations for mothers and children, and in our feedback sessions for mothers.

The group process has nurtured our thinking and our ability to maintain our effort to help the mothers and children who have experienced this unthinkable trauma. We have continuously worked to understand the internal worlds of the children and the mothers who lost their fathers/husbands in such a traumatic way.

Psychoanalytic concepts have been richly applied in various community settings outside the frame of psychoanalytic practice. These settings include, for example, educational approaches for typical and atypical children, parent-infant psychotherapy, and interventions in war-torn communities. Our work with the widowed mothers and young children of September 11 fits in this tradition. In this Project we applied psychoanalytic views of early child development, attachment, representational processes, object loss, and mourning. We also built upon – and extended the meaning of – a rich body of empirical research on mother-infant interaction, attachment processes, self- and interactive regulation, nonverbal behavior, and parental experience.

One of our original hopes was to begin to develop a model for a long term primary prevention project that could be applied to other situations in which mothers, infants and young children suffer trauma and loss. Our observations allow us to reconsider psychoanalytic propositions regarding death, early development and parent-child relationships. Our longitudinal observations and clinical consultations have informed us about the importance of the representation of a lost parent. Many of the children in our project never directly knew their fathers. We responded to the painful circumstances impinging on these families with understandings gleaned in our prior psychoanalytic work. In turn, our primary prevention efforts can further inform psychoanalytic theory and practice.

World Trade Center, 1999

The photos on this page and on the next were taken by Lucille Tortora. Ms. Tortora, a native New Yorker, has always been interested in photographing architecture and nature. To see more of her photography of New York and of the world, please visit her website at www.lucilletortora.com. Reprinted with permission.

Memorial (WTC), 2002

Photo by Lucille Tortora. Reprinted with permission.

Project therapists. Top row (left to right): K. Mark Sossin, Phyllis Cohen, Beatrice Beebe. Bottom row (left to right): Anni Bergman, Rita Reiswig, Donna Demetri Friedman, Suzi Tortora, Sally Moskowitz.

# Introduction

## Beatrice Beebe, Ph.D.

The Project for Mothers, Infants, and Young Children of September 11, 2001, is described in this book. This group of chapters represents 10 years of involvement of a group of eight core therapists, working originally with approximately 40 families who suffered the loss of husbands and fathers on September 11, 2001. We focused our efforts on the families of women who were pregnant and widowed in the disaster, or of women who were widowed with an infant born in the previous year. These therapists are Beatrice Beebe, Phyllis Cohen, Anni Bergman, Sally Moskowitz, K. Mark Sossin, Rita Reiswig, Suzi Tortora, and Donna Demetri Friedman. This highly trained group of therapists specializes in adult, child, mother-infant, and family treatment, as well as in nonverbal communication. Two of Dr. Beebe's former students, Dr. Sara Markese and Adrianne Lange, were intimately involved in running the Project and contributed key chapters. We also invited Dr. Andrea Remez to co-author one of the mother-child treatments, and we invited Dr. Marsha Kaitz of Hebrew University, Israel to discuss the project. The demands of the crisis led us to expand our psychoanalytic training, fostering new approaches to meeting the needs of these families. We sought out these families, offering support groups for mothers and their infants and young children in the mothers' own neighborhoods, and bringing the families to mother-child filming sessions at Columbia University, New York State Psychiatric Institute, courtesy of Dr. Joseph Jaffe. In 2011, marking the 10th anniversary of the World Trade Center tragedy, our Project continues to provide free services for these mothers who lost their husbands, for their infants who are now approximately 10 years old, and for the siblings of these children.

The disaster of September 11, 2001, mobilized the therapeutic community in New York City. The desire to help families in which a parent had suddenly been killed in the attack was universal. This book describes the response of one group of therapists. We focused our efforts on the families of women who were pregnant and widowed in the disaster, or of women who were widowed with an infant born in the previous year. We organized a pro bono primary prevention project, the "September 11, 2001 Mothers, Infants and Young Children Project" (Beebe & Jaffe, 2002). The chapters presented in this book represents 10 years of involvement of a group of eight core therapists, working originally with approximately 40 families who suffered the loss of husbands and fathers. These therapists are Beatrice Beebe, Phyllis Cohen, Anni Bergman, Sally Moskowitz, K. Mark Sossin, Rita Reiswig, Suzi Tortora, and Donna Demetri Friedman (see Notes on Contributors for therapist biographies). This highly trained group of therapists specializes in adult, child, mother-infant, and family treatment, as well as in nonverbal communication.

The demands of the crisis led us to expand our psychoanalytic training, fostering new approaches to meeting the needs of these families. This Project was unique for all the therapists involved. Although we all had extensive experience with trauma, we were not trauma "experts." We sought out these families, offering support groups for mothers and their infants and young children in the mothers' own neighborhoods, and bringing the families to mother-child filming sessions at Columbia University, New York State Psychiatric Institute. In 2011, marking the $10^{th}$ anniversary of the World Trade Center attack, our Project continues to provide pro bono services for these mothers who lost their husbands, for their infants who are now approximately 10 years old, and for the siblings of these children.

The degree to which this trauma continues to impact these families is not generally well understood. Recovery from a trauma such as this one is a long-term process. However, there is no one picture of the effects of this trauma. The families with whom we have worked experienced and coped with the effects of this trauma in unique and personal ways. Despite the magnitude of the ongoing suffering in these families, there is also remarkable resilience and growth.

When we began the Project, we designed the clinical services that we describe in the following chapters based on our own understanding of the potential effects of trauma on infant and early child development, adult functioning, and the mother-child relationship. Over the past decade there have been a number of research documentations and clinical descriptions of the effects of the traumatic events of September 11, 2001, on young children and their parents living in the surrounding areas of the World Trade Center (Chemtob et al, 2010; Chemtob, Nomura & Abramovitz, 2008; Coates, Rosenthal & Schechter, 2003; Danieli & Dingman, 2005; Hoven, Duarte, Lucas, Wu, Mandell, et al., 2005; Mowder, Guttman, Rubinson, & Sossin, 2006; Neria, Gross, Marshall, & Susser, 2006; Schechter, 2003; Schechter, Coates & First, 2001; Wilson, Lengua, Meltzoff, & Smith, 2010). Consistent with our view, these chapters all conclude that parents and young children were highly vulnerable to the traumatic events of September 11, 2001, and that young children and parents would benefit immensely from prevention and intervention efforts in the face of such trauma. None, however, have focused specifically on the group we targeted, in which the mother was pregnant and the husband was lost.

## SEPTEMBER 11, 2001

In the late afternoon of Tuesday, September 11, I met Dr. Anni Bergman by chance on the street in Chelsea, New York City, where we both live, four miles from the World Trade Center. I knew Anni from her work on mother-child psychotherapy, and by this point she had been in a seminar with me for a number of years. We were both in a dazed state, and we offered each other mutual support. In the next several days I learned on the news that there had been 39 pregnant widows from one firm alone, Cantor Fitzgerald. I could not stop thinking about the experiences of these mothers and of their babies still in utero. I wondered how many others there might be. In the aftermath of the terror and confusion, I left New York City for the weekend, and I was fearful as I returned. From the train on the way home at the end of the weekend, I called Dr. Phyllis Cohen, with whom I had collaborated for half a decade on an intensive mother-infant/mother-child treatment. I proposed a collaboration on a primary prevention project for these pregnant widows and their infants, soon to be born. Phyllis agreed. I then immediately called Anni Bergman, who also readily agreed to participate. Shortly thereafter, Dr. Sally Moskowitz joined as part of the initial group.

The September 11, 2001, Mothers, Infants and Young Children Project (from here on, the "Project") has been working with approximately 40 families, in various capacities. About 80 children have been involved in the Project at various phases. In addition, we included several families who were referred to us through the psychoanalytic community. These families lived at the scene of the World Trade Center, and the mother was pregnant or had just given birth at the time of the trauma, but neither parent was lost. All our families have participated in some or all aspects of the services we have offered, including support groups for mothers and children, videotaped mother-child communication consultations and feedback sessions, telephone consultations, individual and dyadic treatment for mothers and children, and referral. Nearly half of the mothers in our Project have at various times participated in individual adult psychotherapy. A small number of the children have participated in their own individual child psychotherapy. We have had the opportunity to work with a remarkably resilient, courageous, and resourceful group of women, most of whom had never participated in any type of therapy prior to this trauma. Anyone enduring a traumatic loss deserves access to therapeutic services. We continue to search for these families who may join any aspect of the Project at any time.

## BACKGROUND OF THE PROJECT

The Project is housed in the Communication Sciences lab, Department of Child and Adolescent Psychiatry, New York State Psychiatric Institute, Columbia University Medical Center, through the generous collaboration of Joseph Jaffe, M.D. This basic research lab was established in 1965 by Dr. Jaffe, and it focuses on the study of nonverbal behavior. I joined in 1969 to work with Daniel Stern, M.D., an infant researcher and psychoanalyst who worked with Dr. Jaffe. Influenced by Dr. Stern, mother-infant communication research has been a significant focus of the lab since the early 1970s. I became a member of the lab in 1980.

I am both a psychoanalyst, trained by Dr. Frank Lachmann among others, and an infant researcher, trained by Drs. Daniel Stern and Joseph Jaffe. Following a decade and a half immersed in basic research on mother-infant communication, in the late 1980s I began to offer a special type of consultation to mother-infant pairs. This consultation was modeled in part on the work of Daniel Stern (1977, 1985, 1995). Our research uses slow-motion film and videotape to identify subtle communication difficulties in distressed mother-infant pairs. In our lab we first film mothers and their infants (or young children) using split-screen video technology. One camera views the mother and one camera the child, yielding a split-screen view of both at the same time. Then, a psychoanalytically informed therapeutic viewing of the videotape with the parent gives the parent "new eyes" to see how both parent and child affect each other, from moment-to-moment (Lyne & Beebe, 2010). This is a new experience for the mother. She becomes aware of subtle aspects of the communication that she could not otherwise be aware of because these are interactions that generally occur out of awareness. This psychoanalytically informed "video bonding and communication consultation" helps the parent identify, reflect on, and change behaviours that may impede optimal communication with the infant or young child (Beebe, 2003, 2005; Cohen & Beebe, 2002).

## THE THERAPISTS OF THE PROJECT

Following the events of September 11, 2001, the psychoanalytic community in New York City was highly motivated and mobilized to help. Many participated in therapeutic activities at Pier 94, where people received multiple emergency services (Schecter et al., 2001). Because of my connections among psychoanalysts interested in infant and early childhood therapy, the core therapists of this Project were able to form a coherent and highly motivated group in response to this traumatic event.

Phyllis Cohen took a class with me in the early 1990s at the New York University Postdoctoral Program in Psychotherapy and Psychoanalysis, the Institute from which I had graduated. When she began treating a seriously depressed mother with a new infant, Phyllis Cohen brought the family for a series of video bonding and communication consultations with me. We collaborated for the latter half of the 1990s on the intensive treatment of this pair, Linda and Dan, from the time Dan was an infant through age 4 (Cohen & Beebe, 2002). Phyllis was the primary therapist in this treatment. She used her family systems background, integrated with her psychoanalytic approach, to enable this family to participate in a remarkably receptive manner. Phyllis had an amazing ability to speak to the strength of the parents at every point. Rather than feeling threatened by the video lab set-up, the parents expressed feeling lucky to be able to participate in these consultations. Phyllis and I forged a powerful personal and professional bond during the work on this case, which paved the way for us to take the momentous step of embarking on this Project. Phyllis became the co-director of the Project.

Also during the latter half of the 1990s, at the suggestion of Anni Bergman, I began a study group of psychoanalytically oriented clinicians interested in video microanalysis study of mother-infant interaction. The group consisted of Anni Bergman, Sally Moskowitz, and Rita Reiswig. With Drs. Margaret Mahler and Fred Pine, Anni had spent many decades studying the psychological birth and development of infants in relation to their mothers, and she pioneered the "tri-partite" treatment of the mother and child together with the therapist (Mahler, Pine & Bergman, 1975). For half a decade prior to September 11, 2001, in our study group we studied how video microanalysis and research in mother-infant communication could inform mother-infant treatment. Powerful personal, professional, and intellectual bonds were formed in this group as well. Without the remarkable, clinically talented, and dedicated collaboration of Anni, Sally, and Rita, this Project could never have developed. Anni and Rita were both child as well as adult analysts; Sally was a psychoanalytically oriented child therapist and an adult analyst. In the 1980s Anni developed a therapeutic nursery at the City University Clinical Psychology program, and Sally joined as a co-director. Anni and Rita began the "Anni Bergman Parent-Infant Training Program" in 1997, and Sally joined as co-director in 2006.

Dr. Suzi Tortora also attended another one of my study groups during this period, beginning in 1999, thanks to Dr. Steven Knoblauch. Suzi's extraordinary talent in observing nonverbal communication became a critical resource for our Project. As a dance-movement therapist, Suzi used video analysis of nonverbal communication in her clinical practice with infants, children, families, and adults. Suzi's observations of the video interactions were essential to our feedback sessions with the mothers. These observations were translated into practical clinical interventions. Suzi, as well as Dr. Mark Sossin, had a deep understanding of movement dynamics and nonverbal process based on the Laban School.

Dr. Mark Sossin was my Ph.D. student when I taught at Ferkauf Graduate School, Yeshiva University, beginning in 1978. That connection began a bond that was always strong but only fully flowered in the context of this Project. Mark's extraordinary ability to engage children in therapeutic play became an indispensable dimension of the video bonding and communication consultations at the lab. His remarkable ability to observe nonverbal communication began with his work with Dr. Judith Kestenberg. Suzi attended Dr. Kestenberg's first training program, which was co-taught with Mark Sossin and others. Mark Sossin and Rita Reiswig went through child psychoanalytic training together at the New York Freudian Society, which included study with Anni Bergman. Anni was an outstanding teacher, who modeled a deeply respectful way of engaging and thinking about children.

Dr. Donna Demetri Friedman was originally one of my Ph.D. students, where she learned the video microanalysis of mother-infant communication. Joe Jaffe was one of her important teachers in the study of mother-infant rhythms of dialogue. Because of her remarkable clinical talent, I invited her to join the Project. She had already begun to work with families of September 11, 2001, at the clinic she directed, the Riverdale Mental Health Association. Donna Demetri Friedman went on to create an early childhood center at the Riverdale Clinic, using videotaped interactions as a component of the intervention.

Without the dedication of this remarkable group of therapists, this Project could never have developed and flourished.

Only gradually did we learn that most of the mothers did not live in Manhattan or Brooklyn but rather in New Jersey and some on Long Island and Staten Island. Thanks to referrals from the psychoanalytic community, and thanks in particular to Drs. James Fosshage and Gerry Costa and the tireless outreach of Phyllis Cohen, we began an intensive search for therapists who might live in towns in New Jersey or Long Island near the widowed mothers.

Ten other therapists were recruited and became essential to the success of the Project in the early years. Dr. Kerstin Kupfermann, a colleague of Anni Bergman, was also briefly in one of my study groups. For several years, along with Mark Sossin and Rita Reiswig, Kerstin was one of the leaders of a mother-child support group until her retirement. Dr. Naomi Hirschfeld was another one of my Ph.D. students at Yeshiva University in the 1980s. Naomi made an outstanding contribution, and she continues to be associated with the Project. Dr. Linda Taylor and I had crossed paths in the 1990s through colleagues active in mother-infant treatment, and I had always admired Linda's work. We were lucky that Linda joined the Project in the early years, and she and Naomi ran a mother-child support group. Dr. Kathryn Adorney was sent to us by Dr. Jim Fosshage. Kathryn played an absolutely pivotal role in organizing the Project in New Jersey. She worked tirelessly for the Project, and we are enormously grateful to her. Kathryn also participated in a mother-child support group in New Jersey with Naomi Hirschfeld and Linda Taylor. Through intense outreach efforts spearheaded by Phyllis and Kathryn, we were also very lucky to meet Drs. Sarah Behr Moaba and

Kristen Peck. Sarah and Kristen ran a mother-child group in New Jersey in the early years and they were a tremendous asset to the Project. Dr. Nancie Senet and Helge Staby Deaton also participated in the early years of the Project, running a mothers' group as well as a children's group in New Jersey, assisted by Rebecca Melon. We are also grateful for the contributions of Dr. Irit Felsen, Lynn Macarin-Mara, and Jane Schacter Walco, who were briefly associated with the Project. Our thanks also go to colleagues who consulted at the beginning of the Project, Drs. Marvin Hurvich, Sarah Hahn-Burke, Susan Coates and Stephen Ruffins.

## LAUNCHING THE PROJECT

Dr. Sara Markese, Dr. Michael Ritter, and Emily Brodie, student research assistants at the time of the World Trade Center disaster, were invaluable to the organization, administration, and lab videotape sessions of the Project. Sara Markese stayed on and administered the Project for six years. Michael Ritter led the filming team for many years. Sara Markese became a principal editor of this *JICAP* special issue and book. Brianna Hailey, Daniella Polyak, and Edward Liebmann were assistant editors of the special issue.

Despite our organizational efforts, we had no idea how hard it would be to find and engage the widowed mothers. Outreach began in November 2001 when Phyllis Cohen visited the firm Cantor Fitzgerald. Thanks to the dedication of Robert Talbot and the assistance of Allison Lutnick, the Project was able to begin in March 2002, when Cantor Fitzgerald began to introduce our team of therapists to the widows. Pro bono clinical services began in April 2002.

## CONCLUSION

The video bonding and communication consultation and supportive group therapy, in conjunction with standard adult and child therapy and continuous outreach, form the foundation of the trauma response provided by the September 11, 2001, Mothers, Infants and Young Children Project. The Project was conceived from the outset as primarily a clinical endeavor but also with a research component. At this point we have not yet conducted any research, but we hope to do so in the future.

An unexpected benefit of the Project has been the reparative effect the work has had on all involved in its implementation, approximately 25 therapists and 50 psychology student volunteer assistants to date. The mothers and children have described to us that they have been helped in manifest ways by our clinical interventions (see Mothers of the Project, Chapter 4). But as we stand now at the ten-year mark and reflect back on the progress of the work, another group of people touched and healed by the Project has surfaced: the rest of us. We sought to empower and support those most directly and tragically touched by the attacks, yet we were all affected in some way by the tragedy and healed by our involvement in this Project.

## ACKNOWLEDGEMENTS

We would like to thank all of the women and children who allowed us into their lives at such an unthinkable moment and shared not only their grief but also their courage and joy. We thank Allison Lutnick and Robert Talbot from Cantor Fitzgerald for putting us in touch with many of our families. We thank "Tuesday's Children" for assisting us in outreach efforts to find our families.

We are grateful to the many foundations and individuals who funded this project. Funds from the Federal Emergency Management Agency, through Project Liberty and Project Phoenix, covered a large portion of program expenses from September 2002 to August 2003. The Margaret Mahler Foundation also made a gift during that time. The Robin Hood Foundation then funded a large portion of the Project through December 2005. Since then, the Project has run largely on a pro bono basis, with small grants from the Hazelcorn Foundation, the Kenworthy-Swift Foundation, an American Psychological Foundation Visionary Grant, the American Psychoanalytic Fund, the Edward Aldwell Fund, the Los Angeles Fund for Infant Research and Psychoanalysis, and individual donations from the psychoanalytic community. We thank Estelle Shane, Ruth Gruenthal, Pauline Pinto and Alexandra Harrison for their fundraising efforts.

We wish to thank the Derner Institute at Adelphi University, the Waldorf School, the St. Georges Church in Rumson, N.J., and the Church of the Nativity in Fair Haven, N.J., for providing space for mother-child support groups. We thank Howard and Miriam Steele for their generous collaboration on this project, and their help in using the Steele Affect Task as a way to assess how the older children of the Project understood their own emotions and those of other people. We thank our colleagues who contributed to our clinical work in this project: Marvin Hurvich, Sara Hahn-Burke, George Downing, Estelle Shane, Frank Lachmann, Jennifer and Peter Kaufmann, and Stephen Ruffins. We thank Mary Sue Moore, who taught us early on about the clinical use of attachment.

The early years of the Project could not have succeeded without the tireless dedication of the Project's first team of volunteer coordinators and filming assistants: Sara Markese, Michael Ritter, Emily Brodie, and Nicholas Seivert.We thank the student volunteer filming team: Jennifer Lyne, Matthew Kirkpatrick, Kari Gray, Nidhi Parashar, Annee Ackerman, Sarah Temech, Danny Sims, and Jake Freeman. We thank the student volunteer project coordinators: Adrianne Lange, Kate Lieberman, Brianna Hailey, Sarah Miller, Christy Meyer, and Daniella Polyak. We thank our student volunteer assistants who participated in the Project: Eddie Liebmann, Claire Jaffe, Kara Levin, Rachel Altstein, Hope Igleheart, Alla Chavarga, Alina Pavlakos, Julia Reuben, Priscilla Caldwell, Jessica Latack, Carol Schiek-Gamble, Josie Moise, Maria Zieher, Suzanne Kwon, Michael Klein, Sam Marcus, TJ Gambrel, Nicole Selzer, Claudia Andrei, Ali Pivar, Jenny Lotterman, Iskra Smiljanic, Abby Herzig, Pat Cremins, Robbie Ross, Gena Bresgi, Adrienne Lapidous, and Linda Rindlaub. We thank John Burke and William Hohauser of ESPY TV for organizing our videotaping set-up.

## THERAPISTS INVOLVED IN THE EARLY YEARS OF THE PROJECT

**Kerstin Kupferman**, M.A., D.E.S., retired, is the former clinical assistant professor, Department of Psychiatry & Behavioral Science, SUNY Stony Brook, N.Y.; faculty and supervisor, Child and Adolescent Psychiatry, Schneider Children's Hospital, LIJ Medical Center; co-director, New York School for Psychoanalytic Psychotherapy, Training Program for Clinicians in Child and Adolescent Psychotherapy.

**Kathryn Adorney**, Ph.D. is a child, adolescent and family therapist in private practice in Bergen County, N.J. She has taught family therapy at Yeshiva University and Montclair State University.

**Naomi Hirschfeld**, Ph.D. specializes in the evaluation and treatment of young children. She consults to the Elizabeth Morrow School in Englewood, N.J., and the Fieldston School in Riverdale, N.Y. She is an adjunct clinical supervisor at Yeshiva University and a child psychologist in private practice in Teaneck, N.J.

**Linda Taylor**, Ph.D. is a clinical psychologist, adult psychoanalyst, and mother-infant, child and adolescent therapist, in private practice in Ridgewood, N.J.

**Sarah Behr Moaba**, M.S.W. is a child, adolescent, and adult psychotherapist in private practice in Summit, N.J.

**Kristen Peck**, Ph.D. is in private practice in Summit, N.J. She was formerly the coordinator of Child Psychotherapy Training in Clinical Psychology at New York University where she taught seminars in child and adolescent treatment and supervised the clinical work of doctoral students.

**Nancie Senet**, Ph.D. is a psychoanalyst/psychologist in private practice in Allenhurst/Loch Arbour, N.J., specializing in psychoanalysis and psychotherapy for children, adolescents, and adults.

**Helge Staby Deaton**, M.S.W. is a child psychoanalyst and a clinical social worker in private practice. She consults to the NYU Education Department Head Start programs throughout New Jersey and teaches for IPPNJ, a psychoanalytic training institute in New Jersey.

**Irit Felsen**, Ph.D. is a clinical psychologist in private practice in Morris County, N.J. She specializes in research and treatment of severe trauma, posttraumatic stress disorder, and the intergenerational transmission of trauma in families.

**Jane Schachter Walco**, Ph.D. is a clinical psychologist in private practice in Mountain Lakes, N.J. She specializes in the evaluation and treatment of children and adolescents. She was formerly assistant clinical professor of psychiatry at Albert Einstein College of Medicine. She has an expertise in child development, parent-child communication, and child abuse and neglect.

**Lynn Macarin Mara** is a psychotherapist, supervisor and educator. She works with children, adolescents and adults on issues of bereavement, marriage, divorce, family dynamics, parenting and step-parenting, eating problems, anxiety, depression, women's and men's issues and communication skills.

## REFERENCES

Beebe, B. (2003). Brief mother-infant treatment: Psychoanalytically informed video feedback. *Infant Mental Health Journal, 24* (1), 24-52.

Beebe, B. (2005). Mother-infant research informs mother-infant treatment. *Psychoanalytic Study of the Child, 60,* 7-46.

Beebe, B., & Jaffe, J. (2002). Support groups for mothers and children, and parent-child video bonding consultations for mothers pregnant and widowed on 9–11. Grant Request, funded by Project Liberty, 2002; by Robin Hood Foundation, 2003. Manuscript, New York Psychiatric Institute.

Chemtob, C., Nomura, Y., Rajendran, K., Yehuda, R., Schwarz, D., & Abramovitz, R. (2010), Impact of maternal posttraumatic stress disorder and depression following exposure to the September 11 attacks on preschool children's behavior. *Child Development, 81*(4), 1129–1141.

Chemtob, C., Nomura, Y., & Abramovitz, R. (2008). Impact of conjoined exposure to the World Trade Center attacks and to other traumatic events on the behavioral problems of preschool children. *Archives of Pediatrics and Adolescent Medicine, 162*, 126–132.

Coates, S., Rosenthal, J., & Schechter, D. (Eds.) (2003). *September 11: Trauma and human bonds.* New York: The Analytic Press/Taylor & Francis Group.

Cohen, P. M., & Beebe, B. (2002). Video feedback with a depressed mother and her infant: A collaborative individual psychoanalytic and mother-infant treatment. *Journal of Infant Child, and Adolescent Psychotherapy, 2* (3), 1-55.

Danieli, Y., & Dingman, R. (Eds.) (2005). *On the ground after September 11: Mental health responses and practical knowledge gained.* Binghamton, NY: Haworth Maltreatment and Trauma Press/The Haworth Press.

DeVoe, E., Klein, T., Bannon,W. & Miranda-Julian, C. (2011). Young children in the aftermath of theWorld Trade Center attacks. *Psychological Trauma: Theory, Research, Practice, and Policy, 3*(1): 1–7.

Hoven, C., Duarte, C., Lucas, C., Wu, P., Mandell, D., Goodwin, R., . . . Susser, E. (2005). Psychopathology among New York City public school children 6 months after September 11. *Archives of General Psychiatry, 62*(5): 545–552.

Lyne, J., & Beebe, B. (2010). *Learning to look: Mother-infant communication* [documentary film]. Presented at the American Psychoanalytic Association National Meeting, New York, January.

Mahler, M., Pine, F., & Bergman, A. (1975). *The Psychological Birth of the Human Infant: Symbiosis and Individuation,* New York: Basic Books.

Mowder, B., Guttman, M., Rubinson, F., & Sossin, K.M. (2006). Parents, children, and trauma: Parent role perceptions and behaviors related to the 9/11 tragedy. *Journal of Child and Family Studies, 15*(6), 733–743.

Neria, Y., Gross, R., Marshall, R., & Susser, E. (Eds.) (2006). *9/11: Mental health in the wake of terrorist attacks.* Cambridge, England: Cambridge University Press.

Schechter, D. (2003). Intergenerational communication of maternal violent trauma: Understanding the interplay of reflective functioning and posttraumatic psychopathology. In S. Coates, J. Rosenthal, & D. Schechter (Eds.), *September 11: Trauma and Human Bonds.* (pp. 115–142). Hillsdale, NJ: The Analytic Press.

Schechter, D., Coates, S., & First, E. (2001). Observations from New York on young childrens' and their families' acute reactions to the World Trade Center attacks. *Bulletin Zero to Three, 22*(3), 9–13.

Stern, D. (1974). Goal and structure of mother-infant play. *Journal of the American Academy of Child Psychiatry, 13,* 402–421

Stern, D. (1985).*The interpersonal world of the infant: A view from psychoanalysis and developmental psychology.* New York: Basic Books.

Stern, D. (1995). *The motherhood constellation.* New York: Basic Books.

Wilson, A., Lengua, L., Meltzoff, A., & Smith, K. (2010). Parenting and temperament prior to September 11, 2001, and parenting specific to 9/11 as predictors of children's posttraumatic stress symptoms following 9/11. *Journal of Clinical Child and Adolescent Psychology*, *39*(4), 445–459.

# THE PROJECT

# Description of the Project: A Longitudinal Primary Prevention Project for Mothers Pregnant and Widowed in the World Trade Center Tragedy of September 11, 2001, and Their Young Children

Beatrice Beebe, Ph.D.
Joseph Jaffe, M.D.

Since spring 2002, the Project for Mothers, Infants, and Young Children of September 11, 2001, has been providing diverse pro bono therapeutic services for women who were pregnant when widowed by the World Trade Center attacks of September 11, 2001. This primary prevention Project attempted to facilitate grieving in the families and to promote optimal relationships between the mothers and their infants and their older children. This article describes the components of the Project.

## INTRODUCTION

We began the Project with approximately 40 participating widowed mothers, their children born in the aftermath of the disaster (now in the spring of 2011 approximately 9 years old), and their older siblings, altogether approximately 80 children. Among these numbers were also several families where the infant was born in the year 2001 prior to the mother being widowed on September 11, 2001, and two families with infants who lived at the World Trade Center site and were traumatized by the tragedy but neither parent was lost. We are continuously involved in outreach, but we have been unable to find or to involve most of the approximately 60 additional families within this population. As time progressed, we have welcomed new families, as well as new fathers and new infants, as many of the mothers have found new partners or re-married. The original letter that we sent to the mothers in 2002 can be found at the end of this article.

Although there was a great deal of therapeutic intervention available in New York City for the bereaved adults of the World Trade Center disaster, their unborn infants and very young children were in danger of being forgotten (see Weinberg and Tronick, 1998; Gaensbauer, 2002). There were no specific programs available to provide services for these infants to be born amidst such traumatic circumstances. However, the value of mother-infant and mother-child therapy has been well documented (see, e.g., Brazelton, 1994; Cramer et al., 1990; Fraiberg, 1980; Hofacker and Papousek, 1998; McDonough, 1993; Murray and Cooper, 1997; Stern, 1995; van den Boom, 1995).

Most programs in New York City targeted traumatized adults, providing services to address their needs as individuals, but not specifically as parents. In contrast, our specialized training allowed us to identify and to respond to the maternal needs of these widowed pregnant women, their young children, and their infants once they were born. As far as we know, our Project has been the only one to provide a longitudinal primary prevention approach in an attempt to address the ongoing effect of this traumatic loss on these families. We address the parent-infant and parent-child relationship, and the ongoing and evolving needs of even the very youngest victims of this unprecedented disaster. In recent years, we have begun to address relationships in these families as they have evolved to include new partners for the mothers. Now in its tenth year, our Project is the longest-running ongoing clinical service, offered at no cost, to families with young children who were traumatized by the events of September 11, 2001.

## RISK FACTORS FOR THESE FAMILIES

More than two decades of research on maternal distress, mother-infant interaction, and infant and child developmental outcomes have shown that infants suffer when a parent is distressed. Because of our backgrounds in mother-infant research and treatment, and child and family treatment, our Project operated on the assumption that all members of the family were at risk, not just the surviving parent. We thus focused on the effects of the trauma and loss in the mother-infant and mother-child relationships, as well as in the widowed mothers themselves (see Beebe and Markese, this issue; Moskowitz, this issue). However, we conceptualize any trauma effects as "normative" in a trauma of this kind, rather than as psychopathology. Moreover, we have no baseline of how these families were functioning prior to the trauma. We can infer family functioning from our understanding of their histories which have emerged, but it is impossible to determine what relational patterns might have emerged without this trauma.

Even highly competent parents can become destabilized in the wake of a loss as sudden and devastating as that experienced by the widows of September 11, 2001. As a group, the women who experienced this trauma were highly competent individuals and parents. However, parents who experience traumatic bereavement are often preoccupied with their own losses and may have difficulty being fully emotionally available to their infants and young children (Buxbaum and Brant, 2001; Brier, Kelsoe, Kirwin, Beller, Wolkowitz, & Pickar, 1988; Garber, 1997; Kranzler, Schaffer, Wasserman, & Davies, 1990; Moskowitz, this issue; Markese, this issue). Maternal depression and anxiety are associated with mother-infant communication disturbances (Beebe, Buck, Chen, Cohen, Feldstein, et al., 2008; Beebe, Steele, Jaffe, Buck, Chen, et al., 2011; Tronick, 1989; Feldman, 2006, 2007; Field, 1995, 2011; Murray and Cooper, 1997; see Markese, this issue). Inconsistent parental support or emotional unavailability can lead to insecure infant attachment and childhood social and emotional difficulties (Beebe et al., 2010; Carlson, 1998; Lyons-Ruth, Bronfman and Parsons, 1999; Main, Kaplan and Cassidy, 1985). In addition to maternal contributions, infants may also bring their own difficulties to the relationship based on constitutional or developmental factors or biological stresses suffered while they were still in utero (Monk, 2001; Monk et al., 2004). Ordinary variations in maternal caregiving are important even in low-risk populations. Infants who receive more tender and affectionate maternal caregiving show less fearfulness to novelty, more positive joint attention, less negative affect, and evidence a lower physiological index of negative affect (less right frontal electroencephalographic asymmetry), even when differences in infant temperament are taken into account (Hane and Fox, 2006; Feldman, 2006, 2007; Tronick, 1989).

Traumatic loss is often associated with depression, anxiety, and difficulty with mourning (Buxbaum and Brant, 2001; Worden, 1982). Traumatic loss also increases the risk of "complicated grief," in which the person becomes stuck in the mourning process and has difficulty reestablishing a fulfilling life (Shear and Shair, 2005). In a study of 700 survivors of September 11, 2001, 50 percent of those who lost a spouse experienced complicated grief in the initial years following the trauma (Neria et al., 2007). Due to the intense and sudden nature of the trauma and the centrality of the loss, we anticipated that these mothers were likely to experience depression, anxiety, and possibly difficulties with unresolved grief following the traumatic loss of their spouses during their pregnancies.

The idea that a mother's emotional distress during pregnancy may influence the development of her fetus has existed since ancient times (Wadhwa, 2005). Recent research documents that, independent of other established obstetric and socio-demographic risk factors, pre- and perinatal stress, such as maternal distress, is a risk factor for fetal development (Wadhwa, 1998; Barker, 1998; Monk, 2001; Monk et al., 2004). Animal models show that prenatal stress predicts decreased infant learning, increased anxiety, and increased withdrawal (see Lange, this issue). The mother's own subjective experience of the stress appears to exert a larger effect on the fetus than the exposure to stress per se (Wahhwa, 2005). Yehuda et al. (2005) studied women who were pregnant on September 11, 2001, but did not lose their husbands. Infants of these mothers showed altered amounts of the stress hormone, cortisol, at one year of age. Cortisol passes through the placental wall and can be directly transmitted from mother to fetus, potentially altering the infant's physiologically based regulation capacities (Wadhwa, 2005; Dozier et al., 2008).

Loss of a parent in early childhood presents unique and profound difficulties for a child's development (Lieberman et al., 2005). Any child who has experienced the loss of a parent directly, as in the case of the toddlers, or indirectly, as in the case of the unborn infants in our Project, will be affected by this loss, whether or not symptoms are present at a particular moment. Opportunity to deal with this loss through play or talk is therapeutic. Interventions earlier on will help prevent later difficulties. With children, much goes underground, and delayed reactions are common (Bergman, 1999). The interventions of our Project have aimed to give children the chance to express their feelings and to help parents understand the feelings of their children, as a means of preventing later difficulties as development proceeds.

We thus anticipated that a primary prevention project would facilitate the mother-infant and mother-child relationships, the development of the infants who were as yet unborn on September 11, 2001, the ongoing development of the toddlers who had lost their fathers, and the mothers' own recovery processes. Instead of "treating difficulties," our goal was the promotion and safeguarding of ongoing development and, where possible, the prevention of difficulties.

The siblings of these infants, often toddler age or older, were included as central to the Project as well. We aimed to assist the mothers themselves, to facilitate mother-infant and mother-child communication, to provide assistance to mothers in handling developmental questions, and to provide mother and child referrals as necessary.

## COMPONENTS OF THE PROJECT

The Project's therapist team is composed of a diverse group of highly experienced clinicians, including those who specialize in the treatment of severe adult disturbance based on early childhood trauma, mother-child and child treatment, family and couples treatment, mother-infant research and treatment, and video microanalysis of nonverbal communication. The services we provide for the families are diverse as well. Mothers and their infants and young children have been involved in supportive parent-child therapy groups, individual child and adult therapy with project therapists or other therapists through referrals from the Project; children's groups (without mothers); mothers' groups (without children); and video communication consultations and feedback sessions (see Cohen, *Video Feedback*, this issue) focused on facilitating the parent-child relationship, explored with the mother and a team of Project therapists.

The Project began with the following components:

1. Ongoing support groups for mothers, and mothers and children together, to address family concerns related to the evolving nature of the disaster's effect and to facilitate maternal as well as child bereavement (see articles on Support Groups I and II in this issue).
2. Children's groups to promote resiliency among children of similar ages with a shared experience of parental loss and family crisis post-September 11, 2001.
3. A bi-annual (or annual) two-session mother-child video bonding and communication consultation. The first component of the consultation, the filming session, takes place at the Communication Sciences lab, Department of Child and Adolescent Psychiatry, New York State Psychiatric Institute. This session videotapes face-to-face interactions between mother and child and therapist and child. The second component, the video feedback session, is held in Dr. Beebe's clinical office. This is a two-hour consultation with the mother and several team therapists. More frequent consultations are available to any mother who wishes to have them.

These consultations are intended to identify and support the strengths of these mothers, and to address any communication difficulties, or emotional difficulties. Regardless of whether mothers or children participate in our support groups, all families are invited to participate in the two-session video consultation to provide ongoing follow-up.

There is also a research component to this Project, although the potential research value has not yet been tapped. We hope to assess the effect of the trauma on maternal levels of anxiety and depression, and on mother-child communication, and to chart the course of recovery of these families, identifying the strengths and protective factors that contributed to their resilience.

## SUPPORT GROUPS

One initial goal of the maternal support groups was to promote healthy mourning, in which the loss of the husband and father of the family could be gradually worked through and accepted by the mothers, allowing them to move forward in their lives to form new, meaningful relationships. The promotion of healthy mourning is tied to the well-being of the children. Protracted, derailed, or overly intense mourning processes have been shown to lead to the clinical phenomenon of complicated grief (Shear and Shair, 2005). We considered it important to facilitate the normal process of mourning in these mothers because it has been shown that unresolved mourning in mothers affects their mood, functioning, and attachment to their children; reciprocally it affects the security of children's attachment to their mothers (Lyons-Ruth, Bronfman and Parsons, 1999; van Ijzendoorn, Juffer and Duyvesteyn, 1995). Mourning is facilitated by the presence of others who are supportive, nurturing, and able to accept the guilt, grief, anger, and helplessness which are part of normal mourning. We thus conceptualized the mourning as a group process which could be facilitated by the presence of other mothers, and our therapists.

A second focus of the support groups was the mother-infant and mother-child relationships. Mothers were encouraged to bring their infants and older children to the groups whenever they liked. The group leaders observed and facilitated discussions of mother-child bonding, the normal difficulties of parenting, and any reactions the children were having to the loss of their fathers (see articles on Groups I and II in this issue).

At the beginning of the Project, we formulated the mother-infant support groups as described below (description courtesy of Rita Reiswig):

> *The format is an hour and a half meeting, in which the first 15 minutes might be "unwrapping" the baby and getting settled, an hour for group interaction, and a final 15 minutes of "wrapping up" and departure. To begin, the mothers introduce themselves and their babies and say whatever they want about who they are. The group process evolves in a non-structured manner, with each group taking on its own individual style. The aim is for the mothers to coalesce as a group. The therapists are not the "experts." The mothers can learn from each other. If the mothers bring up concerns, they are encouraged to share their own solutions with each other. Mothers are told that their babies are welcome. If they bring the baby, they will want to be "showing" the baby. But they are also free to come without the baby, if they prefer. It is their choice. In case the mother also has a preschooler, these children are very welcome. We supply toys and the designated "child therapist" tries to engage the children so that the mothers can "be" in the group together. Children of this age move back and forth, refueling. After each group, therapists are encouraged to spend a half hour processing the group.*

A third focus of the support groups was the bonding of the group itself, so that eventually these groups could become leaderless mutual support groups, that is, a new community of care (Taylor, 2006). Their shared, sudden loss generated a special bond for these mothers, and doing much of the counseling in groups offered a tremendous advantage. Not only were there opportunities for new bonding with mothers and children in a similar situation, but also reactions to the loss were shared so that vicarious learning could take place (Marvin et al., 2002). Looking back, from the viewpoint of spring 2011, this goal of developing and fostering new communities of mutual care has been realized in several of the support groups.

Over time, the mothers' use of the groups has been variable. The mothers' need for the support groups was more pronounced in the early years of the Project. In the first year following the trauma, there were many other types of support groups available in the greater New York City area, although ours was the only one that focused on mothers and young children. Although originally the groups met weekly, currently groups meet once or twice a month, depending on the needs of the group. Of five original support groups, one is ongoing, one has had a changing membership but meets occasionally, and one is no longer meeting but the mothers are in continuous contact themselves; the other two have disbanded.

## VIDEO BONDING AND COMMUNICATION CONSULTATION

All participants are invited to receive a video bonding and communication consultation. The consultation is a two-session sequence composed of a two-hour filming session at the Communication Sciences Lab, New York State Psychiatric Institute, followed by a two-hour feedback session the following week in Dr. Beebe's private office. Both sessions are attended by a minimum of three therapists.

### Filming Session at the Mother-Child Communication Laboratory

The mother is instructed to play with her child as she would at home, while two cameras generate a split-screen videotape of the interaction. The session is designed to last 10 minutes. Following the mother-child play, the child plays with one of the project therapists for another 10 minutes. When the children were infants, they were seated in an infant seat, and the adult was seated opposite. For older children, mother (therapist) and child sit at a small table with a standard set of toys, and the mother is again instructed, "Play with your child as you would at home." When the children were ages 12–18 months, they were given the Ainsworth Strange Situation attachment assessment. This paradigm evaluates the way the infant and the mother manage a reunion following a three-minute separation (see Beebe and Markese, this issue). The results of the Ainsworth attachment assessment were an important source of information in the feedback sessions.

After age 5, in collaboration with Howard and Miriam Steele, we evaluated each child and sibling with the Steele Affect Task, a series of cartoons that assess children's emotional understanding of common social dilemmas (Steele, Steele and Fonagy, 1994; Steele et al., 1999). For example, the cartoon depicts a child with some juice. While his back is turned, a second child drinks the juice; how does the first child feel now? The child is then asked to choose a facial expression that shows how the first child feels. Then the child is asked to identify other ways that the first child could feel and ways that the second child who drank the juice might feel. Thus the Steele Affect Task measures the child's ability to represent emotions, the match between verbal and visual representations of emotion, complex nuances of emotions and their alternatives, and aspects of the child's understanding of the mind of the other. These evaluations were an invaluable additional source of information for the feedback sessions, as well as a basis for research in the future.

The experience at the filming lab is unique. The mother brings the child into an environment away from the distractions of everyday life. She comes knowing that the focus is the effect of the family's loss on her child and on their relationship. In the mother and child face-to-face play session, the mother gives undivided attention to her child, focusing on what the child is doing. In this way, she experiences an interaction that facilitates the child's opening up an emotional level of communication. Any difficulty represented through the infant's or child's interaction or play, or any difficulty in the mother's ability to facilitate the infant's or child's play, can be identified and addressed in the subsequent feedback session.

Next, the infant or child plays with an experienced child therapist. The therapist-child play is an essential aspect of the evaluation, allowing the child's capacity for engagement with a trained, attuned adult partner to be evaluated. The therapist allows the child to take the lead. As the therapist plays with the infant/child, often a larger repertoire is revealed. We were also able to evaluate the infant's or child's ability to deal with the challenge of the novel partner. As the therapist plays with the verbal child, and reflects on the child's concerns, the child's agenda unfolds. When we review the therapist-child interaction with the mothers in the feedback sessions, much is revealed that the mothers would otherwise be unable to see, without the therapist's assistance. The nondirective play situation facilitates the child's ability to communicate to the therapist concerns and preoccupations through the play themes. In various ways, all of the children in the Project have played out themes of danger in the world, loss, and death. Over time, the children began to play out themes of recovery and repair as well. In the feedback sessions, the mothers gain new understanding of how their children experience and represent the early trauma through play themes and how the trauma may continue to affect their children's development.

### Feedback Session of Video Bonding and Communication Consultation

The video feedback approach is informed by psychoanalysis, by research on mother-infant face-to-face interaction using video microanalysis, and by the Laban and Kestenberg methods of observing nonverbal communication (see Beebe and Markese, this issue). We address mother-infant and mother-child interaction patterns visible on videotape. When appropriate we also address the mother's representations of and transferences to the infant (child) as well.

Microanalytic research describing face-to-face patterns has been extensively reviewed elsewhere (see Beebe, 2003, 2005; Beebe and Lachmann, 2002; Stern, 1985, 1995; Jaffe et al., 2001; see Beebe and Markese, this issue). By the time infants are 4 months, the youngest age of any infant we saw in this group, they perceive contingent if-then relations between their own behaviors and those of the parent, and they can anticipate when events will occur. These capacities enable the infant to anticipate how each partner changes predictably in relation to the other's changes, organizing "expectancies" of "how I affect you" and "how you affect me." These infant capacities for the perception of sequence, contingency detection, and the anticipation of events underlie the generation of procedural, presymbolic representations of interactions (Beebe and Lachmann, 2002). Thus intervening into the nature of the mother's interactive behavior can potentially reorganize the infant's emerging procedural representations of "how things go" or what it is like to be with this partner.

This kind of video feedback communication consultation has been used for more than two decades for mothers in the general population experiencing difficulties with their infants and young children (Beebe, 2003, 2005; Cohen and Beebe, 2002; Downing, 2004; Marvin et al., 2002; McDonough, 1993; Stern, 1995; Tortora, 2006; van den Boom, 1995). Generally, the therapeutic intervention attempts to link the "story" of the presenting parental complaints, the "story" of the parent and child seen in the videotape, and the "story" of the parent's own upbringing. An attempt is made to identify specific parental representations of the child that may interfere with the parent's ability to observe and process the nonverbal interaction. In the video feedback method, any difficulties present in the parent-child nonverbal interaction are translated to words, metaphors and themes by therapists and parent together. This process of the parent watching herself and her child interact, and of translating actions into words, is a powerful method of allowing parents to "see" the relationship.

In the case of the World Trade Center disaster, however, mothers were suffering from a devastating loss rather than from specific mother-child difficulties. Most were high-functioning individuals and competent parents. Therefore, the focus of the video consultation was the possibility of a temporary disruption in parenting in the wake of the traumatic loss and the facilitation of the parent's existing capacities to engage the child. We attempted to facilitate an increased awareness of the effects of the parent's nonverbal as well as verbal behaviors on the child, and the effects of the child's behaviors on the parent. Our effort to identify the strengths of the mother-child communication was central to our approach.

In the week following the videotaping at the lab, mothers are invited to attend a feedback session in Dr. Beebe's private office with several team therapists. The first hour of the session is devoted to a psychoanalytically informed clinical interview with the mother. In the first few years of the Project, we focused on her ongoing reactions to the loss of her husband, the effect of this loss on her children, and her experience of her capacity to cope and to continue to develop as a person herself. The second half of the interview is focused on watching the videotape together. Watching the videotape slows down the moment so that the details of the interaction become quite evident. Because nonverbal interaction is extremely rapid, many of the mother's behaviors are out of awareness.

We usually start the videotape at the beginning, rather than select certain portions. As we watch, positive moments of the interaction are highlighted to confirm and admire what the pair already does well. At particular moments, both optimal and difficult ones, the mother is encouraged to try to see what she herself might have been thinking and feeling and to imagine what she thinks her child may have been thinking and feeling. We also ask the mother to see if she can notice how her behavior might be affecting the child and how the child's behavior might be affecting her. This emphasis on the contribution of both partners to the organization of the exchange avoids the temptation to locate the source of any difficulties in only one partner or the other, for example, in maternal intrusiveness or in infant temperament difficulty.

We often replay the video in slow motion or repeat a section to provide the opportunity to see something that is too rapid to be observed easily in real time. It is a powerful way of helping the mother to observe both the effects of her behaviors on the child and the effects of the child's behaviors on her. She is essentially learning the subtleties of her own and her child's nonverbal language, and the way that they both manage the nonverbal (as well as verbal) "dance." The intervention includes positive reinforcement, modeling, and information sharing (including descriptions of research), as well as interpretation where appropriate. Video feedback on a small amount of videotaped interaction (a minute or two) is usually all that is necessary (Beebe, 2003, 2005; Cohen and Beebe, 2002; Stern, 1995). Nonverbal interactions are highly repetitive, and similar patterns can be discerned over and over.

When mothers can see, for example, their muted responses to their infants or distracted reactions to their young children, or can see their children with low-key moods, difficulty engaging, or sad or angry expressions, the mothers are provided the opportunity to observe and reflect. They can consider more deeply their own responses to their children and the nature of their children's responses. In this process they are supported to facilitate optimal communication with their children and to promote nurturing mother-child relationships. This process facilitates the mother's capacity to engage in her own recovery and to nurture the recovery of her child.

The children born in the disaster's aftermath are now in the spring of 2011 approaching 10 years old. Advances in their thinking capacity allow them to question and understand the concepts of death and loss in a different way. Mothers report that their children are increasingly asking more questions about their fathers. During video consultations and parent-child groups, these children have been observed to understand and manage their experiences of the family's trauma through pretend play behavior often rich in representations of loss and recovery. Because young children often do not show their feelings directly, the child's grief process can be assessed through this play behavior (see Demetri Friedman, this issue; Cohen and Sossin, this issue).

## PROJECT ACCOMPLISHMENTS AND A VIEW TO THE FUTURE

A central accomplishment of the project has been keeping these mothers engaged in a supportive community of other mothers and of therapists as they struggle with their own recoveries and the dilemmas of single parenthood. Because of the devastating impact of their loss, they have many competing needs and stresses in their lives. In many cases, we have reached out to mothers many times before they responded. For some mothers, this process took several years before they could develop a trusting relationship with us. It was important for us to hold in mind that we were reaching out to them, that they were not seeking us out. We also felt that we needed to help them get to us. Providing round-trip car service has been critical to the success of the Project, since most of these mothers live approximately two hours outside of New York City.

In the support groups, mothers learned to talk openly about their feelings of loss and despair and about the possibility of hope. Mothers worked on normal developmental issues such as bed-time routines, children sleeping in mother's bed, children's nightmares, and limit-setting, all made more difficult by single-parenting. In the wake of their grief, many mothers have had difficulties with in-laws who were also grieving. Many of the mothers have bonded with each other and frequently arrange to go out for social activities.

It has been important for us to understand that some mothers who wanted to be a part of our Project in the early years are not interested now, and that some mothers who could not use us in the early years remarkably have been able to do so in the last few years. Whereas the support groups are now largely in the background of the Project (with the exception of one ongoing, thriving group), the video consultations and feedback sessions have become the core of the ongoing Project. This approach has become our central way of following the development of the families we have met over the past nine years. Some mothers have used the video feedback consultations in a consistent way throughout the entire Project, some have used it only in the beginning years, and others have used it only in the more recent years.

In both the support groups and the video consultations, we have helped the mothers to become more aware of the needs of their infants and children, as well as more aware of their own needs. We have helped them appreciate that their own ability to experience their feelings, to mourn, and to move forward in their own lives and development is critical to the well-being of their children. We have helped the mothers understand and accept that the infants born after their fathers were lost have also gone through a trauma, both similar to and different from their own trauma but nevertheless a dreadful one.

In the video consultations we confirmed and admired the mothers' strengths. We helped them to read the nonverbal languages of their children and to understand and tolerate the children's distress instead of needing the children to always be happy. We helped them understand the value of children's play as the children's means of communicating inner needs and conflicts and of working on the loss of the father. We facilitated the mothers' ability to enter the children's play and to follow the children's own themes, such as feelings of anger and loss, rather than directing and redirecting the play away from the children's upset feelings. An understanding of the children's angry play themes as an attempt to work through and absorb the violence of this unthinkable tragedy and loss has been a key focus as the children turned 3 to 4 years and older. The mothers' ability to tolerate the intensity of their children's angry play themes of destruction and loss has been critical in facilitating the children's mourning.

Overall, many mothers have been able to make new friendships, date, remarry; some even have new babies. Other mothers are having more difficulty feeling hopeful about the possibility of making new lives, but they continue the difficult process of healing.

Most of these families would never have used psychological help prior to the tragedy. Almost all find it difficult to use psychological help, which frequently carries a stigma. One of our central roles has been to provide continual outreach and evolving kinds of support over the past nine years to help families actually use the services of the dedicated therapists in our Project. The ongoing, longitudinal aspect of our Project has been critical to our ability to help these families.

Our Project targeted a small group of women who were pregnant as well as widowed. We have still not been able to make contact with the remaining approximately 60 families, despite great efforts to reach all of the approximately 100 pregnant and widowed mothers that suffered so greatly in this tragedy. We remain open to new families at any time. On a larger scale, an estimated 10,000 children lost a parent in the tragedy of September 11, 2001. All of these children, as well as the surviving parents, deserve help. We hope that our work may influence thinking about the emotional needs of all infants, even unborn infants, as well as children and adults who have endured the loss of a parent and a spouse, and about the disaster's continuing long-term effect on the parents and the vital parent-child relationships within these families.

## LETTER TO THE MOTHERS IN 2002

*Support Groups and Video Bonding Consultations for 9/11 Mothers and Children*
September 1, 2002: An expanded view of our Project
Dear Mothers,

We are a group of therapists who are trained in helping adults with loss and trauma. We also have special expertise in mother-infant and mother-child communication and bonding. Our purpose is to help women who were pregnant and widowed on 9/11.

As you may know, we have organized support groups for mothers and their infants and any older children. These groups will run for two years. We currently have four groups in New Jersey, one in Long Island, and one in Manhattan. As we continue to look for the other mothers in this situation, other groups could potentially form. These groups, and our other services, are offered free of charge.

We are writing you this letter for several reasons. First, we would like to encourage you to find out about our support groups. These groups will create a space and time for you to gradually work through this incomprehensible loss, and to share your experiences with other women who know what you are going through. In the wake of this disaster, creating a space to experience all your reactions, in a mutually supportive and safe environment, will help you adjust and recover.

Second, when we began our Project, we were focusing on mothers and infants. As we have gone along, we have widened the scope to include all of the children. This has been an important addition. Thus, our support groups are specifically geared toward all of your children.

Third, as your "infant," now a toddler, is approaching 12 months, we are hoping to see you for a video bonding consultation. If you have any older children, we hope to meet them as well. As you may know, in addition to the support groups, we are also offering mother-toddler and mother-child video bonding consultations. The bonding consultations will help you to read your child's nonverbal "language" and to become aware of the ways that you may respond.

The video bonding consultation occurs in two steps. The first step is a visit to Dr. Beebe's mother-child communication lab at N.Y.S. Psychiatric Institute, Columbia Presbyterian Medical Center. Dr. Phyllis Cohen, co-director of the Project will participate in the filming. Video cameras will make split-screen recordings of mother-toddler or mother-child play. Audio recordings will also be made because vocal rhythms have been shown to be a critical part of mother-child communication. In addition to the play, at 12 months your toddler will be filmed during a brief separation from you. This will give us a good picture of how your child is able to use you as a secure base. You will also be asked to fill out some questionnaires about your mood, your loss, your experience of parenting, and your baby's temperament. These questionnaires will be used by Drs. Beebe and Cohen to better understand the filming. This visit takes about an hour and a half.

In the second step of the video bonding, you are offered a video feedback consultation with Drs. Beebe and Cohen in Dr. Beebe's Manhattan office in Chelsea. One and a half hours are set aside for a leisurely discussion of the film, mother-toddler and mother-child communication, and parenting in general. The video bonding consultations are available to you whether or not you join a support group. Both the filming consultation and feedback session are offered free of charge.

Our Project also has a research component, in which you may participate if you wish. The research is concerned with the effect of trauma on infant and child development. Some of us have years of experience in doing research and observations of infant and child development. We believe that such research is of great benefit to parents and caregivers. If you agree to participate in this aspect of the Project, we will simply ask you if we may use our observations, videotapes, and questionnaires for this purpose. All information is strictly confidential; your privacy is protected by using code numbers; there will be no public use of the videotapes; all information is based on the group (no individuals are identifiable). Participation in this aspect of the Project is entirely voluntary, and if you decline, of course all other aspects of the Project are available to you.

We are encouraging you to participate in the various aspects of the Project. Therapist-led support groups have been demonstrated to help people recover in traumatic circumstances. Mother-child communication video consultations have also been shown to be helpful to mothers and children. Referrals for adult individual treatment, individual on-going parent-infant treatment, or medication consultation can be provided upon request at any time. All phases of the Project are strictly voluntary.

In the long term, even after the groups end, we would like to be a resource for you and your children.

Sincerely yours,
Beatrice Beebe, Ph.D. and the therapists of the Project

## REFERENCES

Barker, D. (1998) In utero programming of chronic disease. *Clinical Science*, *95*, 115–128.

Beebe, B. (2003). Brief mother-infant treatment using psychoanalytically informed video microanalysis. *Infant Mental Health Journal*, *24*(1), 24–52.

Beebe, B. (2005). Mother-infant research informs mother-infant treatment. *Psychoanalytic Study of the Child*, *60*, 7–46.

Beebe, B., & Jaffe, J. (2002). Support groups for mothers and children, and parent-child video bonding consultations, for mothers pregnant and widowed on 9–11. Grant Request, Funded by Project Liberty, 2002; by Robin Hood Foundation, 2003. *Manuscript, New York Psychiatric Institute*.

Beebe, B., Jaffe, J., Buck, K., Chen, H., Cohen, P., Feldstein, S., & Andrews, H. (2008). Maternal depression at 6 weeks postpartum and mother-infant 4-month self-and interactive regulation. *Infant Mental Health Journal*, *29*(5), 442–71.

Beebe, B., Jaffe, J., Markese, S., Buck, K., Chen, H., Cohen, P., Bahrick, L., & Andrews, H. (2010). The origins of 12-month attachment: A microanalysis of 4-month mother-infant interaction. *Attachment & Human Development*, *12*(1–2), 3–141.

Beebe, B., Markese, S., Steele, M., Buck, K., Cohen, P., Reuben, J., . . . Jaffe, J. (2011, in preparation). Paths of risk and resilience in 4-month mother-infant interaction: From 6-week maternal depression to 12-month insecure and secure attachment. New York State Psychiatric Institute.

Beebe, B., Steele, M., Jaffe, J., Buck, K., Chen, H., Cohen, P., . . . Feldstein, S. (2011). Maternal anxiety and 4-month mother-infant self- and interactive contingency. *Infant Mental Health Journal*, *32*(2), 174–206.

Beebe, B., Knoblauch, S., Rustin, J., & Sorter, D. (2005). *Form of intersubjectivity and infant research and adult treatment*. New York: Other Press.

Beebe, B., & Lachmann, F. (2002). *Infant research and adult treatment: Co-constructing interactions*. Hillsdale, NJ: The Analytic Press.

Bergman, A. (1999). *Ours, yours, mine: Mutuality and the emergence of the separate self*. Northvale, NJ: Jason Aronson.

Brazelton, T. B. (1994). Touchpoints: Opportunities for preventing problems in the parent-child relationship. *Acta Paediatrica*, *394*(Suppl.), 35–39.

Brier, A., Kelsoe, J., Kirwin, P., Beller, S., Wolkowitz, O., & Pickar, D. (1988). Early parental loss and development of adult psychopathology. *Archives of General Psychiatry*, *45*, 987–93.

Buxbaum, L., & Brant, J. (2001, July/August). When a parent dies from cancer. *Clinical Journal of Oncology Nursing*, *5*(4).

Carlson, E. (1998). A prospective longitudinal study of attachment disorganization/disorientation. *Child Development*, *69*(4), 1107–1128.

Cohen, P. M., & Beebe, B. (2002). Video feedback with a depressed mother and her infant: A collaborative individual psychoanalytic and mother-infant treatment. *Journal of Infant, Child, and Adolescent Psychotherapy*, *2*(3), 1–55.

Cramer, B., Robert-Tissot, C., Stern, D., Serpa-Rusconi, S., De Muralt, M., Besson, G., . . . Stern, D. N. (1990). Outcome evaluation in brief mother-infant psychotherapy: A preliminary report. *Infant Behavior and Development*, *11*(3), 278–300.

Downing, G. (2004). Emotion, body, & parent-infant interaction. In J. Nadel & D. Muir (Eds.), *Emotional development: Recent research advances* (pp. 429–449). Oxford: Oxford University Press.

Dozier, M., Peloso, E., Lewis, E., Laurenceau, J., & Levine, S. (2008). Effects of an attachment-based intervention of the cortisol production of infants and toddlers in foster care. *Development and Psychopathology*, *20*(3), 845–859.

Feldman, R. (2006). From biological rhythms to social rhythms: Physiological precursors of mother–infant synchrony. *Developmental Psychology*, *4*, 175–188.

Feldman, (2007). Parent–infant synchrony and the construction of shared timing: Physiological precursors, developmental outcomes, and risk conditions. *Journal of Child Psychology and Psychiatry*, *48*, 329–354.

Field, T. (1995). Infants of depressed mothers. *Infant Behavior and Development*, *18*, 1–13.

Field, T. (2011). Prenatal depression effects on early development: A review. *Infant Behavior & Development*, *34*(1), 1–14.

Fraiberg, S. (1980). *Clinical studies in infant mental health: The first year of life*. New York: Basic Books.

Gaensbauer, T. (2002). Trauma in infancy. *Infant Mental Health Journal*, *23*(3), 259–277.

Garber, B. (1997). Parent loss in childhood and adult psychopathology. In L. Flaherty & H. Horowitz (Eds.), *Adolescent psychiatry, Vol. 21: Developmental and clinical studies. Annals of the American Society for Adolescent Psychiatry*, (pp. 101–118). Hillsdale, NJ: The Analytic Press.

Hane, A. A., & Fox, N. (2006). Ordinary variations in maternal caregiving influence human infants' stress reactivity. *Psychological Science*, *17*(6), 550–556.

Harris, T., Brown, G., & Bifulco, A. (1986). Loss of parent in childhood and adult psychiatric disorder: The role of lack of adequate parental care. *Psychological Medicine*, *16*, 641–659.

Hofacker, N., & Papousek, M. (1998). Disorders of excessive crying, feeding, and sleeping: The Munich interdisciplinary research and intervention program. *Infant Mental Health Journal*, *19*(2), 180–201.

Jaffe, J., Beebe, B., Feldstein, S., Crown, C. L., & Jasnow, M. (2001). Rhythms of dialogue in infancy. *Monographs of the Society for Research in Child Development*, *66*(Serial No. 265).

Kranzler, E., Schaffer, D., Wasserman, G., & Davies, M. (1990). Early childhood bereavement. *Journal of the American Academy of Child and Adolescent Psychiatry*, *29*, 413–520.

Lieberman, A., Compton, N., Van Horn, P., & Ghosh Pippen, C. (2005). *Losing a parent to death in the early years: Guidelines for the treatment of traumatic bereavement in infancy and early childhood*. Washington, DC: Zero to Three Press.

Lyons-Ruth, K., Bronfman, E., & Parsons, E. (1999). Maternal frightened, frightening or atypical behavior and disorganized infant attachment patterns. In J. Vondra & D. Barnett (Eds.), *Monographs of the Society for Research in Child Development 64*(3), pp. 67–96. Serial No. 258.

Lyons-Ruth, K. (1998). Attachment disorganization: Unresolved loss, relational violence, and lapses in behavioral and attentional strategies. In J. Cassidy & P. Shaver (Eds.), *Handbook of Attachment Theory and Research* (pp. 520–554). New York: Guilford Press.

Main, M., Kaplan, N., & Cassidy, J. (1985). Security in infancy, childhood, and adulthood: A move to the level of representation. In I. Bretherton & E. Waters (Eds.), *Monographs of the Society for Research in Child Development*. Vol. 50(1–2), 66–104.

McDonough, S. (1993). Interaction guidance. In C. Zeanah (Ed.), *Handbook of infant mental health* (pp. 414–426). New York: Guilford.

Marvin, R., Cooper, G., Hoffman, K., & Powell, B. (2002). The circle of security project: Attachment-based intervention with caregiver-preschool child dyads. *Attachment and Human Development*, *4*(1), 107–24.

Monk, C. (2001). Stress and mood disorders during pregnancy: Implications for child development. *Psychiatric Quarterly*, *72*(4), 347–357.

Monk, C., Sloan, R., Myers, M., Ellman, L., Werner, E., Jeon, J., Tager, F., & Fifer, W. (2004). Fetal heart rate reactivity differs by women's psychiatric status: An early marker for developmental risk? *Journal of the American Academy of Child and Adolescent Psychiatry*, *43*(3), 283–290.

Murray, L., Fiori-Cowley, A., Hooper, R., & Cooper, P. (1996). The impact of postnatal depression and associated adversity on early mother-infant interactions and later infant outcome. *Child Development*, *67*, 2512–2526.

Murray, L., & Cooper, P. (1997). *Postpartum depression and child development*. New York: Guilford Press.

Neria, Y., Gross, R., Marshall, R., & Susser, E. (Eds.) (2006). *9/11: Mental Health in the Wake of Terrorist Attacks*. Cambridge, England: Cambridge University Press.

Neria, Y., Gross, R., Litz, B., Maguen, S., Insel, B., Seirmarco, G., Rosenfeld, H., . . . Marshall, R. (2007). Prevalence and psychological correlates of complicated grief among bereaved adults 2.5–3.5 years after September 11th attacks. *Journal of Traumatic Stress*, *20*(3), 251–62.

Shear, M. K., & Shair, H. (2005). Attachment, loss and complicated grief. *Developmental Psychobiology*, *47*, 53–67.

Sroufe, A. (1983). Infant-caregiver attachment and patterns of adaptation in the preschool: The roots of maladaptation and competence. In M. Permutter (Ed.), *Minnesota Symposia on Child Psychology* (Vol. 16, pp. 41–79). Hillsdale, NJ: Erlbaum Associates.

Steele, M., Steele, H., & Fonagy, P. (1994). The affect task protocol and coding guidelines. Unpublished manuscript, University College London.

Steele, M., Croft, C., & Fonagy, P. (1999). Infant-mother attachment at one-year predicts children's understanding of mixed-emotions at six years. *Social Development*, *8*, 161–78.

Stern, D. (1985). *The interpersonal world of the infant: A view from psychoanalysis and developmental psychology*. New York: Basic Books.

Stern, D. (1995). *The motherhood constellation*. New York: Basic Books.

Taylor, S. E. (2006). Tend and befriend: Biobehavioral bases of affiliation under stress. *Current Directions in Psychological Science, 15*, 273–277.

Tortora, S. (2006). *The dancing dialogue: Using the communicative power of movement with young children*. Baltimore: Paul H. Brookes Publishing Co., Inc.

Tremblay, G., & Israel, A. (1998). Children's adjustment to parental death. *Clinical Psychology-Science and Practice, 5*(4), 424–438.

Tronick, E. (1989). Emotions and emotional communication in infants. *American Psychologist, 44*, 112–119.

Van den Boom, D. (1995). Do first-year intervention effects endure: Follow-up during toddlerhood of a sample of Dutch irritable infants. *Child Development, 66*, 1798–1816.

Van Ijzendoorn, M., Juffer, F., & Duyvesteyn, M. (1995). Breaking the intergenerational cycle of insecure attachment: A review of the effects of attachment-based interventions on maternal sensitivity and infant security. *Journal of Child Psychology and Psychiatry, 36*(2), 225–248.

Wadhwa, P. (1998). Prenatal stress and life-span development. In H. Friedman (Ed.), *Encyclopedia of mental health* (Vol. 3, pp. 265–280). San Diego: Academic Press.

Wadhwa, P. (2005). Psychoneuroendocrine processes in human pregnancy influence fetal development and health. *Psychoneuroendocrinology, 30*, 724–743.

Weinberg, K., & Tronick, E. (1998). The impact of maternal psychiatric illness on infant development. *Journal of Clinical Psychiatry, 59*(2), 53–61.

Worden, J. (1982). *Grief counseling and grief therapy*. New York: Springer.

Worden, J., & Silverman, P. (1996). Parental death and the adjustment of school age children. *Omega, 33*, 99–102.

Yehuda, R., Engel, S., Brand, S., Seckl, J., Marcus, S., & Berkowitz, G. (2005). Transgenerational effects of posttraumatic stress disorder in babies of mothers exposed to the World Trade Center attacks during pregnancy. *Journal of Endocrinology & Metabolism, 90*(7), 4115–4118.

Yehuda, R., Southwick, S., Nussbaum, G., Wahlby, V., Giller, E., & Mason, J. (1990). Low urinary cortisol excretion in patients with post-traumatic stress disorder. *Journal of. Nervous and Mental Disease, 178*, 366–369.

Zeanah, C., Anders, T., Seifer, R., & Stern, D. (1989). Implications of research on infant development for psychodynamic theory and practice. *Journal of the American Academy of Child and Adolescent Psychiatry, 28*, 657–668.

# Theory and Research That Informed the Clinical Approach of the Project for Mothers, Infants, and Young Children of September 11, 2001

Beatrice Beebe, Ph.D.
Sara Markese, Ph.D.

We outline the central clinical theories that informed the Project for Mothers, Infants, and Young Children of September 11, 2001. We looked to Bowlby, Winnicott, Mahler, and Ainsworth for the core ideas about the nature of loss and the mother-infant relationship. We also looked to empirical infant research and the microanalysis of videotaped mother-infant interaction to understand early communication patterns. An understanding of nonverbal communication and its use in video feedback was central to our approach. We also describe early childhood psychotherapy and mother-child support groups.

## INTRODUCTION

Our approach was based on the research and therapeutic experience of our group of psychoanalysts, mother-infant clinicians, and researchers who had done significant work in mother-child research and treatment before the attacks of September 11, 2001. There was a great deal of therapeutic intervention available in New York City for victims of the disaster (Barbanel & Sternberg, 2006; Chemtob, Nomura, Rajendran, Yehuda, Schwartz, et al., 2010; Danieli & Dingman, 2005; Coates, Rosenthal, & Schechter, 2003; Schechter, Coates, & First, 2001). However, infants and the mother-infant relationship were not targeted for intervention except by our Project. To those professionals involved in the arenas of infant development and parent-child psychotherapy, the idea was taken for granted that women pregnant and widowed in the face of a sudden, traumatic loss would face particular difficulties. There might be difficulties in maintaining their own emotional equilibrium and in fostering optimal emotional relationships with their newborns and young children. However, as we applied for funding, made outreach attempts to World Trade Center firms, and contacted the women themselves, it became clear that this idea could not be taken for granted.

From the point of view of the general community, these infants born to the pregnant widows were "never directly exposed to the trauma." Consequently, we needed to explain our reasons for thinking that both the infant and mother would benefit from therapeutic support following this trauma. Part of our job was to explain in which ways the trauma might have affected the developing fetus (see Lange, this issue). How and why would maternal states of mind emerging from trauma and loss affect the developing fetus and, later, the infant and the mother-infant relationship (see Markese, this issue)? In short, we needed to make explicit our reasons for offering preventive "well-baby" visits and the theory and research underlying our treatment approach.

In the articles that follow, there are many references to the clinical theory and developmental research that informed our work with these particular women, their infants born after the tragedy, and their older children. Here we outline the central clinical theories and research findings that informed our approach, particularly those that address the effects of distressed maternal states of mind on infant and child development. We refer the reader to the appropriate articles for more detail.

## THEORETICAL FRAMES THAT INFORMED THE PROJECT

To understand how maternal states of mind emerging from trauma and loss might affect the developing mother-infant relationship and infant/child development, we look to the core ideas about the nature of loss itself, and about the mother-infant relationship, of four theoreticians whose ideas continue to inform the field of developmental and clinical psychology: Bowlby, Winnicott, Mahler, and Ainsworth.

Bowlby's extensive work on attachment, separation, and loss informed the Project (Bowlby, 1951, 1969, 1973, 1980). He wrote about the immense difficulties faced within the mother-infant attachment system with the advent of sudden, traumatic loss. He described the powerful impact of psychological deprivation on a child when a parent is preoccupied with intense states of grief. He also described normal grief and complicated grief reactions, the two on a continuum of intensity and time scale (see also Shear & Shair, 2005). Bowlby stressed the inherent risk in complicated grief, when the griever isolates herself from others and shields herself from the outer world to protect against any disconfirming realities that might interfere with the need to hold onto the belief that the loved one is missing, but not gone forever (Bowlby, 1980). Avoidance of the reality of the loss, or "defensive exclusion," which can be protective and normal in healthy mourning, may become unhealthy and dissociative in complicated grief states (Shear & Shair, 2005). This avoidance leaves the mourner disconnected from the present and unable to move forward into the future and to redefine her own life without the lost attachment figure (Bowlby, 1980). Grief symptoms usually resolve as the mourner works to face the loss in phases, to revise her internalized representations of the deceased person in order to incorporate the reality of the death, and to re-define the reality of life without the deceased. Failure to do so results in the syndrome of complicated grief (Shear & Shair, 2005). The implications of prolonged states of complicated grief have begun to be described in the research literature, showing biobehavioral regulation and neurological processing differences in those engaged in the complicated mourning of lost attachment figures (Shear & Shair, 2005). The implications of complicated grief have also been described in the literature on research and treatment of adults with early losses (Beebe, 2004; Brier et al., 1988; Garber, 1997).

D. W. Winnicott advanced the powerful idea that there is no "separate" infant early in development. Rather, every infant exists within a mother-infant relationship (Winnicott, 1965). He held that the infant cannot exist without the mother's physical and emotional care, which shape the infant's development and emerging awareness of self and other. Winnicott's position informs the current view advanced by mother-infant psychologists that a trauma for the mother inherently affects the infant as well.

Margaret Mahler, in collaboration with Fred Pine and Anni Bergman, shared with Winnicott an emphasis on the inter-dependence of mother and infant. She described the mother as "the maternal symbiotic partner," helping her infant to maintain homeostasis of physical and emotional states (Mahler, 1967; Mahler, Pine, & Bergman, 1975; see Moskowitz, this issue). The process by which the mother and the infant together regulate infant states in turn forms the foundation of the developing infant's characteristic neurobiological processes. Thus, in Mahler's view, early interactions between mother and infant, comprising subtle mutual cueing exchanges, shape the processes by which an infant becomes "the child of his particular mother" (Mahler, 1967). Mahler's views set the stage for many aspects of current empirical investigations of the mother-infant relationship.

Mahler described a "rapprochement crisis." This third subphase of the separation-individuation process is characterized by the toddler's return to enthusiastic sharing of experiences with mother, but also by the child's awareness of his/her separateness from the mother. This recognition leads to an acute sense of vulnerability, and the developmentally appropriate and universal rapprochement crisis. The child struggles with all separations as he/she experiences the conflicted positions of wanting to be simultaneously with, and separate from, the mother (Mahler, 1967; Mahler, Pine, & Bergman, 1975).

Anni Bergman further developed this idea (see Bergman & Harpaz-Rotem, 2004; Harpaz-Rotem & Bergman, 2006; see Moskowitz, this issue). "During rapprochement, the mother becomes the narrator of what mother and child experience together, as the child develops language skills and joins the mother in creating stories . . . Rather than seeing the rapprochement crisis solely as a transition to separate self- and object representations, we can see it also as a time when mother and child begin to share their experience of each other and the world through storytelling" (Bergman & Harpaz-Rotem, 2004, p. 564). In the case of those infants born after the loss of their father on September 11, 2001, the story of the lost father became an important influence on the developing mother-child relationship. This proved to be an extremely difficult area in which mothers sought therapists' support and guidance.

Both Winnicott and Mahler theorized that the earliest mother-infant interaction patterns, which reflect the mother's state of mind toward the infant, organize aspects of the infant's developing ways of interacting, of regulating states, and of viewing self and other. Current empirical research has confirmed aspects of these ideas. Particular patterns of reciprocal interactions, ways that infants affect mothers, and mothers affect infants, do reflect maternal states of mind and do predict infant development (Beebe et al., 2007; Beebe et al., 2008; Beebe et al., 2010; Beebe et al., 2011; Jaffe, Beebe, Feldstein, Crown, & Jasnow, 2001; Tronick, 1989; Feldman, 2006, 2007; Field, 1995, 2011; see Beebe, *Description of the Project,* and Markese, *Parental Loss and Trauma*, this issue).

The work of Mary Ainsworth adds another view of the developing relationship between infant and mother. We refer to Ainsworth's work, further developed by three decades of extensive research, as "Attachment Theory." The Ainsworth Strange Situation provides an important means of assessing the security (versus insecurity) of the developing mother-infant relationship once the infant is one year old (Ainsworth, Blehar, Waters, & Wall, 1978). In the Ainsworth "Strange Situation" attachment test, mother and infant go through periods of free play, separations, and reunions. Based on the balance between the infant's ability to use the mother as a "secure base" to calm down after the separation, and his or her ability to return to play, infants can be classified as having secure or insecure attachment styles. Insecurity involves a loss of balance, tilting toward over-involvement with the mother, attempting but failing to use her as a secure base; or over-involvement with independent play and avoidance of maternal contact.

While there would be no reason to think that this particular group of women would have had any difficulties in their relationships with their infants if the World Trade Center disaster had not occurred, the trauma that the women endured put them and their children at risk. When a parent is bereaved or depressed, the ensuing preoccupation, distraction, sadness, or depression will likely in some way compromise the parent's emotional availability for the child (Buxbaum & Brant, 2001; Garber, 1997; Harris, Brown, & Bifulco, 1986; Lyons-Ruth, 1998; Lyons-Ruth & Block, 1996). A large body of research has shown that the security of a child's attachment to the parent is dependent on the emotional availability of the parent (Lyons-Ruth & Jacobvitz, 2008; see de Wolff & van Ijzendorn, 1997, for a review). Research has shown that parental emotional unavailability is more difficult for the child than actual physical separation (Field, 1995, 2011; see Markese, this issue).

Therefore, as a preventive measure for families under great duress with the traumatic loss of the husband/father, we invited mothers and their infants to a bi-annual video bonding and communication consultation, which we viewed as a well-baby visit. In this way, we were able to observe, in collaboration with the mother, both strengths and possible difficulties in the developing mother-infant relationship. By the time the infants were one year old, we were able to observe the infant's attachment style through the Ainsworth "Strange Situation" assessment and to identify attachment insecurity, a predictor of childhood difficulties. We could then address strengths, as well as any difficulties, in collaboration with the mother.

We also drew from Attachment Theory's work on "intergenerational transmission of trauma." This work documents that trauma in the parent's life, even trauma well before the child is born, can be transmitted to the child (Fonagy, Steele, & Steele, 1991; Fraiberg, 1980; Yehuda et al., 1990; Yehuda et al., 2005; Osofsky, 1995; see Markese, this issue). A history of unresolved maternal trauma and loss predicts the development of insecure-disorganized attachment patterns in her infant (Main & Hesse, 1990). The mother's continuing state of fear is thought to be one mechanism linking unresolved trauma to the infant/child's developing insecure-disorganized attachment style. This disorganized attachment style is linked to later oppositional, hostile-aggressive and fearful behavior, lower self-esteem, and cognitive difficulties in childhood (Lyons-Ruth, Bronfman, & Parsons, 1999; Lyons-Ruth & Jacobitz, 2008; Jacobson, Edelstein, & Hofmann, 1994). This disorganized attachment style is also linked to psychopathology, dissociation, and peer difficulties in adolescence and young adulthood (Lyons-Ruth, 2003; Carlson, 1998; Jacobvitz & Hazen, 1999). It remains an empirical question whether an acute, sudden loss, such as that suffered by the families in our Project, rather than trauma and loss in the mother's own developmental history, would generate a higher risk of infant disorganized attachment.

Both for the mother's optimal functioning and the child's optimal development, we saw the mother's state of mind in response to her loss and trauma following the events of September 11 as a potential source of risk. Thus, supporting the mother in processing her grief and sadness over the loss of her husband, and other losses in her life that this trauma may have re-evoked, was one key aspect of our effort to promote both mothers' and children's optimal emotional functioning (see Moskowitz, this issue; Reiswig, this issue).

## RESEARCH THAT INFORMED THE PROJECT

We attempted to conceptualize how the particular trauma of losing a husband while pregnant might affect the mothers, the infants, and the developing mother-infant interaction. Several of our mothers also experienced the terror that they might lose their own lives. A considerable literature now exists on how depressed/anxious/traumatized maternal states of mind may affect mother-infant interaction and infant development (Beebe et al., 2007, 2008, 2010, 2011; Feldman, 2006, 2007; Field, 1995, 2011; Kaitz, Levy, Ebstein, Faraone, & Mankuta, 2009; Murray & Cooper, 1997; Tronick, 1989; see Markese, this issue).

The relevant research that informed the Project can be conceptualized as: 1) the effect of maternal distress on the developing fetus, 2) the effect of maternal distress on mother-infant face-to-face interaction, 3) the effect of mother-infant interaction difficulties on infant/child attachment outcomes and subsequent child emotional development, 4) the effect of loss and trauma in infancy and early childhood on child development, and 5) the potential intergenerational effects of trauma from terror experienced by pregnant mothers, passed on to their infants.

We review the above research in several articles of this issue, including the "Description of the Project: A Longitudinal Primary Prevention Project for Mothers Pregnant and Widowed in the World Trade Center Tragedy of September 11, 2001, and Their Young Children" (Beebe, 2011, this issue), and two extensive, related literature review papers: "Prenatal Maternal Stress in the Development of Fetus and Infant: A Review of Animal Models as Related to Human Research" (Lange, this issue) and "Dyadic Trauma in Infancy and Early Childhood: Review of the Literature" (Markese, this issue).

Because our Project focused on offering support to mothers who were pregnant at the time of the terrorist attacks on the World Trade Center, we may be able to contribute to the compelling work that has been done by other teams on the effects of terror-related trauma in pregnant and delivering women on the mother, the infant, and the mother-infant interaction. For example, Kaitz and colleagues (2009) focused on mothers who were exposed to terrorist acts. They evaluated the risks for their children and particularly how, in some cases, mothers' traumas could be transmitted to their children. Kaitz and colleagues also seek to identify preventive factors by identifying strengths in the parent, in the child, and in the parent-child relationship that moderate risk and promote resilience.

## CLINICAL WORK THAT INFORMED THE TREATMENT APPROACH

In this section, we briefly note the ideas central to the Project's clinical approach. We considered a "multimodal" treatment approach to be essential to supporting parents exposed to trauma and their children (see also Kaitz et al., 2009). As shown in the article, "Early Years of Support Group I: Three Therapists' Views," some aspects of our approach are common tools in psychotherapy and psychoanalysis: individual treatments for mother and for child (see Demetri Friedman's section in Bergman, Moskowitz, & Demetri Friedman, this issue); therapy groups for mothers and their children (see Anni Bergman's section in Bergman, Moskowitz, and Demetri Friedman, this issue; Moskowitz, this issue; Sossin, "Support Group II," this issue; Reiswig, this issue), for mothers alone or for children alone; and dyadic or tri-partite treatments for the mother-child relationship (see Bergman and Remez, this issue; Bergman, this issue). A more unusual feature of our approach is the mother-child and therapist-child video assessment of free play in the split-screen video lab (Cohen & Beebe, 2002; Beebe, 2003, 2005; see Sossin & Cohen, this issue; Tortora, this issue). Another unusual feature of our approach is the structure of the video feedback session in which three or four therapists participate with one mother (see Cohen, "Video Feedback and the Impact of Multiple Therapists," this issue).

Why did psychoanalytically oriented video-assisted mother-infant treatment emerge as one key feature of our approach? Daniel Stern led the way in this method of treatment (Stern, 1995). Microanalysis of film and video by Brazelton, Trevarthen, and Stern in the 1970s revolutionized infant research on mother-infant communication (see Beebe, Knoblauch, Rustin, & Sorter, 2005). Frame-by-frame microanalysis dazzled us with its facilitation of our ability to see the details of the face-to-face exchange. Stern, trained as a psychoanalyst as well as an infant researcher, quickly realized that a video-assisted approach might be able to help mothers see the details of exchanges as well. Originally trained by Stern in the 1970s, Beatrice Beebe began to develop a version of this approach in the late 1980s and 1990s (see Beebe & Sloate, 1982; Cohen & Beebe, 2002; Beebe, 2003, 2005, 2006). By the time the World Trade Center tragedy occurred, she already had considerable experience with the power of this approach.

Our approach has much in common with other treatment models for at-risk parent-child dyads, such as the Circle of Security Project (Marvin, Cooper, Hoffman, & Powell, 2002), Minding the Baby Project (Slade et al., 2005), and the video-based behavioral approach to treating depressed mother described by Malphurs, Field, & Larrain (1996). This model is based on evidence that the early face-to-face interaction between parents and infants is essential to infant development, risk assessment, and therapeutic change (Beebe, 2005; Beebe et al., 2010; Tronick, 1989; Feldman, 2006, 2007).

As the infants turned ages 3 and 4 on, we extended this approach to include assessment and facilitation of the symbolic "pretend" play of older children (Sossin & Cohen, this issue). From the inception of the Project, symbolic play was a primary mode with the infant's older siblings, many of whom were toddlers in 2002. Pretend play provided a rich view into the child's inner emotional world and a way for therapists and mothers to see and understand the child's thoughts, ideas and concerns. By observing the child's play in the feedback sessions, the therapists were able to translate for mothers aspects of the child's ways of self-regulating, communicating, and representing important themes and conflicts (see Sossin & Cohen, this issue).

Another reason why the analysis of nonverbal communication and video-assisted treatment became central to our approach was that three key therapists in the project, Mark Sossin, Suzi Tortora, and Beatrice Beebe, had extensive experience in video analysis of nonverbal behavior and its use in mother-child treatment. Sossin and Tortora were informed by Laban Movement Analysis and Kestenberg movement analysis (Laban, 1975, 1976; Laban & Lawrence, 1974; Kestenberg, 1965a, b, 1967; Sossin, 2002, 2007; Sossin & Birklein, 2006; Birklein & Sossin, 2006; Tortora, 2006; see Tortora, this issue). The Laban and Kestenberg methods brought an additional, invaluable perspective. The Laban method emphasizes "movement qualities," ways of moving with regard to space, weight, and time and with regard to primary spatial dimensions and planes, such as direct/indirect, abrupt/gradual. These perspectives provide additional avenues into the relational dynamics of a mother-child dyad. The analysis of movement qualities differs in some respects from the analysis of face-to-face interaction from infant research. It includes all aspects of nonverbal behavior, including gestures, postures, full body motions, muscle tension levels, the shapes each person's body makes in relationship to the other person, and how each partner navigates her own personal space and the shared dyadic space. The Laban and Kestenberg methods specifically facilitated the continuing observation and treatment of children in the Project after they reached one year of age, when children and mothers engage in more active play and a wider range of movement.

Using methods of analysis of nonverbal communication from infant research on face-to-face communication, as well as from Laban and Kestenberg methods of movement analysis, as we watched the films we asked clinical questions such as: How do mother and infant experience each other? How does each partner affect the other? How does each partner regulate herself/himself? Can we identify specific patterns in the nonverbal exchange that reveal how mother and infant/child are coping as a dyad with their loss?

Why did we develop the approach to the video feedback session in which three or four therapists participate with one mother? This approached developed gradually over the first two years of the project as we came to realize how profound the protective dissociative reactions were in the mothers and the difficulty reaching them in that state (see Cohen, "Video Feedback," this issue). We found that the presence of several therapists at these feedback sessions, the dialogue among the therapists, and the emergence of multiple points of view were very reassuring to the mothers and helped them to participate. As the Project evolved, we discovered that the therapists' dialogue helped the mothers to appreciate the amount of careful thinking required to understand any particular mother-child relationship. This collaborative dialogue among the therapists helped the mothers appreciate that there is no "one" truth or assessment. Instead, the collaborative process helped us to understand a child's particular developmental process. For a detailed description of this approach, see Dr. Phyllis Cohen's article on video feedback (this issue).

## SPECIFIC CLINICAL APPROACHES

### Video Feedback Therapy

Face-to-face play is a rich entry point for intervention. In "video feedback" therapy, we use the videotaped mother-infant face-to-face interactions as part of the therapy. The mother has a powerful experience during the video feedback session of watching herself and her child interact. In the feedback session we collaborate in attempting to describe the "nonverbal language" of both mother and child as they play. We observe, for example, shifts of gaze on and off the partner's face, moments of facial exuberance or facial sobering, postures which reach toward the partner and postures which orient away, rhythms of hand, and foot movements which may be slow and modulated or rapid and agitated. In this way, mothers can learn about the feelings and needs of their children, as well as their own. Therapists attempt to provide parents with a safe context in which to explore and express feelings about what they are seeing and feeling, or might have felt. Parental involvement, sensitivity, and mindfulness have been shown to be positive mediating factors in a child's recovery following trauma and loss (Slade et al., 2005). Such parental involvement also has long-term effect on attachment security, and optimal social-emotional development from infancy through adulthood (Carlson, 1998; Fonagy, Steele, & Steele, 1991; Lyons-Ruth, 2003; Lyons-Ruth & Jacobvitz, 2008).

## The Method of Video Microanalysis in Infancy

Video microanalysis can teach us to observe the subtle, fleeting details of the mother-infant action language. The infant's repertoire during a face-to-face exchange is complex. There is a remarkable range of behaviors at the infant's disposal to initiate, maintain, disrupt, or avoid a face-to-face encounter (Stern, 1971, 1985). The mother is instructed to play with her infant as she would at home. Until 9–12 months, we do not provide toys. The infant is placed in an infant seat opposite the mother, who is seated in the same plane. Two cameras, one on each partner's face and upper torso, generate a split-screen view of the pair interacting.

Videotape played in slowed time, or frame-by-frame, acts like a "social microscope," revealing subtleties and subliminal details of interactions which are too rapid and complex to grasp with the naked eye in ongoing time. It is difficult for anyone to be aware of his or her nonverbal behavior. If the video feedback is handled with great care to protect the parent's self-esteem, it helps the parent to *see how* both infant and parent affect each other, moment-by-moment. Video feedback provides an opportunity for the parent to process and reflect on the successful moments in the interaction, as well as the difficult ones (Beebe, 2003, 2005; Cohen & Beebe, 2002; Fonagy, Gergely, Jurist, & Target, 2002). Thus "mother-infant treatment occurs at a unique intersection of implicit, procedural (repetitive action-sequences) and explicit, declarative (symbolic) modes of processing, and it fosters a greater integration between the two modes" (Beebe, 2003, p. 34).

## Gaze Patterns

We begin by observing the ways that infants and mothers look and look away from each other's face. Mothers tend to look at the infant's face most of the time, and it is the infant who typically "makes" and "breaks" the mutual gaze, looking at mother's face for a period of time, looking away, and then looking back (Stern, 1971, 1974). Looking into the face of a partner can be very stimulating; most humans (and animals) do not sustain long periods of such looking unless they are about to fight or make love (Chance & Larsen, 1996; Eibes-Eiblfeld, 1970). Field (1981) documented that infants organize their look-look away cycles to regulate degree of arousal. She monitored infant heart rate during face-to-face play and showed that the moment that the infant looks away is preceded by a burst of arousal in the previous five seconds. Following the infant's gaze aversion, heart rate decreases back down to baseline within the next five seconds, and then the infant returns to gazing at mother's face. Thus infant gaze aversion is an important means of infant self-regulation. Brazelton, Kozlowski, and Main (1974) first showed that mothers typically pace their amount of stimulation according to this infant gaze cycle, stimulating more as the infant looks, and decreasing stimulation as the infant looks away. Although these are typical patterns, we have also noted a pattern of mutual "eye love" (Beebe, 1973; Beebe & Stern, 1977) in which mothers and infants can sustain prolonged mutual gaze for up to 100 seconds during periods of positive affect. These are special moments, of course, that every parent loves.

Maternal difficulty in tolerating momentary infant gaze aversion is one of the most common pictures observed in mothers and infants who present for treatment. If the mother feels that her infant is not interested in her, or if she feels rejected at the moment that the infant looks away, she may pursue or "chase" the infant, increasing rather than decreasing the amount of stimulation. Maternal "chase" behavior is counter-productive; the infant then requires more time to regulate arousal down sufficiently to return to gazing at mother. Instead, if the mother can be helped to give the baby a "time-out" to re-regulate, "cooling it" when the infant looks away, trusting her infant to return to her, the infant will rapidly re-engage.

In relation to maternal "chase" behaviors above, the infant may "dodge" with increasing degrees of head aversion, as well as arching back, freezing, or going limp and giving up tonus. Through increasing head aversions, arching, or going limp, infants can have a remarkable "veto power" over the possibility of a sustained, mutual gaze encounter (Beebe & Stern, 1977).

## Facial Dialogue

If mother and infant together manage the infant's look-look away cycle so that the infant can comfortably regulate arousal, periods of sustained mutual gaze with infant vis-à-vis orientation can be enjoyed. During these periods, facial and vocal communications take center stage. By 3–4 months the infant's social capacity flowers. The infant's opening and closing of the mouth is a powerful and continuous form of communication. Even without any hint of smiling, a fully opened mouth ("neutral gape") is highly evocative (Beebe, 1973; Bennett, 1971). A fully widened smile by itself, with closed lips, is only moderately positive. As increasing degrees of mouth opening are added to a smile, positive affect increases up and up into the fully opened "gape smile," hugely exciting for both partners. Mothers intuitively *roughly* match the infant's increments of positive affect, so that both build to a peak of positive facial excitement. Often both partners excitedly vocalize at such moments, further increasing the intensity. In general, mothers and infants tend to match the direction of the other's positive-to-negative affective changes, increasing and decreasing together (Beebe & Lachmann, 1988; Beebe et al., 2010). Rarely is there an exact match of facial expression. Elaboration (Fogel, 1993), echo, or complementing (Trevarthen, 1977) are better metaphors than matching or imitation (Stern, 1985). Instead of the romanticized notion that mothers and infants exactly match, or are in exact "synch," Tronick and Cohn (1989) showed that a more flexible process of match, mismatch, and rematch (disruption and repair) characterizes the exchange. Furthermore, a greater likelihood of rapid re-match (within two seconds) predicts secure attachment at one year (Tronick, 1989; Cohn, Campbell, & Ross, 1991). When infants are distressed, typically mothers display a "woe-face." Malatesta, Culver, Tesman, and Shepard (1989) showed that unusual responses such as maternal joy or surprise to infant anger or sadness predict toddler preoccupation with attempts to dampen negative affect (e.g., compressed lips, frowning, sadness). Beebe et al. (2010) showed that maternal surprise faces or smiles in response to infant distress predict disorganized infant attachment. Maternal faces which are overly stable, or "inscrutable," also predict disorganized infant attachment (Beebe et al., 2010). We conjecture that these patterns occur when the infant's distress triggers unresolved distress in the mother.

## Vocal Dialogue

A key feature of the vocal exchange (preverbal as well as verbal) is a turntaking structure. Both partners contribute to turntaking by matching the brief "switching pause" as turns are exchanged. Mothers contribute by slowing their speech rhythms, providing a great deal of repetition, and matching the intonation (shape) of the infant's sounds. Across cultures, a sinusoidal shape indicates approval; a rightward falling shape, disapproval (Fernald, 1993). Mothers also optimally pause sufficiently to give the infant a turn. Mothers who prattle continuously do not permit this; on the other hand, mothers who are silent partners can also disturb the development of vocal turn-taking, an essential building block of language. An approximate matching of the infant's vocal contours and rhythms can be an effective way to make contact with a gaze-avoidant infant. Because such an infant does not have to orient or look, approximately matching the infant's rhythms (vocal or motoric) is a nonintrusive way of helping the infant feel sensed: someone is on his "wavelength."

### Self-Regulation

From birth onward, self-regulation refers to the management of arousal, maintenance of alertness, ability to dampen positive or negative arousal in the face of overstimulation, capacity to inhibit behavior, and stability/lability of behavioral rhythms (Beebe & Lachmann, 2002; Beebe et al., 2010). Infants from birth differ in their ability to regulate sleep, feeding, and arousal (Korner & Grobstein, 1977; Brazelton, 1994). Some infants have special sensitivities to sound, smell, or touch (DeGangi, Di Pietro, Greenspan, & Porges, 1991; van den Boom, 1995).

### Distress Regulation

Mother-infant dyads show important differences in infant ability to manage moments of heightened distress and maternal management of infant distress. Both partners bring capacities to soothe and dampen as opposed to escalating distress. Obviously the mother has greater range and resources in this process. An effective form of distress regulation is a partial or *loosely coordinated* "joining" or matching of the infant's fuss or cry rhythm, with "woe face" and associated vocal "woe" intonations (facial and vocal empathy). In this process, the rhythm (but not the volume or intensity) of the distress is matched and then gradually slowed down (Beebe, 2000; Gergely & Watson, 1997; Stern, 1985).

### Therapist as Novel Partner

Similar to our research assessment, in our Project mother and infant first play face-to-face, followed by infant and therapist. The therapist acts as the novel partner ("stranger"). Over time, of course, the therapists ceased to be "strangers." The stranger-infant interaction has been shown to be a sensitive predictor of infant attachment outcomes (Jaffe et al., 2001; Beebe et al., 2009) and to discriminate treatment and control dyads (Weinberg & Tronick, 1998). Before the end of the first year, when some infants develop "stranger anxiety," the stranger is both a novel challenge and, at the same time, an intensely interesting new partner. Although most 4-month infants are very sociable with the stranger, some infants are wary. We assess the infant's capacity to engage the therapist and to be engaged.

## KEY ROLE OF THE FACE-TO-FACE INTERACTION

An ongoing study in our lab has examined maternal self-report depression at 6 weeks, mother-infant face-to-face interaction at 4 months, and infant attachment at 12 months, in a community sample of 132 families (Beebe et al., 2007, 2008, 2010). Six-week maternal depression and 4-month maternal anxiety were robustly associated with mother-infant patterns of self- and interactive regulation at 4 months, but maternal depression and anxiety did not predict infant attachment outcomes at 1 year. Instead, it was the quality of the 4-month mother-infant face-to-face interaction itself in conjunction with maternal distress that predicted infant attachment outcomes (Beebe et al., 2011, in preparation). One implication is that, in a community sample, distressed maternal states of mind do not necessarily lead to insecure infant attachment outcomes, unless there is also difficulty in the face-to-face interaction itself. This study provides a further rationale for a central goal in our Project, which is therapeutically supporting the quality of the mother-infant face-to-face interaction when mothers are distressed.

## EARLY CHILDHOOD PLAY THERAPY

There were four potential ways that a child could receive play therapy through this Project: (1) in the context of the mother-child support groups (see Demetri Friedman's perspective in Bergman, Moskowitz, & Demetri Friedman, this issue); (2) through children's groups for children, ages approximately 5–10 years old; (3) through referral from within the Project to one of our therapists for individual treatment; and (4) through referral from the psychoanalytic community (see Bergman & Remez, this issue; see also Bergman's perspective in Bergman, Moskowitz, & Demetri Friedman, this issue). All families referred to our Project were included in the laboratory filming and video feedback sessions, in addition to individual child treatment.

Early childhood play therapy emerged as a key additional treatment component. The needs of the infants changed as they turned into toddlers, and the needs of the older siblings became a central concern as well. Whenever possible, we referred these children for treatment with one of our Project therapists, of whom Anni Bergman took the lead. She had extensive experience in developing and implementing play therapy with young children and their parents. However, most of the families were not able to use our referrals of children for individual or dyadic mother-child treatment until the later years of the project.

Anni Bergman writes in her book *Ours, Yours, Mine: Mutuality and the Emergence of the Separate Self:* "In their work with children, Mahler and her co-workers began to notice that the presence of the mothers within the therapeutic situation appeared to have a positive value. Even when the mothers were unable to fulfill the needs of their children, they were able to understand their nonverbal communications and thus aid the therapist. Out of this realization, Mahler developed what she termed the 'tripartite therapeutic design'" (Bergman, 1999, pp. 12–13; Mahler, 1967; Bergman, 1971).

Mahler viewed mothers and their young infants as a sort of "dual unity." She thought that it took a long time for the child to develop a separate psychic structure; therefore, she recommended that mother and child be treated together. In this design, young children were seen together with their mothers in intensive psychoanalytically oriented therapy sessions.

Anni Bergman goes on to describe that mother, child, and therapist join together in the treatment of the child. "Thus, the child's development is re-experienced and re-lived, not only with the therapist, but with the mother as well. Through her participation in the child's treatment, the mother is trained to assume and maintain the corrective symbiotic experience she has seen being developed by the therapist" (Bergman, 1999, pp. xv–xxiv).

Bergman and Remez (this issue) and Bergman (in Bergman, Moskowitz, & Demetri Friedman, this issue) describe the treatment of two children whose families lived at the World Trade Center site. The families were traumatized, but no one was lost in the attack. These multi-layered treatments involved (1) lab filming sessions, (2) parent feedback sessions with our team of therapists, (3) private individual child and tri-partite sessions with Anni Bergman, and (4) private sessions between Anni Bergman and the child's mother, and in the case treated by Bergman and Remez, an individual treatment for the mother by Remez. These two cases powerfully illustrate the transmission of trauma between parents and their children. They also illustrate the flexibility of our multimodal approach, integrating many forms of assessment and treatment.

## COMBINED MOTHER-CHILD SUPPORT GROUPS

In our individual feedback sessions, mothers' mourning of the lost spouse is facilitated. This work is grounded in a psychodynamic exploration of the meaning of the loss as a part of a complex individual adult attachment history. Another approach to a facilitation of the mourning occurred in the context of the support groups. In these support groups we encouraged mothers to process their loss, and to discuss parenting challenges, with other mothers who suffered the trauma.

In spring 2002, we organized several support groups, collaboratively run by two to three psychoanalytically trained therapists. The initial goal was to bring together mothers and their young babies in weekly groups and to help the mothers with the mourning process. Mothers were encouraged to bring their older children as well. We strived to provide a holding environment in which mothers could be free to discuss whatever was on their minds, while one therapist always attended to the needs of their children (see Sossin, this issue; Reiswig, this issue; see also Moskowitz's perspective in Bergman, Moskowitz, and Demetri Friedman, this issue). Our intention as therapists was to be available, to listen and to provide a nurturing environment within which the mothers themselves could nurture and support one another. We believed that much could be gained by attending to the quality of the developing mother-infant relationships in the context of their shared experiences. Both mother and infant were survivors of traumatic loss.

The support groups were essential to the structure of the Project. We felt strongly that a group experience would benefit these women. They could both give and receive support, thus utilizing a uniquely female strength, the motivation to "tend and befriend" that has been identified as a valuable resource for women under stress (Taylor, 2006). We felt that especially in this group of highly independent, resourceful women, it would be important to encourage them to use their strengths to help another, to facilitate a process in which the women themselves could be an essential part of each other's recovery. This process was fully realized in one of our support groups that stayed together and continues today.

## CONCLUSION

Our methods of primary prevention combine psychoanalytically-oriented explorations of the parent's loss and attachment history with educational and behavioral interventions which focus on nonverbal as well as verbal modes of communication in the parent-child relationship. Video-assisted psychoanalytically informed feedback sessions facilitate the mother's capacity to become more aware of the nonverbal "language" of the child and of the patterns of communication that characterize the developing relationship. By helping mothers to reflect on their own experiences in relation to the experiences of their children, these multimodal methods support and empower bereaved parents to engage in optimal interactions despite their distress.

Interactional approaches to treating early parent-child dyadic difficulty, in combination with individual psychodynamic, representational treatment of bereaved parents, integrate short-term and long-term treatment models. These multimodal primary prevention approaches are likely to provide more complex, lasting treatment outcomes by facilitating infant, child, and parental mourning, strengthening the relational development of young children, and simultaneously providing mothers with the capacity to form strong attachment bonds with their children in the face of the loss of their husbands.

## REFERENCES

Ainsworth, M., Blehar, M., Waters, E., & Wall, S. (1978). *Patterns of attachment: A psychological study of the strange situation*. Hillsdale, NJ: Lawrence Erlbaum Associates.

Barbanel, L., & Sternberg, R. (Eds.). (2006). *Psychological interventions in times of crisis*. New York, NY: Springer Publishing Company.

Beebe, B. (1973). Ontogeny of positive affect in the third and fourth months of the life of one infant. (Doctoral dissertation). *Dissertation Abstracts International, 35*(2), 1014B.

Beebe, B. (2000). Co-constructing mother-infant distress: The micro-synchrony of maternal impingement and infant avoidance in the face-to-face encounter. *Psychoanalytic Inquiry, 20*(3), 421–440.

Beebe, B. (2003). Brief mother-infant treatment using psychoanalytically informed video microanalysis. *Infant Mental Health Journal, 24*(1), 24–52.

Beebe, B. (2004). Faces in relation: A case study. *Psychoanalytic Dialogues, 14*(1), 1–51.

Beebe, B. (2005). Mother-infant research informs mother-infant treatment. *Psychoanalytic Study of the Child, 60*, 7–46.

Beebe, B. (2006). Co-constructing mother-infant distress in face-to-face interactions: Contributions of microanalysis. *Infant Observation, 9*(2), 151–164.

Beebe, B. (2011, this issue). Description of the project: A longitudinal primary prevention project for mothers pregnant and widowed in the World Trade Center tragedy of September 11, 2001, and their young children. *Journal of Infant, Child, and Adolescent Psychotherapy, 10*, 156–169.

Beebe, B., Jaffe, J., Buck, K., Chen, H., Cohen, P., Blatt, S., . . . Andrews, H. (2007). Six-week postpartum maternal self-criticism and dependency and 4-month mother-infant self- and interactive contingencies. *Developmental Psychology, 43*(6), 1360–1376.

Beebe, B., Jaffe, J., Buck, K., Chen, H., Cohen, P., Feldstein, S., & Andrews, H. (2008). Maternal depression at 6 weeks postpartum and mother-infant 4-month self-and interactive regulation. *Infant Mental Health Journal, 29*(5), 442–471.

Beebe, B., Jaffe, J., Markese, S., Buck, K., Chen, H., Cohen, P., Bahrick, L., & Andrews, H. (2010). The origins of 12-month attachment: A microanalysis of 4-month mother-infant interaction. *Attachment & Human Development, 12*(1–2), 3–141.

Beebe, B., Markese, S., Steele, M., Buck, K., Cohen, P., Reuben, J., . . . Jaffe, J. (2011, in preparation). Paths of risk and resilience in 4-month mother-infant interaction: From 6-week maternal depression to 12-month insecure and secure attachment. New York State Psychiatric Institute.

Beebe, B., Steele, M., Jaffe, J., Buck, K., Chen, H., Cohen, P., . . . Feldstein, S. (2011). Maternal anxiety and 4-month mother-infant self- and interactive contingency. *Infant Mental Health Journal, 32*(2), 174–206.

Beebe, B., Knoblauch, S., Rustin, J., & Sorter, D. (2005). *Form of intersubjectivity and infant research and adult treatment*. New York, NY: Other Press.

Beebe, B., & Lachmann, F. (1988). The contribution of mother-infant mutual influence to the origins of self- and object representations. *Psychoanalytic Psychology, 5*, 304–337.

Beebe, B., & Lachmann, F. (2002). *Infant research and adult treatment: Co-constructing interactions*. Hillsdale, NJ: The Analytic Press.

Beebe, B., & Sloate, P. (1982). Assessment and treatment of difficulties in mother-infant attunement in the first three years of life. *Psychoanalytic Inquiry*, *1*(4), 601–623.

Beebe, B., & Stern, D. (1977). Engagement-disengagement and early object experiences. In N. Freedman & S. Grand (Eds.), *Communicative structures and psychic structures* (pp. 35–55). New York, NY: Plenum Press.

Beebe, B., Margolis, A., Markese, S., Jaffe, J., Buck, K., Chen, H., . . . Reuben, J. (2009). *Mother-infant vs. stranger-infant: Depression and attachment*. Report to The Psychoanalytic Fund, August 6.

Bennett, S. L. (1971). Infant-caretaker interaction. *Journal of the American Academy of Child Psychiatry*, *10*, 321–335.

Bergman, A. (1971). I and you: The separation-individuation process in the treatment of symbiotic psychotic child. In J. McDevitt & C. Settlage (Eds.), *Separation-individuation: Essays in honor of Margaret S.Mahler* (pp. 325–355). New York, NY: International Universities Press.

Bergman, A. (1999). *Ours, yours, mine: Mutuality and the emergence of the separate self*. Northvale, NJ: Jason Aronson.

Bergman, A., Sossin, K. M., Tortora, S., Lydia (Ryan's mother), Cohen, P., & Beebe, B. (2011, this issue). The team approach to the treatment of a traumatized mother and child: Lydia and Ryan. *Journal of Infant, Child, and Adolescent Psychotherapy*, *10*, 302–316.

Bergman, A., & Harpaz-Rotem, I. (2004). Revisiting rapprochement in the light of contemporary developmental theories. *Journal of the American Psychoanalytic Association*, *52*(2), 555–570.

Bergman, A. & Remez, A. (2011, this issue). The team approach to the treatment of a traumatized mother and child: Christina and Bobby. *Journal of Infant, Child, and Adolescent Psychotherapy*, *10*, 286–295.

Bergman, A., Moskowitz, S., & Demetri Friedman, D. (2011, this issue). Early years of Support Group I: Three therapists' views. *Journal of Infant, Child, and Adolescent Psychotherapy*, *10*, 207–216.

Birklein, S., & Sossin, K. M. (2006). Nonverbal indices of stress in parent-child dyads: Implications for individual and interpersonal affect regulation and intergenerational transmission. In S. Koch & I. Bräuninger (Eds.), *Advances in dance/movement therapy: Theoretical perspectives and empirical findings* (pp. 128–141). Berlin, Germany: Logos Verlag.

Bowlby, J. (1951). *Maternal care and mental health*. Geneva, Switzerland: World Health Organization.

Bowlby, J. (1969). *Attachment: Attachment and loss, vol. I*. New York, NY: Basic Books.

Bowlby, J. (1973). *Separation, anxiety and anger: Attachment and loss, vol. II*. New York, NY: Basic Books.

Bowlby, J. (1980). *Loss, sadness and depression: Attachment and loss, vol. III*. New York, NY: Basic Books.

Brazelton, T. B. (1994). Touchpoints: Opportunities for preventing problems in the parent-child relationship. *Acta Paediatrica*, *394*(Suppl.), 35–39.

Brazelton, T. B., Koslowski, B., & Main, M. (1974). The origins of reciprocity. In M. Lewis & L. Rosenblum (Eds.), *The effect of the infant on its caregiver* (pp. 49–70). New York, NY: Wiley-Interscience.

Brier, A., Kelsoe, J., Kirwin, P., Beller, S., Wolkowitz, O., & Pickar, D. (1988). Early parental loss and development of adult psychopathology. *Archives of General Psychiatry*, *45*, 987–993.

Buxbaum, L., & Brant, J. (2001). When a parent dies from cancer. *Clinical Journal of Oncology Nursing*, *5*(4, July/August).

Carlson, E. (1998). A prospective longitudinal study of attachment isorganization/disorientation. *Child Development*, *69*(4), 1107–1128.

Chance, M., & Larsen, R. (Eds.). (1996). *The social structure of attention*. New York, NY: Wiley.

Chemtob, C., Nomura, Y., Rajendran, K., Yehuda, R., Schwartz, D., & Abramovitz, R. (2010). Impact of maternal posttraumatic stress disorder and depression following exposure to the September 11 attacks on preschool children's behavior. *Child Development*, *81*(4), 1129–1141.

Coates, S., Rosenthal, J., & Schechter, D. (Eds.). (2003). *September 11: Trauma and human bonds*. New York, NY: The Analytic Press/Taylor & Francis Group.

Cohen, P. M. (2011, this issue). Video feedback and the impact of multiple therapists. *Journal of Infant, Child, and Adolescent Psychotherapy*, *10*, 278–285.

Cohen, P. M., & Beebe, B. (2002). Video feedback with a depressed mother and her infant: A collaborative individual psychoanalytic and mother-infant treatment. *Journal of Infant, Child, and Adolescent Psychotherapy*, *2*(3), 1–55.

Cohn, J., Campbell, S., & Ross, S. (1991). Infant response in the still-face paradigm at 6 months predicts avoidant and secure attachments at 12 months. *Development and Psychopathology*, *3*, 367–376.

Danieli, Y., & Dingman, R. (Eds.). (2005). *On the ground after September 11: Mental health responses and practical knowledge gained*. Binghamton, NY: Haworth Maltreatment and Trauma Press/The Haworth Press.

DeGangi, G., Di Pietro, J., Greenspan, S., & Porges, S. (1991). Psychophysiological characteristics of the regulatory disordered infant. *Infant Behavior and Development*, *14*, 37–50.

Eibl-Eibesfeldt, I. (1970). *Ethology: The biology of behavior*. New York, NY: Holt, Rhinehart & Winston.

Feldman, R. (2006). From biological rhythms to social rhythms: Physiological precursors of mother–infant synchrony. *Developmental Psychology*, *4*, 175–188.

Feldman, R. (2007). Parent–infant synchrony and the construction of shared timing: Physiological precursors, developmental outcomes, and risk conditions. *Journal of Child Psychology and Psychiatry*, *48*, 329–354.

Fernald, A. (1993). Approval and disapproval: Infant responsiveness to vocal affect in familiar and unfamiliar languages. *Child Development*, *64*(3), 657–674.

Field, T. (1981). Infant gaze aversion and heart rate during face-to-face interactions. *Infant Behavior and Development*, *4*, 307–315.

Field, T. (1995). Infants of depressed mothers. *Infant Behavior and Development*, *18*, 1–13.

Field,T. (2011). Prenatal depression effects on early development: A review. *Infant Behavior & Development*, *34*(1), 1–14.

Feldman, R. (2006). From biological rhythms to social rhythms: Physiological precursors of mother–infant synchrony. *Developmental Psychology*, *4*, 175–188.

Feldman, R. (2007). Parent–infant synchrony and the construction of shared timing: Physiological precursors, developmental outcomes, and risk conditions . *Journal of Child psychology and Psychiatry*, *48*, 329–354.

Fonagy, P., Gergely, G., Jurist, E., & Target, M. (2002). *Affect regulation, mentalization and the development of the self*. New York, NY: Other Press.

Fonagy, P., Steele, M., & Steele, H. (1991). The capacity for understanding mental states: The reflective self in parent and child and its significance for security of attachment. *Infant Mental Health Journal*, *12*, 201–218.

Fogel, A. (1993). Two principles of communication: Co-Regulation and framing. In J. Nadel & L. Camaioni (Eds.), *New perspectives in early communicative development* (pp. 9–22). London, England: Routledge.

Fraiberg, S. (1980). *Clinical studies in infant mental health: The first year of life*. New York, NY: Basic Books.

Garber, B. (1997). Parent loss in childhood and adult psychopathology. In L. Flaherty & H. Horowitz (Eds.). *Adolescent Psychiatry, Vol. 21: Developmental and clinical studies. Annals of the American Society for Adolescent Psychiatry*, 101–118.

Gergely, G., & Watson, J. (1997). The social biofeedback theory of parental affect-mirroring. *International Journal of Psycho-Analysis*, *77*, 1181–1212.

Harris, T., Brown, G., & Bifulco, A. (1986). Loss of parent in childhood and adult psychiatric disorder: The role of lack of adequate parental care. *Psychological Medicine*, *16*, 641–659.

Harpaz-Rotem, I., & Bergman, A. (2006). On evolving theory of attachment: Rapprochement, theory of a developing mind. *Psychoanalytic Study of the Child*, *61*, 170–189.

Jacobsen, T., Edelstein, W., & Hofmann, V. (1994). A longitudinal study of the relation between representations of attachment in childhood and cognitive functioning in childhood and adolescence. *Developmental Psychology*, *30*, 112–124.

Jacobvitz, D., & Hazen, N. (1999). Developmental pathways from infant disorganization to childhood peer relationships. In J. Solomon & C. George (Eds.), *Attachment disorganization* (pp. 127–159). New York, NY: Guilford Press.

Jaffe, J., Beebe, B., Feldstein, S., Crown, C. L., & Jasnow, M. (2001). Rhythms of dialogue in infancy. *Monographs of the Society for Research in Child Development*, *66*(Serial No. 265).

Kaitz, M., Levy, M., Ebstein, R., Faraone, S. V., & Mankuta, D. (2009). The intergenerational effects of trauma from terror: A real possibility. *Infant Mental Health Journal*, *30*(2), 158–170.

Kestenberg, J. S. (1965a). The role of movement patterns in development: 1. Rhythms of movement. *Psychoanalytic Quarterly*, *34*, 1–36.

Kestenberg, J. S. (1965b). The role of movement patterns in development: 2. Flow of tension and effort. *Psychoanalytic Quarterly*, *34*, 517–563.

Kestenberg, J. (1967). *The role of movement patterns in development, vol. 1*. New York, NY: Dance Notation Bureau Press.

Korner, A., & Grobstein, R. (1977). Individual differences at birth. In E. Rexford, L. Sander, & T. Shapiro (Eds.), *Infant psychiatry* (pp. 69–78). New Haven, CT: Yale University Press.

Laban, R. (1975). *The mastery of movement*. Boston, MA: Plays, Inc.

Laban, R. (1976). *The language of movement*. Boston, MA: Plays, Inc.

Laban, R., & Lawrence, F. C. (1974). *Effort*. Boston, MA: Plays, Inc.

Lange, A. (2011). Prenatal maternal stress and the developing fetus and infant: A review of animal models as related to human research. *Journal of Infant, Child, and Adolescent Psychotherapy*, *10*, 325–339.

Lyons-Ruth, K. (1998). Implicit relational knowing: Its role in development and psychoanalytic treatment. *Infant Mental Health Journal, 19*, 282–289.

Lyons-Ruth, K., & Jacobvitz, D. (2008) Attachment disorganization: Genetic factors, parenting contexts, and developmental transformation from infancy to adulthood. In J. Cassidy & P. Shaver (Eds.), *Handbook of attachment: Theory, research, and clinical applications.* (2nd ed., pp. 666–697). New York, NY: Guilford Press.

Lyons-Ruth, K. (2003). Dissociation and the parent-infant dialogue: A longitudinal perspective from attachment research. *Journal of the American Psychoanalytic Association, 51*, 883–911.

Lyons-Ruth, K., & Block, D. (1996). The disturbed caregiving system: Relations among childhood trauma, maternal caregiving, and infant affect and attachment. *Infant Mental Health Journal, 17*, 257–275.

Lyons-Ruth, K., Bronfman, E., & Parsons, E. (1999). Maternal frightened, frightening or atypical behavior and disorganized infant attachment patterns. In J. Vondra & D. Barnett (Eds.), *Monographs of the Society for Research in Child Development, 64*(3), Serial No. 258, 67–96.

Mahler, M. (1967). On human symbiosis and the vicissitudes of individuation. In *The selected papers of Margaret Mahler, vol. 2: Separation-individuation.* Northvale, NJ: Jason Aronson.

Mahler, M., Pine, F., & Bergman, A. (1975). *The psychological birth of the human infant: Symbiosis and individuation.* New York, NY: Basic Books.

Main, M., & Hesse, E. (1990). Parents' unresolved traumatic experiences are related to infant disorganized attachment status: Is frightened and/or frightening parental behavior the linking mechanism? In M. Greenberg, D. Cicchetti, & E. Cummings (Eds.), *Attachment in the preschool years: Theory, research, and intervention* (pp. 161–182). Chicago, IL: University of Chicago Press.

Malatesta, C., Culver, C., Tesman, J., & Shepard, B. (1989). The development of emotion expression during the first two years of life. *Monographs of the Society for Research in Child Development, 54*(1–2, Serial No. 219), 1–103.

Malphurs, J., Field, T., & Larrain, C. (1996). Altering withdrawn and intrusive interaction behaviors of depressed mothers. *Infant Mental Health Journal, 17*(2), 152–160.

Marvin, R., Cooper, G., Hoffman, K., and Powell, B. (2002). The circle of security project: Attachment-based intervention with caregiver-preschool child dyads. *Attachment and Human Development, 4*(1), 107–124.

Markese, S. (2011, this issue). Dyadic trauma in infancy and early childhood: Review of the literature. *Journal of Infant, Child, and Adolescent Psychotherapy, 10*, 341–378.

Markese, S., Beebe, B., Feldstein, S., & Jaffe, J. (2008, March). *Rhythms of dialogue in infancy and attachment narratives in childhood.* XVI Biennial International Conference on Infant Studies, Vancouver, Canada.

Moskowitz, S. (2011, this issue). Primary maternal preoccupation disrupted by trauma and loss: Early years of the project. *Journal of Infant, Child, and Adolescent Psychotherapy, 10*, 229–237.

Murray, L., & Cooper, P. (Eds.). (1997). *Postpartum depression and child development.* New York, NY: The Guilford Press.

Osofsky, J. (1995). Perspectives on attachment and psychoanalysis. *Psychoanalytic Psychology, 12*, 347–363.

Schechter, D., Coates, S., & First, E. (2001). Observations from New York on young children's and their families' acute reactions to the World Trade Center attacks. *Bulletin Zero to Three, 22*(3), 9–13.

Shear, M. K., & Shair, H. (2005).Attachment, loss and complicated grief.*Developmental Psychobiology, 47*, 253–267.

Slade, A., Sadler, L., Dios-Kenn, C., Webb, D., Currier-Ezepchick, J., & Mayes, L. (2005). Minding the baby: A reflective parenting program. *Psychoanalytic Study of the Child, 60*, 74–100.

Sossin, K. M. (2002). Interactive movement patterns as ports of entry in infant-parent psychotherapy. *Journal of Infant, Child and Adolescent Psychotherapy, 2*, 97–131.

Sossin, K. M. (2007). Nonmentalizing states in early childhood survivors of the Holocaust: Developmental considerations regarding child survivors of genocidal atrocities. *American Journal of Psychoanalysis, 67*, 68–81.

Sossin, K. M., & Birklein, S. (2006). Nonverbal transmission of stress between parent and young child: Considerations and psychotherapeutic implications of a study of affective movement patterns. *Journal of Infant, Child, & Adolescent Psychotherapy, 5*, 46–69.

Sossin, K. M., & Cohen, P. M. (2011, this issue). Children's play in the wake of loss and trauma. *Journal of Infant, Child, and Adolescent Psychotherapy, 10*, 255–272.

Stern, D. (1971). A microanalysis of mother–infant interaction. *Journal of the American Academy of Child Psychiatry, 19*, 501–517.

Stern, D. (1974). Goal and structure of mother-infant play. *Journal of the American Academy of Child Psychiatry, 13*, 402–421.

Stern, D. (1985). *The interpersonal world of the infant: A view from psychoanalysis and developmental psychology*. New York, NY: Basic Books.

Stern, D. (1995). *The motherhood constellation*. New York, NY: Basic Books.

Taylor, S. E. (2006). Tend and befriend: Biobehavioral bases of affiliation under stress. *Current Directions in Psychological Science*, *15*, 273–277.

Tortora, S. (2006). *The dancing dialogue: Using the communicative power of movement with young children*. Baltimore, MD: Paul H. Brookes Publishing Co., Inc.

Trevarthen, C. (1977). Descriptive analyses of infant communicative behavior. In H. Schaffer (Ed.), *Studies in mother–infant interaction* (pp. 227–270). London, England: Academic Press.

Tronick, E. (1989). Emotions and emotional communication in infants. *American Psychologist*, *44*, 112–119.

Tronick, E., & Cohn, J. (1989). Infant-mother face-to-face interaction: Age and gender differences in coordination and miscoordination. *Child Development*, *59*, 85–92.

Van den Boom, D. (1995). Do first-year intervention effects endure: Follow-up during toddlerhood of a sample of Dutch irritable infants. *Child Development*, *66*, 1798–1816.

Weinberg, K., & Tronick, E. (1998). The impact of maternal psychiatric illness on infant development. *Journal of Clinical Psychiatry*, *59*(2), 53–61.

Winnicott, D. W. (1965). *The maturational processes and the facilitating environment*.Madison, CT: International Universities Press, Inc.

de Wolff, M. S., & van Ijzendoorn, M. H. (1997). Sensitivity and attachment: A meta-analysis on parental antecedents of infant attachment. *Child Development*, *68*, 571–591.

Yehuda, R., Southwick, S., Nussbaum, G., Wahlby, V., Giller, E., & Mason, J. (1990). Low urinary cortisol excretion in patients with post-traumatic stress disorder. *Journal of Nervous and Mental Disease*, *178*, 366–369.

Yehuda, R., Engel, S. M., Brand, S. R., Seckl, J., Marcus, S. M., & Berkowitz, G. S. (2005). Transgenerational effects of posttraumatic stress disorder in babies of mothers exposed to the World Trade Center attacks during pregnancy. *Journal of Endocrinology & Metabolism*, *90*(7), 4115–4118.

# The Evolution of the Project: Helping the Mothers, Infants and Young Children of September 11, 2001

Phyllis Cohen, Ph.D.

This article describes the evolution of the Project for Mothers, Infants, and Young Children of September 11, 2001. When a group of pregnant women lost their husbands on 9/11, we knew that traditional approaches would not be sufficient to help them cope with this unthinkable disaster. The unique circumstances of being pregnant and widowed, and having to experience not only the birth of a baby but also pressures from in-laws, government agencies, and stresses of a national disaster that served as a constant reminder, all contributed to the difficulty in launching this project. Begun as an intervention to help with mourning, bonding, developing a community of support, and trying to minimize the transmission of the trauma, our work evolved into a long-term primary prevention project. Eventually a range of services was offered to the mothers and their children, including groups for mothers and babies, videotaped play sessions and video feedback consultations with a team of therapists. These services altered as the needs of families changed over time. The Project created a net of safety to attend to the needs of the therapist team as well.

## CONCEPTION AND PRIMARY OBJECTIVES OF THE PROJECT

I recount here how we approached and engaged a group of women who endured an unimaginable loss, a loss compounded by tragic timing. On September 11, 2001, not only were these women widowed, but also the joy and happy anticipation and predictability of their impending motherhood were abruptly ended. These women were left with a cascade of feelings of fear, anger, resentment, and grief. Beyond the loss of a husband and father for their children, the sudden and unexpected scope of the disaster increased the trauma. Our attempt to launch and implement the Mothers and Young Children Project represented our interest in bringing our psychoanalytic perspective and training out into the community during a time of collective trauma and loss.

The experience of September 11, 2001, was universal. Everyone felt that September 11 had changed everything. The date became a dividing line between a "before" and an "after" (Dudziak, 2003). People tried to make sense of the disaster, yet these events seemed incomprehensible. Amidst the developing international crisis, many people felt that we had entered into a new age of terror, and part of the coping involved people commiserating in their mourning process. Massive media scrutiny made solitary mourning impossible.

Our plan was to help the mothers work through their mourning process and to facilitate their ability to provide a stable, nurturing environment for their children. Our effort, however, was fraught with obstacles. For one thing, we sought out the mothers. This changed the way the mothers were able to receive and participate in our therapeutic intervention. Many of our mothers were constantly rushing and keeping busy, out of necessity in part, but also to keep their feelings of devastation at bay. Others were quietly grieving at home. We invited the mothers to participate in support groups and in video bonding consultations to provide a containing/holding environment for themselves and their infants. We anticipated that when the infants began to acquire language, they would turn to their mothers to understand who their fathers were and what happened to them. The mothers likely would need help handling their children's feelings of anger and loss at that time.

Our specific interventions evolved as we became more familiar with this group of families. In response to the magnitude of the trauma and their complex needs, we developed and expanded our methods of intervention. We used interdisciplinary approaches with teams of multiple therapists. We provided nontraditional services such as home visits, videotaped play sessions, and video feedback consultations.

Since spring 2002, we have had contact with approximately 40 of these widowed mothers, the infants they were carrying on September 11, 2001, and their older siblings, a total of approximately 80 children. We have also had contact with subsequent husbands and the children born into some of these new families. Over the Project's first few years, the infants grew from lap babies to toddlers, and more recently from preschoolers to entering fifth grade in the fall of 2011. As the infants and their siblings have grown, the needs of the families have changed, requiring us to be flexible and creative.

Initially our project team consisted of 18 psychoanalytically oriented therapists trained to work with mothers and infants, children, adolescents, and adults. Some brought specialized knowledge about adult grief and trauma, and one was a dance-movement therapist. Each volunteered in differing capacities with the support groups, video lab, and feedback sessions. The common ground we shared was our understanding of the importance of the earliest relationship (Stern, 1985, 1995).

## REACHING THE MOTHERS: OBSTACLES AND SUCCESSES

We learned that there were approximately 100 pregnant women whose husbands never returned from work on September 11, 2001. These women were pregnant with 103 babies, including two sets of twins. Widowed women who had given birth in the immediate months preceding September 11, 2001, faced many of the same issues as the pregnant widows. Eventually our focus expanded to offer help to these mothers as well. We realized that all of their grieving children were potentially at risk, having suffered the loss of a father, as well as experiencing a grieving mother who was also called upon to care for a new baby. We were asked many times to expand the Project to include other widowed women with older children but who did not also have a baby. With few exceptions, however, we maintained our focus on the smaller group of pregnant and new mothers who had suddenly become widows.

There were many obstacles impeding the early progress of our Project. It took several months to locate the pregnant women in our target group. Understandably, the identities of these families were being protected. Their husbands had worked for many different companies and there was no central registry. They came from a wide variety of professions including firemen, policemen, maintenance workers, Port Authority employees, corporate lawyers, and financial brokers. Most had worked in or near the World Trade Center in New York City, but there were others from Boston, Washington, D.C., Los Angeles, and other cities.

Although we learned that there were a number of pregnant women whose husbands had worked for the financial services company Cantor Fitzgerald, it took many months before we actually met them. Cantor Fitzgerald was located on the 101st–105th floors of One World Trade Center and lost 658 employees, more than any other single entity. We attempted to contact the firm, but our calls yielded no results. After many weeks of calls, we luckily connected with Bob Talbot from the human resources department. Talbot eventually became our main contact, putting us in touch with the wife of the CEO of Cantor Fitzgerald, Allison Lutnick. In spring 2002, she invited us to a series of luncheons that she hosted for the pregnant Cantor Fitzgerald widows. At the luncheons we had a chance to introduce ourselves and speak about our Project. Those luncheons helped us launch the Project.

Meanwhile, our search for pregnant widows whose husbands had worked for other firms at the World Trade Center continued throughout the spring, summer, and fall of 2002. At first, we tried to engage the women by phone or e-mail, which was not effective. Most did not answer their telephones or e-mails, and they rarely responded to messages. We continued to call, repeatedly, until a person could finally be reached on the phone. We developed a way of speaking with those who we reached on the phone. We explained that we were a group of therapists who wanted to help the women who were pregnant and lost their husbands. We needed to communicate our concern while instilling trust. Many times the mothers never came to the phone, and only a sister, mother, babysitter, or neighbor would speak with us.

Over time we realized that we were a group of strangers offering a service that *we* thought they needed, yet this was not what they thought *they* needed. At that point we began to use larger systems for outreach. We visited many of the mothers in their local churches, in hospital outpatient centers, or in various community meetings they already attended. These familiar community sites had offered different kinds of services that many of the mothers found easier to accept. By attending some of their bereavement groups, we then had the opportunity to introduce ourselves in person, to reach out and offer help. However, even this route met with mixed responses, possibly because we were therapists.

## DIFFICULTIES IMPLEMENTING THE PROJECT

Although locating the widows was not an easy task, the logistics was not the only obstacle to launching the Project. Once we connected with a number of women, convincing them to accept the services we offered was still problematic. It is well documented that individuals who have been traumatized often have difficulty availing themselves of help (Barbanel and Sternberg, 2006). We quickly became aware of the complexity of providing support and intervention for traumatized mothers and children who otherwise would not be a population that would utilize mental health services. Most had no previous history of therapy nor any expectation that a therapeutic intervention could be helpful.

Complicating things further, by the time we located the mothers, many of them had been inundated by multiple stressors, including unsolicited offers. Some of these offers, such as photo shoots and the opportunity to be featured in magazines, were at first seen as potentially positive. However, in many families, public exposure was experienced as exploitative. In agreeing to give interviews or to participate in photo shoots, many of the mothers learned that they might be called upon to speak, look, or pose themselves (and their children) in ways that made them feel uncomfortable in order to "get" what was being offered for "free." In addition, many outsiders wanted access to this vulnerable population because of their interesting circumstances. Many of those offering "help" were perceived by the mothers to be voyeuristic.

Furthermore, many of the women did not want to be seen as "9/11 widows." Most felt angry about being in a situation they did not create. Some of the mothers avoided us because we reminded them of events they wanted to forget. Others resisted becoming involved in the Project because of the perceived stigma associated with mental health services, even though they were in a distraught, traumatized state. Although we were offering assistance, we were frequently viewed as outsiders. We were challenged to gain the trust of these women.

During the first year we persevered in trying to launch the Project. Over time we learned that the complications of loss and grief had exacerbated the difficulties that these new mothers faced, difficulties that often kept them from engaging with us. In retrospect, many of the women described feeling "numb" and "out of it." In addition, an oppressive amount of paperwork was required of them, for the government, insurance companies, and lawyers. Also weighing heavily on the women was pressure from in-laws, some of whom felt that theirs was the greater loss. Naturally, in addition to all of these demands, the mothers found it difficult to deal with basic self-care needs and responsibilities to their children. For some of the mothers, they were able to participate only after they heard that we were already working with other mothers who reported they were benefiting from the Project.

Even after connecting with a number of mothers, we realized that many still were ambivalent about attending group or individual appointments that we tried to arrange. Eventually, we became aware of some of the mothers' unfamiliarity and/or discomfort with the world of psychotherapy. Instead of offering "therapeutic" services, we explained that our groups would provide a community of support. We were offering to videotape the mothers interacting with their babies so that they could learn about the infant's and preverbal child's "nonverbal language." This would provide an opportunity for the mothers to see how their babies were doing, like a "well-baby" check-up.

After the Project was launched, we needed to find a way to facilitate the mothers coming into the city to attend video sessions with their children and to attend the follow-up feedback sessions. Once we were funded, we began to offer a car service to pick up and return these families from their homes. In this way, we were able to ensure a greater reliability in attendance. Because most of the mothers lived two hours outside of Manhattan, we needed funding to be able to offer this car service. The car service became essential to the Project.

## SUPPORT GROUPS FOR MOTHERS AND INFANTS: FINDING THERAPISTS AND BUILDING COMMUNITY

In response to this unprecedented disaster, many therapists in the New York City area experienced a profound sense of upheaval. They were highly motivated to help those who were most directly affected. At first we thought most of the pregnant women lived in or near the New York City area. We expected that they would be seen in New York City where we had access to many highly qualified therapists who were willing to volunteer their time to work with the women. We soon learned that almost none of the affected families actually lived in the New York City area.

Many of the families lived in towns from which husbands commuted as much as two hours to work at the World Trade Center. Furthermore, many of the women would not travel into the city. For some, New York City was a location to be avoided at all costs. This required us to locate and recruit therapists in the outlying suburban areas close to where the mothers actually lived.

Early in spring 2002, we arranged an orientation meeting for all the therapists we had recruited, most of whom we had not met, nor had they ever met each other. We laid out a map of the areas surrounding New York City in New Jersey, Long Island, and Staten Island. We located towns where mothers lived and towns where therapists lived. In this way we organized five support groups near the towns where the mothers lived.

We then decided to arrange regular meetings of the therapists, initially to coordinate what was going on in the Project, and later to offer peer supervision to all the therapists. Our bimonthly peer supervision group evolved out of this need (see below).

We organized mothers' groups in Long Island; North, South, and Central New Jersey; and Manhattan. Each mother was invited to participate in a group with her infant and, if it pertained, her older toddler or preschooler. Our initial goal was for the therapists to bring together mothers and their babies and young children in weekly groups. We attempted to place in each group two or three therapists with three kinds of expertise: adult trauma, child trauma, and mother-infant treatment. We hoped that by seeing the mothers and children as a group we would be able to attend to the quality of the developing relationships among the mothers and children in the face of their shared loss (see Bergman, Moskowitz and Friedman, *Support Group I;* Sossin, *Support Group II;* and Reiswig, *Support Group II*, this issue).

The therapists were instructed to help the mothers coalesce as a group to provide support for each other. The therapists were not to be the "experts" but rather would encourage the mothers to share their own solutions with each other. The focus would be on mourning, mother-infant bonding, and any current needs and/or problems the mothers might be facing, including with their infants, other children, or extended family.

Each group was unique with regard to relationships among mothers, needs of each mother and child dyad, and the relationships among collaborating therapists. The mothers varied in their capacities for empathy, group participation, and reflection, as well as age, length of marriage, living circumstances, prior experience of trauma, number of children, education, career, economic status, husband's career, and family relations. Until the women got to know each other, the diversity within the groups was often challenging to the facilitation of empathy. Some of the husbands had worked in civil service while others had worked in business and finance, creating a large cultural gap. The women were also in different places with regard to their psychological needs, their courses of healing, and their relationships with their children. We observed differences in how the mothers reacted based on their acute versus chronic problems. We kept in mind a basic psychoanalytic principle that the best predictor for how the children would develop was the mother-child relationship (Fonagy et al., 2002).

At the height of our Project, we were running five groups. Some of the groups of mothers and children met weekly and others met biweekly or monthly. All of the groups were run by the female therapists in the Project except one that was co-led by the only male therapist in our Project, Dr. Mark Sossin. In the group with Dr. Sossin, the mothers had the opportunity to experience both a male (Dr. Sossin) and a female therapist (Rita Reiswig) who, at times, served as a "father-mother" pair as well as a "couple." In addition, the third therapist in that group, Dr. Kirsten Kupferman, was often seen as a supportive and wise "grandmother figure." In relation to Dr. Sossin, some of the mothers were more aware of their newly emerging identities as single mother and single woman in relation to a male figure (Sossin, 2006; Cohen and Sossin, 2006). In another group, the children had an opportunity to relate to each other in a play group with a trained child therapist while the mothers met separately with a separate adult therapist.

## VIDEO BONDING CONSULTATIONS AT NEW YORK STATE PSYCHIATRIC INSTITUTE

All of the mothers were offered the opportunity to be videotaped interacting with their babies and older children. This two-session intervention involved the mother and child coming to the lab at New York State Psychiatric Institute (NYSPI) and a feedback session for the mother approximately a week later at Dr. Beebe's clinical office. The lab videotaping session occurred in two parts. The mother and child were videotaped playing together first, and the mother was instructed to play with her child as she would at home, for about 10 minutes. Next, the child played with one of the Project therapists, generally Dr. Beebe when they were infants and Drs. Cohen or Sossin when the babies became toddlers and preschoolers (see Sossin and Cohen, this issue). In the feedback sessions, the mother viewed sections of the videotape with the therapists, and she was able to understand aspects of the communication patterns between herself and her children (Beebe, 2003, 2005; Cohen and Beebe, 2002).

The mothers who participated in the "video bonding and communication consultations" were told that "the therapists in the Project were concerned with the effect of trauma on infant and child development and the course of healing for the widowed families," and that "some of the therapists have had years of experience in doing research and observations of infant and child development." We explained to the mothers that the Project had a research component, which we were planning. If research were carried out at a later point, such research could potentially benefit children, parents, and caregivers who might find themselves in a similar situation. The mothers were assured that their participation in the research aspect of the Project was entirely voluntary, and that if they declined, all other aspects of the Project would still be available to them.

We found that all of the mothers who received our services agreed to participate in both research and clinical components of the Project. They were committed to help others who might find themselves in a similar situation. The same questionnaires that the mothers were asked to complete for the clinical aspect of the Project (regarding their mood and their loss) would be an aspect of the research component at a later point.

During the first year, all feedback sessions were conducted by Drs. Beebe and Cohen as a team. Over time we discovered the value, for everyone involved, of having more than two therapists participate in these intense and painful sessions. Our model eventually evolved to utilize multiple therapists (see Cohen, *Video Feedback*, this issue). Although we had thought the mothers might be overwhelmed by three or four therapists in the feedback sessions, the mothers never seemed to experience the session this way. In fact, they have consistently reported that meeting with a group of therapists is a powerful and generous event.

Prior to each feedback session, the therapists meet to discuss areas of strength and concern and ways we might intervene with each mother. As we watch the video, the therapists identify video segments during which the mother-child pair generates positive moments. At times we may also identify problematic moments of interactions if we feel the mother is receptive. In the feedback session, we aim to create an environment in which the mother can look at the video and see her child in a new, potentially transformative way. At times, a mother may avoid seeing the video altogether, while at other times the therapists might decide not to show the video because we may sense the mother's vulnerability and lack of readiness to see herself or her child. Or we may decide that, in this particular session, the mother's own needs take precedence. Our interventions in any one session were always psychodynamically oriented, and they might also include a combination of positive reinforcement, modeling, and information giving, as well as interpretation when appropriate.

As the children have grown older, we have shifted our focus to helping the mothers learn to communicate with their children through their play (see Sossin and Cohen, this issue). When we watch the video with a mother, we offer her a way to join her child by following the child's lead in the play story. Upon seeing her child construct themes with angry, aggressive, painful, or fearful content, the mother's first reaction is usually to try to diffuse or repair the traumatic play themes. We help the mother to tolerate her child's angry or fearful themes. We help the mother find ways to help her child express meaning for herself rather than imposing her own thinking and narratives on her child (Fonagy et al., 2002). We encourage the mothers to join the play in such a way that they can facilitate the child's process of mourning and healing.

Over time, we have observed the mothers grow to appreciate the value of the play. They learn to step back and allow the internal process of the child to unfold, rather than redirecting the play. Most of the mothers have developed the capacity to allow their children to express sadness, anger, and fear. We have encouraged the mothers to set aside a special 10–15 minute block of time to play with their children whenever possible, even daily. We have also tried to help the mothers find ways to facilitate their children's representations of their fathers (see Reiswig, this issue; Sossin and Cohen, this issue). Many mothers have been reluctant to tell their children even the most basic information about how the fathers died. We have spoken about what and how the child can be told about what happened to the father, and how this may change as the children grow older.

Using the video has been a powerful means to help a mother learn to read the subtleties of her child's communication. For example, is the child directly oriented to her or partially oriented away? Does the child make any eye contact? Is the child calm or fidgety? The video helps her observe both the effects of the mother's behavior on the child and the effects of the child's behavior on herself. Each mother-child dyad has been invited back for video and feedback sessions every six months to a year. As the children have grown older, they have become more verbal, sharing more intimate details with the therapists during the child-therapist videotaping. As a result, it has become necessary for us to protect the child's confidentiality during videotapings with the therapist. When the children were infants, toddlers, and very young children, we gave copies of the video recordings of both mother-child and therapist-child play sessions, for mothers to review at home. Now we give mothers only a copy of their own interaction with their children.

Over the years of the Project we have observed an incremental effect on the mothers and children. Each session builds on what happened in the previous sessions. While specific themes and content have changed over time, deeper issues and patterns of interaction have been consistent from one time to the next. It has been gratifying for the therapists to hear from the mothers and children how something we may have said a year before had changed things for them in a positive way. On the other hand, as all of the children have grown, many of the mothers are becoming reticent to take them out of school to attend the video sessions. We are now offering mothers the opportunity to meet with our team of therapists, whether or not the lab visit with the children has been possible.

## PEER SUPERVISION GROUP FOR THERAPISTS AND THE TRANSMISSION OF TRAUMA

Our motivation to become involved in the Project was influenced by our desire to reach out and help a vulnerable group at a time when we too felt helpless and vulnerable. Choosing to work specifically with women who were pregnant and widowed or had very young babies carried a very deep, personal meaning for each therapist. Some of us carried legacies of intergenerational trauma and loss, while others associated to our own experiences as mothers with our own infants and young children (see Beebe, Cohen, Bergman, Moskowitz, Sossin, Reiswig, et al., this issue). Influenced by our individual histories and styles of coping, we were affected by the situations of these widowed women in complicated and personal ways.

The most important factor that helped us stay connected to our work with these families has proven to be our peer group forum. We created the peer group in response to the clinical difficulty of the work and the logistical complexity of coordinating the support groups, video bonding consultations, and feedback sessions. The therapist group was a place where we could process disruptions and rejections and where we could contain our own anxiety and disappointments. Knowing we might be vulnerable to the secondary trauma of working with people suffering from a traumatic event (otherwise known as "vicarious traumatization" or "compassion fatigue") (McCann and Pearlmen, 1990; Pearlman and Saakvitnek, 1995; Figley, 1995), we began to use the peer group to process our experiences, consider clinical strategies, and discuss our evolving relationships with each other, and clinical strategies. The peer group has met in mutually supportive two-hour sessions every other week since the Project began in the winter of 2001.

Despite many obstacles, notably the uncertainties of working with this severely traumatized group of families, we have persevered because of the coherence of our therapist peer group. Eventually, the group became a forum for the therapists to discuss the transmission of trauma. Early in the Project, the mothers told stories of the initial moments, hours, and days after the attacks on September 11, 2001. Most of the mothers cried, but some did not. Often in the feedback sessions, one of the therapists would be tearful, even if the mother was not. At times it was as difficult and painful for the mothers to speak about their grief or to talk about the potential effect of the loss on their children as it was for the therapists to hear and metabolize the mothers' painful experiences.

In the beginning of the Project, many of the mothers expressed: "You can't help us . . . our families and friends can't help us . . . no one can help us . . . ." At times we joined the mothers in their feelings of helplessness. They could not help their husbands; they could not do anything to prevent what happened, and neither could we. We offered to help, but we could not help. Here we were, all these "helpers," wanting to help—yet at times we felt helpless ourselves. In a parallel process, the helplessness that the mothers felt was transmitted to us. We went through these stories many times with all of the women in the Project. At times we felt overwhelmed. At other times we felt discouraged.

As the Project evolved, we came to understand that some aspects of the mothers' trauma were transmitted to the therapists in the experience of helplessness and "not-knowing." Thus, whether the mothers attended a scheduled group session or not, we encouraged our group therapists to meet together at the scheduled times. When mothers did come, the therapists would spend an hour together after the session, without the mothers present, discussing the group's themes and process. They would discuss their personal reactions and thoughts, as well as their concerns for the children, the mothers, and/or for each other. When the mothers did not come, the therapists spent that time discussing what the mothers might be feeling and what the therapists were feeling.

Our peer group has helped the therapists of the Project grow professionally and personally. It has enabled us to monitor and manage the complex emotions related to the transmission of trauma between family and therapist. We depended upon each other to contain our personal feelings so that we, in turn, could help the mothers to contain their own and those of their children.

## DIFFICULTIES SECURING FUNDING

We began our work on a pro bono basis. We did not have any idea if the Project would succeed or how long it would last. Initially, we thought we might run the Project until the infants reached the age of 2. However, over time, it became clear that much more time and effort were needed than we had anticipated.

We attempted to apply for funding to continue the work, a daunting process. Our specific challenge was to address the needs of the grieving widows and children while at the same time requesting support for the Project. We needed to write and submit proposals for grants, in essence, to translate what we thought would be most helpful into something that would "fit" the requirements of a funding source. There was a great need for philanthropic support in the early days following the attacks on the World Trade Center, and the foundation world was overwhelmed by requests for help.

We submitted approximately 50 proposals for grants. During this time when we were having difficulty getting funded, the Margaret Mahler Foundation gave us a small but inspirational gift. After almost one year of frustration, we eventually received funding from Project Liberty and Project Phoenix, which covered our Project from September 2002 through August 2003. We were then able to receive funding from the Robin Hood Foundation from September 2003 through December 2005. These two grants covered a large portion of the costs of the Project at that time. While securing these grants definitely contributed to a feeling of being supported, administering the funds was difficult. For one grant in particular, a great deal of time was needed to attend to a significant amount of required paperwork. In addition, even though we had support groups running in both New York and New Jersey, some grant funding was earmarked for one region and not the other.

By December 2005, most of the federal funding as well as private charity support for grants for work related to September 11, 2001, had ended. Since then, we have been fortunate to have received partial support for the Project from the Hazelcorn Foundation, the Kenworthy-Swift Foundation, and a small grant from the American Psychological Foundation and the American Psychoanalytic Fund. Also, individuals from the psychoanalytic communities in New York City and Los Angeles have generously made personal donations. Since December 2005, despite this partial support, most of the work has been performed pro bono.

## THE PROJECT TODAY AND BEYOND

Today, in the spring of 2011, almost 10 years after the day that changed history, our Project continues to evolve. As the families continue to recover, no two look alike. Each develops in a unique way, requiring a unique approach. As the children grow, we continue to provide support and resources for the long-term effects of this traumatic loss on the subsequent life developments of mothers and children.

This year, the children whose mothers were pregnant on September 11, 2001, will turn 10. As their cognitive abilities flourish, we continue to observe how they and their older siblings have been affected by their losses. For the infants born after September 11, 2001, losing their fathers before they were born has had an effect on their development across the domains of learning, emotion, and relationship styles. As the children grow, their cognitive and emotional developments add new dimensions to the Project. Interacting with the children during lab visits, we continue to observe repetitive themes generated by the loss of a father who is known through the preverbal experiences of the mother's traumatic loss and through representations transmitted by the mother (see Reiswig, this issue; Tortora, this issue).

More than half of the mothers contacted in those early painful months still visit us. Some of the mothers now come for individual consultation sessions with our team of therapists, without bringing the children to the lab videotaping sessions. Initially, support groups were as central to our approach as the video feedback consultations. However, in latter years the communication and feedback consultations have emerged as the core of the Project. One of the original five support groups continues to meet. This remarkable group of mothers remains committed to looking at the evolution of their trauma as they discuss their new life challenges. Many of our mothers have nurtured new relationships, remarried, or had one or more new babies. Some are facing the new challenge of sustaining blended families. Many strive to maintain a balance between integrating a new father into their children's lives while keeping alive the memory of the father lost on September 11, 2001 (see Reiswig, this issue).

Some mothers have returned to graduate school or to the workforce or have become community leaders who direct foundations or memorials in their lost husbands' memories. Some of the mothers do not visit us anymore, either from a feeling of closure or because we continue to represent frightening, out-of-control moments in time. Still, there are many mothers and children we have not yet found, mothers to whom we would like to offer the benefits of what we have learned over these years. We still remain open to new families.

As for the cohort of eight therapists who remain in the Project, we continue to think about all the mothers and children—those who still attend our sessions, those with whom we have lost contact, and those we have never met. We still meet every other week to deepen our understanding of the work we have done and continue doing with the families and to discuss its effect on us. Our mutual support and ability to evaluate our work together has sustained the Project all these years. As we continue to help the mothers and children shape coherent narratives of their stories of loss and pain in the context of their new life challenges, we ourselves continue to grow.

## PRESENTATIONS OF THE PROJECT AS THE PROJECT EVOLVED 2002–2011

### 2002

Beebe, B. & Jaffe, J. (2002), Support groups for mothers and children, and parent-child video bonding consultations, for mothers pregnant and widowed on 9/11. Grant funded by Project Liberty 2002, Robin Hood Foundation 2003. New York Psychiatric Institute.

Beebe, B. (2002). Mothers and infants of 9/11: A model for a program of primary prevention. In: Trauma, loss, and communal grieving: The experiences of pregnant women, new mothers, and maternity care providers after 9/11. Presented at New York Academy of Medicine, November, New York City.

## 2004

Bergman, A. & Cohen, P. (2004), The intergenerational transmission of trauma following 9/11. In: Lost in translation: A study of trauma across generations. Presented at Austin-Riggs Center, October, Stockbridge, MA.

## 2005

Bergman, A. (2005), The case of Bobby. Presented at meeting of Division 39 of American Psychological Association, April, New York City.

Cohen, P. (2005), Multi-layered holding environments and parallel processes. Presented at meeting of Division 39 of American Psychological Association, April, New York City.

Sossin, M. (2005), Widowed mothers and infants of 9/11: A model for a program of primary prevention and intervention. Presented at meeting of Division 39 of American Psychological Association, April, New York City.

Beebe, B. (2005), Video bonding consultations. Presented at meeting of Division 39 of American Psychological Association, April, New York City.

Sossin, M. (2005), Comments on the mother-child video analysis in the NYSPI 9/11 Project. Presented at meeting of Division 39 of American Psychological Association, April, New York City.

Cohen, P. & Bergman A. (2005), A video-feedback session with Bobby's parents. Presented at meeting of Division 39 of American Psychological Association, April, New York City.

Bergman, A. (2005), What have we learned? Trauma, risk, coping, resilience, and models of intervention. Presented at meeting of Division 39 of American Psychological Association, April, New York City.

Bergman, A. (2005). Introduction to the 9/11 mothers and young children Project. In: Intergenerational transmission of trauma: What we have learned in our work with mothers and infants affected by the trauma of 9/11. Presented at meeting of Institute for Psychoanalytic Training and Research, May, New York City.

Reiswig, R. (2005). What is transmitted from the mother to the child about the father lost on 9/11: Preliminary sketches of three styles of transmission. In: Intergenerational transmission of trauma: What we have learned in our work with mothers and infants affected by the trauma of 9/11. Presented at meeting of Institute for Psychoanalytic Training and Research, May, New York City.

Sossin, M. (2005). Trauma transmission: Mother-child dyads in the wake of 9/11. In: Intergenerational transmission of trauma: What we have learned in our work with mothers and infants affected by the trauma of 9/11. Presented at meeting of Institute for Psychoanalytic Training and Research, May, New York City.

Tortora, S. (2005). The use of nonverbal movement analysis during the lab visits. In: Intergenerational transmission of trauma: What we have learned in our work with mothers and infants affected by the trauma of 9/11. Presented at meeting of Institute for Psychoanalytic Training and Research, May, New York City.

Moskowitz, S. (2005). Primary maternal preoccupation disrupted by trauma and loss. In: Intergenerational transmission of trauma: What we have learned in our work with mothers and infants affected by the trauma of 9/11. Presented at meeting of Institute for Psychoanalytic Training and Research, May, New York City.

Cohen, P. (2005), Discussion of intergenerational transmission of trauma: What we have learned in our work with mothers and infants affected by the trauma of 9/11. Presented at meeting of Institute for Psychoanalytic Training and Research, May, New York City.

Sossin, M. (2005), Transmission of disillusionment. Mother-child dyads in the wake of 9/11. Presented at International Psychoanalytic Congress, July, Rio de Janeiro, Brazil.

Tortora, S. (2005), The use of nonverbal movement analysis during the lab visits. Presented at International Psychoanalytic Congress, July, Rio de Janeiro, Brazil.

Bergman, A. (2005), Introduction to the 9/11 mothers and young children project. Presented at International Psychoanalytic Congress, July, Rio de Janeiro, Brazil.

Reiswig, R. (2005), What is transmitted from the mother to the child about the father lost on 9/11: Preliminary sketches of three styles of transmission. Presented at International Psychoanalytic Congress, July, Rio de Janeiro, Brazil.

Moskowitz, S. (2005), Primary maternal preoccupation disrupted by trauma and loss. Presented at International Psychoanalytic Congress, July, Rio de Janeiro, Brazil.

Sossin, M. (2005). Play in the wake of traumatic loss. In: *Support groups and mother-infant video bonding consultation for mothers pregnant and widowed on 9/11*. Presented at MI-AIMH 28th Biennial Conference, Michigan Association for Infant Mental Health, October, Ann Arbor, MI.

Tortora, S. (2005), The use of nonverbal movement analysis during the lab visits. Support groups and mother-infant video bonding consultations for mothers pregnant and widowed on 9-11. Michigan Association for infant mental health (MI-AIMH), October, Ann Arbor, MI.

## 2006

Tortora, S. (2006), The use of nonverbal movement analysis in the treatment of women pregnant and widowed on 9-11. Intergenerational transmission of trauma: What we have learned in our work with mothers and infants affected by the trauma of 9/11. IPTAR, May, New York City.

Cohen, P. & Bergman, A. (2006), 9/11 mothers and young children project: A model for primary prevention and intervention for trauma and loss. Presented at Bank Street, June, New York City.

Demetri Friedman, D. (2006). Themes and techniques in the mother-infant groups. In: Support groups and mother-infant bonding consultations for mothers pregnant and widowed on 9/11-01. Symposium conducted at meeting of World Association for Infant Mental Health, July, Paris.

Sossin, M. (2006). Play and interactive styles in mother-child dyads: Longitudinal follow-up following 9/11 loss. In: Support groups and mother-infant bonding consultations for mothers pregnant and widowed on 9/11-01. Symposium conducted at meeting of World Association for Infant Mental Health, July, Paris.

Reiswig, R. (2006). What is transmitted from the mother to the child about the father lost on 9/11: Preliminary sketches of three styles of transmission. In: Support groups and mother-infant bonding consultations for mothers pregnant and widowed on 9/11-01. Symposium conducted at meeting of World Association for Infant Mental Health, July, Paris.

Reiswig, R. (2006). The compromises of motherhood. In: Support groups and mother-infant bonding consultations for mothers pregnant and widowed on 9/11-01. Symposium conducted at meeting of World Association for Infant Mental Health, July, Paris.

Tortora, S. (2006). The use of nonverbal movement analysis during the lab visits. In: Support groups and mother-infant bonding consultations for mothers pregnant and widowed on 9/11-01. Symposium conducted at meeting of World Association for Infant Mental Health, July, Paris.

Cohen, P. & Sossin, M. (2006), Mother-infant groups, video feedback consultation and interventions for those who suffered traumatic loss: Considering loss and 9/11. Invited presentation at meetings jointly sponsored by Kansas City Association for Psychoanalytic Psychology and Greater Kansas City-Topeka Psychoanalytic Center, October, Kansas City, MO.

## 2007

Reiswig, R. (2007). What is transmitted from the mother to the child about the father lost on 9/11: Preliminary sketches of three styles of transmission. In: *Longitudinal impressions from the World Trade Center project: Following families who lost*. Symposium conducted at meeting of Division 39 of American Psychological Association, April, Toronto, Canada.

Moskowitz, S. (2007). Primary maternal preoccupation disrupted by trauma and loss. In: Longitudinal impressions from the World Trade Center project: Following families who lost. Symposium conducted at meeting of Division 39 of American Psychological Association, April, Toronto, Canada.

Tortora, S. (2007). The use of nonverbal movement analysis in the treatment of women pregnant and widowed on 9/11. In: Longitudinal impressions from the World Trade Center project: Following families who lost. Symposium conducted at meeting of Division 39 of American Psychological Association, April, Toronto, Canada.

Demetri Friedman, D. (2007). Pre-natal loss of the father and related difficulties in mother-child and adult attachments. In: Longitudinal impressions from the World Trade Center project: Following families who lost. Symposium conducted at meeting of Division 39 of merican Psychological Association, April, Toronto, Canada.

Sossin, K. M. & Cohen, P. (2007). Play processes and the themes as evidenced in young children during their first five years. In: Longitudinal impressions from the World Trade Center project: Following families who lost. Symposium conducted at meeting of Division 39 of American Psychological Association, April, Toronto, Canada.

## 2008

Cohen, P. (2008). Who is my father, and what happened to him? Video feedback with 9/11 widowed mothers. In: Children playing with a background of loss: Development and clinical inferences gleaned from the World Trade Center project. Panel conducted at meeting of Division 39 of American Psychological Association, April, New York City.

Sossin, M. (2008). Young children coping with the loss of their fathers on 9/11: Implicit and explicit processes in dyadic play. In: Children playing with a background of loss: Development and clinical inferences gleaned from the World Trade Center project. Panel conducted at meeting of Division 39 of American Psychological Association, April, New York City.

Beebe, B. (2008). Discussion of Cohen and Sossin, 9/11 mothers and young children project. In: Children playing with a background of loss: Development and clinical inferences gleaned from the World Trade Center project. Panel conducted at meeting of Division 39 of American Psychological Association, April, New York City.

Moskowitz, S. (2008). Primary maternal preoccupation disrupted by trauma and loss. In: New perspectives in Mahler's separation-individuation theory. Presented at International Margaret Mahler Symposium, May, Padua, Italy.

## 2010

Cohen, P. & Sossin, M. (2010), Adapting a psychoanalytic frame in the shadow of loss: New methods and findings from a project helping the grieving mothers and children of 9/11. Sponsored by Division 39 Outreach Committee of American Psychological Association, April, Chicago.

Cohen, P. & Sossin, M. (2010), Trauma and resilience in the 9/11 families: A primary prevention project. Presented at New York City Chapter, Zero to Three Conference, May, New York City.

Demetri Friedman, D. (2010), Treatment case of siblings who lost their father in the World Trade Center disaster [Panel discussion], presented at New York City Chapter, Zero to Three Conference, May, New York City.

Moskowitz, S. (2010), Primary maternal preoccupation disrupted by trauma and loss. Presented at New York City Chapter, Zero to Three Conference, May, New York City.

Reiswig, R. (2010), Creating space for mourning a lost father and husband after September 11: A therapist's reflections. Presented at New York City Chapter, Zero to Three Conference, May, New York City.

Tortora, S. (2010), Beyond the face and words: How the body speaks. Trauma and resilience in the lives of young children and their families. New York Zero to Three Network, May, New York City.

Tortora, S. (2010), The nonverbal transmission of trauma as it relates to the developing attachment relationship. Military projects & Zero to Three National Training Institute, May, Phoenix, AZ, co-presented with Mulrooney, K., Military families and complicated parental death: Supporting the youngest child in the context of traumatic loss and suicide.

## 2011

Demetri Friedman, D. (2011), Treatment case of siblings who lost their father in the World Trade Center disaster [Panel discussion, Growing up with 9/11]. Presented at Academy of Critical Incident Analysis, July, New York.

Cohen, P., Sossin, K. M. & Tortora, S. (2011), Using play and video feedback: New methods and findings from a project helping the grieving mothers and children of September 11, 2001. One-day training with Dr. Lisa Mennet and the Seattle Group, February, New York City.

Tortora, S. (2011), Beyond the face and words: How the body speaks. Using play and video feedback: New methods and findings from a project helping the grieving mothers and children of September 11, 2001. One-day training with Dr. Lisa Mennet and the Seattle Group, February, New York City.

Reiswig, R. (2011), Creating space for mourning a lost father and husband after September 11: A therapist's reflections. Panel on working with the dying patients and their families, our practice today: Treatment and transformation. Presented at Mount Sinai Medical Center, March, New York City.

Demetri Freedman, D. (2011), The 9-11 mothers and young children project at the 10-year mark. With Gerald Fromm, Austen Riggs, July, New York City.

Sossin, K. M. (2011), Transforming communal trauma into a community of memory: 9/11's legacy. Memorialization and the tenth anniversary of 9/11/2001. Sponsored by Division 56 and APA Annual Meeting of American Psychological Association, August, Washington, DC.

## BIBLIOGRAPHY

Barbanel, L. & Sternberg, R.(Eds.) (2006). *Psychological Interventions in Times of Crisis*. New York: Springer Publishing Company, Inc.

Beebe, B. (2003). Brief mother-infant treatment using psychoanalytically informed video microanalysis. *Infant Mental Health Journal, 24*(1): 24–52.

Beebe, B. (2005), Mother-infant research informs mother-infant treatment. *Psychoanalytic Study of the Child, 60*, 7–46.

Cohen, P. M. & Beebe, B. (2002). Video feedback with a depressed mother and her infant: A collaborative individual psychoanalytic and mother-infant treatment. *Journal of Infant, Child, and Adolescent Psychotherapy, 2*(3), 1–55.

Cohen, P. M. & Sossin, K. M. (2006). Mother-infant groups, video-feedback consultation and interventions for those who suffered traumatic loss: Considering loss and 9/11. Invited presentation, Kansas City Association for Psychoanalytic Psychology and Greater Kansas City-Topeka Psychoanalytic Center, Kansas City, MO.

Dudziak, M. L. (2003). *September 11th in history: A watershed moment*. Durham, NC: Duke University Press.

Figley, C. (1995). *Compassion fatigue*. New York: Bruner Mazel, Psychosocial Stress Series.

Fonagy, P., Gergely, G., Jurist, E. & Target, M. (2002). *Affect regulation, mentalization and the development of the self*. New York: Other Press.

McCann, L. & Pearlman, L. (1990). Vicarious traumatization: A framework for understanding psychological effects of working with victims. *Journal of Traumatic Stress, 3*(1), 131–49.

Pearlman, L. A. & Saakvitne, K. W. (1995). *Trauma and the therapist*. New York: WW Norton & Co.

Sossin, K. M. (2006). Trauma transmission: Mother-child dyads in the wake of 9/11. Presentation (with collaborators P. Cohen, A. Bergman, R. Reiswig, S. Tortora & S. Moskowitz) on NYSPI 9/11 project for mothers and children. Institute for Psychoanalytic Training and Research, New York City.

Stern, D. (1985). *The interpersonal world of the infant: A view from psychoanalysis and developmental psychology*. New York: Basic Books.

Stern, D. (1995). *The Motherhood constellation*. New York: Basic Books.

# The Mothers' Experiences of the Project

Mothers of the Project, Anonymous *(Quoted with permission by Beatrice Beebe, Ph.D.)*

In the Project for Mothers, Infants, and Young Children of September 11, 2001, mothers brought their children to the lab for a filmed play session. After having run the Project for several years, we began to ask the mothers at each lab visit to let us know how the Project might have helped them and how we might improve our Project. We have permission to reprint the following comments.

"This Project has helped me so much because I used to feel so alone and scared after 9/11. It was comforting to know that the people doing this Project really want to help me and my daughter. I knew that I was not alone. I knew that I could get support when I needed it."

"This Project gave me greater insight into each of my children. Throughout, one or two children are videotaped. I was able to speak about issues among and between all of them. The feedback I was given was invaluable to each child and the way I connect with them. Your group has pointed me in the direction of local counselors and even found one to come to my home. It was always easy to get here and 'chauffeured' gave me one-on-one time with my children. I am very grateful! Thank you."

"This Project has benefited us immensely. The video bonding and consultation in particular lets you see yourself as you relate to your child in a way you would not have an opportunity elsewhere. Because of my experience with 9/11, my bond with my child is very strong. At times maybe it was too strong—the video lets you see it. I learned to step back and let go a bit and let him 'drive the bus.' In my desire to protect and be everything for him, I was trying too hard. Now it is much more organic. This process also has made me aware of how important it is to reach out for help and that I was not ok after 9/11 and that it will always be a part of me. It has shaped who we are."

"This Project has been and continues to be an amazing experience for me. It has helped me understand my child at every stage, allowing me to be a truly effective parent. I share an incredible bond with my child—due in large part to my ability to truly understand my child. This Project is now helping me to help my child through feelings of grief over the loss of our father/husband. I don't know what I would have done without Dr. Beebe and her team to help me through my tragedy and help me gain the understanding and confidence I needed to be the very best parent I can be."

". . . I believe the Project has truly helped me cope with the death of my husband. I am the type that probably wouldn't have consulted a therapist on my own . . . Losing my husband and being pregnant at the same time was the most difficult thing I have ever gone through . . . Without their guidance and support I would have been constantly questioning my actions, my mothering, and whether my children were O.K. Everyone says children are resilient, they get over things. This may be so. However, if I didn't have the support and guidance we may have just *moved on* and not properly grieved. I am so thankful for these Projects and these people. It is difficult to truly express what they have done for me and what it means to me."

"This Project has benefited me in so many ways. I've been able to process my grief and emotions, etc. I believe the greatest benefit I received from this Project has been my understanding of my child . . . I have been able to take what I've learned during every stage of my child's life and truly connect. We have a great relationship. I know so much of that comes from what I've learned in the last six years with this Project."

". . . I want to be able to be there for my children, be attentive to their needs, and Dr. Beebe, Mark, and Phyllis really help me to see my children with a clearer perspective. This study is important because although my children are "normal," they have experienced a great loss at a young age, which has changed the course of their lives. They will carry this loss with them always, but they don't need it to define them or hinder their joy in life. Because this study focuses on 9/11 children, the therapists are able to help me help my children continue to grow and develop in a healthy way."

"The first thing I always felt that was very good for me was the fact the therapists came to our group and made it very easy for us to get help. They called *us* and didn't leave it up to us to call them. I probably wouldn't have called. These therapists have helped me raise my children in a way I'm happy about. They helped me with grief, and most importantly with the difficulties of raising strong willed children."

"This Project benefits my family by providing a touchstone for where we are today, our growth, our changes as a family since 9/11 rocked our stability and took our father/husband. Mostly because I gain confidence in my mothering when I am guided/evaluated by professionals! I appreciate you keeping track of my path towards loving, confident, able-to-handle-all-things mothering."

"This Project has been enormously useful for our family. Initially we were all terrified after 9/11; we worried about the health and emotional consequences of the event on our kids. This group helped us make sense out of what was going on with our child, it gave us a forum for dealing with our feelings and worries after 9/11."

"Being without their Dad is an ongoing process through life. There are so many ups and downs. People don't understand what we go through on a day-to-day basis. Dr. Beebe, Dr. Mark Sossin, Phyllis, and Rita Reiswig are so helpful listening and caring in our lives. As a mom I work so hard to make sure my kids are happy and feel so guilty and sad if they are not. I travel two hours each way every month. I love our meetings and need them."

"By watching your child play, I've learned that you can really learn a lot about what they're feeling and the fears that they have. This Project has helped me to understand and to listen to my children better and to follow their lead."

"This Project has benefited me because I am able to have a team of people helping me observe my interactions with my child. I see myself in a way that is not possible, but for the videotaping and feedback. The support of the group watching the interactions keeps me aware of our behavior and helps us improve our relationship."

*One child's comment*: "We get to see our friends and stuff, and it's fun to play, and it's nice to figure out what they want to say about us."

"This Project has been an extremely valuable on-going support to our family. I feel fortunate to have had the opportunity to share our experiences surrounding 9/11 in this on-going study. All of our worries, concerns, and questions surrounding the effect of 9/11 on our child have been addressed by the group. It has been reassuring to have the support for me as I try to support my child."

"This Project has been a God-send for me. First it helped me deal with being a single Mom to my infant. I learned to understand my child in ways I may not have if I didn't have the expertise of the psychologists involved in the Project. They helped me address my grief and my child's grief. Now that my child is getting older, the grief is evolving and new issues are arising. This Project continues to be a source of information and assistance to help me raise an emotionally healthy human being. My child and I have a very strong bond. I am confident that I have done right by my child thus far. I am also confident that the knowledge I gained through this Project has played a huge role and will continue to play a huge role in allowing me to understand and raise my child. I am eternally grateful to the psychologists for creating this Project, offering their expertise and continuing to care for those of us who were and continue to be profoundly affected by the events of 9/11."

"As our child grows older, we are grateful for the ongoing support and feedback that we receive from this group of therapists. It has been a privilege to have the multiple perspectives integrated with insight on the development and needs of our son. It helps us clarify the schools, therapies, etc., that we are doing with him and gives us help in ongoing areas of concern."

"I must tell you that I am forever grateful to you (and everyone) for the time you have dedicated to helping me/us work through everything. It is truly probably the one place where I feel like I can safely share just about anything. And that is invaluable."

"As months and years pass, coming to see Dr. Beebe and her associates always connects my family to the past and to each other by creating a touchstone, a reference, a day of sharing our thoughts and feelings when we so often don't take time in our busy lives to reflect. We learn about each other and where our 'heads' are at this moment, and we always leave feeling better. Better about how far we've come since 9/11 and hopeful about the future. The only thing that would improve the Project is if we could see everyone and speak about ourselves more often!"

"We enjoy coming to this program. I feel that Dr. Beebe, Dr. Cohen, and Dr. Sossin are like family. They have helped us through very difficult times and they really care. I feel very comfortable seeing them. I think it is very helpful for my children to talk to the team."

# MOTHERS AND CHILDREN IN THE EARLY YEARS OF THE SUPPORT GROUPS

## Introduction to the Support Groups

K. Mark Sossin, Ph.D.

Multiple groups were formed in New Jersey, Long Island, and Manhattan. Each had two or three therapists, most of whom were psychoanalytically trained. The three therapists could share and exchange roles as they saw fit. An overarching model emerged wherein two therapists usually focused most closely on the group discussion with the mothers, while the third therapist focused on the siblings of the infants and later on the infants as they became toddlers and preschoolers. This third therapist closely observed the children, offering play materials to them and directly engaging them. We attended to the communication between mother and child, the mother's capacity to reflect about her own state of mind and that of her child, the meaning of the child's emerging play style and themes, as well as each mother's contribution to the group discussion. All served as focal points for clinical observation. The mothers shared a great deal about their emotional pain, as well as their stress from innumerable external demands.

Groups varied in regularity of attendance, duration, and dynamics. However, the goals guiding therapists across groups were generally shared. There were efforts to foster the support that mothers could offer each other. We attempted to augment mothers' use of other social supports and to create space for narratives of the loss, framed in the present and relating to the longed-for recent past. We helped mothers to become aware of those historical elements that might further complicate the bereavement of their husbands' loss. We tried to appraise the mental health condition of each parent, child, and each dyad, and to use that understanding as we interacted with each individual. The lab observations and video feedback consultations deepened our understanding.

In our mother-child groups, a lot of attention focused on the down-to-earth but complicated management of mothers' lives, such as endless forms to fill out, press requests to respond to, communication with the medical examiner's office, questions of when and how to memorialize their lost husbands, and harmonies and conflicts with in-laws and other family members. Some discussions focused on articulating grief and some on thinking about their children's development, or on what to tell children now or in the future. Our approach varied from problem-solving to psycho-education to insight. Mothers felt listened to in distinctive and supportive ways compared to their usual day-to-day experiences, and the groups became an increasingly trusted holding environment.

Early on, the mothers shared their last experiences with their husbands, and the nature of how they learned of their husbands' deaths. Gradually these women began to separate the memory of their husbands from the hope that he might still be alive, a difficult process comparable to traumatic loss in other contexts (Fogelman, 1988). Because of the lack of concrete remains soon after the World Trade Center attacks, and the surreal nature of the post September 11 situation, many mothers shared the hope that their husbands would still be alive. Our underlying idea was that the experience of "unreality" and of "nonmentalized states" (Sossin, 2007) could impinge on the mother-child relationship.

## REFERENCES

Fogelman, E. (1988). Intergenerational group therapy: Child survivors of the Holocaust and offspring of survivors. *Psychoanalytic Review*, *75*, 619–640.

Sossin, K.M. (2007). Nonmentalizing states in early-childhood survivors of the Holocaust: Developmental considerations regarding treatment of child survivors of genocidal atrocities. *American Journal of Psychoanalysis*, *67*(1), 68–81.

# Early Years of Support Group I: Three Therapists' Views

Anni Bergman, Ph.D.
Sally Moskowitz, Ph.D.
Donna Demetri Friedman, LCSW, Ph.D.

This three-part article describes the early years of one of the mother-baby-children groups of the Project for Mothers, Infants, and Young Children of September 11, 2001. The goal of the group was to help prevent the effects of trauma and loss from disrupting the relationships among the mothers, their infants, and growing children. View I by Anni Bergman describes the mothers' states of minds as the group began, when they felt that their worlds had collapsed under them. View II by Sally Moskowitz focuses on the clinical experience of working in the group, transference and countertransference themes, helping the mothers and children with their mourning process, and helping the mothers' relationships to each other, their babies, older children, family, and friends. The evolution of a casual, familial-type atmosphere and format came to be seen by the therapists as very important. The therapists wanted to provide whatever small feeling of normality and comfort possible in the context of the mothers' anguish. This routine atmosphere provided the backdrop against which the mothers could talk about what seemed like unspeakable events, thoughts, and feelings, and process the horrific events, in their magnitude and details. View III by Donna Demetri Friedman describes the play therapy treatment of two preschool-aged siblings in the context of the support group. The children's father had been killed in the World Trade Center attacks. This section describes the themes of the children's play and how they worked through the experience of the loss of their father, the birth of their sibling, and their mother's grief. It also describes their progress a decade later.

## THERAPIST VIEW I: CREATING A SPACE FOR MOTHERS AND BABIES AFTER SEPTEMBER 11, 2001
### ANNI BERGMAN

The nature of the loss suffered by the widows of September 11, 2001 was unique. It was totally unexpected, violent, and shared with the whole world. When the mothers first came to the support group, they were in the middle of this trauma. There were feelings of anxious confusion and helpless despair. These emotions permeated all of the groups. As therapists and fellow New Yorkers, we were relieved that we could find a way to be helpful. However, being helpful turned out to be more difficult than we expected. At the time of the trauma, the mothers could not even envision what they wanted or needed. They could not imagine that they could get help in the face of such a devastating loss.

In all the groups, the mothers came with their babies. We tried to create a space for them where they could freely express their feelings. Our first instinct was to create a refuge, but this turned out to be only a temporary solution as many of the mothers were not yet in a state to receive help. How could there be help for a situation that was as confusing and desperate as this? They did not know what had happened, why it had happened, and what would happen in the future. There was a feeling that in such an unthinkable disaster, in the midst of such real and emotional chaos, no one could really help. What would help actually be? They were not in an inner state where they could really be helped. In their state of shock, they did not yet have the ability to accept and use help because they simply did not believe anything could make things better for them. The first step we took with these mothers was to help them come to some understanding of what help might be.

Sometimes mothers did not show up for a scheduled group, despite many confirming contacts beforehand. It became very important that we met anyway, as therapists, and discussed the groups, even if the mothers themselves were not able to come. They must have somehow known that we kept them in our minds. The belief that help was possible, the hope that they could be helped, needed time to develop. In some ways, at first, the mothers experienced our early attempts as an imposition. We added to the people trying to help them, and everything seemed like an overwhelming undertaking. We encouraged them to talk about whatever they wanted, and for some of them it was enough. We accepted their sense of helplessness and confusion, and gradually we began to be able to contain it. While it seemed to us in the early months that it was hard for them to take in anything new, maybe they did.

The mothers felt that their worlds had collapsed under them. They often described the unavailability of their families. Often they felt that the people around them did not really understand what they were going through. To foster hope felt like such an enormous task.

They knew, and we knew, that we could not bring their husbands back, which was what they most wanted. So much had been destroyed in their lives. We hoped that by creating a group where they could share this longing, and their loss, that it would be helpful to them. These women lost the man who would protect them. They lost the family unit. It was very difficult to restore for these women the feeling that some sense of safety and protection was possible. We were not consciously trying to, but we did seem to restore some sense of family for them.

In our group we attempted to provide an open, accepting atmosphere. We did not have to interpret but rather to bear witness to their fear, grief, and anger. We tried to create an atmosphere in which the mothers felt that whatever happened could be accepted and understood. This turned out to be so important because they often felt that in the outside world, few people could really listen to their experiences, including their families, their friends, the government, the country, the world.

## THERAPIST VIEW II: FOSTERING CONNECTIONS BETWEEN MOTHERS AND THEIR INFANTS AND CHILDREN WITHIN A MULTIGENERATIONAL SUPPORT GROUP

SALLY MOSKOWITZ

Support Group I met once a week for an hour and a half at Anni Bergman's home. We had three therapists: Anni Bergman and Sally Moskowitz, who focused primarily on the mothers and babies, and Donna Demetri Friedman, who focused primarily on the older children. Donna took the older children to another room to play when they were ready. Afterwards, Donna talked with the mothers about their children's concerns. We began with five mothers and babies and three children between the ages of 2 and 3. The group's composition changed over time, with some new mothers, babies, and young children joining the group and others leaving. Many of those who left stayed in touch with the Project by participating in the video consultation sessions with Beatrice Beebe, Phyllis Cohen, and Mark Sossin, and sometimes mothers stayed in touch individually with one of the group therapists.

This article will focus on the clinical experience of working with these bereaved young women and children and with the babies who had just been born into a family context of trauma and loss. Our hope at the group's inception was to help prevent the effects of trauma and loss from disrupting the connections and relationships among the mothers, their infants, and growing children. Many groups were available to the mothers or to somewhat older children affected by the World Trade Center attacks, but none that we knew of focused on the babies or the relationships between them and their mothers. Following are some thoughts about the group at its beginning and as it evolved in the first few years, the transference and countertransference themes, how we tried to help with the mourning process, and how we tried to help with the mothers' and babies' relationships to each other, their older children, and with family and friends.

We began by modeling the physical design of the group on the Mahler nursery (Maher, Pine and Bergman, 1975). We wanted the mothers and children to be able to talk with each other as freely and naturally as possible, as well as to have time with the therapists. We designated an area for the older children to play with Donna and a separate room for the mothers and babies to be with Anni and Sally. The rooms were within easy access of each other so that the children could reconnect with their mothers as they needed. The mothers could talk with one another, their children, and with us, as they wanted and felt comfortable. We hoped the setting would feel as natural as possible despite the incredibly unnatural context.

In a short time, as much by circumstance as by design, the meetings took on some of the feeling of a family-like gathering. We met on the parlor floor of Anni's brownstone home rather than in her office. We were a multigenerational group of therapists working with two generations of patients. Anni was the mothers' grandmothers' age, Sally was the mothers' mothers' age, and Donna was their contemporary. The children and babies were a fourth generation. We provided muffins, strawberries, juice, and tea at the dining room table around which we all gathered as the mothers and children arrived. We mingled, talked, and ate for a while. The atmosphere (at least to us) came to feel familial and to a degree normal, with women talking with some lightness of feeling about events of the week, commenting on how cute the children looked, or on one of the babies' new developmental achievements. Once everyone had arrived and had a bite to eat, we settled in the living room to talk, the older children milling around and then playing with Donna, and the babies nestling on the mothers' laps or settling in infant seats.

Early on, the therapists noticed the enormous importance we placed on this casual format and atmosphere. We worked to enhance it and to feel comfortable with it, despite its considerable difference from the usual context of our work with patients. We noticed and remarked with some humor and perplexity that we spent a lot of time talking to each other about the "strawberries and muffins," making certain they were provided and finding the best ones. The meaning the food and casual atmosphere held for us at the time was not clear. In retrospect, however, we can see it felt very important to provide some small feeling of normality and pleasure. We wanted to help the mothers and children feel that pleasurable details and comforts of life were recoverable and available to them in the midst of their anguish. If they could experience a bit now, it might help them find a way back to more later. Without quite realizing it, we tried to be a link to normality, talking with the mothers about food, clothing, schools, and activities for the older children, trying to contain and stem the panic and dread. The focus on normality was an important link for us as well. We and our families were also New Yorkers, part of the attacked community, frightened and uncertain about our future safety. We, too, needed to hold on tightly to what felt like familiar customs and comforts (see Beebe, Cohen, Bergman, Moskowitz, Sossin, Reiswig et al., this issue).

This routine atmosphere provided the backdrop against which the mothers talked about what seemed like unspeakable events, thoughts, and feelings. Sometimes a mother might quietly mention during the arrival period a new circumstance, and later in the group proper one of us might ask about it if the mother did not bring it up again. Talking about a new circumstance ahead of time while milling around the muffins and strawberries seemed to be a way of testing the waters. So much of what the mothers experienced and wanted to speak about had been treated as unspeakable by many others in their families and lives. Other people did not want to know the details, or told them not to dwell on such painful subjects. Or often people were mourning and unavailable themselves, or simply denied and dismissed their experiences, saying time or God would heal their wounds and they would "move on." We found the mothers needed to talk about and process the horrific events, in their magnitude and details, and to discuss what had occurred and was still occurring. The themes the mothers brought up in the group are discussed more fully in other articles in this issue, but these included the mother's altered states of disbelief, denial, and dissociation immediately following the World Trade Center attacks; their attempts to find their husbands, whom they assumed might be alive and hurt; the gradual realization and horror that the buildings had been incinerated; the uncovering of some bodies and body parts; the missing bodies; funerals; the lonely and anguished births of the babies; rifts with or help from family, in-laws, and friends; feelings of envy, disappointment, overwhelming fatigue, and sadness; and fears about their children's futures.

Deciding what to attend to in the group was often difficult, and we came to see that our difficulty reflected the mothers' difficulty. Our main purpose in the group had been to help strengthen the relationships between the mothers and their babies. But the effects of trauma and the task of mourning often interfered with and took precedence over the mothers' capacities to consistently and deeply immerse themselves in paying attention to the babies (see Moskowitz, this issue). In addition, the group offered an opportunity for the mothers to focus on themselves in a context in which they were supported and encouraged to speak, and so attention to the babies sometimes was secondary. The mothers were aware of feeling pulled in different directions by so many intense and conflicting feelings. They talked about the difficulty soothing a crying baby or playing with an engaging baby when feeling so sad and depleted. The group offered them time to talk with each other about their common experiences. Sometimes we directed their attention to a baby's glance or smile by pointing it out or "speaking for the baby." Sometimes we held or responded to the baby ourselves, highlighting the baby's capacity for reciprocal communication. We often asked pointedly how the baby was doing in a particular area in which we thought the mother might not have been able to monitor in these circumstances as well as she might have otherwise. In these ways, we tried to help the mothers feel pleasure in their emerging mothering capacities and in the babies' growing development. We attempted to provide continuity in thinking about the babies, yet at the same time we did not want to detract from our attention to the mothers' needs for care.

The mothers struggled from the beginning to understand what it would mean to the babies, as they grew older, to have lost a father they had never known. They wanted their babies to know about these beloved men. On the other hand, the mothers did not want to burden the babies with feeling a greater loss than they imagined the babies would already feel in not having a father. We answered and discussed the mothers' many questions and concerns about child development and children's capacities at different developmental stages to think about and understand death. The older children's presence seemed particularly helpful to the first-time mothers in this regard. They looked to these children as models of what their babies might be like in the future. The mothers saw their profound sadness and confusion at having lost their fathers, but also found hope seeing the children sometimes joyful in play and coping and developing generally very well. We had to find a delicate balance between addressing the mothers' mourning processes, which differed for each of them; their enormous practical concerns and decisions; and their relationships to their babies and children. It was very difficult. We often felt, perhaps in our own countertransference, that no one was receiving as much care and attention as was needed.

When we started the group, we expected the mothers to be deeply grieving, but we were not prepared for some of the mothers' disorganized states more characteristic of the effects of trauma. We often felt anxious waiting for them, not knowing if they would remember the group. We came to believe that our own countertransference feelings recalled the mothers' own experiences during the early hours and days after the World Trade Center attack, when they waited for word from their husbands. The therapists met after each group to talk about what occurred. We also stayed during the group time on the occasions that no one came and ate the strawberries and muffins ourselves, while trying to understand the states of mind of the mothers, babies, and children, as well as our own states of mind. We paid close attention to each other's thoughts and experiences and to connections to our own histories of loss and trauma revived in us by the current situation. These intimate conversations with each other proved to be a very important vehicle for understanding the experiences of the mothers, children, and babies, and for helping us to maintain balance and perspective in our work.

During the second and third years of the group, we met less frequently, but there was more predictability and stability in the mothers' attendance. When the babies were 3 years old, at the request of the mothers, we met separately with the children in a play group. We also met with the mothers, but at a different time, to discuss the issues and themes expressed in the children's play. Their play poignantly demonstrated the children's knowledge and attempts to comprehend and process the devastation of their families and deaths of their fathers. The children had absorbed far more than the mothers thought. They struggled to understand what had happened to their fathers, the effects on their mothers, and what it meant for the future. In our group with the mothers, we worked to help them accept what the children knew and to find ways to talk with them about their questions and feelings.

The babies are now school aged, and our group has ended. Almost all the mothers have remained in touch with the Project, coming to Dr. Beebe's lab, and some of them and their children continue to work individually with one of the group therapists. Although these families are remarkable in their capacity to embrace life, the effects of trauma and loss have been deep and lasting.

# THERAPIST VIEW III: CHILD THERAPY IN THE CONTEXT OF THE MOTHERS' SUPPORT GROUPS

DONNA DEMETRI FRIEDMAN

Ellie and Sue are preschool-aged siblings who came to Support Group I with their mother and baby sister, who was born shortly after September 11, 2001. Their father was killed in the World Trade Center attacks. Like the other mothers in this Project, their mother was faced with mourning the loss of her husband while caring for a newborn and two preschoolers.

The preschool years are a critical stage in early psychological development. When all goes reasonably well, a child is launched into the school years with confidence and a strong sense of self. Having a sibling close in age also brings with it a range of both positive and negative possibilities. The birth of an additional sibling before the age of 3 has its own special challenges. Add to this the tragic death of one's father, and there is the potential for a developmental storm. I will discuss our work with these two preschool aged siblings who were faced with all of these challenges simultaneously.

## Themes of Play

Some of the themes of the play included childbirth and caregiving, finding the lost object, building and maintaining structures, and fixing broken objects. Although these are themes that all children play, we observed how their play was invaded by the traumatic context. I will explore the themes of the play and how Ellie and Sue attempted to work through the simultaneous loss of their father and the birth of a sibling.

## Childbirth and Caregiving

Early in the treatment, the siblings spent a lot of time taking care of the baby dolls in the playroom. They fed and bathed the dolls. The baby dolls always needed to be taken care of. In addition, pregnancy, and birth were central themes in the play. The siblings, particularly Ellie, pretended that I was pregnant. She would stuff my belly with pillows and reenact a delivery. This was a very serious matter that required attention and concern. Both siblings were involved in the process. Their own births represented a time when their father was still alive. Ellie imagined his delight upon their arrival. The birth of their baby sister, however, was associated with his death. At one point when we were playing this theme, their mother came into the room. Ellie in particular did not want her to see what we were playing. She firmly instructed her mother to leave. Perhaps she wanted to protect her mother from remembering the past and becoming sad. In protecting her mother, she would be protecting herself.

## Finding the Lost Object

Another early play theme was hide and seek. Sue found that the way the shower doors in the bathroom opened up were like an elevator. Sue put herself in the shower as if she were in an elevator. In the game she was in the "elevator," and she pretended to slip behind as if to be caught inside the elevator shaft. During this time, the mother had expressed concern about what she had told her daughters about the father's death and about how much they had picked up from what they had heard. We do not know if the children knew about people being caught in an elevator during the World Trade Center attacks or if they imagined an elevator could have saved their father.

In her concern about how much she told the children about what happened on September 11th, their mother explained to me that she had told them that an accident had happened at work and that Daddy had fallen and hurt himself.

## Building and Maintaining Structures

In several of the early sessions, the theme of building and maintaining a structure was initiated by Ellie who built what she referred to as a "tower" out of small blocks. This tower was very high, and she placed it precariously on the coffee table in front of us. In one poignant session, she asked me to read a book that she had enjoyed. We sat on the couch facing the tower. She wanted to sit very close to me. Her sister quickly wanted to join in on this intimate moment. I read the book with the girls. At one point, Ellie looked up at me and said, "I love you." Her comment surprised me because it was early in our meetings. I began to feel that in erecting the tower, Ellie felt her Daddy was alive, and she had arranged for her and her sister to be happy with mommy reading to them. I was the transferential mother, available to play with them and feed and nurture them.

In one session Ellie took a plastic toy piece and put it in front of the tower. I asked her what it was and she replied that it was an elevator. She then took a little girl figurine and made it climb up to the top of the tower. I asked her what the little girl was doing, and she said she was looking to see if the tower would stay up. She was focused on keeping this tower up. I wondered if this was a way of keeping her father alive. Because the tower was so high, it kept falling down. Her sister Sue knocked it over once on purpose, and this made Ellie very upset. Another time Sue asked if she could knock it down and Ellie pleaded, "Please, no." At that point, I think Sue realized how important it was to Ellie and respected her request. This was characteristic of their relationship. Many times in the play they were quite supportive of one another.

A couple of times Sue bumped into the tower "accidentally." Ellie soberly asked Sue to fix it. Then, one time Ellie herself bumped into the table by mistake, and the whole tower crashed to the floor. She got very upset and looked at me and asked, "Why? Why did it fall?" I felt that she was asking at that moment why the real towers had fallen. Upon reflection, I felt in that moment perhaps what the mothers had felt. What do I tell her? How could I explain?

Sue quickly interjected her thoughts about the real towers falling. They began to discuss what they knew about the events that occurred on September 11. Ellie explained that the way it was hit by the plane was what made the tower fall. She then put the tower back together and left it there.

The next thing Ellie did was to take a cow and a dog and make them fall. She wanted to save them, but she could not save them by herself. She had to use a string. She asked me to tie it to them and hoist them up slowly. It was not working well, and they were slipping out of the string. She was getting frustrated, and I acknowledged this. This was toward the end of the session. When it was time to go, she took the harness that she had made with the string for the cow and ceremoniously put it on the shelf. Sadly she said, "Goodbye."

## Fixing Broken Objects

Sue often liked to play with a construction truck that made a sound like a real truck when it backed up. Sue made the sound with the truck over and over. At one point she lost the truck driver in the play and was distressed. I was reminded of the trucks that removed the debris from the World Trade Center disaster site. I later realized that every week, on their way to our group meetings, they drove right by the site of the World Trade Center where they saw trucks picking up the debris.

In another session, Sue focused on a basket of figurines, many of which had missing parts. She asked, "Where is the head? Where is the foot?" She then took little plastic tools and tried to fix the toys. The play alternated between fixing and breaking the figurines. Sue was interested in inspecting a figurine whose ear had fallen off. We discussed how to fix it. In a previous session, we had looked at a puppet that did not have a nose, and together we made one. Ellie later wanted to inspect the puppet and found that the nose was still there. This was very important to her. The repair had been maintained. Ellie tended to be much more verbal than Sue and was more focused on the repair. Sue was more focused on the actual objects, their falling apart and breaking, and on their vulnerability.

Sue needed to touch base with her mother more than Ellie. She often returned to her mother during the session. She had a difficult time being separated from her. She often needed to see that everyone was still there. Then she would come back to the playroom on her own. When the group was first organized, I would go to check on her, but eventually that was not necessary as she became more secure.

The siblings were very attuned to one another. This seems to have served them well as they grieved the loss of their father. They willingly shared the muffins that we fed them and truly seemed to enjoy one another. They played with one another and rarely fought. They were sensitive to each other's space and mindful of each other's needs in a strikingly mature way, perhaps as if knowing that their mother needed them to demand little.

## The Anniversary

Six months after we had been meeting, close to the anniversary of September 11th, Ellie and Sue had a birthday celebration for me, although it was not my birthday. Ellie made a cake and imbued it with special powers. She used it to destroy and fix things. I wondered if it was their way of remembering the anniversary of September 11th, which was in six days. The cake was made with red toy bricks. It was a strawberry cake. Each week we had served strawberries as one of the treats for them. We ate the pretend cake together. The tower that Ellie had rebuilt each week stood before us.

My overall impression of the older siblings (of the babies who were in utero on September 11, 2011) was that they had a striking compassion for each other. They seemed to understand that they were all in the same vulnerable situation of having lost their daddies and having mommies who were very sad. For example, one of the therapists working with the mothers and babies observed that Ellie had come to their room that day. One of the babies was playing with a whisk on the floor. Ellie wanted to use it to make her strawberry cake. The therapist noted that Ellie was clever and sensitive in how she took the whisk away from the baby. When the baby looked at something else, Ellie was looking at him and looking at the whisk. She watched to see if he would become distressed. When he looked at something else, she slipped the whisk away and then she kept it hidden, still watching him closely. When he was distracted and not upset, she slipped away and rejoined the play groups upstairs.

## Summary of Interventions

The children were supported throughout the time we worked together to express all of their feelings, good, bad, angry, or sad, both verbally and symbolically in their play. Throughout their sessions, I validated their feelings. In each session they played out conflicts related to the loss of their father, and they played out the effect that his loss had on their mother. They were able to use me transferentially as a "good enough" mother. I was someone who could tolerate the loss, whereas their mother at this early point could not. The children were aware of that. I could "hold everything together" like the building that we constructed again and again.

Facilitating play involving the birth and caring of babies by providing dolls, bottles, and diapers was crucial. This gave the siblings the opportunity to explore their own births, a time when their father was still alive, as well as the birth of their baby sibling, which was fraught with conflict because it was associated with the loss of their father.

Supporting the themes of "hide and seek" was an opportunity for children to be in control, to find the lost person, and to be found. The initial working through reflected their need to have some understanding of where their Daddy was, what had happened to him, and to have mastery over locating him. They represented this when they talked about him watching over them.

Helping in the play of fixing broken objects and games of repair was important. There was a need to go back to a time when the object was not lost. This was a period of undoing, during which the entire event was undone. The tower was erected and watched over so that it would remain intact. The anniversary of the loss of the father was acknowledged in the birthday party.

## Follow-up at 11 Years Old

Ellie and Sue are currently doing well socially, emotionally, and academically. They continue to express a desire for a father. Ellie will often state that she wants her mother to find a husband so her mother would not be lonely. The siblings have had an opportunity to get to know what their father was like through a charity in which their mother got involved. Friends and family have gathered annually to celebrate his memory. Ellie and Sue speak of that event as the most important day of the year for them.

Ellie's and Sue's ability and willingness to use me, each other, and the play; to work through the loss their father, the birth of their sister, and their mother's grief, made me feel hopeful for them. The work with these children has shown their incredible capacity to face their trauma. Their amazing ability to master their fear, sadness, and sense of loss demonstrates a remarkable resilience.

## BIBLIOGRAPHY

Beebe, B., Cohen, P., Bergman, A., Moskowitz, S., Sossin, K. M., Reiswig, R. . . . Demetri Friedman, D. (2011, this issue). The therapist group: A transformational process. *Journal of Infant, Child, and Adolescent Psychotherapy, 10*, 317–325.

Bowlby, J. (1958), The nature of child's tie to his mother. *International Journal of Psycho-Analysis, 39*: 350–73.

Erikson, E. (1950), *Childhood and society*. New York: Norton.

Furman, E. (1974), *A child's parent dies: Studies in childhood bereavement*. New Haven, CT: Yale University Press.

Mahler, M., Pine, F. & Bergman, A. (1975), *The psychological birth of the human infant: Symbiosis and individuation*. New York: Basic Books.

Moskowitz, S. (2011, this issue). Primary maternal preoccupation disrupted by trauma and loss: Early years of the project. *Journal of Infant, Child, and Adolescent Psychotherapy, 10*, 229–237.
Stern, D. (1985), *The interpersonal world of the infant: A view from psychoanalysis and developmental psychology*. New York: Basic Books.
Winnicott, D. (1965), *The maturational processes and the facilitating environment*.Madison, CT: International Universities Press, Inc.

# Support Group II: An Evolving Approach: Reflections on Group Process in the Early Years

K. Mark Sossin, Ph.D.

In the Project for Mothers, Infants, and Young Children of September 11, 2001, one form of intervention was group work with mothers and young children whose husbands and fathers had died. Multiple therapists facilitated the group process. The evolving process of one group is described, including grief support, affect sharing, and emerging trust among mothers and therapists, manners of therapist collaboration, and children's developing social interactions and communications through play. Therapeutic listening in the group influenced the ways that the mothers attended to each other and, in turn, the ways that the mothers attended to their children. The importance of state-awareness on the part of therapists is underscored. Although personalities, histories, sorrows, coping strategies, child needs, parenting styles, and later experiences of romance were distinct, the group work fostered ways in which the lost husbands/fathers were held in mind by wives and children. Shared understanding of traumatic loss and the group process fostered self-reflection among the mothers and reflective parenting.

While some aspects of group process early in the course of this Project generalized across groups, my observations here derive from a single group, which also gave rise to Rita Reiswig's considerations of representations of the lost father (see Reiswig, *Support Group II*, this issue). Rita and I were joined during the first two years of our ongoing group by Kirsten Kupfermann. This article focuses on a few key issues regarding the group process during the initial years. It considers the place of emotions in the group process, how we collaborated as co-therapists, how the mothers and children were held in our minds, and how these factors influenced our interventions.

After meeting in a university setting for the first seven months of the group, we moved to a school environment, in which an early childhood room was kindly made available to us for weekly meetings with the mothers and children. Blocks, dolls, puppets, a large dollhouse, a toy kitchen, and many other toddler- and preschool-friendly playthings were readily available, although much space was quite open. In the main space there was a large carpeted area (often where mothers, therapists, and children convened). There was another hard-floor area with a large set of tables, chairs, and a sink. We provided food, such as fruit, nuts, and drinks. If a child did enter into play with one of the therapists, he or she was usually within 20 feet of his or her mother. Even if the child wandered to the other end of the room, the mother was always in sight.

We shared the concern that without early "preventive" intervention after traumatic loss, serious symptoms could surface later. We operated differently from those bringing manualized trauma/grief-focused groups and child-centered interventions into postwar regions (see Lane et al., 2001; Bragin, 2007). These mothers and their children did not experience a direct threat to their own lives. However, the perpetrated violence of September 11, 2001, the repetitive television witnessing of the World Trade Center destruction, and the communal/societal terror that followed all cast complexities upon the mourning process and parenting challenges that could complicate early caregiving interactions. We knew the risks to such early care, as demonstrated by depressed and anxious mothers (Beebe et al., 2008; Beebe, Steele et al., 2011; Field, 1995; Tronick, 1989). We also recognized that group treatments in the wake of trauma involve the development of trust and the communalization of the trauma within a cohesive group. Kingsley (2007) recently discussed this process in work with veterans who developed combat-related posttraumatic stress syndrome (PTSD). We also knew that responses to death and stress are highly individualized. As Piper, McCallum and Azim (1992) articulated in developing group interventions for those who suffer loss, the more ambivalent the relationship with the deceased, the more complicated one can expect the grief to be (Shear and Mulhare, 2008). We thus offered a group approach that could attend to the highly individualized experiences of each mother and each family.

As the group began, a profound loss and aloneness was palpable. Gradually the mothers and therapists together developed a capacity to catalyze some degree of connection and change. Most individuals who have had a traumatic loss cannot readily trust, or even imagine, that another individual can feel what she/he feels. Thus, especially when the "absolutisms of everyday life" are shattered, there is reduced expectation of empathic responsiveness (Stolorow, 1999; Walker and Dudley, 2004; Sossin, 2007). In our group, it became clear that much about the loss was shared among the mothers. Each mother told and retold her tale of the day's events of September 11, 2001. The telling itself helped to assuage the experience of isolation.

Over time, the mothers' discussion gained a central place. Gradually, each mother took a turn at being the focal speaker. Therapists kept in mind the time to be sure that each mother had sufficient time in each session. Originally, the other mothers said little unless they had a directly analogous story. In time, however, each took on an increased role in giving other mothers feedback.

## AFFECT SHARING IN GROUP PROCESS

In this particular group, the majority of group members had relatively long and strong marriages. Research has found that when a higher percentage of patients in a therapy group have had a history of relatively more mature relationships, there is a better outcome for all patients in the group, despite many other distinguishing factors (Piper et al., 2007).

A fairly balanced degree of positive and negative affect expression emerged in our group. Of course, the negative affects of sorrow, grief, and anxiety were given much space. However, positive affects, most readily tagged to the children's emerging acquisitions, comical actions, and pleasure-seeking, were a source of shared delight. A parent's woeful accounts of a lonely evening and in-law stresses were quite likely to be balanced by focus on a child's new discovery, endearing imitation, or winsome smile. This "balance" was enhanced because of the presence of the babies, toddlers, and preschoolers in the group room. As one therapist facilitated the children's play, the mothers could readily hear the child's shouts of glee upon finding a colorful balloon flying outside the window, and mothers would share stories about each of their children's relished funny sides;

the mothers would speak with pride and amusement. Such "balance" is particularly important in light of research that demonstrates that a balance of positive and negative expression is beneficial to group therapy outcomes (Piper et al., 2003). Piper et al. hypothesize that greater balance leads to greater tolerance and acceptance of the expression of conflicted feelings.

## THERAPIST COLLABORATION AND REFLECTION ON AFFECTS IN THE GROUP

The therapists routinely met afterwards to discuss that day's group process. We would reflect on particular participants and the way they interacted with each other. In talking with each other after a group meeting, for example, one therapist observed that a one-year-old boy "loved" playing with the blocks, taking them out of a box and putting them back in. Another therapist added that the boy showed particular reciprocity with the therapist who was most directly involved in playing with him, and the third commented on an affectionate way in which the young boy approached the face of the therapist. We all agreed on that day that this child, who often avoided warm face-to-face interactions, approached his mother warmly several times and seemed "cuddly." The mother, though, had apologized to the group, saying: "He's clingy because he must be sick." Where we all had seen a positive embrace, the mother had seen clinginess. We reflected on a therapist's comment at the time, regarding the "delicious" way in which the boy held a soft cuddly toy dog in his arms as he was held by his mother so enjoyably. This vignette exemplifies how therapists often reinforced their impressions of the motives or intents of the child, which in this case involved quite positive attachment-seeking.

In reflecting on that day's group afterwards, the therapists among themselves then shared frustration with the mother who, on that day, had attributed a less healthy motive to her child than we thought pertained. Perspective sharing among therapists was important to substantiate our impressions of a healthy core in this child. We also recognized that the mother was not in any way malevolent but rather overwhelmed, and at that time was less able to discriminate between attachment-seeking and clinginess. It led to our raising questions about the qualities of the mother's own attachments. We recognized that the mother's sense of security would need to be heightened before she could offer greater security to her child. Gradually, we learned a great deal about how insecurely attached this mother was to her own mother. The ambivalence and anger that often rose toward her nonetheless beloved child was parallel to an anger and ambivalence she felt toward her own mother. The sharing among therapists gave us clear impressions of how we each understood what was going on with the mothers.

We heard many stories of mothers sleeping with children for extended periods of time. We puzzled over what we heard. There often seemed to be confusion between the child's need to sleep together versus the mother's need. Our wondering about this aloud with each other furthered our ability to wonder with the mother in a subsequent group if and when the issue next arose.

At the end of 2002, a mother was considering what her five-year-old child was ready to hear about the events of September 11, 2001. Although each therapist perceived that the child needed to know more than she did, the intervention in the mother's group was to ask the mother to think about what her child already knew, what questions the child had, and what advantages or disadvantages would follow from the child knowing more. By thinking aloud, we gleaned other important facts to inform our overall response. We found out that the child did not yet "formally" know that the buildings had fallen. Many other facets of this simple "professional advice" seeking emerged. For example, we heard how strong this mother's need was to control the information flow to her children. This took on heightened compensatory meaning in relation to her helplessness. Moreover, we gained a picture of the dead husband as quite claustrophobic. Giving her child facts that could enhance the child's ability to picture the father as "crushed" (clearly an image the mother herself had) was profoundly sad and intolerable to her. She realized what this way of dying would mean to her husband in light of his claustrophobia. We realized that as this mother sidestepped her own grief work through high activity, it was harder for her to create a climate within which her son could grieve. The mother spoke of feeling guilty in day-to-day experiences if she found herself laughing or happy. Being unhappy was experienced as a link to her dead husband; feeling happy felt like abandoning him.

We also learned that this mother held secrets, a defensive coping method she had used for a long time. She had coped by separating information into small bits and by not allowing others to validate the information. This became clearer as she sought to share a secret with one of the therapists and to keep it from the others in the group. This method of coping complicated her grieving. Not until a year and a half after her husband had died did this mother acknowledge "feeling anything." She had described feeling completely numb. The secret-zone was somewhat like the numb-zone. If she did happen to make any real contact with anyone, it went unacknowledged. However, she gradually shared her experience of numbness with the other mothers. After finding out that they had at least some variant of the same experience, especially the more-than-year-long numbness and gradual reawakening, she allowed herself to be more "known" by the other mothers, and, in turn, she became more curious about them.

Over time, the children grew in their rapport and playfulness with each other. We noticed marked differences in children's manners of managing pain or frustration. One child cried with a clearly directed plea for comfort by her mother. Another child, with a higher threshold for pain, often reached the point of crying and yet never sought comfort from anyone, particularly his mother. Eventually we came to realize that this mother took pride in her child's autonomous functioning. We tried to put into words what her child seemed to be feeling and thinking. Gradually this mother became more aware of her child's distressed states.

With time, a major focus of the group became the interest and ambivalence each mother had about seeking new relationships with men. The mothers were concerned about the complications of their children's reactions, their family's reactions, their guilt about their lost husbands, and their shame in revealing their wishes. They all expressed a deep desire and hope to create a strong relationship with a new man.

The mothers gradually developed intense relationships with each other. Sometimes jealousy and envy were expressed as one mother seemed to have something another one longed for (such as exploring an exciting new relationship on a trip away from the children). They also expressed admiration and genuine concern for each other. From time to time one mother might be judgmental about another mother's choices or parenting style. However, a heightened bond among the mothers grew as so much became shared among them. Special group meetings were held in each mother's home, especially to mark the occasion of a move or redecorating effort. Special meetings were held in the homes of therapists as well. This openness derived from the group therapy experiences but extended to major events in their lives outside of the usual session boundaries. This openness and sharing seemed to supersede differences among the mothers, and facilitated more therapeutic progress in the group.

From the start, our goal of facilitating trust was crucial, but trust was difficult to achieve. The mothers were initially ambivalent about accepting a treatment that they themselves had not sought. As psychoanalysts and primarily individual therapists, we felt some initial consternation over these impediments. We recognized a need to shift our frame. Over time, the therapeutic process clearly deepened. As the mothers became more able to talk about their own feelings, they became more available to attend to the feelings of their children.

## THE GROUP'S CONTRIBUTION TO REMEMBERING AND IMAGINING THE LOST HUSBAND/FATHER

The older siblings lost their world as they understood it to be. They lost their fathers, and the bereaved mother was not the same one they had known before. Our observations of these children confirm Nickman, Silverman and Normand (1998), who argue that children are better able to cope with loss and change when they can maintain a connection to the dead parent by "constructing" an inner representation. But what of the children who never "knew" their fathers? As the surviving parents, the mothers greatly influenced the early construction of the representation of the deceased fathers. We saw that the representation that the mother was able to create was influenced by the way the group was able to articulate their images of the lost husbands, while a close observation of the infants and toddlers was simultaneously in progress. We believe that having the children in the group influenced how the mothers created representations for the children who were not yet born on September 11, 2001. It was different for the older siblings, who knew their fathers. "The surviving parent can help render the previous introject more serviceable to the child and more accessible to consciousness in the deceased parent's absence" (Nickman et al., 1998, p. 127). We witnessed the process by which the mothers constructed representations of the fathers that were woven together with each child's own wish for a father. These representations offered a nurturing influence and sense of rootedness for each child (see Reiswig, *Support Group II*, this issue).

The group supported the mother's capacity to remember her husband for herself, as well as for her children. A strong aversion to hearing the child's early inquiries about the lost father—because of the sadness it evoked—gradually gave way to more tolerant and even welcoming attitudes. The mothers began to be able to be more reflective and emotionally flexible when the children expressed curiosity about their dead fathers. The group facilitated the mother's compassionate listening in place of defensive dismissal or distracting instruction. Our ability in the group to observe the child and the mother-child dyad and to engage the mother in thinking about the child's own thoughts and feelings, while simultaneously listening to her own thoughts, promoted more open communication at home. The manner in which we attended to the mother's remembering had intergenerational consequences. Her children were then able to construct representations of the deceased father that contributed to the child's sense of feeling cared for and experience of continuity. Occasionally direct conversations about the father, or the availability of photos, videos, or keepsakes, facilitated this process.

As group leaders, we found we stretched beyond our usual limits regarding self-disclosure in our goals of scaffolding empathic and resonant moments and of encouraging more reflection in the mothers. Although innumerable subjects, across social, developmental, familial, and practical domains came up in the group, we always maintained the centrality of emotional experience. We exposed more of ourselves than we would in our practices in psychoanalysis or psychotherapy. Perhaps showing a degree of vulnerable involvement by the group leaders themselves contributed to the promotion of change (Livingston, 2003). As the process unfolded, we found ourselves increasingly aware of subtle nonverbal indicators of emotional states in the mothers, and we became aware of our own state-sharing moments (Beebe and Lachmann, 2002; Lachmann and Beebe, 1993). Our own self-experiences often informed us about important inner experiences in a mother even when her state apparently seemed to be more benign. These nonverbal and self-state experiences of the therapists influenced our shifts in attention and exploration and heightened our ability to use these feelings, to understand them in each other as co-therapists, and, ultimately, to facilitate these feelings among the mothers themselves. For example, one group leader felt tremendously sad when a mother was describing in all-too-matter-of-fact, though irritated, terms, a conflict with her new boyfriend. The therapist's attentiveness to a personal feeling of sadness opened a window into the mother's sadness, linked to remembrances of the lost husband. Our deep involvement with the experiences of these women allowed us to take risks, and allowed them to take risks. They shared their feelings in ways that they may not otherwise have been inclined to do. In turn, this process increased their abilities to think about their children's experiences.

Trust did emerge, albeit slowly and gradually. It appeared that the empathic resonances attained in the group therapy experience awakened or facilitated potentials among the mothers to address prior traumas and stresses, especially their affective intensities, which would have otherwise stayed defensively deadened. It seemed that the mothers felt that if the group could process and show responsiveness to the tragic loss of September 11, 2001, perhaps buried painful memories could also finally emerge from imposed phenomenological seclusion, and be shared.

Death is usually conceived as leaving the bereaved with only the representation of the lost person. But the babies whose fathers died prior to their births had to construct such a representation. The mother's parenting behavior bore significantly on the child's capacity to develop an internalized image of the father. Having followed these children and families for almost 10 years now, it is our impression that such a developmental acquisition has well served the child's own self-development and sense of personal integration. Alongside the other interventions of our Project, such as video feedback, and the personal therapies that some mothers, and some children, engaged in, the group experience significantly contributed to constructing and sustaining the internalized image of the husband/father. The early phase of this group experience prompted the mothers and the children to use the group for potent emotional expressions that they did not usually risk sharing elsewhere. Moreover, over time the group experience seemed to increase the ability of each mother to reflect on her own emotions, to revisit her grief reactions, and to think about her children's thoughts, feelings, and emerging personalities.

## REFERENCES

Beebe, B. & Lachmann, F. (2002). *Infant research and adult treatment: Co-constructing interactions*. Hillsdale, NJ: The Analytic Press.

Beebe, B., Jaffe, J., Buck, K., Chen, H., Cohen, P., Feldstein, S., & Andrews, H. (2008). Six-week postpartum maternal depression symptoms and 4-month mother-infant self-and interactive contingency. *Infant Mental Health Journal*, *29*(5), 442–471.

Beebe, B., Steele, M., Jaffe, J., Buck, K., Chen, H., Cohen, P., . . . Feldstein, S. (2011). Maternal anxiety and 4-month mother-infant self- and interactive contingency. *Infant Mental Health Journal*, *32*(2), 174–206.

Bragin, M. (2007). The psychological effects of war on children: A psychosocial approach. In E. Carll (Ed.), *Trauma psychology: Issues in violence, disaster, health, and illness, Vol. 1: Violence and disaster*. Westport, CT: Praeger, pp. 195–229.

Field, T. (1995). Infants of depressed mothers. *Infant Behavior and Development*, *18*, 1–13.

Fogelman, E. (1988). Intergenerational group therapy: Child survivors of the Holocaust and offspring of survivors. *Psychoanalytic Review*, *75*, 619–640.

Kingsley, G. (2007). Contemporary group treatment of combat-related posttraumatic stress disorder. *Journal of the American Academy of Psychoanalysis & Dynamic Psychiatry*, *35*(1), 51–69.

Lachmann, F. M., & Beebe, B. (1993). Interpretation in a developmental perspective. In A. Goldberg (Ed.), *Progress in self psychology*, *Vol.* (pp. 3–15). Hillsdale, NJ: Analytic Press.

Lane, C., Pynoos, R., Saltzman, W., Arslanagic, B., Black, M., Safjak, N., . . . Hourston, R. (2001). Trauma/grief-focused group psychotherapy: School-based postwar intervention with traumatized Bosnian adolescents. *Group Dynamics: Theory, Research, and Practice*, *5*(4), 277–90.

Livingston, M. S. (2003). Vulnerability, affect, and depth in group psychotherapy. *Psychoanalytic Inquiry*, *23*, 646–77.

Nickman, S., Silverman, P., & Normand, C. (1998). Children's construction of a deceased parent: The surviving parent's contribution. *American Journal of Orthopsychiatry*, *68*, 126–34.

Piper, W., McCallum, M., & Azim Hassan, F. (1992), *Adaptation to loss through short-term group psychotherapy*. New York: Guilford Press.

Piper, W., Ogrodniczuk, J., Joyce, A., Weidman, R., & Rosie, J. (2007). Group composition and group therapy for complicated grief. *Journal of Consulting and Clinical Psychology*, *75*, 116–125.

Piper, W., Ogrodniczuk, J., McCallum, M., Joyce, A. & Rosie, J. (2003). Expression of affect as a mediator of the relationship between quality of object relations and group therapy outcome for patients with complicated grief. *Journal of Consulting and Clinical Psychology*, *71*, 664–671.

Shear, M. K. & Mulhare, E. (2008). Complicated grief. *Psychiatric Annals, 38, Special issue: Bereavement-related depression*, 662–670.

Sossin, K. M. (2007). Nonmentalizing states in early childhood survivors of the Holocaust: Developmental considerations regarding child survivors of genocidal atrocities. *American Journal of Psychoanalysis*, *67*, 68–81.

Stolorow, R. (1999). The phenomenology of trauma and the absolutisms of everyday life: A personal journey. *Psychoanalytic Psychology*, *16*, 464–468.

Tronick, E. (1989). Emotions and emotional communication in infants. *American Psychologist*, *44*, 112–119.

Walker, T. & Dudley, S. (2004). Trauma and recovery: A story of personal transformation and healing amidst the terror of September 11. *Progress in Self Psychology*, *20*, 109–123.

# Support Group II: Maternal Representation of the Lost Father

Rita Reiswig, M.S., L.P.

In the Project for Mothers, Infants, and Young Children of September 11, 2001, we conducted a support group for women who were pregnant when their husbands died on that date. The trauma of their husbands' death triggered complex and contradictory needs in these pregnant women who would soon be new mothers. This article explores ways in which the women with their babies used the therapy group to understand and grieve their loss. It documents how the therapeutic process, including the therapists' participation, represented the lost father/husband based on the understanding of him as conveyed by each mother. The article also describes how the group and the therapists supported the concurrent needs to grieve while at the same time to nurture a new baby.

The women of the September 11, 2001, Mothers and Young Children's Project were pregnant when their husbands died in the Twin Towers. They experienced an exceptionally poignant situation, having to confront a sudden trauma, grieve for the lost husband, and, at the same time, give birth to a child who would be fatherless. These circumstances made for a complex concurrence of events and emotions that merited special attention and study. Unique therapeutic interventions attuned to these women's particular experiences were needed, and the women played a strong role in shaping the therapeutic trajectory.

I will focus on several themes from our group that relate to how the absent father was held in the mind of each mother. First, I address how the mother's representation of her lost husband became part of the ongoing discourse of the mothers' group. Second, I look at how the therapists, when possible, represented the absent father and partnered with the mother to create a therapeutic environment where change could occur. Third, I focus on how the group supported the mothers' efforts to grieve the loss of the husband/father. Finally, I note how the group's discourse helped to inform and support the mothers' efforts to parent their children.

My contact with these mothers began in spring 2002, when I and two other therapists began weekly group meetings with the mothers and their newborn children. Since then, we have met regularly for nearly nine years. Although our location and format have evolved and changed according to the needs and schedules of the mothers and children, we continue as an ongoing support and therapy group to this day. The group comprised mothers who lived in suburbs of New York City. Their husbands had commuted daily to their jobs at the World Trade Center.

Some of the women had older children; others became first-time mothers. None of the women knew each other prior to meeting in the group.

When beginning the group, we sought to find a place to meet that was centrally located. The therapists also traveled to this location. We met there for almost a year until we needed more space for the toddlers to spread out and play with toys. We approached an adjacent school, and they offered us a spacious and well-appointed classroom. We took up residence there and met weekly for several years until the children in the group were ready for nursery school. When the children entered school, we began to meet with the mothers only on a monthly basis. In addition, each year we planned a reunion in August that included the mothers, all the children (including older children), new spouses, and stepchildren.

Initially, we were three therapists: Mark Sossin, Kerstin Kupfermann, and Rita Reiswig, all child and adult psychoanalysts. In the third year of the group, Kerstin retired and her participation in the mother/baby group ended.

From the beginning, the post–September 11, 2001 chaos experienced by the mothers made it difficult to establish a cohesive group. Weekly phone contact with the mothers between scheduled group meetings helped them remain engaged with the therapists and other group members. The call was a check-in with the mothers to see how they were doing, to offer a steady voice at the other end of the phone, and to encourage their involvement and connection. Sometimes the mothers did not answer the phone, and so a message was left, such as the following: "Hi. I'm calling to be in touch with you. I'm reminding you of our meeting on Tuesday. I hope to see you there and I just wanted to let you know that I am thinking of you. I look forward to seeing you at our next meeting. Goodbye for now." In retrospect, this message, which seemed like merely a pragmatic matter at the time, offered a holding and containing function. In essence the message was saying: "We are going offer a structured space and time, attending to your feelings of loss and grief, and to the child you created with your husband. We will think about the relationships and connections you are forming with the other group members in a way that is not otherwise structured into your lives." The father's death, who he was when he was alive, and how he might play an ongoing role in his children's lives was embedded in the discourse of the group from the beginning.

The group format was similar each week and evolved as a multitasking, intergenerational community. The mothers spoke of their immediate situations, histories, and memories while the therapists listened. All of the adults simultaneously attended to the children. By the second year, in the nursery school space the mothers sat in a semicircle on child-size chairs or on the carpet. Two of the therapists either sat with the mothers or stood by the edge in proximity. The babies were then toddlers. They typically began a session on the mothers' laps but then ventured off to the play area. They were free to return to the mother at any point, and the mothers were always visible to them. The third therapist was especially available to the children in the play area, facilitating play and motoric activity, and responding to shifts in the children's mood. The group met for one and a half hours. A snack of fruit, cheese, and crackers was always provided for the mothers, the children, and the therapists. Our eating together further identified our group as being somewhat distinct from a typical therapy. Along with the occasional hosting of the group in a therapist's home, this created an atmosphere of giving that was reciprocated by each mother as time went on. Rather than diminishing the therapeutic nature of the group, it seemed that this collective effort and more flexible set of parameters enhanced the therapeutic process.

Early on, the therapists were aware of a number of primary issues. These included helping the mothers cope with the loss of their husbands; attending to the needs and evolving personalities of the babies; and attending to the needs and feelings of the older children in the family as reported by the mothers. The mothers' relationships with other family members, especially in-laws, permeated their concerns. Furthermore, identification of the remains of the husbands, memorialization, participation in journalistic activities related to September 11, 2001, and abundant paperwork all contributed to their overwhelming lives. Over the years, new issues evolved, as new relationships emerged, marriages were considered and entered into, step-parenting roles surfaced, and new children were born.

Although these topics and others were often discussed in the group, there was always the central, continuous thread of the lost husband's presence and absence to think about. In sharing their thoughts about their lost husbands, the women gradually began to transform their past marital and childrearing experiences with their husbands into something different.

Over time the mothers talked about wanting to visit each other's homes, and so the format of meeting at the school was altered. This emerged from many conversations about what it was like to be alone in their homes without their husbands. The idea of home-visiting also arose during the first summer after September 11, 2001, when one of the therapists hosted a summer meeting at her home. All the older siblings were included at this reunion. While the mothers talked together, their infants sat on their laps or played nearby. The older children played outdoors with balls, ran through the sprinklers, and had fun chasing each other. The reunion was a mixture of celebration and sadness. One could feel the lost husbands' presence and absence. The occasion resembled the kind of visit one would make at the time of a death to convey respect for the deceased and sympathy with the grieving. Yet there was a celebratory tone, since food was offered, conversation was plentiful, and there was a heightened mood.

During the home visits, it became clear that some mothers wished to preserve aspects of their husband's lives, such as his clothing, photos, and personal artifacts. At the same time, they found themselves rearranging and divesting, constantly working to adjust in some manner to their sudden trauma. One mother, who moved in with her parents after September 11, 2001, later purchased a home of her own. After she renovated it, she wanted the group to see it. In the spirit of a field trip, we traveled to her home and had a housewarming party, where we also met her father. The group was filled with admiration for her accomplishment in situating herself and her children in a colorful, beautiful home. We were shown poignant reminders of the lost husband and father of her children.

The home-visiting had some unique aspects—we often brought gifts of plants or something for the home. These occasions seemed to further bond the mothers, toddlers, and therapists together into a traveling collective. These visits often provided a vivid and intimate look into the home where the husband had previously resided, where he slept and ate and lived with his family. We sometimes had lunch or a snack and sat in the kitchen or in the dining room where we could imagine the husband's presence on an everyday basis. When seated at the table, it seemed easier to talk about him and to imagine him in his family setting with his wife and children. All the mothers were keen to show us around and to show photos of their husbands at special events and vacations. We looked at wedding albums, and on one occasion we saw a video of one father with his older child on a family vacation.

In each home we were struck by the continuity of each family's life—how the memory of the husband was kept alive, recorded, and displayed inside the house. On the other hand, we were shown concrete displays of how each mother was coming to grips with the husband's absence, such as efforts to redecorate an area of the house or to divest of the husband's clothing. In these ways the mothers sought incrementally to redefine themselves in their environments as someone single, albeit widowed. The husband continued to exert his personality via the mother's memory of him, her attachment to him, and the ways she represented him in conversation. This continuity was often juxtaposed with a startled realization of his absence and her aloneness in making decisions and in caring for the children in a wholly altered life.

Initially, when parenting topics were brought up in the group, the mothers were inclined to take turns speaking individually, directly addressing the therapists, while the other mothers listened. Over time, the group developed a more dynamic format. The mothers talked to each other, having become effective and trusted listeners and participators.

Each therapist developed a style of relating to each individual mother while simultaneously promoting the group process. As one of the therapists was male and the other female, a couple's model was evoked, injecting verve into the themes of marital relationships and pointing to the tragically truncated marriages. As the group came to know each absent husband and held him in a shared representation, the conversation seemed to move the mourning process forward. Each therapist asked questions, made comments, and often worked to create a location for, and a representation of, the father within the discourse. A therapist might ask, for instance, "How do you think he would feel about this?" "How would things be different if he were here now?" The therapists kept in mind what the mothers had told them about the husbands, the details, postures, jokes, and views of the world, so that some of these attributes might be reflected back to the mothers. There was a gliding back and forth between current reality and memory.

The therapists lent themselves into the spousal, parental space and, in the process, hoped to facilitate grieving and mourning. For each mother, the therapists thus had the ongoing potential to become temporary placeholders for the husband and in this way to represent aspects of him. This experience was spontaneous in the conversation but not fully interpreted in the way it might have been if the person had been in individual treatment.

Over the years, there were a variety of impediments that made it difficult for some of the mothers to move forward and establish relationships with new men. Some mothers, who had not remarried, conveyed many layers of their stories of their relationships with their lost husbands and numerous boyfriends past and current. They tended to maintain idealized memories of the dead husbands. For some mothers who remarried, the new husbands became at times targets of dissatisfaction: the new husbands were so different from the lost husbands. There was a wish that the new man should fit into something similar to what was experienced with the former. Some of the women had difficulty with the feeling that they might be "betraying" the memory of the lost husband. Sometimes, it seemed they expected something from the new husbands to compensate them for their loss.

Often the mothers had suffered estrangements and strains with their dead husbands' families. They wanted to maintain connections with their former mothers-in-law because there had been affection between them when the husbands had been alive. These mothers also wanted to give their children a reference point to their dead fathers. However, without the presence of the husband/son, the relationships between mothers-in-law and daughters-in-law often faltered.

The older siblings experienced a dramatically altered world. They lost their father, inherited a bereaved mother, and acquired a new sibling. Our observations of these children confirmed that they had all struggled to maintain a connection to their fathers. They were better able to cope with loss and related changes when they could maintain a connection to the dead father by constructing an inner representation of him. The mothers' capacity to give shape and dimension to those representations was essential, generating aspects of the lost father that the older children held onto.

Differentiated from older children who had some personal memories of their fathers, the younger children who lost their fathers while in the womb experienced their absent fathers at first only through their mothers' sadness and moods. Over time, the younger children absorbed the representations of their mothers and siblings. Gradually they developed their own explanatory ideas and fantasies about their fathers' absence through their own experiences with the larger world.

The mothers shaped the early construction of the representations of the deceased fathers for their children. In turn, each mother was influenced by the representations of the other group members, including the input of the therapists who were representing the absent fathers in the discourse. In this way, the group supported the capacity of the mothers to remember their husbands, for themselves, as well as for their children. We saw in the group a gradual transition from idealized images of the dead husbands to more complex and emergent ideas of the lost husbands/fathers. These men could gradually be seen, recalled, and remembered with additional dimensions. Early strong aversions, evoked by sadness, to hearing inquiries about their husbands gave way to more welcoming inclusive attitudes in which the mothers could convey more complex ideas of the lost fathers to their children.

After following these mothers and families for more than nine years, the group experience seems to have contributed significantly to the construction and sustaining of vivid and differentiated internalized images of the lost fathers/husbands. These internalized images have allowed the mothers to traverse the often treacherous landscape between the loss of their husbands and the birth of their children.

# THEMES ARISING FROM THE SUPPORT GROUPS

## Primary Maternal Preoccupation Disrupted by Trauma and Loss: Early Years of the Project

Sally Moskowitz, Ph.D.

Working in the Project for Mothers, Infants, and Young Children of September 11, 2001, I focus in this article on some of the ways in which normal states of mind essential to "good enough mothering" were significantly disrupted and altered by the effects of trauma and loss following the events of September 11$^{th}$. Themes mothers talked about and patterns of mother-infant/mother-child interaction observed during the first two years of the group are discussed in the contexts of pregnancy and Winnicott's concepts of primary maternal preoccupation and holding. Pregnancy, childbirth, new motherhood, loss, and trauma are all life-transforming events, each having particular states of mind, psychic tasks, and challenges associated with them. Although the mothers in our Project were heroic in their attempts to simultaneously experience and process these highly contradictory states, we found the work of mourning largely incompatible with the work of primary maternal preoccupation. It did not seem possible for the psyche to be consumed with the lost object in mourning and at the same time to be consumed with the infant in primary maternal preoccupation. This article also touches on the mothers' ongoing difficult task of telling their babies, now children approaching 10 years old, about their fathers and their fathers' deaths.

I will talk about some ways in which normal states of mind essential to good enough mothering were significantly disrupted and altered by the effects of trauma and loss following the events of September 11, 2001. I will focus on pregnancy, primary maternal preoccupation, and holding in the first two years of the Project, which began in spring 2002. I will talk about themes we heard in the groups, patterns we saw in some of the mothers, and interactions between them and their babies. Although most of the mothers in our Project were high functioning, economically privileged young women with strong family and friend supports, the degree of disorganization and chaos they experienced in these first two years was staggering. On the other hand, the mothers' courage, determination, and investment in their babies' well-being have been remarkable, incredibly poignant, and impressive to us throughout the Project. The babies have also shown incredible resilience.

Even when all goes as hoped, pregnancy and the period of primary maternal preoccupation are times of extreme vulnerability and upheaval (Benedek, 1970; Bergman, 1999; Kestenberg 1976; Lester & Notman, 1988; Pines, 1972; Raphael-Leff, 1996; Rustin, 1989; Stern, 1995). The mother-to-be faces an irreversible psychic change, which demands a new identity and reorganization of her sense of self to include the coming baby. Enormous practical changes in work, home, and relationships are about to occur as well. During pregnancy, there is a normal heightened narcissism and a turning inward to focus on the dramatic changes in the body and on the fetus growing inside. There can be a euphoric sense of well-being, intense connection to the expected baby, and fantasies about the future. There can also be an increasing and disorienting sense of loss of control over one's body. For some women this loss of control can bring resentment and, in some instances, fearful feelings of being inhabited by a foreign and potentially destructive creature. For all women, identity and self concept are transforming from "daughter of mother" to "mother of baby." Both archaic wishes for nurturance and conflicts about separation from their own mothers are reactivated. There is a strong regressive pull to become re-entwined in the lives and minds of their families of origin. During this time of developmental transformation and psychic reorganization, under optimal circumstances the prospective mother's partner provides care, support, and another focus for her wishes, enormously helping her to contain anxieties and to stem regression.

It was during this already vulnerable time of loosened defenses and permeable boundaries that the women in our Project experienced devastating loss and trauma—their minds unable to assimilate the horrifying magnitude of their experiences. Nina's circumstances on the morning of September 11 are paradigmatic (Nina represents a composite of several mothers' experiences). While she was at a prenatal visit, her husband was at his office in the World Trade Center. He would have gone to the obstetrician with her as he usually did, but Nina had encouraged him to go to an important business meeting instead. She had spoken to him by cell phone just before their respective appointments, and she looked forward to telling him about her visit afterwards. As Nina viewed a sonogram image of their baby-to-be, her husband was killed in the incinerating fireball and collapse of the towers. She learned of the attack as she left the doctor's building. She wandered the streets in a fugue state, trying frantically to reach her husband. Days later she found herself at her parent's apartment, still believing she would find him but simultaneously knowing in another part of her mind that he was gone and her life was shattered. For Nina and the other mothers-to-be, thoughts of the baby were supplanted by floods of memories of their husbands, horrific images of the ways they had died, and devastating feelings of loss, anxiety, and deprivation.

Winnicott (1956) describes primary maternal preoccupation as "a very special state of . . . heightened sensitivity during [which] mothers . . . become preoccupied with their infant to the exclusion of other interests" (p. 301). Mahler (1967) talks about this state and the mother's holding patterns as the "symbiotic organizer" promoting structuralization of the baby's mind. Anni Bergman (1999) describes primary maternal preoccupation as "regression in service of the baby," an extremely delicate and complex state requiring the mother to ". . . feel secure enough within her own self to be able to move in and out of states of loss of interest in other relationships so that she can lose herself in empathy and intimacy with her infant" (p. 116).

For the mothers in our Project, it was virtually impossible to be preoccupied with their infants in this way. Their beloved anchors were gone. In our early group meetings, with new babies in tow, discussions of the details of their babies' lives, how nursing was going, how the babies slept, their first smiles—invariably gradually turned to details of the traumatic event and its aftermath. Filled with anguish, guilt, and anger, the mothers talked about how their husbands might have been saved, the last times they spoke, how they had tried to find them, their husbands' wishes for the new baby, and funeral and memorial services. They talked about how they first fell in love and what their dreams had been for the future. The complicated task of mourning, of ". . . hyper-cathecting and detaching" (Freud, 1917) from the hopes and memories bound to the lost object, placed these women's already burdened internal worlds in states of further disarray.

Freud talked about the feelings normally involved in mourning: "painful dejection, abrogation of interest in the outside world, loss of the capacity to love, and inhibition of all activity . . ." He said, "[there is]. . . . an inhibition and circumscription of the ego . . . which leaves nothing over for other purposes or other interests" (p. 243). We found the mothers sometimes heroic in their attempts to simultaneously work on mourning and on mothering a new baby. We also found the work of mourning largely incompatible with the work of primary maternal preoccupation. It did not seem possible for the psyche to be consumed with the lost object in mourning and at the same time to be consumed with the infant in primary maternal preoccupation. Both states demand profound and absorbing focus on the object. Each elicits intense affects contradictory to the other. In the early period of our Project, we saw powerful states of sorrow and loss interfere with and sometimes supplant the new states of joy and love felt for the babies.

Further compounding this incompatible requirement to mourn and to be in "primary preoccupation" with their babies was the traumatic nature of the losses and the trauma sustained by the mothers themselves during the attack. Mourning and mothering were made even more difficult by the confusing, shocking, and terrifying circumstances of September 11 and their husbands' deaths. They confronted the terror of the attack, fearing for their own and their older children's safety, knowing other friends, relatives, and colleagues who were killed, and suffering images of their husbands' violent deaths in the fire and collapse of the towers. After the initial horrific events, often there was no body recovered, or at various times mothers were notified about body fragments having been found. The mothers' grief was very public. They were confused and overwhelmed by the outpouring of sympathy, pity, and curiosity from strangers. One mother cried that in addition to everything else she had to think about, she now had to write more than 300 personal thank you notes. Many of the mothers questioned their trust in their country and religion for the first time.

As our Project evolved, we understood more about the profoundly disruptive effects of traumatic loss on the mothers' minds. Blum (2003), Varvin (2003), and Rosenbaum and Varvin (2007) recently described the significant disturbances in self experience typically seen as a result of trauma: there are profuse feelings of helplessness, insecurity, anxiety, loss of basic trust, and fragmentation of perspective on one's own life. There is a continuous threat of chaotic mental states and a disturbance of the symbolizing function. Freud (1920) described trauma as a flooding of the psyche by overwhelming stimuli, the consequences of which are disorganization, confusion, and disruption of basic physiological cycles such as sleep and eating.

Hofer (1998, 1994, 1996) has suggested that the chaotic physiological and psychological states experienced by people who have suffered the loss of a love object may be at least partially due to the way in which that person provided biologic regulatory functions to the survivor, much as the mother provides these functions to her infant. That is, the disorientation and disregulation experienced in bereavement may have an actual biological base. All through the life cycle, people have physiological dependence on their love partners and on the internal representations of them throughout the rhythms of the normal course of daily life. Thus, the mothers in our Project were faced with massive effects on their psyches of pregnancy, childbirth, new motherhood, mourning and trauma.

In the early months following September 11, other prominent themes emerged in addition to those related to mourning. These other themes often dominated group sessions, further eclipsing the mothers' focus on their babies. The content and intransigence of these themes seemed related to the already vulnerable psychic state induced by pregnancy and childbirth in which the mothers' psyches were already unsettled by their bodies and minds accommodating to a new infant, and then made more difficult to resolve because of the effect of traumatic loss.

Many of the mothers were absorbed by and enmeshed in conflicts with their families of origin. Some women had moved to live with or near their original families immediately after the loss of their husbands. The degree to which they were later able to extricate themselves and leave again varied. Many expressed profound disappointment with parents and in-laws and reported enhanced or resumed rivalries and resentments with siblings and close friends. The deepened need for their own mothers that had already been activated by pregnancy became a different kind of need for them in actuality at this time. In the years following, disengaging from dependence and conflict with their families and reestablishing separateness has been very difficult for some.

The mothers' feeling of loss of control of their bodies, which began in pregnancy, was heightened and made intolerable by the loss of control brought by their husbands' deaths. Many mothers made changes in plans for their babies' births, scheduling the deliveries earlier than their due dates. Some mothers decided to have induced labors and fully anesthesized deliveries rather than allowing the births to occur in their own time and being conscious during delivery, as they originally had planned. Inasmuch as the babies represented all that was left of their husbands, the mothers desperately longed to see them. However, at the same time, thoughts of the babies often were infused with sadness, grief, anxiety, and lost hope. The actual presence of the baby inside lent power to fearful fantasies and feelings of loss of control, and for some mothers this took on great proportions. Allowing their bodies and minds to be overcome by labor and delivery, without the support of their husbands, seemed intolerable.

Disturbing feelings of uncertain and unwanted identities were also discussed a great deal in our early groups and individual sessions. The normal shifts in maternal identity already initiated by pregnancy were further heightened and shaken by their husbands' deaths. Not only was there a change from the newly forming identity as mother back to "daughter in need," but also, paradoxically, there was an instant transformation from young wife to widow and single mother. An identity as widow normally would not have been reached, if ever, until the ends of their lives. Many women talked of feeling very old, worn, and nonsexual, and they could not imagine ever reconstituting themselves as young, sexual women. Many women also talked about how they never would have chosen to have a baby alone and could not imagine connecting with other single mothers. They felt pitied at a time when they had imagined they would be envied. It was the worst time in their lives instead of the best. Although the groups were set up to help the mother-baby relationship, the mothers often more urgently needed to talk about these themes before turning to focus on the babies.

More than 50 years ago, Winnicott (1960) began to conceptualize the elements which comprise "good enough" maternal care, and to describe the "holding environment" associated with "primary maternal preoccupation." Mahler (1967) at around the same time talked about the mother as a symbiotic partner who helps maintain her infant's homeostasis, which in turn forms the foundation of neurobiological patterns and processes in the infant. Gratification-frustration sequences and mutual cuing exchanges create the complex pattern that becomes what Mahler calls "the leitmotif" for the infant becoming the child of his particular mother. More recently, psychoanalytic infant researchers (Beebe & Lachmann, 1988; Beebe, Lachmann, & Jaffe, 1997; Stern, 1985; Tronick, 1989) have identified in detail some of the countless nonconscious and conscious, minute yet highly complex mother-infant action sequences that constitute the totality of mothers' empathically reliable provision of routine care. Winnicott and Mahler thought, and now we know it to be true, that what is physical between mother and baby becomes part of the infant's psychology. The caregiver is the co-regulator of infant states. Maternal body warmth affects the infant's neuroendocrine system; maternal touch affects infants' growth hormone production and heart rate. Vocal, facial, and bodily interactional patterns between caregiver and infant literally organize the infant's brain, affecting the function, structure, and neurochemical architecture and forming the sensory-motor foundations of the later sense of self and of self and object representations (Beebe & Stern, 1977; Beebe, Lachmann, & Jaffe, 1997; Shore, 1994). In Mahler's words:

> . . . .the mother conveys—in innumerable ways—a kind of "mirroring frame of reference," to which the primitive self of the infant automatically adjusts. If the mother's "primary preoccupation" with her infant—her mirroring function during earlier infancy—is unpredictable, unstable, anxiety-ridden, or hostile; if her confidence in herself as a mother is shaky, then the individuating child has to do without a reliable frame of reference for checking back, perceptually and emotionally, to the symbiotic partner. The result will then be a disturbance in the primitive "self feeling," which would derive or originate from a pleasurable and safe state of symbiosis, from which he did not have to hatch prematurely and abruptly. (1967, p. 750)

Mahler goes on to say that if the infant has to take over functions from the mother, premature ego development in the form of "false self" or "as if" mechanisms can occur.

There is already a large body of research demonstrating the disrupting effects of depression on maternal "provision of routine care," and in turn, on the social and cognitive development of the babies of depressed mothers (Field, 1995, 2011; Murray, 1992; Tronick, 1997; Weinberg & Tronick, 1998). Even in low-risk community samples, maternal depression has an important and disturbing effect on mother-infant communication (Beebe, Jaffe, Buck, Chen, Cohen, Feldstein, & Andrews, 2008). Babies of depressed mothers may be intermittently attended to, and the babies' spontaneous gestures may sometimes be interfered with, intruded on, or ignored. Depressed mothers may present babies with affectively flat facial expressions or provide little scaffolding of infants' activities. Infants may become hypervigilant of their mothers' emotional states, have difficulty in emotional regulation, and show delays in cognitive function and language development. They also may become emotionally constricted and limit their own arousal and excited states. Clinically, we know that infants of depressed mothers can become "caretaker" children, attempting to enliven or placate their mothers.

Engaging victims of trauma in treatment is often difficult from a practical standpoint because of the very effects of the trauma. Moreover, the therapeutic relationship itself can be experienced as threatening because the traumatized person may have difficulty accessing good internal object representations and may fear re-experiencing in treatment feelings connected to the traumatic event. Basic trust that others can help has often been profoundly shaken. Even the practical aspects of setting and keeping appointment times can be enormously difficult because of the dysregulation and disorganization caused by the effects of trauma on the ego.

In the first year of our Project we hoped we could help strengthen the connection between the mothers and their babies. We hoped to help the mothers to distinguish the work of mourning and the effects of trauma from the work of caring for their babies and children. We hoped to help them surmount some of what interfered with keeping the babies in mind so they could feel empathy and pleasure in caring for them. We tried to hold the mothers so they could hold their babies. We provided a comfortable space, with food and beverages, encouraged them to tell us whatever they wanted, and attended very closely, looking for moments during which we could point them to their infants to see a smile or potentially gratifying response. We sometimes offered clarifications or interpretations of dynamic issues relating to families. We tried to facilitate their relationships to each other as they poignantly and uniquely understood each other's situations. The work was very difficult. The material was often searingly painful. The mothers were often disorganized, preoccupied, absent-minded, or unable to focus. We had to provide calls to remind them of the group because they often could not remember what day it was.

It was very difficult simultaneously to address the mothers' traumatized states and their grief while attempting to help them in their interactions with their babies. Under optimal circumstances, the new mother's vulnerable and permeable psychic state is used to identify with her baby and to be stirred up emotionally by her baby. For the mothers in our Project, however, identifying with the baby's helplessness, neediness, and dependency at times felt too overwhelming. It compounded their own states of helplessness. Many mothers at times found themselves sadly withdrawing from intimate connection to their babies. At those moments, empathy and affective resonance with the baby seemed to be threatening. One mother described that she could not soothe her crying baby because when he cried in her arms, she began to cry too. Another mother began crying as she looked at her baby in his infant seat and imagined he felt alone and afraid. At times it was extraordinarily difficult for these mothers to identify with and contain their babies' distress because it too easily dissolved into and intensified their own. Conversely, they also at times withdrew from their babies in an effort to protect them so as not to inflict their sadness on them, and so, left the babies with others whom they thought provided better care. At other times mothers were anxious about and had difficulty leaving their babies at all, relying on them for comfort and companionship, sleeping with them and taking them everywhere, so as not to feel alone. Most mothers had significant trouble regulating their babies' sleep and feeding schedules, particularly since they were having difficulty regulating their own sleep and eating cycles.

Disconnection, unpredictability, and loss often infused the mother-baby relationships in the early years of the Project. It was unbearable for the mothers to think that in addition to growing up without a father, their own traumatized and mournful states might affect the babies as well. The mothers' trauma was being transmitted to the babies through the myriad ways in which the early maternal functioning was unavoidably temporarily disrupted. Yet they came to our mother-baby group and project and gradually, although still partially, their grief receded, and they came to accept that they were now single mothers and to understand that they were very much needed by their babies.

We found that each developmental step in the babies and children brought renewed challenges and grief to the mothers. Mothers' usual thrill in seeing their children achieve something new was at times marred by the reminder that their husbands were not there to witness the accomplishment. In turn, the renewed grief led at times to momentary withdrawal from the babies. Sometimes there was renewed sadness as mourning progressed and the mothers realized the extent to which they had not been able to be as psychically available to their babies as they would have wished. In the second year, they talked a great deal about how painful it was that they remembered so little of their babies' first year and had missed their babyhoods. The toddlers' practicing periods brought additional stresses and anxieties as the toddlers physically separated and began crawling, walking, and running away from their mothers. Some mothers watched too closely, some did not watch closely enough, and some inconsistently did both. Yet, throughout, the mothers' courage and determination, and their investment in their babies' well-being was remarkable, incredibly poignant, and impressive throughout.

The babies, now children approaching 10 years old, have been for some time asking about, and representing in play, their fathers and their fathers' deaths. As they began to develop language and to notice other families with fathers, they directly asked their mothers questions about where their fathers were and what had happened to them. The mothers struggled a great deal with how, when, and what to tell the children. The children's questions themselves frequently reawakened in the mothers the anguished feelings from which they had begun to recover and from which they wanted to shield their children. The mothers wanted their children to know their fathers but also wanted to protect them from the pain that the knowledge of their fathers' deaths would bring. Some of the mothers felt they could not talk to their children about their fathers' deaths at all, that it was unimaginable. Some mothers found it difficult to answer their children's questions and attempted to distract them. Others told very vague and partial stories. For several years, many mothers did not believe their children already knew much of what happened because they had not told them. Laub and Auerhahn (1993) described the difficulty translating the experience of trauma and loss into words. Because trauma involves a radical break from normal experience, the usual structures of meaning and categories of thought are not available and do not apply. Helping the mothers tolerate and process their understanding and feelings about their children's understanding of and feelings about the loss of their fathers has been a challenging but essential focus of our work.

The children who never knew their fathers have been posed with the very complex psychic task of constructing representations of fathers with whom they have had no direct sensory history. At the same time, the children have had to struggle with understanding their fathers' deaths and managing the feelings of loss and anxiety that entails. In addition, they have been faced with the potentially traumatizing knowledge of their fathers' causes of death, which contain terrifying images and concepts: murder, crashing airplanes, collapsing buildings, and fire.

Research has demonstrated that mothers' capacity to reflect on loss and process grief predicts the attachment security of their children (Fonagy, Steele, & Steele, 1991; Steele, Steele, & Model, 1991; Hesse & Main, 1990). The mothers in our Project have helped their children think about and contain feelings about their fathers and about their own babyhoods. This capacity to reflect will help to prevent the stories and the telling of the stories from being traumatizing. In our mother-child groups, mothers' groups, video consultations, and individual treatments, we have been working to help the mothers to think through their own experience, and thus to help their children to think as well.

## REFERENCES

Beebe, B., & Lachmann, F. (1988). The contribution of mother-infant mutual influence to the origins of self- and object representations. *Psychoanalytic Psychology*, *5*, 304–337.

Beebe, B., & Stern, D. (1977). Engagement-disengagement and early object experiences. In N. Freedman & S. Grand (Eds.), *Communicative structures and psychic structures* (pp. 35–55). New York, NY: Plenum Press.

Beebe, B., Lachmann, F., & Jaffe, J. (1997). Mother-infant interaction structures and presymbolic self- and object representations. *Psychoanalytic Dialogues*, *7*, 133–182.

Beebe, B., Jaffe, J., Buck, K., Chen, H., Cohen, P., Feldstein, S., & Andrews, H. (2008). Six-week postpartum maternal depressive symptoms and 4-month mother-infant self-and interactive contingency. *Infant Mental Health Journal*, *29*(5), 442–471.

Benedek, T. (1970). The psychobiology of pregnancy. In A. Anthony & T. Benedek (Eds.), *Parenthood: Its psychology and psychopathology*. Boston, MA: Little, Brown.

Bergman, A. (1999). *Ours, yours, mine: Mutuality and the emergence of the separate self*. Northvale, NJ: Jason Aronson.

Blum, H. P. (2003). Psychic trauma and traumatic object loss. *Journal of the American Psychoanalytic Association*, *51*, 415–431.

Field, T., Healy, B., Goldstein, S., Perry, D., Bendell, D., Schanberg, S., . . . Kuhn, C. (1988). Infants of depressed mothers show "depressed" behavior even with nondepressed adults. *Child Development*, *59*, 1569–1579.

Field,T. (2011). Prenatal depression effects on early development: A review. *Infant Behavior & Development*, *34*(1), 1–14.

Fonagy, P., Steele, M., & Steele, H. (1991). The capacity for understanding mental states: The reflective self in parent and child and its significance for security of attachment. *Infant Mental Health Journal*, *12*, 201–218.

Freud, S. (1917). Mourning and melancholia. *The Standard Edition*, *14*, 237–258.

Freud, S. (1920). Beyond the pleasure principle. *The Standard Edition*, *18*, 7–66.

Hesse, E., & Main, M. (1999). Second-generation effects of unresolved trauma in nonmaltreating parents: Dissociated, frightened, and threatening parental behavior. *Psychoanalytic Inquiry*, *19*, 481–540.

Hofer, M. (1988). Relationships as regulators: A psychobiological perspective on bereavement. *Psychosomatic Medicine*, *46*, 183–197.

Hofer, M. (1994). Early relationships as regulators of infant physiology and behavior. *International Forum of Psychoanalysis, 3*, 197.

Hofer, M. (1996). On the nature and consequences of early loss. *Psychosomatic Medicine*, *58*, 570–581.

Kestenberg, J. (1976). Regression and reintegration in pregnancy. *Journal of American Psychoanalytical Association*, *24*(Suppl.), 213–250.

Laub, D., & Auerhahn, N. (1993). Knowing and not knowing massive psychic trauma: Forms of traumatic memory. *International Journal of Psycho-Analysis*, *74*, 287–302.

Lester, E., & Notman, M. (1988). Pregnancy and object relations: Clinical considerations. *Psychoanalytic Inquiry*, *8*, 196–221.

Mahler, M. (1967). On human symbiosis and the vicissitudes of individuation. *Journal of the American Psychoanalytic Association*, *15*, 740–763.

Murray, L. (1992). The impact of postnatal depression on infant development. *Journal of Child Psychology and Psychiatry*, *33*, 543–561.

Pines, D. (1972). Pregnancy and motherhood: Interaction between fantasy and reality. *British Journal of Medical Psychology*, *45*, 333–343.

Raphael-Leff, J. (1996). *Pregnancy: The inside story*. Northvale, NJ: Aronson.

Rosenbaum, B., & Varvin, S. (2007). The influence of extreme traumatization on body, mind and social relations. *International Journal of Psychoanalysis*, *88*, 1527–1542.

Rustin, M. (1989). Encountering primitive anxieties. In L. Miller, M. Rustin, M. Rustin, & J. Shuttleworth (Eds.), *Closely observed infants* (pp. 22–51). London, England: Gerald Duckworth & Co.

Schore, A. (1994). *Affect regulation and the origin of the self: The neurobiology of emotional development*. Hillsdale, NJ: Lawrence Erlbaum Associates.

Steele, M., Steele, H., & Model, E. (1991). Links across generations: Predicting parent-child relationship patterns from structured interviews with expectant parents. *Bulletin of the Anna Freud Centre*, *14*, 95–113.

Stern, D. (1995). *The motherhood constellation*. New York, NY: Basic Books.

Tronick, E. (1997). *The neurobehavioral and social emotional development of infants and children*. New York, NY: W. W. Norton.

Varvin, S. (2003). Extreme traumatisation: Strategies for mental survival. *International Forum of Psychoanalysis*, *12*, 5–16.

Weinberg, K., & Tronick, E. (1998). The impact of maternal psychiatric illness on infant development. *Journal of Clinical Psychiatry*, *59*, 53–61.

Winnicott, D. (1956). Primary maternal preoccupation. In *Through paediatrics to psycho-analysis* (pp. 300–305). London, England: Hogarth Press.

Winnicott, D. (1960). The theory of the parent-infant relationship. *International Journal of Psycho-Analysis*, *41*, 585–595.

Yehuda, R., Engel, S., Brand, S., Seckl, J., Marcus, S., & Berkowitz, G. (2005). Transgenerational effects of posttraumatic stress disorder in babies of mothers exposed to the World Trade Center attacks during pregnancy. *The Journal of Clinical Endocrinology & Metabolism*, *90*(7), 4115–4118.

# Creating Space for Mourning a Lost Father and Husband After September 11: A Therapist's Reflections

Rita Reiswig, M.S., L.P.

This article describes how a mother, shortly after the loss of her husband on September 11, 2001, keeps the father in mind, conveying his essence to her children and to the therapists and mothers' group, in the Project for Mothers, Infants, and Young Children of September 11, 2001. A particular bird, a cardinal, that appeared and disappeared from her yard, became a symbol that gave shape and meaning to her mourning for her and for her children. Over time, as one of the therapists, I came to know the lost husband through the accounts of the mother. I gradually held a place in the discourse for him and his point of view. In this way I helped to facilitate the process of incremental mourning, filling a similar role to that of the cardinal, a fleeting symbol of the lost husband and father.

I am a therapist in one of the support groups that has met for nine years with mothers who were pregnant on September 11, 2001, and lost their husbands on that day. The child's idea of the father, never known by the child, will be shaped by how the mother keeps him in mind, how her fantasies and thoughts give shape to her representations of him, how she sorts these bits and pieces of his personality, and how she conveys his essence, both consciously and unconsciously. In addition, the mother and any children already born to the parents at the time of September 11 must find a way to understand the loss.

Each mother's reaction to the immediate trauma of the father's loss unfolded in ways that were influenced by the mother's response to past loss, her experience of being a mother, and her relationship with her husband before he died. Some aspects of the loss were transmitted from the mother to the baby through the mother's state of mind and what she said and did. But other pathways of transmission were observable over time at the microanalytic level. These were set in motion from the beginning of the baby's life and were nonverbal, happening at the body-to-body level through holding, gaze, smile, tone of voice, vocal rhythm patterns, look/look away cycles, and self and interactive regulation patterns (see Beebe and Markese, this issue; Tortora, this issue; Markese, this issue). An additional layer of loss was in some cases created by the mother's diminished psychic availability due to her state of shock and literal distraction.

The nature of the loss and its ensuing trauma was sudden and specific. Initially, the mothers searched for their husbands around the Twin Towers site. They inquired at local hospitals trying to determine if their husbands were still alive. The mothers were crying, sleeping irregularly, eating abnormally, and involuntarily exposing their fetuses to an intrauterine experience of considerable stress. The stress continued postpartum. Each mother's state of shock and grief altered her availability and attunement to her infant. In early meetings of the mothers' group, the mothers often appeared stunned, numb, and in a state of disbelief as they responded to a daily barrage of events, memorials, paperwork, identification of body parts, and legal matters. Their phones rang constantly. At times they did not respond. They were treated as public figures, as "negative celebrities," as one mother described it. In meetings, the mothers might hand their babies to a therapist to hold, as they faced each other sharing their grief in excruciating detail.

Among the women, no two experiences of loss were the same. Likewise, their psychological profiles, their marriages, and their support systems varied widely. The particular mother I will focus on managed to find a creative, metaphorical way of dealing with her loss and conveying something meaningful about it to her children, both with the newborn baby and her two older children.

The following vignette about Louise, told with the mother's permission, describes her interactions with the older children. It illustrates her way of transmitting her feelings and ideas about the lost father to them. Moreover, it is a description of my work with this mother in the group.

Louise developed transitional ideas to represent the lost husband and father, both for herself and her children. Within days after September 11, she had been looking for a sign that her husband was somehow still connected to her and that he was looking out for her and the children. One day she noticed a particular cardinal at the bird feeder in their backyard. She pointed out the cardinal's daily arrival to her older children. They were sure by a particular marking that it was the same cardinal who returned each day. Before long, Louise found herself talking to the children about the cardinal being special, a friend—maybe even the spirit of Daddy—visiting them, watching over them. As they watched the cardinal, they felt the cardinal also watched them. Louise created this symbol as a way to feel the husband's presence, to hold on to him, and to talk to the children about him. There were days, however, when the bird did not appear, and Louise was confronted with the idea that the symbol she created for her husband to visit was unpredictable, like the day her husband did not come home. The bird itself symbolized both the husband's presence and his absence.

When they traveled to their country house, they saw some cardinals there, too. The children speculated about whether it was the same cardinal from the bird feeder at home. They wondered, was Daddy watching over them there, too?

Louise told the group that she had said to her children, "I know he isn't the bird, but his spirit resides in the bird." This imagery that Louise and her older children created allowed the children a way to take in and begin to make sense of the loss of their father. The cardinal also became important to Louise as a transition from one psychic state to another—an intermediary between disbelief and belief, between shock and dawning awareness. Although the cardinal was a symbol, it also had vitality and a reality of its own, even if only a fleeting one, to Louise and her older children. The conversation between mother and children about the cardinal was alternately playful and serious. Through these conversations, over time, the mother invested the symbol of the cardinal with meaning about the father, giving the idea shape and language, and conveying that meaning to her children. The cardinal, a fleeting image, set the stage for less symbolic ways of conveying the missing father to her children, even to her newborn. The children, as a result, will hopefully over time be able to give their own shape and meaning to the father's absence.

Week by week, in the mothers' group meetings, I became increasingly aware that Louise used the image of the cardinal not only to convey something to her children but also as a flexible container for her own mourning. The symbol was playful and allowed Louise to both engage and evolve her understanding of her loss over time.

In addition, through her descriptions of her husband, I developed a picture in my mind of how he looked, how he smiled, and of the ebullient nature of his personality. Louise's presentation of her husband was alternately lively and sad. She spoke about how he had always talked things over with her. I heard how they met, about their long courtship and some of the bumpy times they had prior to their marriage, and some of the intimacies they shared. She told about his parents and his tight-knit Italian extended family, what he liked to eat on his birthday, and the traditions the family shared at Christmas. I heard he was generous but liked things a certain way. I formed an idea of how his mind worked and how he used it to become successful at work. I knew about his devotion to his children and how he sometimes took them out early in the morning so Louise could sleep a little longer.

At the summer house, he played with the kids at the edge of the bay looking for stones and shells. Sometimes he just piddled around with them. Sometimes they all stayed in pajamas and he fed them breakfast. On Friday nights they always stayed home and had pizza and watched a movie together. Louise described how he gave everyone a kiss and how much she loved remembering that.

When the World Trade Center was bombed in 1993, her husband was there and helped a woman down 16 flights of stairs, saying to her, "You're coming with me." He survived that day. When the tower he worked in was attacked on September 11, he made a phone call to their home and left a message for Louise. She missed the call because she was taking her daughter to her first day of school. Then he called her at work, left a message saying he was okay but wanted to speak to her urgently. In her mind, she saw him as a survivor, as active in pressing to get out of the tower. She believed he was working his way down the steps, helping people and thinking about others that he loved. She knows he thought he would get out. Louise held that idea in her mind. She told the mothers' group how she turned on the television and from those images realized he had probably died. While she had no evidence, she believed he probably died without too much pain and suffering.

What she had conveyed to her children by using the cardinal as a symbol, she now conveyed to the group through verbal representations of her husband. Although Louise's husband was dead, his essence, his spirit, remained alive in Louise, who in turn conveyed that essence to me. In an attempt to face his death, Louise had painted in contrast a strikingly alive portrait of him. From her account I could see him clearly in my mind. Her details created a place in my mind that held him. I knew that behind his presence was his absence. As a result, he became so tangibly present in group conversations that I came to identify with him.

On occasion, I then began to represent Louise's husband to her. I felt I could better comfort her since I had taken him in. I kept in mind what I knew from her about him, the details, postures, jokes, and positive views of the world, so that I might reflect some of these attributes back to Louise. There was a gliding back and forth between current reality and memory. She told me and the group things she would have told her husband.

Getting to know her husband as Louise conveyed him to me, holding mental images of him in my mind, feeling a spousal connection to him and to her, lending myself temporarily into that space where he used to be, helped me to co-parent with Louise by imagining and sometimes representing his point of view. For example, Louise had taken to heart what I said about allowing her now 7-year-old daughter to have fancier clothes and allowing her to wear a bracelet. Louise described how elated her daughter had been when she saw a photo of her mother on her wedding day. Her daughter asked about the dress, which was plain but had some sequins and pearls on the bodice. "What do you have on your dress?" she asked. "What is all that stuff?" I asked her whether her husband might have enjoyed the daughter's fancier choices. She was then able to negotiate with her daughter the purchase of things that were a bit different from her own taste. She could see her daughter as separate and admire her.

I felt I could help her with her sadness by symbolically standing in for her husband. I felt I could give her a sense of his aliveness in the present and a sense of what she might imagine he would have wanted for her and their children in the future. Although he was dead, he was accessible and reachable through word, memory, and mental representation.

All this created an atmosphere in which mourning could occur. As I felt a profound connection to Louise's loss, I understood more fully that I stood in for her husband. Of course, I was not her husband. At other times, I stood in for the father of the children and could represent what I thought his point of view might be. In reality, I was not their father, either. My shifting roles were mere moments in time with Louise; they were fleeting markers in the slow evolution of her mourning. I, too, had participated, as had the cardinal, in creating a transitional idea, a shadow play, part reality and part fantasy, something that was internal and external at the same time.

# MOTHERS AND CHILDREN IN THE VIDEO LABORATORY CONTEXT

## Beyond the Face and Words: How the Body Speaks

Suzi Tortora, Ed.D., BC–DMT, CMA

This case study presents a microanalysis of interactions of one mother-infant dyad videotaped at four and fourteen months, in the Project for Mothers, Infants, and Young Children of September 11, 2001. It provides an intriguing window into the infant's experience within the context of loss and trauma. The observational method utilizes the D.A.N.C.E. tool developed by this author and the Laban movement analysis system. The integrated rhythms of the actions, the timing of gestures and the spatial shifts of posture comprise each individual's core choreography in the dance of relating.

This article illustrates how observations of nonverbal behavior in mother-infant dyads can inform a clinical understanding of early relational patterns, through a description of one mother in our Project and her 4-month old infant. An analysis of the next follow-up visit when the child was 14 months will also be presented. These observations are made with mother and infant seated face-to-face. This mother has given us permission for this description; names and identifying features have been changed to preserve confidentiality.

Celina at 4 months is in an infant seat on a table. Mother is seated in a chair, so that their heads are in the same plane. One camera captures the infant's body and hands, and another camera captures the mother's upper body and hands, generating a split-screen view of each seen "head-on." The following vignette is a one-minute nonverbal analysis segment of a 10-minute face-to-face interaction. The words in italics are my personal reactions as I observe this interaction, guided by a self-observation form that will be described later in the article.

### CELINA AND HER MOTHER AT 4 MONTHS

Mother's light gentle touch begins the play with Celina age 4 months old. Ever so slightly, Celina pulls her head in and down, simultaneously sucking on the neckline of her shirt and finger with a quick pulsing rhythm, as she intently looks up at her mother. Her face brightens as her eyes meet her mother's eyes, and they each burst into a smile in perfect synchrony. Continuing with her gentle gestures, her mother retrieves the shirt collar out of Celina's mouth. She takes Celina's wrists with a light touch, directing her arms through the air, to a slow rhythmic finger play nursery rhyme, pausing through each verse. The unhurried phrasing of Mother's gestures has a measured controlled, yet punctuated quality, creating an action-pause sequence.

Their interaction takes on the qualities of a slow-motion dance, completely directed by Mother. Here is the dance: Mother takes Celina's hands and pauses for 1-2-3 counts / tap hands together at midline . . . swing, open arms wide and then together *again;* and 1-2 pause / open and close, tap hands, open and close, and open arms *again*; pause / press left-arm down onto Celina's lap, and pause . . . / follow with right-arm down to meet the left, and pause / up go both arms widening, and, pausing, as mother and baby burst into a fresh smile.

*Comment.* The mother does all the work of organizing the rhythm of actions and pauses. The pauses punctuate the mother's rhythm rather than the baby's rhythm.

There Mother goes *again*, tapping Celina's hands center again – boing! Open arms wide again; bicycle arms up and down through the air, in a soft slow directional beat, 1-2-3. Now down *again* onto Celina's lap as her mother glides her fingers along Celina's belly in a long even stroke . . . pause. Back up go Celina's arms as her mother brings them out and then to center *again*. This arm dance is serenaded by her mother's soft sing-song yet strained voice. Now her voice pauses with her actions, taking time to look at Celina for a moment as she continues directing Celina's arms. Mother's face is animated, with a wide smile and intermittently lifted arching eyebrows. Celina watches intently in a quiet, relatively still alert state, only occasionally blinking. She takes her eyes off her mother's face just once for a slight moment, 58 seconds into this sequence. The action is subtle. Celina slightly slides her gaze to her right. Immediately Mother reacts, looking down, with a sobering look.

*Comment.* This moment catches my eye. Celina's gaze away is just a second. She momentarily disengages with her mother, and her mother loses her smile so quickly. I wonder, are we getting a glimpse of the mother that reveals a side of her that seems to belie a deeper unexpressed feeling? I need to review this moment to analyze it more fully. I slow the tape down to get a closer look.

We now turn to a discussion of what this nonverbal dance between baby and mother can tell us about this dyad, several months after the tragic loss of the father. How are they experiencing each other, and how is this experience co-created by each of them? Are there specific elements revealed through their unspoken dance that provide details about how the experience of loss may be affecting the development of their relationship? Moreover, how might the multisensory-based experience of the mother, compromised by grief and trauma, influence the trajectory of the infant's developing procedural action-based representation of self-in-relation-to-other?

I attempted to answer these questions by analyzing mother and infant's individual and dyadic movement styles using elements of a specific nonverbal observation system called Laban Movement Analysis (Bartenieff, 1973; Bartenieff & Lewis, 1980; Laban, 1975, 1976; Laban & Lawrence, 1974; Lamb & Watson, 1979; Tortora, 2004, 2006, 2010). This system takes into account five movement categories: body, shape, space, phrasing, and effort. For a thorough explanation of these elements, see Tortora (2006).

I have combined specific elements of the Laban system with infant mental health theory, research, and practice to develop an observational tool that provides a lens into the underlying dynamics of a dyadic relationship. This nonverbal lens has been essential in helping us understand, in the video laboratory setting, the specific relational elements involved in the experiences of these mothers and their babies.

## ELEMENTS OF THE NONVERBAL ANALYSIS SYSTEM

The specific nonverbal elements that inform observations of mother-infant dyads follow:

1. *Body.* How each person moves the body as a whole, and as individual body parts, including full body alignment and how weight is shifted and balanced through the body.
2. *Facial expressivity* and *quality of eye gaze.*
3. *Body shapes.* The shapes a person makes within her own body and in relation to dyadic partner
4. *Quality of the movement actions.* These qualities include the tension, fluidity, speed, strength (strong, gentle, light), and spatial focus of the actions.
5. *Interactional space.* Space created by the dyad, including how each person occupies her personal private space (known as the "kinesphere") and moves in the surrounding general space; the changing distances between the dyad, involving the mingling, merging, overlapping and separateness of individual kinespheric spaces; how frequently they move in proximity to each other; and "embraced space." This term defines the intimate space that is created when two people are relating deeply and emotionally. It refers to an intimate connection that is not confined to a specific spatial distance. It can exist in close proximity or across the room.
6. *Physical contact.* The quality and amount of touch and/or physical contact between partners.
7. *Phrasing.* The rhythm and tempo of each person's nonverbal movement sequences.
8. *Vocal patterns.* How the tone and tempo of each person's vocal/verbal utterances support, complement, or juxtapose their individual nonverbal movement styles.
9. *Regulation and co-regulation.* How nonverbal behavior supports regulation or dysregulation of the individual and/or the dyadic interaction, including the infant's methods for regulating her internal system physiologically, emotionally and socially (such as breath patterns, tactile stimulation through self-touch and/or rubbing an object such as clothing).
10. *Coherence.* What is the level of harmonious connection, or "forming a whole" in the dyad? Is there a sense of contingent responsiveness within the dyadic interactions? Is there congruence between what the person says and what her nonverbal actions reveal?

A lack of congruence can become apparent in two ways: through a verbal-nonverbal discrepancy or through discrepancies within the individual bodily communication in different modalities, such as smiling but with extreme body tension. Nonverbal analysis includes but goes beyond the study of facial expression. It includes all aspects of body movement: gestures, postures, full body actions and muscle tension levels, as well as the shapes each person makes with her body in relationship to the partner, and how each person moves within her personal spatial surroundings, and the surrounding space shared by the dyad. It is through such nonverbal analysis that a more nuanced, in-depth picture of a person's internal state can be illuminated.

The nonverbal analysis method described is highly detailed and intricate. It does not simply describe what the participant's physical actions are but rather describes the movement qualities used to perform the actions. The qualities of action reveal meaning in a movement, or what I think of as the "dance" of the interaction and relationship. This method goes beyond a basic description of physical nonverbal behavior. It moves to a clinical method of describing the *quality* of nonverbal behavior that may provide insight into psychodynamic organization and feeling states.

### Sense of Body

The psychodynamic relevance of the body, and body experience, stems from the concept that the body and movement-based experiences are the initial conduits from which knowing and being known emerge (see Beebe et al., 2010; Tortora, 2006). I use the term *sense of body* to highlight this primary stage of the baby's developing sense of "self" (procedural, action-based representations) within the context of others and the surrounding world (Tortora, 2004, 2006, 2010). It is from embodied experiencing that is sensorial, kinesthetic, and somatic in nature that all other levels of knowing develop. I believe this embodied sense of knowing is the primary source that informs mental states, intersubjective experience, reflective functioning, and mentalization. Sense of body underlies the regulatory and co-regulatory bi-directional nature of the early attachment relationship. It informs how I analyze this mother-infant pair.

### Nonverbal Nature of the Dyadic Relationship

I have developed a set of questions about the qualitative aspects of nonverbal interaction within a dyad to analyze the nature of the relationship (Tortora, 2006). These questions, guided by the nonverbal qualitative elements discussed above, act as the lens through which I observe both the mother-child and the therapist-child dyadic exchange.

1. How are turn-taking interactions organized? How does each person "open" and "close" the possibility of either partner taking action? Specifically, how does each partner *initiate*, *withdraw* and *resume* contact?
2. How do mirroring, attuning, misattunement, and repair cycles occur in the body movement dialogue?
3. Does the adult make room for the child's expression before intervening, or does she respond without attending to the child's cues?
4. Is there an interactive congruence in the nonverbal styles of the partners, creating a complementary, synchronous, or harmonious dialogue?

Using these guidelines, I create hypotheses about the relation between the nonverbal interaction patterns and the psychodynamics of the evolving relationship. The pattern of initiation, withdrawal, and resumption of contact is especially significant in the analysis of the mother-infant dyad described above.

### "Self-Observation" as an Element of Nonverbal Analysis

I conducted the nonverbal analysis by initially viewing the videotape of Celina and her mother (described above) with the sound off. As I watched this mother and baby I remained receptive and attentive. I closely tracked the details of the nonverbal dialogue and my own reactions (*italicized*), which might involve thought, emotion, or a somatic reaction. This specific self-observation process has two purposes: to decipher what might constitute a counter-transference response and to notice how my somatic reactions identify implicit information about themes that may underlie the dynamics of a dyad. I want to experience this dyad as their nonverbal exchange unfolds, to be viscerally present in their experiencing of each other. I continually ask myself what it might feel like to be a member of this dyad.

I listen to the verbal dialogue only after I have a clear nonverbal understanding, to keep my nonverbal analysis separate from the tone and meaning of the verbal utterances. Typically, the verbal content is so compelling it can distract the viewer from fully capturing the unspoken exchange. Once I have a deep sense of this nonverbal exchange, I add the sound to see how my nonverbal impressions correlate with the verbal and vocal expressions.

### "Self-Observation" as I Watch Celina and Her Mother at 4 Months

I am initially a bit puzzled by the seemingly paradoxical feedback I sense within myself as I watch the video of Celina and her mother. At first glance, I feel calmed by her mother's slow, even pace. Her tempo is deliberate and regular, with each gesture occurring in a cycle of 4 to 7 beats followed by a pause. As the interaction continues, a feeling of being overwhelmed emerges in me. I realize I am holding my breath. Despite her slow pacing, I have to stop, start, rewind, and replay this sequence many times. I begin to wonder: do I do this to map accurately the correct order of her actions, or do I need a break from the reactions I am having? What is the underlying message I am picking up from her actions?

## FOUR-MONTH VISIT: INITIAL NONVERBAL ANALYSIS OF CELINA AND HER MOTHER

I turn to the baby's part in the nonverbal dialogue to gather more clues about the relationship. The baby is tracking her mother's contact so diligently, vigilantly, following Mother with her gaze yet maintaining stillness in her trunk and limbs. Most often she is looking up at her mother with her head shifted down and slightly pulled back. At times she has a slight and rapid increase in the flow of her breath. Intermittently there is a subtle lengthening and shortening of her torso or fluttering of her limbs, defined in Laban movement analysis as *shape-flow* actions. These subtle actions and her changing breath rhythms create a fluid sensation within the confines of the torso and can serve a self-regulatory function.

Each time Mother begins to smile, Celina responds immediately with a similar smile. Although Mother is smiling and her eyebrows rise, there is a stillness in her eyes and a tightness to her smile. Celina's brightened smile is not accompanied by the usual full body fluttering so typical in mother-baby nonverbal dialogues. I wonder, does Celina note this tightness in Mother as well? That increasing, almost ecstatic infatuation, so commonly seen as mother and baby "talk" to each other with their bodies, seems missing. Celina maintains her vigilant tracking of Mother with a full body stillness, despite her facial responses.

Again I review the moment about one minute into the filming when Celina took her eyes off her mother's face for an instant, mother's facial expression sobered, and Mother looked away.

Mother's visual disengagement is almost imperceptible. Almost instantly she follows Celina's downward visual gaze. She swoops down and lifts Celina's left foot to plant a sustained kiss on it. Mother comes closer still, leaning in with directness, folding her arms across the baby seat. *As I observe this I notice that I slightly pull myself back in reaction to Mother's close contact. I am holding my breath and become curious about Celina's breath pattern.*

As Mother comes in close, Celina maintains her alert state with little observable action, except a rapid eye blink and a short quickness in her breath. She holds back her smile, watching her mother closely. Throughout much of the interaction Celina keeps both her bodily and facial actions reserved and contained. Her physical responses are limited to slightly widening her mouth in response to Mother's widening smile; and subtly pulling her head into her body, down on her chest, alternating with faintly lifting her head by lengthening her neck. At times there are quiet gurgles from Celina, but they are almost inaudible because Mother's dialogue is constant. While she is not overtly distressed, Celina appears to be in a hyper-aroused state, noted by her full body stillness, quick short breathing, increased eye blinking, and her continuous visual attention on her mother.

Throughout the 10-minute playtime, Mother repeatedly maintains contact with Celina through multiple concurrent channels of touch, voice, and vision. Her even, rhythmic, stop-and-go tempo at first appears sensitive to Celina's needs. However, I interpret the pace as too constant. The pauses do not seem long enough to give Celina a chance to respond, or to initiate her own actions. I begin to wonder if the pauses are actually in response to Celina or more a reflection of Mother's own tempo and rhythm. I wonder if the mother is perhaps unconsciously hypervigilant for signs of Celina's attention wavering. What role does Celina play in supporting her mother's emotional needs? How does this co-constructed relationship support both of their needs?

At this point, I turn up the volume to hear if Mother's verbal dialogue is consistent with her nonverbal one. She states, "Your turn – are you going to talk to me – Hmm, Hmm," as Celina looks away, about one minute into their play. Following Celina's gaze away, Mother looks away as she sweeps her body even closer to Celina. The fluid and constant overlapping of her nonverbal and verbal expressions do not ever provide a complete pause. Instead, Mother creates a sequence of constant input. She moves closer. Now Celina receives all of her mother's auditory, visual, and kinesic input in a heightened way. Celina is drawn back in.

In the next sequence there is a slight variation in tempo through subtle accelerations in how Mother phrases her actions. She punctuates her actions by pausing between and within movement phrases, while she maintains steady eye contact with Celina. Mother leans her own body very close to Celina's by folding her arms across the baby seat over Celina's legs. The intensity level of her contact is constant. *Now that Mother adds tactile input to the other sensory modalities, will Celina continue to be able to receive all of this input with such undivided attention?*

Celina adapts by using behaviors that support central body awareness and that can be very self-organizing. She follows her mother's nursery song and hand gestures, lifting her head by lengthening up and forward through her upper spine and performing small fluid (shape flow) actions in her torso and legs. Mother finishes the song and grabs Celina's hands. Mother brings her own hands together, pauses, then embraces Celina's hands, and shakes them together with a vibratory phrase. After her slowly paced stop and pause phrasing, this more active vibration has a recuperative function. Mother bends forward kissing Celina's left hand, moves back momentarily and then sweeps forward again, kissing Celina's belly. There is a fluid swing-like quality in the timing of this movement phrase, as Mother slightly increases and decreases her tempo. Through the use of her full body to create these actions, Mother forms a circular spatial pathway toward and away from Celina. The timing of her phrases has only slight occasional increases or decreases in tempo.

The overall even-tempo, repetitiveness, and fluid spatial organization of Mother's phrasing style constructs predictability in mother's actions. Mother clearly wants to engage her daughter. Celina finds a way to maintain self-regulation, while organizing all of her mother's input. Mother continues to initiate the engagement with Celina, with her eyes bright and wide. Celina follows and responds with continuous eye contact and affective excitement. She brightens her face by squinting her eyes, and she holds a smile for a moment. She vocalizes and articulates with her mouth and lifts her arms following Mother's vocal input.

*Comment.* It appears that Celina is working with effort to maintain self-regulation. Celina follows her mother, but she does not frequently initiate. It is after this point that a sense of overload is increasingly detectable in both the baby and the mother.

At times her mother's face seems frozen in bright smiles and widened eyes, which lack modulation. Celina's actions become more still. She shortens her neck as she pulls her head deeper down, and increases her sucking behaviors. Mother flutters her fingers for a moment close to Celina's face, then she walks her fingers up Celina's belly and taps her on the nose.

*Comment.* As I watch I am aware of my somatic reactions. I put myself in the baby's body. It is as if I can actually feel her mother's articulating fingers. Mother has such clear fine motor control and her actions are steady and continuous. Although the contact is gentle and the increasing tempo has a slow pace, I feel a mounting tension, a sensory overload. There is so much visual and tactile input. Mother's moving fingers are framing her facial expressions, punctuated by her vocal utterances. I need a rest from all of the contact. How is Celina feeling, I wonder?

Celina begins to suck on her fist, in a chewing rhythm, and slightly turns her head to the side while still looking at her mother. Mother adds her own bent finger to Celina's mouth, for a momentary suck. *Now an oral element is also added to the multisensory stimulation.* As Celina continues to suck her own hand, her mother shifts her tactile focus to Celina's legs. Mother pumps her legs up and down, to a slow regular beat. Mother encourages Celina, "talk to me," and she repeats a vocalizing "raspberry" sound. Celina responds with a slight increased smile and attempted tongue thrust forward with her tiny mouth, while maintaining eye contact. Only occasionally does Celina look slightly away.

*Comment.* I feel tension arising in my own body. I realize I am waiting for Celina to protest in some way — to look away, to turn away, or slide her body off to the side. I am surprised to see that Celina continues to keep her steady gaze on Mother, smiling at moments in harmony with her mother's smiles.

Almost halfway into the segment, as Mother sings and swings Celina's legs, Celina begins to fling her own arms out. She widens and then arches her arms over her head as she vocalizes in a deep guttural manner, complementing Mother's swinging of Celina's legs. *Ah, a moment of initiation from Celina that expands Mother's actions.* Mother then makes a sad face, pulling her eyebrows in, shaking her head side-to-side, and opens her own hands, complementing Celina's arm gestures. *But Mother's sad expression and head shake are incongruous with the infant's active initiation.* As Celina brings her arms down and continues to vocalize, her mother puts her own knuckle into Celina's mouth again. *I notice I have taken a quick breath. Mother seems to have interpreted Celina's initiation of arm movements as distress. Mother moves to soothe Celina.*

Celina's actions stop as she stares into her mother's eyes. She blinks once and slightly lifts her left leg up, almost imperceptibly. Then all of her actions cease, and she keeps her eyes on her mother. Mother puts her fingertip into Celina's mouth. She adds pressure by rubbing her gums in a steady side-to-side stroking rhythm. "Your teeth are bothering you. Do they hurt? Do they hurt?" Celina stares at Mother and then lifts her head up and looks away, at the ceiling. *Again Celina initiates an action, but this time she disengages her visual attention.* Mother follows Celina's gaze, verbalizing "What's that?" as she increases her rubbing. Celina looks down and then extends her arm in a fluid gesture while looking away. Mother plays with Celina's feet again. Celina shifts her head to the left side and attempts to suck her own hand. She increases her vocalizations while lengthening and shortening her torso, with occasional fluid leg actions. She then makes eye contact with Mother, using peripheral vision from the corner of her eyes.

*Comment.* I feel startled. I realize I am reacting to the mother's continual and varied forms of touch as stimulation overload. But something is working for them. Celina is so intently watching and absorbing her mother's actions, and she does not lose control physically or vocalize distress. I put myself in the mother's body. She is working so hard. She vigilantly watches every move of her baby. Is she worried? She is so alert to any movement away, gaze away, or any possible distress. Is the pattern that I sense as overstimulation the mother's own attempt to stay very involved with her baby? Does Celina pick up on this? Celina somehow manages to keep herself regulated, despite such a high level of stimulation. Is Celina's own vigilant attentiveness wariness or an attempt to maintain engagement with her mother, or both?

## FOUR-MONTH VISIT: INTERPRETATION OF NONVERBAL DYADIC EXCHANGE BETWEEN CELINA AND HER MOTHER

I bring these observations to our bi-weekly therapist's group discussion. I describe how this mother's actions set the tone for the interaction and how Celina finds a way to regulate herself to stay engaged. Celina does this through sucking and her torso's slight undulating movements, which provide central body awareness and organization. Celina maintains visual focus on her mother, and she adjusts to her mother's continuous stimulation. They have created a mutual adaptive coping dynamic that supports their relationship. Celina's vigilant visual tracking and carefully contained slight smiles reflect an impressive self-regulation. The mother's slow, deliberate, continuous stimulation may reflect her effort to stay connected to her daughter, while she is making such an effort to keep her sadness at bay. Celina is even-tempered, never giving up on her mother. Through her vigilance and hyper-aroused state, Celina co-regulates the relationship by reducing her own initiative to balance her mother's overstimulation. This enables Celina to get the nurturance that her mother has to offer.

Despite her sadness, this mother offers so much. For the baby it seems to be worth the vigilant attention she must pay and the effort she makes to stay so still in order to get her mother's engagement. As mother's multisensory input heightens, Celina's increasing breath flow, rapid eye movements, and sucking, juxtaposed by overall bodily stillness, portray effort and weariness as the infant tries to stay regulated and engaged. But Celina stays emotionally responsive to her mother's efforts, and able to share smiles. Celina has figured out a way to stay connected to her mother. But her own initiative looks compromised.

In summary, Celina has learned to regulate herself rather then becoming disorganized. Her overly still body posture, rapid breath, small retreating actions, head movements which pull her head down and into her body, fisted hands, bringing hands together at midline and sucking, and rapid blinks as Mother comes closer all reflect an inhibitory adaptation. They indicate this infant's attempts to contain her high autonomic arousal (Papoušek, 2007). She stays contained, in the face of so much stimulation, while giving her mother encouraging feedback through her genuine smiles. Celina allows her mother to manipulate her body in an even-paced, accented way. She responds mostly facially, and she watches her mother intently (at times simply staring). This adaptation succeeds in allowing the infant and mother to stay engaged.

Discussion in our therapist peer group turns to the depth of sadness that seems to lie behind the exaggerated facial expressions Mother employs to engage Celina, and it is also revealed during moments of sobering when Celina fleetingly looks away. We begin to discuss how an infant, even at age 4 months, can adjust to be able to stay engaged, adapting to her mother's state (see Beebe & Lachmann, 2002). This pattern is evident in the analysis of the micro-moments of this mother-infant interaction. Our conversation underscores how even at this preverbal stage, infants can adapt to maintain the engagement.

It is remarkable how creative this baby is in developing a coping and regulatory style that adapts to what her mother can provide. I wonder if this nonverbal movement style will continue to manifest in other settings and as the child grows. Analyzing Celina's reactions to the "stranger" during this same lab visit provides more clues.

## FOUR-MONTH VISIT: INTERACTION BETWEEN CELINA AND "STRANGER" (DR. BEEBE)

In this interaction, Celina sits face-to-face with Dr. Beebe. Because Celina had objected to being left alone with Dr. Beebe, the mother is seated to the side of Celina, and is instructed not to talk. However, she can comfort the baby physically if necessary. Celina vigilantly watches Dr. Beebe. She sucks her right fingers, breathing rapidly, and slightly raises her right leg in an undulating manner. Occasionally, a small controlled smile is visible behind Celina's fisted hand as she sucks. Dr. Beebe is facially animated, softly smiling, with her eyebrows raised in slow bursts of expressiveness, which she maintains as the baby watches her. Celina looks at Dr. Beebe's face but orients her body away from Dr. Beebe toward her mother. Her sucking increases to include her other fist and shirt collar. She appears a bit wary of Dr. Beebe but still curious, with a rapport building as Celina stays intermittently visually engaged with Dr. Beebe.

At one moment, she looks at Dr. Beebe, and then turns her head away completely toward her mother, and increases her sucking. Celina appears half present and half turned away. *This stance creates an attitude that seems to say, "I am looking at you. I am staying with you, but I am not sure I really want to stay engaged. . . . But I will stay and watch you anyway." Although Celina is attending to Dr. Beebe, I am left wondering if she is attending because she is curious or because she is vigilant.*

I turned to an analysis of the next videotaped lab visit, which occurred when Celina was 14 months old. How will these behaviors manifest when Celina is older? Will she continue this method of adaptation? How might the dyadic nonverbal exchange develop as their needs change?

## 14-MONTH VISIT: CELINA AND MOTHER

Celina and her mother return to the filming lab after 10 months with an expanded repertoire of communicative skills and nonverbal relational patterns. Mother's slow predictable phrasing pattern is still present. She continues to direct the play, but now she more often facilitates engagement through their shared "embraced space," connecting spatially by creating emotional intimacy from a far. Thus there seems to be more space for Celina.

Both Mother and Celina create this space by shifting their upper torsos forward toward each other rather than relying as much on physical contact. In this sequence mother has added puppet play activities to the finger play songs of four months. She often brings the puppet close to Celina, using it to physically touch Celina on different parts of her body, rather than using her own fingers directly.

Celina now takes more initiative spatially as well. Since she has outgrown the infant seat she now sits in the highchair. She frequently folds her upper torso over her legs, reaching out to her mother and gestures for her water bottle. She holds onto her mother briefly and then lets go, shifting her torso back in one sweep, then re-engaging with her mother or another object. In addition, her still-body vigilance and visual watchfulness continue to be present, but she shifts her gaze and turns her body away from her mother more frequently. She flings her upper torso to hang it over the right arm of the chair, looking away. She smiles less in response to the mother's smiles. She shows increased strain, shifting her head back, squinting her eyes, tightening her face, and crying out when her mother verbally acknowledges her request for her water bottle but does not comply.

Mother now gives Celina the water bottle she is requesting. Celina sucks on the bottle, which appears to help Celina self-regulate sufficiently to maintain engagement with her mother. But soon Celina sweeps her body forward again, reaching directly toward her mother with extended arms. She seems to be asking to be taken out of the highchair. Mother hugs her momentarily. Celina lets go of her, sweeping back in the chair to look at her mother with a sober face and motionless body, as Mother tries to re-engage Celina with a finger play song. Celina does not respond as quickly this time. Instead she reaches out toward her mother and again gestures to get out. Gradually Celina regains composure and does get absorbed in play with her mother, who has abandoned the song and finds a puppet to interest Celina. When her mother attempts to have the puppet "eat your nose," Celina lifts up her leg instead. Mother follows her lead, stating, "Oh you want her to eat your toes again." Celina's own initiative is acknowledged by her mother.

Celina's increased use of space, including her continual reaching out into full torso and limb extension, demonstrate her growing ability to communicate her needs. Her dominant use of the sagittal (forward – backward) spatial domain fosters her growing sense of agency. At one point she even uses her legs to push against the chair, causing it to lift and rock back. The Laban system theorizes that use of this sagittal spatial domain in early movement development fosters independence. It enables the baby to physically experience entering into and retreating from the environment.

With her increased communicative and physical skills, Celina is able to express her desire to do something different from her mother's agenda. However, she ultimately does adapt to her mother's play. She gets absorbed in her mother's play activities, but at the same time she maintains her own physical spatial body boundaries, intermittently pulling or turning away from her mother. By continually interjecting her own wishes in between moments of adaptation to her mother's behavior, she never abandons her own internal desires, even if her requests are not met. At age 14 months Celina has expanded her ability to communicate her needs nonverbally. Although she continues to engage on her mother's terms, Celina also co-regulates their relationship by staying composed and receptive, thereby receiving the pleasure of her mother's loving attention.

## 14-MONTH VISIT: CELINA AND "STRANGER" (DR. BEEBE)

In this interaction, Celina again sits face-to-face with Dr. Beebe. Her mother sits to the side of Celina and is again instructed not to talk. However, she can comfort the baby physically if necessary.

A similar adaptive relational style continues to be observed in Celina as she interacts with Dr. Beebe during this visit. Celina initially sits in the highchair with the right side of her body concave, as she rotates away from Dr. Beebe and leans to reach and touch her mother. She cycles between moving and pausing, as she looks toward and away from Dr. Beebe, from this stance of orientation to her mother. She seeks oral comfort indicating her wish for her water bottle. Mother lightly strokes Celina's head and upper body and intermittently hugs her.

Three and a half minutes into the session Dr. Beebe suggests that Celina be held in her mother's arms. At four minutes, Celina has turned her back to Dr. Beebe. Mother and baby are very still, with sober staring facial expressions. Mother and Celina look away in opposite directions from each other. Despite being in her mother's arms, Celina is holding her own body weight with integrity, lightly holding onto her mother rather than nestling into her.

*Comment.* The sustained, deeply still quality of their joint posture creates an image of a stop-frame action. This moment is striking in the sadness it conveys. Who is comforting whom? Initially it seemed that Celina's request to be in her mother's arms was to satisfy her own need for a secure base. But as I watch them both, in such physical stillness and emotional distance, it appears as if Celina is comforting her mother as much as Mother is comforting Celina. Celina joins her mother's quiet stillness. It is striking how well matched their nonverbal styles seem to be as they both are contained and trying to cope. The tempo of their movement phrases is synchronized. I feel a sadness as I watch this pair, both holding on in silence – embraced through touch and space yet simultaneously seeming so alone, together.

Dr. Beebe quietly waits during this moment. Then Dr. Beebe resumes an attempt to play. She adopts a similar phrasing style to Celina's mother's, using slow and steady concentrated facial gestures and providing constant attention with ample pauses. She does not give up on her wish to relate to Celina. Mother shifts her own body, shaping it to form an embracing space around Celina. Mother occasionally rhythmically taps Celina's back as Celina begins breathing more fluidly. Safe in her mother's nurturing space, Celina begins to rotate her body around to view Dr. Beebe, even using her mother's body to push and turn her own body toward Dr. Beebe. She visually turns to check on her mother's face from time to time. Eventually she begins to show interest in watching and playing with Dr. Beebe. *Her ability to recover and to begin to play with Dr. Beebe shows Celina's remarkable capacity.*

## CONCLUDING DISCUSSION

We observed this mother-baby pair by examining the role of multisensory kinetic experiences, affect exchanges and the dynamic moment-to-moment organization and re-organization of the nonverbal rapport. The quality of the nonverbal exchange will organize expectations of what will happen next, as a sense of self-with-other develops (see Beebe & Lachmann, 2002; Beebe & Stern, 1977; Beebe et al., 2010).

Nonverbal analysis of this mother baby dyad at 4 and 14 months provides an intriguing glimpse of the co-constructed relational dance. At age 4 months, Celina's motivation to maintain engagement with her mother was clearly evident. Celina's earliest nonverbal engagement style revealed a pattern of waiting, watching, and assessing before taking action. Acquiring this style supported her mother's style of taking the initiative. It enabled Celina to maintain contact with Mother without disturbing her mother's sadness that loomed in the background. Celina learned very early on through her *sense of body* experience that to look away from her mother, or to initiate, might cause her mother sadness or dissonance — even if it was momentary.

Mother was caught in a devastating conflict between needing to mourn her husband's death and needing to embrace the maternal instinct to love and welcome a new baby. The mother's measured, persistent carefulness showed her determination to connect to the present moment with her baby, despite the painful grief that might be distracting her. Even with her slow tempo, she could not fully focus on interpreting her baby's nonverbal cues. Although she worked very hard to continually engage the baby, she could not relax, pause, wait, and see what the baby might be able to initiate. She directed the interaction, keeping the conversation going as the lead partner in their pas de deux. In turn, Celina did not elaborate her own expressiveness. This is the way that Celina experienced and participated in her mother's loss. She more often watched in stillness, cooperatively responding, rather than finding her own way to initiate the engagement. Like her mother, Celina has adopted the resilient coping strategy of persistence as she maintains engagement with her mother. These co-constructed interactions regulated the relationship and shaped both mother's and infant's styles as the attachment process proceeded.

At age 14 months, when we see Celina beginning to voice her needs, Celina continues the 4-month adaptation in which compliance provides more gains in the relationship than escalating to protest. By 14 months, her mother used less tactile input and provided more space for Celina. Consistency, persistence, and resilience prevailed in both of them. At 14 months, Celina used increased gaze avoidance to regulate her arousal. She maintained her communicative efforts while complying with her mother's directives. Thus at 14 months, in contrast to 4 months, there was a greater balance in Celina between initiation and adaptive following of her mother. However, often her actions shifted from communication to compliance. It appears as if her central motivation is to align herself with her mother's interests, supporting both of their needs for companionship and trust. The continued directiveness of her mother's actions seems to have dampened Celina's ebb and flow of attention and initiation of play themes.

*Comment.* I wonder, has Celina's vigilant coordination with Mother compromised her sense of agency? Although it has become an adaptive way of achieving satisfaction, is Celina sacrificing aspects of her developing sense of self? Will she have the opportunity to experience the pleasure of taking initiative in her world and feeling a response in return? Will her ability to adapt and respond to her mother become a burden for her, as well as an adaptive style that strengthens her self-image and maintains their bond?

## CONCLUSION

Despite what may appear to be these potential difficulties, Celina does seem to feel, and to respond to, her mother's underlying intention to love, care for, and connect to her. Celina's ability to stay engaged with her mother and her mother's persistent efforts to keep Celina engaged attest to this mutual devotion to the relationship. In her interactions with the strangers, Celina shows that she can be cautious and curious at the same time.

Interpreting this co-constructed relationship within the context of the transmission of trauma, we may speculate further. The dynamics of the trauma, loss, sadness, and grief have become an integral aspect of how this mother and baby have related to each other. Driven by a biologically primed capacity to communicate and to develop shared affective experiences, Celina is learning about her mother's experiences though their shared bodily communications. The traumatic events that occupy her mother's mind and body have affected how Celina has learned to regulate her own needs, to communicate through affective expressions, and to form a relationship with her mother.

As depicted in this mother-baby pair, our deepest thoughts, experiences, and intentions are revealed through the language of our bodies in active dialogue. The intricate rhythms of our actions, the timing of our gestures, and the spatial shifts of posture comprise each individual's core choreography in the dance of relating. These nonverbal patterns shape the infant's developing expectancies of self-in-relation-to-other (see Beebe & Stern, 1977; Beebe & Lachmann, 2002). Although the patterns begun in infancy set a trajectory in development, this trajectory can be transformed through the continuing verbal and nonverbal relational dance.

## REFERENCES


Bartenieff, I. (1973). The roots of Laban theory: Aesthetics and beyond. In I. Bartenieff, M. Davis, & F. Paulay (Eds.), *Four adaptations of Effort theory in research and teaching*. (pp. 1–27). New York, NY: Dance Notation Bureau.

Bartenieff, I., & Lewis, D. (1980). *Body movement: Coping with the environment*. New York, NY: Gordon and Breach Science Publishers, Inc.

Beebe, B., & Lachmann, F. (2002). *Infant research and adult treatment: Co-constructing interactions*. Hillsdale, NJ: The Analytic Press.

Beebe, B., & Stern, D. (1977). Engagement-disengagement and early object experiences. In N. Freedman & S. Grand (Eds.), *Communicative structures and psychic structures* (pp. 35–55). New York, NY: Plenum Press.

Beebe, B., Jaffe, J., Markese, S., Buck, K., Chen, H., Cohen, P., . . . Feldstein, S. (2010). The origins of 12-month attachment: A microanalysis of 4-month mother-infant interaction. *Attachment & Human Development*, *12*(1–2), 3–141.

Laban, R. (1975). *The mastery of movement*. Boston, MA: Plays, Inc.

Laban, R. (1976). *The language of movement*. Boston, MA: Plays, Inc.

Laban, R., & Lawrence, F. (1974). *Effort*. Boston, MA: Plays, Inc.

Lamb, W., & Watson, E. (1979). *Body code*. London, England: Routledge & Kegan Paul.

Papoušek, M. (2007). Communication in early infancy: An arena of intersubjective learning. *Infant Behavior and Development*, *30*(2), 258–266.

Tortora, S. (2004). Our moving bodies tell stories, which speak of our experiences. *Zero to Three*, *24*(5), 4–12.

Tortora, S. (2006). *The dancing dialogue: Using the communicative power of movement with young children*. Baltimore, MD: Paul H. Brookes Publishing Co., Inc.

Tortora, S. (2010). Ways of seeing: An early childhood integrated therapeutic approach for parents and babies. *Clinical Social Work Journal*, *38*(1), 37–50.

# Children's Play in the Wake of Loss and Trauma

K. Mark Sossin, Ph.D.
Phyllis Cohen, Ph.D.

In the Project for Mothers, Infants, and Young Children of September 11, 2001, children were longitudinally observed and filmed playing and interacting with mothers and therapists as an extension of the mother-infant/stranger-infant face-to-face play paradigm (Beebe, 2003). Children included those still in the womb on September 11, 2001, when their fathers died, as well as older siblings. Play observations contributed to the assessment of risk and resilience and were used in follow-up video feedback sessions with mothers. Implicit and explicit features of play interactions are described with regard to developmental acquisitions, symbolization, and play themes. Mother-child play is sometimes marked by joining on the part of the mother and sometimes by overriding. Maternal diversion and overriding was particularly evident when themes of aggression emerged. In play episodes, children demonstrated intense efforts to express feelings, worries, and queries. Play themes frequently pertained to death, destruction, rescue, irretrievaibility, and risk taking. Therapists aimed to be nondirective and facilitative of elaboration. Video feedback of children's play with mother and therapist addressed insecurities of mothers and fostered greater recognition of children's grief and more sharing of affect between mother and child. A case example of play and videofeedback is described. Children were helped to develop and hold paternal represention and to use play as a means of expression.

We address in this article the play of the children whose fathers died on September 11, 2001. Many of the children were still in the womb at that time. Our purpose is to illustrate how we understood and helped the mothers to understand the play of their babies, toddlers, and older children. As the two therapists most frequently interacting with the children in the videotaped face-to-face play sessions in the laboratory, we reflect on the nature of the nondirective pretend play that emerged. Each child who came to the lab was filmed with two cameras, one focused on each person, generating a split-screen image (Beebe, 2003, 2005). The children played in our split-screen filming chamber, first with their mothers and then with a therapist, for 10 minutes each. We had a standard set of toys for each developmental phase. The mother was instructed to play with her child as she would at home. The therapist had the goal of following the child's play and, for toddlers and adult children, putting the story line of the play into words.

From a therapeutic rather than research perspective, we wondered about the nature of the play in the therapist-child dyads and on the meanings deciphered. We also wondered about the nature of the play in the mother-child dyads. Did the children play differently with their mothers than they did with a therapist? How did the children who never knew their fathers represent the fathers in play? What about the play of these children's siblings who knew their fathers before losing them? Could we observe any meaningful differences between the siblings as a function of their ages at the time of loss? We also wondered about the relational styles of mother-child interaction in the grieving and preoccupied mothers in our Project. Did the mothers create and hold a distinctive mental space for their children?

For the youngest babies, our focus was largely on dyadic process, such as tempo, pausing, and affective connection. As the children developed into symbolic/representational players, our focus expanded to the themes the children brought into the play and how the dyadic interaction followed the themes so as to allow for expansion. Close observation of the children's pretend play in the lab as they shared their imaginings with their mothers and with the therapists, offered us a lens through which to observe emotional sharing within the mother-child and therapist-child dyads and the themes permeating the play. In our sessions we assessed how mothers joined in their children's play, their ability to follow the child's lead, and whether the mothers' capacity for keeping their children in mind may have been undermined by their traumatic loss (Fonagy & Target, 2008).

At first, while the children were still very young, ages one to two, each mother usually remained in the filming/play room while her child played with a therapist. In these sessions, each mother was instructed not to verbally engage her child, although she could provide other forms of support if necessary. As the children grew older, the child-therapist relationship deepened, which allowed for the child to remain in the room with the therapist without the mother. When they were able to understand, the children were told that we were a group of therapists meeting with children who lost their fathers in the World Trade Center.

The play at the lab was unique. It was time-limited, in an unusual setting. In the therapist-child interaction, we encouraged the children to initiate the play. Instead of being seen weekly or biweekly, most of the children visited the lab at one-year intervals. Many of the babies born after September 11, 2001, were seen in the first six months of life while other mother-infant dyads were not found until later. Many of the children's older siblings, ranging from one to 12 years of age at the time of the trauma, have also participated in filming sessions over the years. We have followed most of these children, and their play, since spring 2002.

When we began the Project, we saw the mother-child and therapist-child play video sessions as an extension of the mother-baby/stranger-baby play paradigm applied by Beebe (2003, 2005), Stern (1995), and Weinberg and Tronick (1998), among others. It was conceived as an "assessment" opportunity in which an experienced child clinician could evaluate whether risk factors called for a more comprehensive evaluation or therapeutic intervention. In light of emerging research on stress and trauma, we knew that our mothers and young children would be susceptible to dialogic mismatches (Beebe, Jaffe, Buck, Chen, Cohen, Blatt, Kaminer, Feldstein & Andrews, 2007, 2008; Beebe, Jaffe, Markese, Buck, Chen, Cohen, Bahrick, Andrews, & Feldstein, 2010; Beebe, Steele, Jaffe, Buck, Chen, Cohen, Kaitz, Markese, Andrews, Margonis, & Feldman, 2011; Sossin, 2002; Sossin & Birklein, 2006) that, if left unrepaired, could negatively affect the long-term development of the children. With the older children we viewed the nondirective play interactions as an opportunity to understand what was on each child's mind.

In addition to filming nondirective play sessions, we assessed attachment classifications at 12–18 months with the Strange Situation paradigm (Ainsworth, Blehar, Waters, & Wall, 1978). We used standard methods with the mothers and babies at 12–18 months and then used modified methods as the children grew older (Main & Cassidy, 1988; Marvin & Britner, 1999). We were influenced by attachment studies indicating that 12-month attachment status predicts the child's unfolding qualities of symbolic play, understanding of mental states, and executive functioning (Meins, Fernyhough, Russell, & Clark-Carter, 2001; Belsky, Gardugque, & Hrncir, 1984; Lyons-Ruth, 1998). Early attachment also predicts socioemotional development and expressive language skills, although Belsky and Fearon (2002) have demonstrated that this effect varies as a function of social context risk.

As the children grew older, in collaboration with Howard and Miriam Steele, we administered the Steele Affect Task to preschool and school-aged children (Steele, Steele, Croft, & Fonagy, 1999), extending the therapist-child play time. This task involves a series of cartoon stories depicting social and emotional challenges typically faced by young children. For example, the child is shown a picture of a child being dropped off at school by the mother. The child is then prompted to answer: how does the child in the picture feel? Then: how does the mother feel? The Steele Affect Task prompts the child for attributions while assessing an awareness of complex emotions (Steele et al., 1999). Data derived from this protocol will be discussed at a later date.

Our lab filming sessions with the mothers and children served as springboards to the video feedback consultations scheduled with the mothers shortly after each lab visit. These consultations aimed to help the mothers to reflect upon their losses and personal needs, as well as upon the play interactions that they co-constructed with their children. Each mother followed her own trajectory of grief work. In our video feedback sessions, a special coherence-building and sharing generally unfolded with the mothers (see Cohen, "Video Feedback and the Impact of Multiple Therapists," this issue). The feedback sessions included discussions of our impressions of various aspects of the children's play as we sat with the mothers and watched segments of the videotaped interactions. Together we considered challenges that the children presented regarding how easy or difficult it might be for a particular mother to enter or join her child's play. We considered the extent to which the mothers' joint attention, shared affect, coordination of rhythms, need to be in control, and facilitation of symbolic play might affect their children's play and development. In our feedback with the mothers, we discussed how joining and developing a verbal narrative could enhance their children's play in light of their particular complexities of personal history and styles of interaction. Our aim in playing with the children was to support their efforts to communicate and represent and to absorb frustration and loss, lending meaning to their play. Through our video feedback sessions, we encouraged the mothers to join their children in their play at home, even for short 15-minute intervals. We found ourselves frequently helping mothers to recognize and appreciate their children's sense of agency. Over time, many of our mothers reported numerous vignettes in which they had begun to notice their children in new ways through joining their play and letting the children take the lead during brief one-on-one play interactions.

## PLAY AND DEVELOPMENTAL FACTORS IN THE CONTEXT OF TRAUMA AND LOSS

Child therapists and analysts have long recognized the importance of nondirective pretend play as a tool for relationship building (Freud, 1946), communication (Watson, 1994), affective organization (Fein & Kinney, 1994), reconstruction and reenactment (Levy, 1939), and understanding via symbolization and representational processes (Winnicott, 1965). Traumatic experiences can also be reworked toward some degree of mastery in play (Erikson, 1940). Therapists working with crisis-laden children have relied on play, symbolization, and metaphor to help children work through conflicts (Webb, 2004, 2006). Nondirective play can be used to facilitate symptom alleviation and improved coping skills. As Watson notes, " . . . play may be a repetition of real life in order to rework and master a conflict head-on, a wish fulfillment in relation to real life in order to compensate for a lack of positive affect, or an escape from the anxiety-provoking situation altogether in order to avoid anxiety that is simply too intense to deal with at the same time" (1994, p. 37).

As we sought to understand the experiences of the mothers and young children in our Project, we were open to considering an amalgam of factors. These factors included the child's exposure to increased maternal cortisol levels *in utero* and other perinatal risk factors associated with proximity to the World Trade Center (Engel, Berkowitz, Wolff, & Yehuda, 2005); complex intergenerational transmission processes anchored in parental states of mind and representations; and the relational expression of the trauma within the parent-child interaction (Baradon & Steele, 2008; Schechter, Zygmunt, Trabka, Davies, Colon, Kolodji, & McCaw, 2007).

A body of research has explicated the manner in which trauma experienced in the preverbal period can lead to posttraumatic stress disorder (PTSD) in young children, manifested by reenactments and emotional reliving, as well as numbing of general responsiveness, not unlike what older children experience (Terr, 1988; Sugar, 1992; Gaensbauer, 1995; see Markese, this issue). We were concerned that elements of anxious attachment (Slade, 1987), as well as a reluctance to relax in the service of fantasy and impulse-expression, could compromise the play of many of the children. From the earliest days of their lives, the children in our Project were exposed to their mothers' grief and profound efforts at regulative processes, in the context of their loss and the concomitant stresses.

Our understanding of the vulnerability of the mothers and children in our Project is anchored in research-based models of mother-child interaction. The capacity for forms of joint coordination begins early in life. For example, a 2-month-old infant is ready to respond sympathetically to his or her mother's face and to communicate feelings (Beebe, Rustin, Sorter, & Knoblauch, 2003; Beebe, Knoblauch, Rusin, & Sorter, 2005; Trevarthen, 2005; Meltzoff & Brooks, 2009). Considerable research has focused on the origin of mind as essentially "dyadic, dialogic and (presymbolically) representational" (Beebe et al., 2003). In healthy development, mother-child co-construction of reciprocally influenced joint action is already evident in the face-to-face play of 3–4-month-old infants (Beebe & Lachmann, 2002; Stern, 1985; Tronick, 1989; Cohn & Tronick, 1988; Jaffe, Beebe, Feldstein, Crown, & Jasnow, 2001). By four months, a mother's dependency and self-critical depressive experiences can influence maternal speech, infant exploration and agency, and mother-infant self- and interactive contingency during face-to-face play (Kaminer, Beebe, Jaffe, Kelly, & Marquette, 2007; Beebe et al., 2007). Heightened maternal depressive symptoms at infant age six weeks are associated at four months with lowered predictability in the mothers' and infants' rhythms of nonverbal behavior, and with atypical interactive regulation. Specifically, mothers and four-month infants lower their gaze coordination but heighten their affective coordination (Beebe et al., 2008). In this pattern, mothers are overly thrilled when babies are positive, but overly disappointed when babies sober or become distressed. At the same time, however, mothers are insufficiently attentive to whether babies are actually available for visual engagement. The nature of mother-infant contingent coordination at four months predicts secure and insecure attachment outcomes at one year (Beebe et al., 2010).

Normally, the capacity to play is anchored in satisfactory provisions by an empathic caregiver — necessities for spontaneity and creativity. Impingement and disruption can thwart spontaneous play. Fonagy, Gergely, Jurist, and Target (2002) have suggested that pretend play with a facilitative partner promotes developmental understandings of mental states: "Pretending requires a mental stance involving the symbolic transformation of reality in the presence of, and with a view to, the mind of the other" (p. 48). Achieving the capacity for pretend play is a landmark in a child's development. Over time, a child whose play is minimally or unreliably followed or validated cannot easily engage in pretend play (Fonagy & Target, 1996). We were concerned that the children in our Project would potentially be caught in their mothers' preoccupation with grief, and thus would become overly vigilant to their mothers' emotional reactions, or feel the need to regulate their mothers' moods (Verheugt-Pleiter, 2008).

A mother's capacity to reflect on her own state of mind has been linked to her child's state of mind and mental health status (Fonagy et al., 2002). Fonagy and colleagues (2002) specifically connect a mother's capacity to reflect on her own state of mind, and on her child's state of mind, with secure attachment in the infant/toddler, and later with resilience in the face of disadvantage and heightened stress. The mother's capacity to reflect is also believed to promote the child's capacity to reflect. The child who can reflect on the mother's intentions can tolerate a mother's periodic unresponsiveness with fewer ill-effects than a child who cannot. Therefore, a child's capacity to think about the mother's mind is a developmental acquisition enhanced by the parent's capacity to think about the child's mind.

Harris (2003) describes how a grieving woman whose husband was lost on September 11, 2001, helped her young child build a complex representation of a lost father who would continue to bear a positive influence on the child's life. This mother's own reflective capacity fostered her ability to evoke an image of a mentalizing father who could hold his child in mind. Harris's case report underscores how complex a mother's task can be in the wake of such loss. The mother's tasks include helping to create narrative memories for the child, constructing some aura of continuity of the father, and conveying the experience of collaborative and protective parents. This was not an easy task for the grieving mothers in our Project, especially while tolerating, albeit painfully, their children's innumerable efforts to grasp and accommodate to the reality of their father's death.

## THEMES OF CHILDREN'S PLAY IN RESPONSE TO PARENTAL LOSS

As we listened to the themes of the children's play, we began to understand many factors related to their experiences of loss and the nature of their relationships with their mothers and others. In addition to the nonverbal behavior of the infant, the preschool child introduces narrative themes through pretend play. We saw the emerging temperament and personality features of the children, their growing capacity to represent their lost fathers, and their efforts to comprehend what happened on September 11, 2001. We saw the ability of the children to express grief, anger, and destruction in an attempt to regain a sense of safety and control. In some cases, we saw mothers join their children and share affects while in other cases we saw mothers attempt to rewrite their children's scripts. Such factors were seen in the video-taped interactions. For example, one child struggled for control with her mother who anxiously tried to steer the play her own way. Another child suddenly put on a cheerful face while trying to make eye contact at a moment when his mother was looking somber and depressed. Still another child set up toy figures and suddenly sent them flying off the table. Either no one rescued them, or a supernatural force was conjured up to save the day.

Trauma, death, destruction, rescue, and irretrievability were prominent themes in the play of most of the children in this Project. We witnessed over and over the children playing out themes of building towers that fell, people who fell from rooftops, people being killed, and all of the cars, dogs, cats, and houses ending up flying onto the floor. Very often, the play table was left utterly empty. We also saw many attempts to rescue or reconstruct seemingly hopeless situations. These themes were seen when, for example, a toy lizard would be run over, time and again, by trucks and tanks. The lizard would die, but it would not really die. Instead it might come back with enhanced strength after its ordeal and eventually protect all the other lizards. In response, the therapists would never cease their reactions of being "wowed" or duly impressed at the "amazing powers" at work. Here, as elsewhere, we saw the children's symbolic play incorporating repair themes with the wish for an idealized father to return to protect the family. Many of the children played out their wish for a father-identified-self to develop super-human strength and armor to protect one from the peril that had consumed their dads. For children to employ magical thinking in early defensive and coping efforts is not unusual. However, what was notable in the children of this Project was the intensity of their play, and the repetitive nature of the destruction (and repair) themes, as if, with enough magic, an imagined event could actually come true. At times, play themes reflected a search for someone to protect the family. Some children seemed to bear the burden of feeling the responsibility to protect the family themselves.

Another common play scenario involved risk taking when the children reached the age of four or older. Their play figures took huge risks, making high jumps and marvelous twirls. In the play with their mothers, when the figures reached unfathomable heights, the children were at times cautioned by a worried mother, who listed all the various body parts that could break if one of these feats were to actually be carried out. In these situations, the children's attempts at mastery in the pretend mode were met not by a play-absorbing, attuned mother, but by a traumatized mother who may have had only one tiny body part of her husband to bury.

The World Trade Center tragedy was a shared experience among the children we saw and its repercussions affected their play interactions with their mothers. As would be expected, in many of the mother-child dyads, we observed maternal interruption and diversion of certain play themes, especially themes of loss or aggression. In these dyads, we saw mothers who reacted concretely to their children's play actions, stepping out of the pretend play mode, unable to join the symbolic and representational meanings of the play when their own uncomfortable feelings were evoked. As the children became older, they began to use play in a different way. For both the older siblings who had known their lost fathers, as well as for the babies of the Project as they grew in their capacity for symbolization, themes emerged that often corresponded to the mothers' own traumatic grief and/or fears. At times this led to "discordance" in the play in which the emotional quality of the mothers' interactions may not have matched those of her child (Sossin & Birklein, 2006; Shelby, Avina, & Warnick, 2010).

In rare moments in the play with the therapists, some of the young children made direct reference to the World Trade Center disaster, but this was more likely seen in the play of the older siblings. For example, a child who was three years old on September 11, 2001, while visiting the lab at age five, played out the role of rescuer when he picked up a large empty object. Pretending it was supremely heavy, he said, "This is a building. It is the North Tower. I will hold it up until everyone gets out. I can do it!" In contrast, at times we saw some children playing out an identification with the aggressor as they created scenarios of danger and disaster. This was another area of divergence between the child-mother play and child-therapist play. For example, a child might play a good-guy/bad guy scenario with the mother, yet most of the figures would end up safely in their homes. With the therapist, however, the child might play out a total killing off of everyone. We observed this scene often in the child-therapist play. With their mothers, when the children did play out their wish to become the destroyer, in their efforts to retaliate for their father's death, invariably their mothers would step out of the pretend play mode and react to their children in the "reality mode" and try to stop them.

We frequently observed the children's aggressive themes burrowing into hiding when the mothers reacted to their destructive play concretely and disallowed it. In some dyads, the mother's discomfort was observed in her correction or re-direction of her child's play, or in a lack of acknowledgement. In some of these situations we would hear mothers saying, "We don't play like that . . .," or "Be nice . . ." Some of the mothers did not support their children's aggressive play themes, such as blowing up buildings or creating fires, for fear that their children would actually become aggressive. They did not recognize that the child was well within a zone of safety offered by the pretend play. In contrast, while playing with the therapist, the children were not discouraged from exploring aggressive themes.

The mothers in our Project fell along a wide spectrum of play skills regarding imagination, turn-taking, following the child's lead, and emotional comprehension. Their play styles were not only reactive to their losses and circumstances, but were also anchored in their own childhoods, based on their own psychic realities. As we came to understand in the feedback sessions, the disparate play skills parents demonstrated were most often developmentally continuous with their own childhoods. Parents who reported little play with their own parents often showed the least proclivity for imaginative play. Representational play may be strongly linked along intergenerational pathways, with notable experiences with other caregivers or peers being required to acquire playfulness. Even mothers who may have had a taste for play, however, can readily be impeded in playfulness by traumatic loss. The lively affectivity and associative freedom in play are avoided when managing traumatized self-states. Following Fonagy and colleagues (2002), caregivers who are experiencing heightened stress or trauma themselves cannot "play with" the most burning, conflictual, and uneasy aspects of the child's thoughts because they are the most troubling and unacceptable thoughts and feelings for the adult as well. Rather than joined in the pretend mode, the child reverts to a more concrete, "psychic equivalent" manner of experiencing reality, parallel to that of the parent.

We conceptualize two streams of play interaction operating in parallel to each other, one explicit and one implicit. The explicit stream incorporates the shared imaginings, words, and comprehended story-lines that are co-constructed by mother and child. The implicit stream, so central in infant-mother interaction, has been explicated by many key infant researchers and theorists. The implicit level of engagement never becomes outgrown, and it pertains to the undercurrent of the interaction. It can be observed, for example, in facial expression, gaze patterns, the rhythms of tension changes, and body contour adjustments. These implicit, generally nonverbal processes are equally as important as the symbolically developing play themes.

For example, during play with her mother, a 7-year-old girl seemed to have one side of her body stabilizing her, almost immobile (but not inert), while the other side of her body was active. At the same time, she pressed her lips close together ("compressed lips") with high intensity, frequently not speaking, even though her mother made efforts to engage her verbally. It seemed that as she played, she was "holding on" and "holding in." These patterns were elementally communicative about her anxiety, as much as her play theme of people at risk. As the session went on, her mother became more abrupt, interruptive, and intrusive. The mother's heightened tension was both a response to, and perpetuator of, her child's anxiety. This implicit level of their interaction was operating outside of the awareness of both. Our observations and video feedback consultations with the mothers addressed both the explicit and implicit levels of communication between mother and child.

Early in the Project, these differences between mother-child and therapist-child play became apparent, especially with regard to following the child's lead, both ideationally and affectively. The nondirective approach used by the therapists seemed to facilitate the children's opening up in ways that did not happen with the mother. The therapist-child play that emerged became quite meaningful on multiple levels, including implicit process, and explicit content and themes. In the therapist play with the children, we aimed to heighten patterns of mirroring and following, and we elaborated the children's story lines more often than the mothers. Many factors likely contributed to the children's greater ease in expanding their traumatic themes more easily with the therapist. They were naturally sensitive to their mothers' discouragement of such themes. We also hypothesized that they were not as invested in regulating the therapist's mood as they were in regulating their mother's moods. Another possibility was that our fixed sequence of mother-child play, followed by therapist-child play, may have contributed to the differences between mother-child versus therapist-child themes. For example, in one session, while in play with the mother, a bird simply went flying about to and fro. In the play with the therapist, however, the same bird got "lost" or was "hiding," or otherwise became the object of an emotionally charged "search." Regardless of the sequence of the children's play with the mother and therapist as play partners, we realized that the differences in purposeful following versus directiveness, in therapists versus mothers, would become an important area of focus for intervention in our work with the mothers.

All of the women in our Project had lost their "assumptive world," and this loss was also experienced by the children (Goldman, 2002; Stolorow, 1999). The mothers' experiences of security, control, choice, protection, and predictability were compromised with the events of September 11, 2001. As the Project babies developed from infants to toddlers to preschoolers, and later to school-aged children, we noticed how they were often denied experiences of safety, comfort, and connection. While the mothers varied in their reactions, all of the babies were born to grieving women who went through a period of being frozen in time and in motion. By the time many of the mothers were ready to engage with their babies, they found that they had "missed" the babyhood period and that they needed to re-awaken their capacities to play with young toddlers they hardly knew. It was hard for them to understand that the children had absorbed far more of what had happened than they thought. Despite their efforts to "protect" the children, the children knew, in their own way, that something terrible had happened. While these mothers would have been joyful upon the birth of their children, the death of their husbands had disrupted many wonderful opportunities for early attunement, accurate affect attributions, developmentally needed scaffolding, and symbolic elaborations with their babies. Thus, the mothers' experiences of loss contextualized their children's experiences. This was seen in the children's play, regardless of whether or not they had known their fathers.

Despite the discordances noted above between the children's needs to represent the horrors of loss in pretend play, and the mothers' needs not to enter this domain, we also observed a tremendous resilience in many dyads (Fonagy, Steele, Steele, Higgitt, & Target, 1994). Many mothers demonstrated capacities for responsiveness and repair in the mother-child interchanges that, along with the children's own creative and affirmative capacities, created an impressive developmental foundation in these children. It was our impression, reinforced by what mothers came to share with us in considering the effect of this Project, that our method seemed to succeed in its preventative aims, building on these resilient capacities. The "lab play" experience allowed us to closely observe the mother-child interaction on both implicit and explicit levels, and the therapist's play with the child allowed us to gain a sense of the mind of the child. All these facets contributed to the efficacy of the feedback consultations with the mothers. Hence, the resilience observed reflected resourceful traits in both mothers and children, but also our ability to make the Project useful to them.

## INCORPORATING THEMES OF PLAY IN THE VIDEO FEEDBACK CONSULTATIONS

Video feedback sessions were scheduled with the mothers the week following the video filming session in the lab. The videotape was reviewed by the therapists prior to each feedback session. The therapist team would prepare ways to intervene, always attempting to hold the mothers' self-esteem in mind (see Cohen, *Video Feedback*, this issue). In the feedback sessions, we highlighted the importance of the children's play styles and themes by observing with the mother the video-taped play interactions of mother-child and therapist-child taken at the lab. The mothers would take on the role of observer as they watched the video with us (Cohen & Beebe, 2002). This position facilitated an emotional reverberation and, later, an increased availability to be open to their children's intense and difficult feelings.

In the play of a 5-year-old boy, in this case an older sibling, the boy gathered figures into a story with a clear theme. Various people entered a house one by one, some going "upstairs." The house, though, was surrounded by angry critters, including lizards, horses, a lion, a dog, and a bird, as the boy called upon the available toy figures. Then the bird flew into the upper window of the small doll-house, while the other angry animals knocked the house down (off the table, to the floor). This scene was repeatedly enacted. The mother, who was playing with her son, interjected that the people would be okay; the boy insisted they would not. The mother suggested that the police would rescue and protect the people; the boy clearly included the police among the casualties (they fell off the table, too, pronounced "dead"). The boy was showing determination and high emotional intensity; he was involved in serious business in this play. The mother was trying to reassure him, but also to make light of the matter, alternating with joking and admonishing. Her own efforts at pleasantries and more lighthearted themes were belied by her furrowed brow and look of consternation. When the mother's efforts to edit and re-direct the story did not succeed, she attempted to limit, control, and divert her son's play in other ways. Perhaps they could play a familiar paper-and-pencil game they frequently engaged in, she suggested. After all, they shouldn't mess up the room; the toy figures should stay on the table. In our video feedback consultation with this mother, she began to think about what her child's emotions were, and her own, during this scene. Over time, she increased her capacity to stay with the difficult themes of her child's play.

In the videotaped play of one 3-year-old with his mother, when the child hid a dog figure under the doll house, he said, "Doggie go bye-bye." The mother first responded with laughter (an affective "discordant" divergence, possibly due to her discomfort with the theme of loss or abandonment). Then, when she observed her child's upset facial expression, she sobered and said, "Bye-bye?" In response, her son apparently was still upset (since he had been seriously trying to communicate his sad feeling of something lost). In the play, he then abruptly switched the play object, picking up a doll figure (see Erikson, 1940). The mother, in turn, picked up another doll, and her son began to hit her doll as he looked intently at his mother.

Understandably, the mother was stunned at this behavior and reminded her son, "We don't hit like that." Following this filming session, when the therapists watched this play sequence on the video, the mother was at first perceived to be attentively following her child's lead, since she did respond with "Bye-bye" after noticing her son was upset. However, the fact that the child had abruptly changed the play theme from expressing loss to expressing anger suggested to us that he had been looking for his mother to affectively join him in a way that she had not. In this case, in the video feedback context, the therapists empathically supported the mother while watching the moment-to-moment clash that arose between her son's play theme of disappearance, and her initial defensive response of laughter. We attempted to enter the mother's state of mind at the moment she laughed. We helped her to imagine what she might have been thinking and feeling. This type of support given to the mothers, while they observed "affective mismatches" and "play disruptions," created the opportunity for the mothers to share their own feelings of sadness, anxiety, frustration, and bewilderment. In the feedback sessions, we would often join the mothers in their experience of grief as they cried about their losses, not only the loss of their husbands but also of the mother they would have been and the life they would have led. In turn, the mothers grew in their capacity to repair and to connect empathically with the childlike, often disguised, expressions of loss represented by their children in their pretend play.

Much of the time we observed that the mothers were capable of following, scaffolding, and elaborating their children's play, as long as the play themes did not trigger their own painful and conflicted issues related to loss or aggression. At these moments, the mothers understandably tended to become concrete and intrusive, and to divert the play themes, as they attempted to avoid their own painful affects. During feedback sessions with the therapists, the mothers were often supported in seeing painful meanings in their children's play. The tower-building, structures crashing, fire-rescue, death-by-crushing, figures dying, disappearing and jumping off the table, crashing all the toys and figures off the table in one big swoop, and various forms of hiding-and-seeking were gradually understood by the mothers as reflecting the children's efforts to work through their anxieties and experiences of loss and helplessness.

Some of the mothers negated or minimized their children's negative play themes and preoccupations out of their well-intended efforts to protect the children from painful feelings of loss and depression. But this negation almost invariably led to the escalation of traumatic play themes. Some of the mothers were afraid that their children would carry out their symbolized expressions of death wishes and destruction in other settings, inward or outward, now or later. In the feedback sessions, we addressed the mothers' heightened fears, insecurities and need to let go of the past and "move on." For some, protective motives were entwined with their own defenses.

As noted earlier, most of the children showed the therapists much more than they showed their mothers, especially regarding themes of trauma. Many of the children revealed to the therapists very early on that they knew more about what happened on September 11, 2001, than their mothers assumed. It was common to find that the children had drawn upon sibling, familial, peer, school, and community sources of information and upon posters, ads, or even glimpses of TV, no matter how hard the mothers had tried to shield the children. Children intuitively knew not to share with their mothers, even through play, their knowledge of the events of September 11. They seemed to know that their mothers were not yet prepared to know of their knowledge. Sometimes not showing their knowledge of September 11 appeared anchored in the children's self-protective maneuvers to avoid the pain of losing their mother's collaboration. At other times, it appeared anchored in children's characteristic ways of protecting their mothers, and these were not necessarily mutually exclusive. Many of the mothers maintained their "belief" that their children did not "know," simply because their children had not told them. In the feedback sessions, we would gently approach these topics, supporting our understanding of the child's awareness and concerns, while taking into consideration the mother's readiness or lack of readiness to help her child know, at a developmental level that the child could absorb.

During the filming, and in the video feedback sessions, the mothers often became painfully aware of what their children knew of their losses, and of how representational the play was. Gradually, the mothers realized how actively they had tried to elicit positive affect in the play, thus shifting their children's play away from themes of death, loss, or destruction. This realization led to discussions of the mothers' powerless feelings of being unable to protect their children. It was so difficult to embrace the reality that this tragedy really happened. Even years after September 11, 2001, some of the mothers were still waiting to tell their children until they could have an adult type of dialogue about the disaster. In the video feedback sessions, many mothers began to understand that, in the pretend play itself, there were many rich opportunities for the child to express thoughts and concerns about the father's death, along with many opportunities for "direct conversation." We focused on the power of pretend play, both as a way for the child to communicate, and to gain mastery over, fears and uncertainties. The mothers gradually came to know that being open to all of the play themes, including those of destruction, was a way of protecting their children, even though it was counterintuitive and so painful.

Eventually, most of the mothers began to see the themes and related feelings that their children were playing out with the therapists as ones that they too had experienced in response to their own losses. In the video feedback sessions, mothers developed the capacity to achieve a heightened sense of shared affect with their children. This empathic position enhanced the mothers' ability to imagine and validate their children's representations of their lost fathers through their wishes and magical thinking, such as in bringing the father back or joining him in heaven. Although there were many individual differences in maternal capacities to reflect on their children's minds, in the feedback sessions the mothers became able to be more interested in knowing their children.

Regardless of whether the mothers were following their children's play themes, we consistently noted the children's attempts to engage their mothers, seeking attention for their concerns. Even when the children's minds were drawn to emotional "hollows" from which these mothers were retreating, the dynamics of the dyad would become refocused by the child's intense efforts to contact the mother, to express intense feelings, and the child's need to know. In many of these situations, we would work with the mothers to help them understand the developmentally appropriate stages of their children's grief. At times, when many of the mothers had thought that the subject was long ago put to rest, as the years passed we would help the mothers realize that they were still being called upon by their children to revisit stories from the past. For example, the children asked to view videos of the parents' wedding, or asked how the parents had originally met. Or the children asked about what happened to their fathers, or where their fathers were. The questions changed as the children became developmentally ready to understand more details of their history in newly matured ways.

In the feedback sessions with the mothers, we often pointed out when the children's play showed a premature sense of responsibility to protect others, especially their mothers. When the mothers would notice these themes, either spontaneously or with our help, they would cry about what they and their children were missing. We would then discuss the possibility of other adult (generally, male) figures closely connected to the family who might offer themselves in substitutive father-figure roles. In one play session, when we observed the child putting a lizard-parent-figure to bed while all kinds of dangerous activities were happening to the baby lizards, we thought that this child's mother might be taking to her bed while unknowingly leaving her child feeling abandoned. In that play scenario, the therapist responded, "Wow, that mother lizard seems awfully tired while the baby lizards are still awake. And it must be pretty scary." In these situations, as in others, we were often faced with some difficult choices about whether and how to approach these topics with the mothers. In the feedback sessions, we aimed to help the mothers to see how their children were trying to communicate their worries and concerns, thus empowering the mothers without being critical.

Throughout the years, we were often impressed with the love and maternal capacity we witnessed. We saw mothers who worked hard to know, understand, and provide for their children. For some mothers, the stresses of September 11, compounded with unresolved past grief, were overwhelming. At times we observed patterns that, for some of the children, elevated risks for their development. In some families, we noted in early observations that there were problems with over-stimulation, tolerating the infant's distress, or turn-taking. In feedback sessions, we worked with many of the mothers to help them become aware of how their grief and preoccupation with their loss might be affecting their children, and to find ways they might "see" and "sense" their children's nonverbal language more. A central issue in the feedback sessions focused on the mothers' ability to tolerate their children's destructive play and on their capacity to follow their children's lead into aggressive play. We focused on their ability to understand pretend play as indeed pretend, as a way for the children to play out, represent, and ultimately repair these terrifying images. In some of these situations, we made referrals for outside support, or we referred a mother or a child for some individual treatment with one of our own therapists, while we continued seeing these families regularly over the years.

## EXAMPLE OF VIDEOTAPED PLAY OF MOTHER-CHILD, THERAPIST-CHILD, AND VIDEO FEEDBACK

Carl was a young boy of almost three years when his father failed to come home from work on that fateful day of September 11, 2001. His mother was pregnant with a younger sister who was born the following spring. Since September 12, Carl had insisted on spending his days glued to his father's chair at home and refused to allow anyone else to use the chair. The mother was very concerned. First seen in June 2002, at the age of 3-and-a-half, Carl was unusually attentive to the video equipment in the filming room. He vigilantly watched and listened to the camera's movements. He interrupted his play by focusing on the microphone and other procedural sounds that most of the other children did not attend to. Notably, there were a few other children who were also hypervigilant to the camera and other noises, yet Carl seemed to experience a greater degree of anxiety.

As the mother-child play unfolded, Carl was often the protagonist in search of something that he could not find. He did not elaborate on this theme, nor did the mother advance the play, even though she appeared to be loving, attentive, and sufficiently available to Carl. Carl and his mother seemed to be engaged in joint attention but not in shared meanings. The mother and Carl spent more time looking at whether the dollhouse door could physically open or close than developing a play theme. Carl's own disposition was to veer from the pretend play in favor of a detail. Throughout the play with his mother, Carl looked anxious and he engaged in an unusual degree of self-regulatory behaviors with the play objects, such as fidgeting with a toy in his hand, and many self-touch movements.

Within the first minute of interaction, Carl and his mother began to explore the doll house. His mother made suggestions as to which room "guests" might stay in. Carl, in turn, would say, "No, it doesn't go there, mommy." Yet the mother continued to pick up new items and ask where they went. At times the mother rushed a bit, as if trying to race ahead of Carl's proclivity to focus on the camera and the door. By two minutes into the play, both the mother and the child were each influencing the tempo, manner, and themes of the other. Then the roles reversed. Carl began asking his mother where something would go, only to say "No" to her after she answered. This interaction continued with Carl asking for help and direction and then finding the answers unacceptable. When we watched the video of this play sequence in the therapist group, we hypothesized that this interaction may have evolved in reaction to Carl's mother's unacceptable answers to his queries about what happened to his lost father. On the other hand, Carl seemed trusting and comfortable with his mother. His nay-saying did not seem to be defiant but rather an attempt to cope with the intolerable loss that he could not discuss with his mother.

By three minutes into the play with his mother, Carl introduced a Playmobil figure and named it "Carl." The mother and Carl then joined in creating a story of going to school. The plastic play toilet took on a charged meaning as both mother and Carl recognized that he himself was in need of the bathroom about then. This led to shared laughter in reaction to the Playmobil toy that Carl had used to represent the play toilet. After a bathroom break, the play session continued as Carl and his mother began depicting themes of the school experience. We later learned that the bathroom reference was not only about Carl's having to go to the bathroom. In the subsequent feedback session, the mother explained that Carl had recently mastered his toileting body function and that he was afraid of losing control.

After 10 minutes of mother-child play, the play session with the therapist began. Again, Carl initially focused on the microphones and the cameras, but he quickly moved into symbolic puppet play that he had begun with the therapist in the waiting room prior to his play with his mother. Carl re-introduced the names and roles he had already created for a bird figure and a plastic cow. The bird was a female and the cow was male, and there was a romance between them. Then Carl moved the cow to the side of the play area and announced that the cow had gone off to work. Next Carl looked sad and said that the cow was not coming home. The therapist empathically said, "Ohhhhh." It seemed quite possible to us that he was playing out what happened on the day his Dad went to work and never returned home. Quickly however, Carl disrupted the play (Erikson, 1940). He switched gears and picked up the play theme where he left off with his mother about the toilet. In retrospect, although the therapist had joined Carl in that painful moment when he said the cow was not coming home, it seemed that it was too difficult to be expanded into the play context at that time. Carl then changed the play theme to being driven to school. He told the therapist to take the car and go look for the cow (the male figure that had previously not returned home) to bring him home. We wondered if he was expressing a wish that the therapist would be able to find his father. Carl then repeatedly hid the bird and suddenly announced the cow's reappearance. In this play between Carl and the therapist, themes of disappearance and reappearance seemed related to the lost and remembered father, and the wish for the father to reappear.

Initially, the play of the mother-child and therapist-child were similar. Carl was distracted by sounds of the microphones and cameras in the lab, and then he moved into a school-based play theme. However, with his mother, he stayed with enacting his school experience. With the therapist, he started to play out a school theme but quickly shifted into more symbolically elaborated pretend play. He played out the memory of his father's loss and his wish for his father's return. This theme was developed when he introduced themes of disappearance and reappearance with various play figures that could and could not be found. Thus, the play was more revealing with the therapist. As the 10 minutes passed, Carl became increasingly assertive, and his play themes became more creative. These themes reflected Carl's loss, and the play offered him an opportunity to experience empathy and empowerment with the therapist. As the session unfolded, Carl continued to develop more symbolic ways of communicating his intense inner feelings.

As Carl and his mother were preparing to leave the lab, Carl decided that he wanted to take home one of the play figures he had used. He was told that these are toys for all the children and that he would have to leave it in the lab until his next visit. Carl began to cry. His crying escalated until he worked himself up into a state of uncontrollable sobbing. His mother took him on her lap to try to comfort him. After about 20 minutes he gradually calmed down. His mother told us that this was the first time that she had seen Carl cry since September 11, 2001.

In the feedback session, Carl's mother reported that she was less worried about Carl after their visit to the lab. Using the video, we were able to discuss what we understood of Carl's thoughts and concerns as revealed in the play themes. In the mother-child play, there were many beautiful moments of playful matching between them that we pointed out to the mother. Initially, Carl had been hypersensitive to his surroundings, revealing concerns for his safety and that of his mother. We suggested to the mother that although Carl had not spoken to her about his father, his wish to stay on the father's chair seemed to be an attempt to hold onto his father, and to gain some control over remaining connected to his father. The mother cried as she recalled how it was for her in the days following September 11, being pregnant and having to deal with Carl's confusion and grief. We pointed out how the play at the lab enabled Carl to communicate what was on his mind, in manageable doses. The mother was sensitive to Carl's experience in the lab and its importance. We also suggested that Carl's wish to take the doll home and his not being allowed to do so may have symbolized the reality of the loss of his father. His ability to let out a torrent of sobbing after not being allowed to take the doll home seemed to confirm this interpretation.

A couple of weeks after her feedback session, the mother reported that not long after Carl's visit to the lab, with his brief 10 minutes of therapeutic play with his mother and 10 minutes with the therapist, Carl no longer insisted on sitting in his father's chair. We wondered how such a resolution could come about so shortly after Carl's lab visit. In retrospect, Carl had been supported within the play in taking a step for which he was primed and ready. He became more confident as he represented his ideas, questions, and formidable feelings in his symbolic play. Moreover, with his mother's newly acquired ability to understand and permit Carl's expression of his grief and pain, she also helped him to let go of something he had previously needed to hold onto. Thus, he did not remain stuck in the previously repetitive pattern of his trauma and loss, sitting in his father's chair. We all felt that he had found some new sense of comfort.

The case of Carl exemplifies an "older" sibling of a child who was in the mother's belly on the day of the trauma. The mother was quite concerned about Carl when she brought him to the lab at the age of 3-and-a-half She was not worried about his baby sibling who was a few months old at the time. Carl's play with one of the therapists was carefully followed and met concordantly in emotional tone and in the pretend play themes. Preoccupying issues of loss, helplessness, searching, the finality of death, activity, and passivity all began to emerge in Carl's first visit to the lab, as they did over time with all of the children in our Project. For some of the children, referrals were made for follow-up with an individual therapist for the child or mother. For other children, the mother may have already been participating in one of our groups and/or awaiting the next scheduled visit to the lab. In the case of Carl, both he and his mother benefited from the experience of play in the lab, and his mother benefited from watching the play in her video feedback session with one of her other children. In this case, Carl's mother was very receptive to our ideas, and it appeared from follow-ups that she clearly employed them. A year later, we helped Carl's mother find a suitable therapist for her son when new symptoms developed.

## CONCLUSION

Our experiences of playing with the children whose fathers were lost defy simple generalizations. Each case warrants individualized reflection, especially regarding aspects of the family support system, personality, temperament, and relational differences, along with varied resilience factors. In the year following the disaster of September 11, 2001, the responsiveness of many mothers to their children was understandably askew in their ability for shared emotion and joint attention. In the first few months of their baby's lives, often these loving but preoccupied mothers would direct or divert their infants' and children's attention rather than follow their leads. We observed, moreover, that babies who were in the belly at the time of their father's loss frequently had heightened sensitivities. In their early years, these children were highly attentive to their mothers' emotional responsiveness. For many of the mothers, engaging in a pattern of pause-wait-and-follow would leave them too vulnerable to sadness and/or depression.

As the babies grew and became old enough to engage in pretend play, they frequently experienced from their mothers a type of veto over some of the aggressive and destructive themes that emerged. At that time, many of the mothers had great difficulty in validating feelings of loss, aggression, grief, and wishes to repair. As the children grew older, most were strongly inclined to create pretend play themes of loss and symbolizations of death, aggression and heroics. Father-rescuer role depictions seemed to be driven by the curiosities of the children to know, to gain mastery, and to reconstruct what happened to their fathers. Many of the mothers had understandable reluctance to "go there" with the children as these themes emerged in their play.

As the children developed more capacity for symbolization, they increasingly knew not to bring destructive or painful representations into the play with their mothers, even though they would almost always do so with the therapists. Thus we observed differences in the children's play with mothers and therapists. The standard sequence in the lab was mother-child play followed by therapist-child play. Our observations were limited to this paradigm, and we do not know what the opposite sequence would have produced.

After several years of our participation in lab videotaping sessions with the children and mothers, and in video feedback consultations with the mothers, we saw increasing evidence of our effectiveness in sensitizing mothers to instances when they interrupted their children's play processes, particularly around painful themes. Many facets of this Project (as reflected in this volume) contributed to an evolution of trust, enabling mothers to benefit from their increased awareness. The mothers began effectively modifying their play styles, their mentalizing ability, and their overall relationships with their children. Gradually we observed a lessening of the repetitive, driven, aggressive quality in the children's play themes, and an emergence of a greater flexibility in their play.

We have witnessed a great deal of growth in the families with whom we have worked. We have come to appreciate anew how helping a mother to listen, to "see," and to follow her child's lead, facilitates the child in play, and helps the child to integrate his or her experience. At times during the play sessions and often following the entire experience in the video lab sessions, the therapists felt overwhelmed by the power of the children's intense affect. The children's play conveyed their seeking of containment, recognition, and safety in a world that was beyond their, or our, control. Our implicit encouragement and permission facilitated the children to play out whatever was on their minds, without any censoring on our part. Their responses were often painful for us as we worked with the mothers and children in this Project.

In summary, we observed that when mothers were supported by the therapist team, this support reinforced their capacity to provide a joining and scaffolding of their children's play. Over time, the mothers developed an increased flexibility that advanced their children's capacity for emotionally rich pretend play. Each new stage of development has offered new opportunities for repair and for the mothers to help their children represent the fathers whose presence would have made such a great difference in their children's lives.

## REFERENCES

Ainsworth, M., Blehar, M., Waters, E., & Wall, S. (1978). *Patterns of attachment: A psychological study of the Strange Situation*. Hillsdale, NJ: Lawrence Erlbaum.

Baradon, T., & Steele M. (2008). Integrating the AAI in the clinical process of psychoanalytic parent-infant psychotherapy in a case of relational trauma. In *Clinical applications of the adult attachment interview* (pp. 195–212). New York, NY: Guilford Press.

Beebe, B. (2003). Brief mother-infant treatment: Psychoanalytically informed video feedback. *Infant Mental Health Journal, 24*(1), 24–52.

Beebe, B. (2005). Mother infant research informs mother-infant treatment. *The Psychoanalytic Study of the Child, 60*, 7–46.

Beebe, B., Jaffe, J., Buck, K., Chen, H., Cohen, P., Blatt, S., . . . Andrews, H. (2007). Six-week postpartum maternal self-criticism and dependency and 4-month mother-infant self and interactive contingencies. *Developmental Psychology, 43*(6), 1360–1376.

Beebe, B., Jaffe, J., Chen, H., Buck, K., Cohen, P., Feldstein, S., & Andrews, H. (2008). Six-week postpartum depressive symptoms and 4-month mother-infant self- and interactive contingency. *Infant Mental Health Journal, 29*(5), 442–471.

Beebe, B., Jaffe, J., Markese, S., Buck, K., Chen, H., Cohen, P., . . . Feldstein, S. (2010). The origins of 12-month attachment: A microanalysis of 4-month mother-infant interaction. *Attachment and Human Development, 12*, 1–135.

Beebe, B., Knoblauch, S., Rustin, J., & Sorter, D. (2005). *Forms of intersubjectivity in infant research and adult treatment*. New York, NY: Other Press.

Beebe, B., & Lachmann, F. (2002). *Infant research and adult treatment: Co-constructing interactions*. Hillsdale, NJ: Analytic Press.

Beebe, B., Rustin, J., Sorter, D., & Knoblauch, S. (2003). An expanded view of intersubjectivity in infancy and its applications to psychoanalysis. *Psychoanalytic Dialogues*, *13*(6), 805–841.
Beebe, B., Steele, M., Jaffe, J., Buck, K., Chen, H., Cohen, P., . . . Feldstein, S. (2011). Maternal anxiety and 4-month mother-infant self- and interactive contingency. *Infant Mental Health Journal*, *32*(2), 174–206.
Belsky, J., & Fearon, P. (2002). Infant-mother attachment security, contextual risk, and early development: A moderational analysis. *Development and Psychopathology*, *14*, 293–310.
Belsky, J., Garduque, L., & Hrncir, E. (1984). Assessing performance, competence, and executive capacity in infant play: Relations to home environment and security of attachment. *Developmental Psychology*, *20*, 406–417.
Cohen, P. M., & Beebe, B. (2002). Video feedback with a depressed mother and her infant: A collaborative individual psychoanalytic and mother-infant treatment. *Journal of Infant, Child, & Adolescent Psychotherapy*, *2*(3), 1–55.
Cohn, J., & Tronick, E. (1988). Mother-infant face-to-face interaction: Influence is bidirectional and unrelated to periodic cycles in either partner's behavior. *Developmental Psychology*, *24*(3), 386–392.
Danis, A., Bourdais, C., & Ruel, J. (2000). The co-construction of joint action between mothers and 2–4 month-old infants: The mother's role. *Infant and Child Development*, *9*, 181–198.
Erikson, E. (1940). Studies in the interpretation of play: I. Clinical observation of play disruption in young children. *Genetic Psychology Monographs*, *22*, 557–671.
Engel, S., Berkowitz, G., Wolff, M., & Yehuda, R. (2005). Psychological trauma associated with the World Trade Center attacks and its effect on pregnancy outcome. *Paediatric and Perinatal Epidemiology*, *19*, 334–341.
Fein, G., & Kinney, P. (1994). He's a nice alligator: Observations on the affective organization of pretense. In A. Slade & D. Wolf (Eds.), *Children at play: Clinical and developmental approaches to meaning and representation* (pp. 188–205). New York, NY: Oxford University Press.
Fonagy, P., Gergely, G., Jurist, E., & Target, M. (2002). *Affect regulation, mentalization, and the development of the self*. New York, NY: Other Press.
Fonagy, P., & Target, M. (1996). Playing with reality: I. Theory of mind and the normal development of psychic reality. *The International Journal of Psychoanalysis*, *77*, 217–233.
Fonagy, P., Steele, M., Steele, H., Higgitt, A., & Target, M. (1994). The theory and practice of resilience. *Journal of Child Psychology and Psychiatry and Allied Disciplines*, *35*, 231–257.
Fonagy, P., & Target, M. (2008). Attachment, trauma, and psychoanalysis: Where psychoanalysis meets neuroscience. In E. Jurist, A. Slade, & S. Bergner (Eds.), *Mind to mind: Infant research, neuroscience and psychoanalysis* (pp. 15–49). New York, NY: Other Press.
Freud, A. (1946). *The psychoanalytical treatment of children*. New York, NY: International Universities Press.
Gaensbaurer, T. J. (1995). Trauma in the preverbal period: Symptoms, memories, and developmental impact. *Psychoanalytic Study of the Child*, *50*, 122–149.
Goldman, L. (2002). The assumptive world of children. In J. Kaufman (Ed.), *Loss of the assumptive world: A theory of traumatic loss* (pp. 193–204). New York, NY: Brunner-Routledge.
Harris, A. (2003). Relational mourning in a mother and three-year-old after September 11. In S. Coates, J. Rosenthal, & D. Schechter (Eds.), *September 11: Trauma and human bonds* (pp. 143–163). Hillsdale, NJ: Analytic Press.
Jaffe, J., Beebe, B., Feldstein, S., Crown, C. L., & Jasnow, M. D. (2001). Rhythms of dialogue in infancy: Coordinated timing in development. *Monographs of the Society for Research in Child Development*, *66*(2), vi–131.
Kaminer, T., Beebe, B., Jaffe, J., Kelly, K., & Marquette, L. (2007). Mothers' dependent and self-critical depressive experience is related to speech content with infants. *Journal of Early Childhood Infant Psychology*, *3*, 163–184.
Levy, D. (1939). Release therapy. *American Journal of Orthopsychiatry*, *9*, 713–736.
Lyons-Ruth, K. (1998). Attachment disorganization: Unresolved loss, relational violence, and lapses in behavioral and attentional strategies. In J. Cassidy & P. Shaver (Eds.), *Handbook of attachment theory and research* (pp. 520–554). New York, NY: Guilford Press.
Main, M., & Cassidy, J. (1988). Categories of response to reunion with the parent at age 6: Predictable from infant attachment classifications and stable over a 1-month period. *Developmental Psychology*, *24*, 415–426.
Marvin, R., & Britner, P. A. (1999). Normative development: The ontogeny of attachment. In J. Cassidy & P. R. Shaver (Eds.), *Handbook of attachment: Theory, research, and clinical applications* (pp. 44–67). New York, NY: Guilford.
Meins, E., Fernyhough, C., Russell, J., & Clark-Carter, D. (2001). Security of attachment as a predictor of symbolic and mentalising abilities: A longitudinal study. *Social Development*, *7*, 1–24.
Meltzoff, A. N. & Brooks, R. (2009). Social cognition and language: The role of gaze following in early word learning. In J. Colombo, P. McCardle, & L. Freund (Eds.), *Infant pathways to language: Methods, models, and research disorders* (pp. 169–194). New York, NY: Psychology Press.

Schechter, D., Zygmunt, A., Trabka, K., Davies, M., Colon, E., Kolodji, A., & McCaw, J. E. (2007). Child mental representations of attachment when mothers are traumatized: The relationship of family-drawings to story-stem completion. *Journal of Early Childhood and Infant Psychology, 3*, 119–140.

Schore, A. (2002). Dysregulation of the right brain: A fundamental mechanism of traumatic attachment and the psychopathogenesis of posttraumatic stress disorder. *Australian and New Zealand Journal of Psychiatry, 36*, 9–30.

Shelby, J., Avina, C., & Warnick, H. (2010). Posttraumatic parenting: A parent-child dyadic treatment for young children's posttraumatic adjustment. In C. Schaefer (Ed.), *Play therapy for preschool children* (pp. 69–87). Washington, DC: American Psychological Association.

Slade, A. (1987). Quality of attachment and early symbolic play. *Developmental Psychology, 23*(1), 78–85.

Sossin, K. M. (2002). Interactive movement patterns as ports of entry in infant-parent psychotherapy. *Journal of Infant, Child and Adolescent Psychotherapy, 2*, 97–131.

Sossin, K. M., & Birklein, S. (2006). Nonverbal transmission of stress between parent and young child: Considerations and psychotherapeutic implications of a study of affective movement patterns. *Journal of Infant, Child, and Adolescent Psychotherapy, 5*, 46–69.

Steele, H., Steele, M., Croft, C., & Fonagy, P. (1999). Infant-mother attachment at one year predicts children's understanding of mixed-emotions at six years. *Social Development, 8*(2), 161–178.

Stern, D. (1985). *The interpersonal world of the infant: A view from psychoanalysis and developmental psychology*. New York, NY: Basic Books.

Stern, D. N. (1995). *The motherhood constellation: A unified view of parent infant psychotherapy*. New York, NY: Basic Books.

Stolorow, R. (1999). The phenomenology of trauma and the absolutisms of everyday life: A personal journey. *Psychoanalytic Psychology, 16*, 464–468.

Sugar, M. (1992). Toddlers' traumatic memories. *Infant Mental Health Journal, 13*(3), 245–251.

Terr, L. (1988). What happens to early memories of trauma? A study of twenty children under age five at the time of documented traumatic events. *Journal of the American Academy of Child & Adolescent Psychiatry, 27*(1), 96–104.

Trevarthen, C. (2005). First things first: Infants make good use of the sympathetic rhythm of imitation, without reason or language. *Journal of Child Psychotherapy, 31*, 91–113.

Tronick, E. Z. (1989). Emotions and emotional communication in infants. *American Psychologist, 44*(2), 112–119.

Verheugt-Pleiter, A. J. E. (2008). Treatment strategy. In A. Verheugt-Pleiter, J. Zevalkink, & M. Schmeets (Eds.), *Mentalizing in child therapy* (pp. 41–68). London, England: Karnac.

Watson, M. (1994). The relation between anxiety and pretend play. In A. Slade & D. Wolf (Eds.), *Children at play: Clinical and developmental approaches to meaning and representation* (pp. 33–47). New York, NY: Oxford University Press.

Webb, N. (2004). The impact of traumatic stress and loss on children and families. In N. Webb (Ed.), Mass trauma and violence: Helping families and children cope. *Play therapy crisis intervention with children* (pp. 3–22). New York, NY: Guilford.

Webb, N. (2006). Crisis intervention play therapy to help traumatized children. In L. Carey (Ed.), *Expressive and creative arts methods for trauma survivors* (pp. 36–56). London, England: Jessica Kingsley.

Weinberg, K., & Tronick, E. (1998). The impact of maternal psychiatric illness on infant development. *Journal of Clinical Psychology, 59*, 53–61.

Winnicott, D. (1965). The theory of the parent-infant relationship. *The maturational processes and the facilitating environment* (pp. 37–55). Madison, CT: International Univ. Press.

# THE FEEDBACK SESSIONS

## Video Feedback and the Impact of Multiple Therapists

Phyllis Cohen, Ph.D.

In the field of parent-infant therapy, psychoanalytically informed video feedback has been applied as a dyadic intervention for more than 15 years by Daniel Stern, Beatraice Beebe, and others. Expanding upon this approach with women who were pregnant and widowed in the Project for Mothers, Infants, and Young Children of September 11, 2001, we learned that a collaborative method with a team of therapists enhanced our efficacy. This approach provides a multidimensional lens through which different therapists can understand what is on the minds of both mothers and children, fostering an increased sensitivity to their vulnerabilities and strengths. A visit to the lab is followed by a two-hour video feedback session in which team members take on predictable roles to enable the mother to develop a transference to the group as the agent of change. This approach includes cultivating an observing ego, securing a therapeutic alliance while minimizing shame and avoiding potential ruptures, integrating past and present, and emphasizing positive moments to enhance each mother's self-esteem while normalizing, empowering and consolidating gains.

The model of multiple therapists working simultaneously with one mother evolved as we created this Project. The women who became widows on September 11, 2001, while they were pregnant or had just become new mothers had raw, immediate, and urgent needs. As therapists who responded to this trauma, we did not have the luxury of slowly developing a therapeutic relationship and allowing trust to build over time. We usually saw each family only once a year, in a two-session format of a two-hour lab videotaping session, followed by a two-hour feedback session during the next week. Sometimes we saw a particular family twice a year. The mothers were unable to come more often. We needed an approach that would allow us a brief, concentrated, and accelerated intervention, one that would provide a large number of mothers and children maximum exposure to getting help in the shortest amount of time.

The author wishes to thank Rachel Altstein and Dr. Mark Sossin for their help in this article.

While we were organizing groups to provide a community of support for the mothers in areas close to their homes (see Bergman, Moskowitz, & Demetri Friedman, *Support Groups I, II and III,* this issue; Sossin, *Support Group II,* this issue; Reiswig, *Mourning a Lost Father,* this issue), we were also developing our model of "video feedback" sessions for mothers, with three or four therapists working together. Video feedback has been used in the field of parent-infant therapy (Stern, 1995; Beebe, 2003, 2005; Cohen & Beebe, 2002; Reck et al., 2004). In our method, families first visit the filming lab of Dr. Beatrice Beebe and Dr. Joseph Jaffe at the New York State Psychiatric Institute. In a two-hour session, the mother and her baby (and older children) are videotaped interacting in a nondirective play session for 10 minutes, followed by 10 minutes with one of the therapists of the Project acting as the "stranger" or novel partner. During the mother-child play session, other therapists from our team, including Dr. Beebe and Dr. Suzi Tortora, a movement therapist, watch the filming on a monitor. In the next week, after both the mother and the therapists have had a chance to reflect on the filming, we meet for a two-hour psychoanalytically informed consultation within which video feedback is embedded.

At the very beginning of the Project, Beatrice Beebe and I met together with individual mothers in feedback sessions. As we got to know many of the grieving women, when we learned that a mother was in her own individual therapy, we invited her therapist to the feedback session. If the mother was participating in one of our mothers' groups, the group therapists were invited as well. We soon learned that conducting a feedback session with three or four therapists was extremely effective and meaningful and, under the circumstances, the method of choice. Three or four therapists turned out to be far more effective than two therapists.

The feedback sessions are conducted at Dr. Beebe's clinical office. Typically, she escorts the mother into the room where the therapists are already assembled, and we warmly greet her. At that point we have met briefly before the session to review the video and plan our strategy for the most positive way to help the mother. We aim to keep in mind how vulnerable the mother is and how we must protect her from any feelings of humiliation. Watching a video of oneself playing with one's child in front of several therapists can be uncomfortable for any mother.

The seating arrangement of the room has been consistent through the years. The mother is directed to a seat on the couch to the left and next to Dr. Beebe, and Dr. Cohen is seated at a right angle to her other side. Sitting opposite the mother are Dr. Sossin and any other therapist involved with the family (either from within the Project or from outside). Occasionally, others participate in the session, such as a boyfriend or a new spouse. This person sits next to the mother on the couch. This seating arrangement is not accidental; it allows the mother to have direct contact with each of the therapists and allows each of us to have visual contact with each other without excluding the mother. The close proximity of the mother to the therapists seems to provide a comfortable holding environment to contain whatever difficult material might emerge. It allows me or Dr. Beebe to reach out and possibly touch the mother's hand without changing our physical positions, for example at a moment when she might begin to cry as the material becomes searingly painful.

In this two-hour session, time seems to disappear. In the first hour or more, we catch up on what is going on in the mother's life and whether she has any concerns about how her children are doing. In the second hour we may observe portions of the videotape if we feel that the mother is ready to see the complex communications between herself and her child. Either the mother or one of the therapists may segue into turning on the video. Watching only a minute or two of the play session is usually enough. From such a small sample of the play the mother can gain new eyes for seeing the dynamics of the communication between herself and her child, and she can relate what is happening in the play to the trauma of September 11, 2001, or to her own personal history of being parented. This integrative process can transform the experience of loss, as well as past conflicts, into a healing narrative for both the mother and the child.

In this article, I describe how we worked together as a team to help the mothers endure the painful process of grieving, while also attending to the needs of their children. To date, we have held consultations incorporating both video and feedback sessions with 41 mothers, observing together their interactions with their infants and older children. Some of the mothers have been seen as many as 10–12 times. While this is a small number of sessions in the traditional field of therapeutic intervention, it has generated a far greater impact than the number suggests.

Our video feedback method with multiple therapists working together involves a unique group process. Observing segments of the video interaction together is usually only a small portion of the two-hour session. More of the time is spent reflecting and reframing developmental and family issues, current relationships, and other concerns that the mother may have. All of the mothers have requested "feedback" on "how am I doing?" We have used the feedback sessions to help them cope with their tragic loss while providing the opportunity to reflect upon themselves as mothers in relation to their children. During these sessions, the therapists build upon each other's comments, each from a different lens. This process creates deeper meaning through our multiple perspectives, while also helping the mother build coherence and safety for herself and her children.

As the children have grown, our feedback sessions have evolved (see Sossin & Cohen, this issue). Not only do we encourage a mother's reflection, but we also highlight the benefits of joining her child's play by allowing the child to take the lead and by seeing the child's play as a communication. In these sessions, we help the mothers to cope with their own personal traumas as well as to help their children cope with their losses, especially in relation to representing the lost father. In this process we attempt to shift both internal representations and interaction styles.

The collaboration of the multiple therapists in the feedback sessions seems to both "slow down" the process and to "speed up" a mothers' capacity to think about difficult material. The ratio of three to four therapists to a single mother seems to have a paradoxical effect. Instead of feeling overwhelmed, the mothers are put at ease; instead of shutting down and feeling self-conscious, the mothers open up. We thought about why this might be the case. First, if the mother seems to be overwhelmed, the therapists talk to each other about our observations of the process. Second, if one therapist misunderstands the mother's communication, another therapist interjects another perspective or requests clarification from the mother. Third, if the mother's grief is so overwhelming that she is frozen in response to her terrible story of loss, one or more of the therapists can join in her sadness, while others can verbalize her unspeakable pain.

In the feedback sessions the mother has a chance to be understood and feel cared about, while her complicated feelings in response to her loss are addressed. Following each of these sessions, the therapists meet to process our reactions and to reflect on and critique our work. We discuss our differences in perspective and approach as we prepare for future sessions, not only for that particular mother, but for other mothers as well. As we have developed our method of seeing one mother in an extended consultation with several therapists, we have learned that this model can lessen the transmission of trauma from a grieving mother to her children. It supports the therapists as well, because the grief is held by the therapists together. This approach may also be useful in other settings addressing trauma and complicated mourning.

## EXCERPT FROM A TYPICAL FEEDBACK SESSION

I now turn to excerpts of a session based on a compilation of notes written by Beebe and Cohen. This feedback session with "Justine" in 2003 was her second one. Her first visit to the filming lab, and her first feedback session, had occurred six months earlier. Justine has come by herself to talk about her concerns and receive feedback on the video filmed with her two children, "Barry," her infant, and "Stephanie," her older child. This session is attended by Drs. Beebe, Cohen, and Sossin. Justine has given us permission to discuss this session.

These notes show the process of how our team worked together in the second year of developing our model of a multiple therapist feedback session. In this nondirective model we can never predict what will come up. The therapists encourage the mother to share whatever is on her mind. The therapists participate, building upon one another as sensitively as possible, as aspects of the mother's story of her trauma unfold. In writing these session notes, I have interspersed process comments in italics.

After the mother is escorted into the room and is seated, Dr. Beebe usually begins the feedback session with some comment that may relate to the mother's previous video session and/or help the mother to "open up." In this session we have been talking about how the mother is doing. When she starts talking about how difficult things are for herself as a mother, Dr. Beebe gives her an honest compliment.

*Beebe*: We were impressed to see you so natural with your children in the lab.

*Justine*: My sister is the one who is natural, not me. She's the pied piper with the kids.
*Justine has tried to take the focus away from herself, perhaps reflecting her discomfort with the compliment.*

*Sossin*: You were quite attentive and lively with the children in the lab
*Dr. Sossin has seen Justine with one of her older children for some consultations. Justine begins to cry as she remembers something painful. Dr. Sossin again brings the focus back to Justine*

*Sossin:* All of the mothers in our Project are grieving in different ways about different things. You're alike in what you've been through, but very different in how you express feelings. Justine, your openness with your feelings is special.
*Dr. Sossin has universalized Justine's experience, and Dr. Beebe now punctuates Dr. Sossin's comment:*

*Beebe:* I have heard from Dr. Mark that your openness in the support group has helped the group members open up.
*This is an example of how the therapists enhance and build upon one another in order to highlight something we think is important.*

*Justine*: Well, we're all experiencing the same thing. We've all been "going crazy." But in our group sessions, we're learning to be very open with each other.
*Justine has echoed what was said previously by Dr. Sossin.*

*Cohen:* It sounds like your group is really bonding.

*Justine*: Yes. And it helps me to know I'm not going out of my mind when I feel these feelings . . .
*The process so far has allowed Justine to go back to what was said in a previous mothers' group session. She shares a deep fear that she's had that she may have been*

*"going crazy." Her response tells us that she is in touch with what she's experiencing and that she is now ready to address this important issue. It seems that the process of the multiple therapists has allowed her to step outside of herself, and to reflect and share something about herself. Also, the "universalizing" seems to have resonated with her, since she now acknowledges she is not alone in her reactions.*

*At a later point in the session there is some discussion about differences in marital relationships with deceased husbands among various mothers that she knows. Since Dr. Sossin has had some individual consultations with Justine in relation to her older child, he explains something to the other therapists.*

*Sossin:* Justine's marriage was very special . . . but as time goes on, she also remembers some of the struggles in her marriage.

*This is an example of how the therapists talk to each other in the session. Dr. Sossin speaks to the therapists; this enables Justine to observe herself.*

*Cohen*: So, your relationship with your husband was both good and sometimes difficult?

*Justine nods in agreement*

*Sossin:* . . . So it was a less than perfect marriage . . . but, let's not overlook the good relationship that you had – there's always complexity in human relationships.

*Beebe:* If we can acknowledge the good *and* the difficult, it helps the mourning process. . . . there is less need to rigidly protect some image.

*Justine*: Yes, and I see that this could happen with my kids. Stephanie is now 7. She was 5 on 9/11. She wants to talk about her Daddy. She needs someone to talk to. I know how much she misses her father.

*Justine has brought the focus onto her kids.*

*Sossin*: For some things, you are the best person for her to talk to. For other things, someone else might be better for her to talk to – maybe someone she can't affect so much.

*Dr. Sossin is leading up to a possible outside referral for Stephanie.*

*Justine*: Recently, Stephanie told me she's mad. I said, "You SHOULD be mad. You lost your Dad."

*Justine is now crying, but she continues talking.*

*Justine*: I told her, I'm so glad you're telling me . . . *[She's still crying.]* She'll never have a father again . . . So many men try to be nice to Stephanie. It's too much. They're all overcompensating. I don't want people to be nice to her for that reason. Otherwise she might think people are nice to her only because she lost her father, rather than for *herself*.

*Some time passes as Justine continues to cry. Dr. Beebe reaches out and touches her hand.*

*Justine*: If Stephanie sees me cry, she closes up. And it upsets her when I yell at her . . . But I come from a screaming family . . . My father had it in him.

*This is Justine's first reference to her own father. She has changed the topic from her marriage, to her child's reaction to a tragic loss, and now to her family of origin . . .*

*Cohen*: What is it like when you scream?

*Justine:* Like. . . . I have a tone – I only do it in my family. My father was like that. I sound like, "STEPHANIE, GET IN HERE!!"

*Sossin:* So, Stephanie isn't the only one who gets mad!!

*Sossin:* And [*to Justine*], how do you deal with your anger?

*Justine:* I pray a lot.

*Sossin*: I see that's important. And what else could you do?

*Cohen:* Well, she could wait and count . . . or she could walk away . . . But when you've grown up with screaming in the family, it's really hard. . . .

*This reference back to Justine's screaming father lets her know that we understand how hard it must be for her.*

*Beebe:* What kinds of things set you off?

*Justine*: When we're doing a million things and there's a glitch . . . like when Stephanie doesn't get to dancing school on time . . .

*Sossin:* And you have shared with me that you know you are a perfectionist.

*Justine:* Yes. If we're out, I don't have that tone. It's mostly in the house, or when we're trying to get out of the house in the morning and the kids have to have breakfast. I start screaming and then Stephanie tells me to stop.

*Cohen:* You mean they can't just have a cereal bar for breakfast?

*Humor has been used and Justine laughs.*

*Justine*: They *have* to eat healthy! I know it doesn't make sense and it's perfectionistic, but I just can't help it.

*Beebe:* This is important. We've just pinpointed a problem. How can we think about this?

*Justine:* I want to control so many things, to have it come out just the way I want, but I can't. It's inborn.

*Sossin:* Seeing this is a good start. You have a difficult time relinquishing control, but such proclivities *can* change.

*Cohen*: And Stephanie is the one asking you not to scream like that. She can help you change.

*Justine:* Yes, and my son Barry also stops me dead in my tracks when he says, "When you talk to me like that, I won't listen to you. I won't do what you say."

*Sossin:* So, you've empowered Stephanie and Barry to be able to complain, to call you on it. And you respect them for it.

*Dr. Sossin is constructing the idea that Stephanie and Barry talking back to their mother resulted from Justine's helping her children to speak their minds. He is reframing a negative behavior into a positive one, empowering Justine.*

*Beebe:* This is something that we need to think about. What used to set your father off?

*Dr. Beebe has brought the focus back to Justine's family of origin to understand more about her past that she is bringing into the present.*

*Justine:* My father lost his father when he was in his teens. My parents are from authoritarian families. They used to say, "Children are children; keep them in their place. Case closed." . . . . My father had great ideas, but lacked self-confidence, and he couldn't accomplish a lot. My husband was a wonderful father – not like my father. My father gave me a very hard time.

*Beebe:* Your father was difficult.

*Dr. Beebe has decided to keep the focus on Justine's family of origin. She will address the comparison between Justine's father and Justine's dead husband at a later time.*

*Justine:* My father was a wonderful man on the outside *[she defends her father but then says]*, but inside he was *not* a good father.

*Sossin*: There are those differences that we've spoken about before – between the outside and the inside. You seem so confident on the outside. What about on the inside?

*Dr. Sossin has used information gleaned from the mothers' support group.*

*Justine:* I'm not confident. I'm not good at introducing myself. I feel stupid. I used to think everyone else was smarter than me . . .

*Sossin:* There's a part of you that feels stupid, like your father may have felt, but another part knows you're smart.

*Justine*: I've always wanted to be smart, but I wasn't . . . *[Justine laughs.]*

*Beebe:* There goes your perfectionistic attitude. It's the same one that gets you into trouble with Stephanie.

*Justine:* My father was like that – a perfectionist. He withdrew around people he thought were smarter . . .

*Sossin:* Your father worked hard to manage his self esteem. You shouldn't have to work so hard.

*Beebe:* We've pinpointed an area to think about. This is how your father was, but this is not who you want to be. You don't have to be like your father . . . It's easier to look at your anger and self-esteem when we see how your children are affected.
*[Later in the session.]*

*Justine:* Stephanie is strong willed. We have our battles, but I think they're less intense lately since the last time I came here. We've been able to talk things through. She storms off to a corner but comes back. She says, I don't want you to squash me . . .
*Justine stops to think and we wait. She has brought up the idea that something has improved, connecting it to our work together six months ago.*

*Justine:* Stephanie is dying for a father's attention. Ugh! She's hanging onto men — anyone who will give her attention. She won't let go. I'm afraid she's always going to look for a man's attention.

*Beebe:* This is a very serious aspect of the trauma for all the children. It'll be one of their biggest tasks and challenges and it will take a lot of work to modulate this.
*Dr. Beebe has normalized a problem that we have seen in many of the children in the Project who lost their fathers*
*At an opportune point in the session when we feel that Justine is ready, one of the therapists asks if she would like to see some of the video, to look at how Justine and the children are communicating. We begin to watch a sequence of Justine with Stephanie. At this point in the video, Stephanie was giving Justine a very difficult time and was frustrated in her play with her mother.*

*Beebe:* Would you say that what we see on this film reflects a typical day for Stephanie? Is this typical of how she behaves?
*Justine* [with an edge in her voice]: It was typical of her with strangers around.
*Justine's comment gives us the feeling that Justine has pulled back, possibly because she was beginning to feel that she was going to be criticized. She was not happy with the way her daughter was interacting with her. Dr. Cohen now speaks to the group in an attempt to take the pressure off Justine.*

*Cohen:* Did you notice how Justine showed that she really "gets it" with Stephanie? Justine was so patient with her when Stephanie was being really difficult. She tried so many things, and in the end she even conveyed her faith in Stephanie that she can do it herself, while Stephanie was pushing her mother to do it for her.
*Dr. Beebe now responds to Dr. Cohen.*

*Beebe:* Yes, Justine's a very talented mother. First she acknowledges her daughter's distress, and then after a moment she tries to slightly shift it. And her pace is nice and slow . . .

*Once again, following this conversation among the therapists, Justine is able to see herself from the outside in. She no longer feels as defensive as she did a few moments earlier, and her facial expression tells us she had begun to take in some positive feedback. In this situation, the work of more than one therapist building on each other has prevented a possible momentary therapeutic rupture. Although Dr. Beebe's question about whether the interaction we saw in the video was typical, it was meant to inquire into how Stephanie's behavior might or might not be reflective of a problem that would need to be addressed. Upon being asked about Stephanie's provocative behavior, Justine seemed not to have been ready to go in that direction. If one of the therapists had been working individually with Justine, he/she would have eventually become aware of how Justine was processing this line of inquiry. However, in the Multiple Therapist model, a therapist "outside" the interaction can pick up on subtle cues early in the interaction to prevent a possible "disruption" in the therapy.*

*After a minute or two of watching Justine and Stephanie engaging in a power struggle, we fast-forward the video to allow Justine to see an interaction later in the videotaping. We feel this interaction may help her with her daughter.*

*Beebe:* Look at how this shows that Stephanie is ready to tell you more about what's on her mind. Justine, if you continue to hang back and give her space, as you just did, this will enable her to tell you even more . . .

*Justine:* Yes, I just noticed how Stephanie said, "Mommy let me finish . . ." on the tape. I see that she's asserting herself, and she started to talk to me when I backed off . . .

*Justine's response has shown us that, once again, she "gets it."*

*As the two hours of the session are nearly finished, we typically switch gears to give the mother a chance to review the important points of the session.*

*Beebe:* So, what are you going to be thinking about after the session and taking home with you today?

*Justine:* What have I learned? Well, that my father was easily intimidated, and so am I. I'm aware of my tone – I have to learn how to work with it, to stop it. And it *is* stoppable!

*Beebe:* And what are you taking with you about *you* as a mother?

*Justine:* That I *am* listening to Stephanie, and I'm responding to what she needs.

*Beebe:* Especially to the distress. You're allowing it.

*Cohen:* And that's why Stephanie is doing so well.

*Justine:* Yes, but is there anything else I should be thinking about until the next time we meet?

*Sossin:* We have seen that all of the children in the Project know something of what they lost, but not who their father was as a person. This will be your task for Stephanie. She lost her Dad when she was very young. And Barry never knew his Dad. Representing him is an important job that you've started doing with your children – to help them "know" their father.

This was the way this particular session ended with Justine. Since that session, in total, Justine has had eight visits to the lab with her two children, each visit followed by a feedback session building on the one preceding it. She continues to participate in one of our mothers' groups. Justine has consistently reported that she has been helped by her participation in our Project.

At the end of the feedback session, we encourage the mother to be in contact with us by phone or e-mail, to share any residual thoughts or feelings with us. This is also the time when we may make referrals if indicated. We let the mother know that we hoped to see her in six months to one year, giving her plenty of time to take in and incorporate changes in response to the feedback. Once the mother leaves, the therapist group sits down to process the multiple levels of what transpired, both for the mother and for ourselves. This 15-minute debriefing allows us to unpack a very layered and powerful two-hour session from each of our personal and professional perspectives.

## SOME MUTATIVE FACTORS IN THE FEEDBACK SESSIONS

While each feedback session is as unique as the mother who sits at its center, we have found surprising consistency over the years in how the therapists have worked with each mother. In reviewing the previous feedback session with Justine, one can see how, organically, we have taken on various roles in the session. We seem to wear our own particular hats throughout a session, based on each of our individual frames of reference. This may, in fact, enhance the mother's experience by contributing to a feeling of continuity and predictability among the therapists. As we have worked together over time, we have observed a repetition of themes that have recurred throughout many of our two-hour feedback sessions, with individual mothers over time, as well as with different mothers.

All of the therapists in our Project share a common psychoanalytic perspective on the value of the earliest relationships. Nevertheless, multiple therapists working together bring multiple theories into play, and we each seem to focus on different levels from which truths operate. In analyzing the notes of the foregoing session with Justine, a number of methods and themes emerged that seem to reflect some of the mutative factors of the Multiple Therapist Model:

### Shared Transference

What happens to the transference when multiple therapists consult with one person? Rather than the transference being multiplied, the central transference is to the Project. The transference to each of the therapists is spread out in smaller doses. With the transference diffused, the mother is *more* prone to absorb and internalize the therapists' observations, rather than needing to put up her guard as she might with one individual therapist. Using the multiple therapist model, "A family is created in which the mother could be the baby, nurtured by all of us, without having to bear the burden of a transference relationship to just one of us" (A. Bergman, personal communication, February 23, 2009). At all times there is always at least one therapist whom the mother experiences as totally in synch with her.

### Cultivating an Observing Ego

In the feedback sessions the mother gains insight into herself by observing the therapists engaged in conversation with each other about her situation. As she listens, she processes what is being said about her. Paradoxically, rather than making the mother feel self-conscious or pressured, this seems to heighten her ability to step outside herself, to view her situation from a distance, as she develops an "observing ego."

Each of the therapists in the group has different areas of expertise, and we often enter into the mother's process from different perspectives (e.g., nonverbal interaction, movement theory, or family systems). The therapists may not always agree with each other. For example, one of us may have felt the need to slow down the conversation just as another of us was making a facilitative, forward-moving intervention. Nevertheless, we have always respected each other. We do not become competitive. Each mother has benefited from observing us sharing our different perspectives and resolving our differences, while keeping her best interests in mind.

### Keeping Mothers on Track While Avoiding Potential Ruptures

When a mother is faced with a disturbing thought or uncomfortable situation, or, in contrast, when she may receive a compliment from one of the therapists, at times she may shift the attention away from herself and onto another person or theme. The mother might be feeling that she cannot face what she is hearing or seeing at that time. Or she might be feeling undeserving or uncomfortable being complimented. In the feedback sessions we have noticed a pattern of one or more of us bringing the focus back but in a gentle yet persuasive way. Or alternatively, one of the therapists might sense a possible impending momentary disruption and might verbalize the mother's lack of readiness to proceed in this direction. Then one of the other therapists might simply change the focus with a comment that redirects the conversation. Eventually, the mother may allow herself to come back to the original difficult topic. These moments have been experienced as reparative as well as clarifying and enlightening, while the mother's ability to process difficult material is facilitated.

### Mobilizing Change by Observing the Video

Watching oneself on video interacting with one's child is a very powerful experience. It can be illuminating, but it can also be anxiety-provoking. We are not used to watching ourselves in this way. It is a deeply emotional experience for a mother, and it requires the therapists to be particularly sensitive to her timing and to her need for support and validation. As the mother sits shoulder-to-shoulder with the group of therapists, we watch the film together, and we develop our understanding of it together. We encourage the mother to reflect on her thoughts, associations, and reactions to what she sees on the videotape. We try to point out positive moments that work in the interaction. We minimize or hold at bay those dimensions of the interaction that we feel could be improved upon, until we feel the mother is sufficiently secure with us to be able to observe and comment on her own behavior. Events revealed on video often serve as launching points for discussing deeper issues in the mother's life. We check in with the mother from time to time to see how she is processing the experience of watching the video as it is happening.

### Integrating Past and Present

Memories of the mother's own childhood and relationships with her family of origin are often evoked in her experiences in the filming lab, in the feedback sessions, and in watching herself on the video. During the video feedback session we navigate back and forth between the mother's personal history with her own parents and siblings and the mother's present experience with her current nuclear family. More recently, with some of our mothers we have helped them to integrate a new boyfriend, new husband, step-children, and even new babies into painful past lives. The mother's comparisons between her own father and her child's father (the lost husband) are frequently a theme, as are her memories of her own childhood and her perspective on her child's experience of childhood. All of these themes are held in mind by the group of therapists as we help the mothers make connections. Together we integrate associations and memories of the past with our observations of the present. In so doing we help the mother to appreciate her strengths, and to develop a coherent narrative, so that she can see options in her current situation.

### Use of Reframing and Positive Connotations

During a feedback session we emphasize positive moments to highlight and reinforce the mother's awareness of her own competence and to consolidate her self-esteem. This positive approach has been a critical dimension of our sessions. We offer new and positive "reframing" language to describe interactions that may have been observed by one of the therapists or that may have been considered "negative" by the mother. This positive reframing empowers the mother. She often leaves the session with a greater sense of mastery and acceptance of herself as a good-enough mother.

### Punctuating

Throughout the feedback session one of the therapists inevitably wears the hat of punctuating the conversation, with powerful echoes and reinforcement. One of us follows up on an important point and reinforces it by saying something such as, "This is really important," or "Let's try to understand this." Punctuating is a critical intervention that marks a moment as poignant. It stops the action and focuses the mother's attention on something that we feel is worthy of being noticed and experienced more deeply.

### Translating into the Mother's Own Language

As we meet with the mothers we often hypothesize about various meanings of what we see and hear. We have found it critical to bring it back home to the mother in words that she can understand and take in. The "translator" of the group does just this, choosing an interpretation that has been formulated by one of the other therapists and paraphrasing it from the theoretical to the practical and concrete. At times an interpretation might be in response to the sharing of very personal details of a mother's life, while at other times, it might come directly from the videotape.

### Universalizing and Normalizing

We frequently observe that the mothers think their anxiety or upset feelings are unique. In some cases, a mother's feelings are complicated by her specific life challenges, in addition to the double tragedy of being pregnant and widowed on September 11, 2001. In the feedback sessions, we frequently employ the technique of "universalizing," or "generalizing" in order to decrease the personalization of her feelings. Generalizing has the effect of normalizing her feelings as she comes to see that she is not the only one in her situation; that what she and her children are going through is similar for others in our Project.

### Consolidating Gains

In the last 15 minutes of a feedback session, one of us will ask the mother a simple question: "What are you taking home with you today?" This open-ended query invites the mother to package for herself the highlights of the session. Over the years we have been consistently impressed with how the mothers have been able to recall salient issues that were covered during the present session, or in a past session, even when more than a year may have passed. In taking the time to sum up, we can also assess the mother's state as she leaves and whether a follow-up intervention will be needed. At this time, when indicated, we discuss the possibility of a referral for additional help. Many mothers spontaneously write down a few notes. We encourage mothers to e-mail or call us with any residual thoughts or feelings they have following our two-hour in-depth session. Many have taken the time to e-mail us feedback on their reactions to the session and on plans to follow through with our suggestions.

### Relationships Among the Therapists Serve as a Model

In working with three or more therapists in this model, each of us brings his/her unique style of working, as well as different areas of expertise. Within our collaborative process, we present a model of repair as we react to the mothers and adjust to one another from moment-to-moment. We take turns and we often defer to one another. At times one of us may give an alternate interpretation in juxtaposition to another's comment. As the mother sees each of us letting someone else take the lead, she has a model that may facilitate her own ability to follow her child's lead – a key theme of the feedback sessions. She sees the deep respect and appreciation that we have for one another. In parallel, she learns that her child can have his/her own mind and thoughts, as she observes what happens when the therapists do not see things the same way, and may even disagree. Yet inevitably, we find a way to integrate our differences into a coherent frame.

## SUMMARY

In light of what was known about the importance of the interactions between mothers and young children, after September 11, 2001, we needed to find a method of helping the group of traumatized widowed mothers to integrate their grief and mourning while also attending to their children. Time was of the essence. We gradually developed our model of brief therapy using the Multiple Therapist Model in feedback sessions. This method has added a depth, focus, and momentum that would ordinarily be absent in a traditional individual treatment. Moreover, it enabled us to provide an intervention with approximately 40 families, with approximately 80 children, seeing them only once or at best twice a year. As Dr. Beebe and I observed in an earlier mother-infant treatment using the method of video feedback, the interactive organization of a mother and child can shift at the behavioral level, even before the mother is able to reorganize her inner representations of herself as a mother in relation to her child (Cohen & Beebe, 2002).

Dr. Beebe explains, "The success of the video method depends on the therapist [team]'s sensitive capacity to 'hold' the mother: to follow her lead and be her advocate; to sense the moment to suggest the video and how long to watch it; to maintain a collaborative rather than didactic stance; and to stay with the parent as the video is shown, alert to any signs of parental distress, particularly shame or feeling criticized, using these empathically to deepen our understanding of the parent's experience of the infant, and of her own inner world" (Beebe, 2003, p. 45). In practice, our multiple therapist approach has enabled us to be extremely sensitive to the vulnerability of the mothers in our Project because we are able to check each other as the sessions unfold.

The multiple-therapist model has offered the mothers a chance to observe a group of professionals working together, looking at her situation through different lenses, yet all focused on the well-being of herself and her children. When asked about her experience of working with a team of therapists at the same time, one mother said, "While you all voice differences of opinion, at the same time you reaffirm each other's analysis and interpretations," and this felt reassuring to her. Through this group process we have addressed the mothers' grief, anxiety, depression, anger, and disappointment. We have given voice to what was on the child's mind and on the mothers' mind. We have attempted to help the mothers to help their children find a way to represent the lost father. We have linked the present to the past, unlocking "ghosts in the nursery" for many, as we have underscored various repetitions in the mothers' lives. While sharing empathic responses, we have also considered the effect of intergenerational transmission of trauma (Fraiberg, 1975).

Working collaboratively in this way has culminated in an innovative, rich and powerful experience, not only for our mothers but also for ourselves. This method has enabled us to think about the mother's experiences when they have at times seemed to be unthinkable. It has helped us to bear the grief, knowing that we can share our own intense reactions with our co-therapists. We have been able to reach mothers emotionally when they might otherwise have been too frozen or dissociated to participate. Our method has helped us to assess the impact of the session on the mother from multiple points of view. And finally, it has helped us to have the courage and determination to pursue this searing, difficult, yet immensely gratifying work, knowing that we have the support of the other members of the team.

## BIBLIOGRAPHY

Beebe, B. (2003). Brief mother-infant treatment using psychoanalytically informed video microanalysis. *Infant Mental Health Journal, 24*(1), 24–52.

Beebe, B. (2005). Mother-infant research informs mother-infant treatment. *Psychoanalytic Study of the Child, 60*, 7–46.

Cohen, P. M., & Beebe, B. (2002). Video feedback with a depressed mother and her infant: A collaborative individual psychoanalytic and mother-infant treatment. *Journal of Infant, Child, and Adolescent Psychotherapy, 2*(3), 1–55.

Fraiberg, S. (1975). Ghosts in the nursery: A psychoanalytic approach to the problems of impaired mother-infant relationships. *Journal of the American Academy of Child Psychiatry, 14*(3), 387.

Reck, C., Hunt, A., Fuchs, T., Weiss, R., Noon, A., Moehler, E., . . . Mundt, C. (2004). Interactive regulation of affect in postpartum depressed mothers and their infants: An overview. *Psychopathology, 37*, 272–280.

Stern, D. (1995). *The motherhood constellation: A unified view of parent-infant psychotherapy*. New York, NY: Basic Books.

# MOTHER-CHILD TREATMENT WITH A TEAM APPROACH

*In this section we present two child treatment cases in which Anni Bergman was the therapist. In the first case, Dr. Andrea Remez was the mother's therapist in an individual treatment. Dr. Remez also made the referral of this mother and child to our Project. Both children in these two cases were treated in individual and tri-partite sessions with Dr. Bergman, as well as in videotaped consultations and feedback sessions with the team. Both cases were different from the original frame of the Project because no parent was lost; instead, both were traumatized families who lived at the site of the World Trade Center. However, in each family, the child we treated had been very young at the time of the World Trade Center attacks. In the first family, the child was a fetus in the seventh month of pregnancy; in the second family, the child was a three-month-old infant. We considered these two families to be just as central to the Project as all the other families where the father was lost. In addition, these were the only families who sought an intensive treatment with us for the child at an early age. This work illustrates a highly unusual integration of a psychoanalytic approach to child treatment with ongoing video consultations from the team. In the first case, it illustrates an unusual collaboration between the mother's individual therapist and the Project team.*

# The Team Approach to the Treatment of a Traumatized Mother and Child: Christina and Bobby

Anni Bergman, Ph.D.
Andrea Remez, Ph.D.

This article describes the treatment of a child in the context of the Project for Mothers, Infants, and Young Children of September 11, 2001. The child's symptom was biting himself when distressed or angry and occasionally biting his parents. His mother had been pregnant during the trauma of September 11, 2001, and lived across the street from the World Trade Center. When the catastrophe occurred she ran out of the house feeling that she had to save her life as well as the life of the baby she was carrying. After the mother was in therapy with Dr. Remez, Dr. Beebe was consulted and referred the mother and child for treatment with Dr. Bergman. Joint play sessions with Christina and Bobby were used as the main therapeutic technique, along with video consultations from the Project team. The mother continued her individual treatment with Dr. Remez. The therapy succeeded in resolving the child's acute symptom and also contributed to the mother's ability to increase her understanding of her child and to become more emotionally available to him.

This article describes a unique approach to the treatment of trauma involving a mother and child. The defining features of this model are the use of a team of therapists who regularly meet and talk among themselves, and with the parent periodically; and the use of the following therapeutic modalities: individual adult psychotherapy for the mother, individual child psychotherapy, tripartite therapy with mother and child, individual meetings between the therapist and the mother, video assessments of mother-child communication, and video feedback consultations for the mother (and father) with the team of therapists.

On September 11, 2001, Christina, seven months pregnant and living across from the World Trade Center, was forced to leave her apartment and run for her life. Christina's husband, John, had already left for work and was out of contact for several hours. Their son, Bobby, was born two months later while they were living in a temporary residence. They were unable to return to their home for six months.

## INDIVIDUAL ADULT PSYCHOTHERAPY WITH DR. REMEZ

Christina entered therapy with Dr. Andrea Remez 18 months after the September 11, 2001, trauma. She rarely mentioned the disaster as a significant event in her life. She was referred by her physician who felt that psychotherapy would help lower stress levels that were aggravating a number of Christina's physical conditions. She suffered from chronic migraines, gynecological and gastrointestinal problems, and an autoimmune condition that created painful skin lesions all over her body and caused significant hair loss.

The identified source of stress for Christina was her extremely difficult relationship with her mother. Although it would take several years to fully appreciate the extent of Christina's mother's problems, it was apparent early in Christina's individual treatment that this relationship was a cause of considerable anguish.

This very attractive woman seemed quite depressed to Dr. Remez. Her voice and facial affect had a dampened quality and her eyes looked lifeless. Gradual progress was made identifying the important variables in Christina's relationship with her mother. She was slow to reveal the extent of the relational trauma she experienced as a child. What became clear in the early stages of therapy was that Christina's mother was extremely reactive to any attempt by Christina to live her own autonomous existence.

Opening up in therapy was not easy for Christina. She had little experience being with an attuned and responsive partner, and she had considerable difficulty getting in touch with and expressing her feelings. Christina needed to learn to trust the therapist and the therapeutic process. She had always kept her feelings of distress hidden from others. The somatic channel was the only means she permitted herself to show distress. It took several years for Christina to fully acknowledge that this was the case.

## PLAY AND PARENT-CHILD THERAPY WITH DR. BERGMAN

In 2003, after almost a year of therapy with Dr. Remez, Christina's son Bobby, then about one and a half years old, developed an alarming symptom. He frequently bit himself when he was distressed and angry, and he occasionally bit Christina and his father, John. This was the first time Christina viewed her relationship with her child as problematic. Bobby's pediatrician suggested behavioral techniques for the parents to use that were aimed at diminishing the child's negative symptom. However, Dr. Remez thought that these techniques would in no way address the mutual regulatory system of the family and that Christina and Bobby would benefit from seeing a therapist together. It was at this point that Dr. Beatrice Beebe was consulted. When she learned of Christina's trauma on September 11, 2001, and that Christina ran for her life when she was seven months pregnant, Dr. Beebe invited Christina to join the World Trade Center Mothers and Young Children Project. Dr. Anni Bergman, a member of Dr. Beebe's team, agreed to see Christina and Bobby for weekly individual and tri-partite mother-child therapy.

## VIDEO CONSULTATIONS AND FEED BACK SESSIONS WITH DR. BEEBE AND THE PROJECT TEAM

At the same time that Dr. Anni Bergman began seeing Christina and Bobby in therapy, they were also invited to Dr. Beebe's lab for the video consultation offered to all mothers in the Project. Christina and Bobby were videotaped playing together, and Bobby was also videotaped separately while playing with psychologists on the team. A similar filming assessment occurred at regular six-month intervals over the next five years. In the week following the filming session, Christina and Dr. Remez, as well as Dr. Bergman, would attend video feedback sessions led by Beebe along with team therapists. These regular six-month visits to the lab, together with the feedback sessions, played an integral part in the therapeutic process. Reviewing videotapes with the team provided detailed information as to how Christina and Bobby were relating to one another. Christina learned a great deal by seeing the relationship from this new perspective and by getting feedback from several of the therapists involved in the Project. Then, in her individual therapy sessions, she continued to process what she had learned with Dr. Remez. This treatment will be discussed in more detail below.

The adult treatment by Dr. Remez of Christina went through a radical transformation when Dr. Beebe, her team, and Dr. Bergman became involved. The treatment received an immediate transfusion of care and expertise. This newly energized individual therapy with Dr. Remez infused hope into the process. This mother and child received a complex degree of coordinated attention rarely administered on an outpatient basis. The additional support helped to override Christina's wariness. With Dr. Remez, Christina exhibited a greater readiness to explore and reorganize her internal world and her interactions with others. Bobby's biting of himself had become the distress call Christina herself was unable to make. The immediate response from her new team of therapists became a powerful motivator for Christina to focus on her own healing. Also, Dr. Remez felt supported, knowing that there were other therapists involved in this case.

The fact that Dr. Remez brought others into the therapeutic system allowed Christina to experience Dr. Remez outside the transference,and to begin to trust her. Her alliance with Dr. Remez became solidified and continued to grow in strength. Christina was able to tell Dr. Remez her story of the day of September 11, 2001, in more vivid detail. She was beginning to believe that others were genuinely interested in hearing about what had happened to her. This interest helped her find the courage to do the difficult work of formulating her experience and bringing it to life.

Christina told the following story. She lived very near the World Trade Center with her husband, John. She was seven months pregnant when the towers were struck. She was unable to reach her husband, who had already left for work. Not being able to reach him made Christina feel frantic and utterly terrified. She remembered the disturbing and unrelenting sounds of the sirens. She ran with neighbors out of the building but then was told by police that it was not safe to be on the street. She had to wait a long time until it was announced that it was safe. A man offered to carry her, but Christina refused his help and ran all the way to Canal Street.

Christina and her husband were not allowed to return to their apartment for several months. All the clothes and equipment purchased for the new baby were destroyed by the debris residue and had to be discarded. At first they stayed with friends and then moved to a furnished apartment, where they lived until it was safe to return to their home. Their temporary residence did not feel like home and was uncomfortable. Bobby was born two months after the towers fell, after a long and difficult delivery. Christina found it difficult to soothe her infant, not realizing that she herself felt desolate, bereft, and traumatized. The only time she felt at peace was when she walked the cold winter streets with Bobby very late at night, trying to quiet him.

When they returned to their own apartment near Ground Zero, difficulties continued with Bobby, who often contracted respiratory infections that eventually developed into asthma. There were also feeding issues that caused Christina much concern. Bobby seemed quite frail. Christina felt lonely and afraid and spent a great deal of time with her parents, hoping for containment and nurturance, which were unfortunately in short supply.

Christina was so determined to be a confident, attentive, adoring, and happy mother that she was reluctant to acknowledge that her relationship with Bobby was in crisis and that this crisis began before he was born. She presented a façade of normalcy for her son and husband and hid from herself and others any feelings or evidence that betrayed that façade. The façade began crumbling when Bobby's self-biting symptom emerged. It was a symptom so severe that she had to reexamine her life in relation to her own traumatic experience on September 11, 2001, and in relation to her own traumatic childhood.

Christina described being born as a "replacement child" for a sister who died at birth. She was often told that she was a "miracle child." She was told that she was the only reason her mother had for being alive. From the beginning, Christina's main purpose in life was to heal her grieving mother. Christina felt subordinated to her mother's needs and preoccupations. She felt she was never seen for herself but rather for the role she played in taking care of her mother.

Christina was born prematurely. Interestingly, Christina's birth trauma occurred at approximately the same gestational time as the World Trade Center disaster occurred in her own pregnancy with Bobby. She was born six weeks early, weighing less than four pounds, which necessitated a stay in intensive care. Her mother informed Christina quite recently that she did not visit Christina in the hospital. This information confirmed in Christina's mind that her feelings of abandonment extended back to the very beginning of her life. Christina remembers that whenever she went to her mother feeling vulnerable, her mother would tell her she was crazy and laugh.

Christina struggled her whole life to achieve greater independence from her mother. She moved across country after college in an effort to feel free of her mother's constant hovering. She was a great deal happier when living far away from home. Her mother, however, developed a quasi-delusional anxiety about Christina falling ill with a terminal disease. Christina claims that her mother's anxiety was so acute she felt literally stalked by her mother's constant calling. Christina eventually returned to New York, changed careers, and got married. Her investment in her work, which she loved, and her new marriage afforded her a hard-won independence from her mother. The traumatic events of September 11, 2001, and the birth of Bobby undermined Christina's newfound independence. Much of Bobby's babyhood was spent at his grandparents' suburban home, where Christina now found refuge away from the city and frightening memories. With Dr. Remez, Christina gradually began to acknowledge that the events of September 11, 2001, and the disruptions they caused in her life shook her confidence to the very core. She had expected that after delivering the baby, she, her husband and her baby would be safe and happy in their own home to begin their life as a family, independent from her family of origin. Instead she found herself "homeless," walking the late-night streets of Manhattan with her difficult-to-soothe baby. She had experienced a profound failure in her ability to adequately protect her unborn child, despite her best efforts and intentions. Her expectation that she would be able to protect her baby and herself from the isolation and unhappiness of her own childhood was smashed. This failure evoked a great deal of shame, which she tried to conceal with a normalized façade.

Before Christina entered therapy with Dr. Remez, she had not felt safe enough to acknowledge to herself or anyone else her fear of annihilation and anxiety over her adequacy as a mother. Memories of terror and feelings of desolation remained unformulated and unexpressed. The risk was too great to her already fragile state of mind to acknowledge that her traumatic experience on September 11, 2001, had opened a Pandora's Box. This left her dissociated from her feelings and unable to communicate openly. This dissociation and the subsequent loss of agency left her feeling barely functional. She went through the motions, presenting herself as if she felt adequate. She somatized her distress, which likely contributed to chronic migraines, gynecological and gastrointestinal problems, and an autoimmune condition, which led to her referral by her physician to psychotherapy. She fell back into an enmeshed relationship with her parents. Despite her valiant attempts to protect her child from her own distress, Bobby demonstrated that he felt his mother was not fully present and engaged, and he sounded the alarm.

When Dr. Anni Bergman first saw Bobby in 2003, she had little knowledge of the family's history. All she knew was that the mother ran for her life on September 11, late in her pregnancy, and that the now two-year-old boy had a self-biting symptom. Brought to this first session by both parents, Bobby was a beautiful and somewhat fragile looking two-year-old with big brown eyes. He looked more like an older child in a small body than a toddler. He had great difficulty relating to or responding to Dr. Bergman or his surroundings. He made minimal eye contact and spoke very little. He was not able to focus on any of the toys in the room. Bobby would not turn to either parent for play, communication, or help. Although it was a cold winter day, Bobby suddenly decided that he wanted to go outside. As he attempted to open the door to the outside, his parents seemed terrified, yet looked at one another knowingly, saying that if they stopped him, he would surely bite himself. The father discovered a little playhouse with a clock on top and with great relief he said, "Bobby loves clocks, and he will love this." He was able to engage Bobby's attention and Bobby finally agreed to stay indoors. Dr. Bergman wondered about the significance of the clock. Perhaps it represented the longed-for qualities of reliability and predictability that Bobby may have felt he was missing.

Not long after the initial session, Dr. Bergman participated in the dyad's first video consultation and a subsequent video feedback session with Christina and Dr. Remez and members of the Project's therapist team. Dr. Bergman then learned about Christina's traumatic relational history with her mother and the details of her experience with Bobby on September 11, 2001. At this feedback session, as well as the ones to come, efforts were made by the team to understand the present-day trauma and how it related to Christina's childhood trauma.

Dr. Bergman observed during the video consultation that this mother and child were in a highly dysregulated state: both were easily aroused, fearful, and distracted. At the same time, both seemed vigilant to the moves of the other. It was difficult for Christina to give Bobby space and to allow him to lead the play. There was an intrusive quality driven by anxiety in her interactions with him. Her affect seemed quite flattened. It was also evident how much the mother was trying to appear normal, to give a good impression. It was heartening to see that when Bobby interacted with members of the team, and was allowed to lead the play, he responded positively, although with slightly dampened affect, and his vigilance and anxiety appeared significantly reduced.

Although Christina had difficulty giving Bobby freedom to play at his own developmental level and at his own pace, she also did not intervene when it would be appropriate to do so. The mother described, for example, how at night, when she and her husband were asleep, Bobby would get up and wander around the house. Christina and John did not know how to effectively deal with this behavior. Bobby had a very hard time accepting any limits, and his parents had a hard time setting and enforcing limits. Bobby's nighttime behavior was indicative of his feeling insufficiently held. His mother often misread his signals for help and was unable to provide firm and consistent holding. We understood Bobby's biting himself as an expression of his frustration and anger at his mother's inability to really know his state of mind.

A few weeks after Bobby's first therapy session, Christina asked to speak with Dr. Bergman privately. She recounted a story of an accident that she had with Bobby when he was four months old. Christina had traveled uptown by subway, with Bobby in his stroller, and they both fell down a flight of stairs. They were picked up by an ambulance, separated, and taken to a hospital, where they had to stay for several hours. They were unable to make contact with John for quite some time. Eventually contact was made and John came to the hospital. Bobby and Christina were not physically injured and were discharged from the hospital. Remarkably, this incident echoed the experiences of Christina, Bobby, and John on September 11, 2001. Christina felt that the story of this accident was important, but she did not want to tell it in Bobby's presence.

Thus, only six months after the trauma of September 11, 2001, Christina and Bobby had once again gone through a terrifying event together, and John was, at first, nowhere to be found. It is likely that by sharing this story Christina felt less burdened by feelings of shame and fear that she was a danger to her child. That Dr. Bergman was able to listen and respond to this story, compassionately and without judgment, was important to Christina. The airing of this story and Dr. Bergman's response was a tremendous relief. Something shifted at this point. Christina became less anxious, and her relationship with Bobby gradually began to be less anxiety-laden.

Bobby's acute symptom of biting himself subsided soon after his mother managed to recall and talk about this second terrifying event that had occurred when he was four months old. His language development improved, as did his ability to play. It now felt safer for Bobby and his mother to be together. It is possible that Dr. Bergman's sensitive listening helped Christina begin the process of transforming her feelings of failure and inadequacy into a more reality-based sense of accomplishment. She had guided her own and Bobby's survival on September 11, 2001, as well as six months later after their fall down the subway steps. It is likely that the Project team's involvement was important in this shift as well. The Project therapist team at the feedback sessions emphasized Christina's successful coping throughout Bobby's infancy. Long-held notions of failure and inadequacy were beginning to lose their grip on Christina's image of herself.

Although this therapeutic breakthrough promoted Bobby's developmental growth, and mother and child's ability to play together, some symptoms of disruption persisted in Bobby's behavior. He would quite suddenly, and often without apparent provocation, experience a need to leave whatever he was doing and ask to go home. When he did not get his way, he would demand to leave the session. Perhaps this was his way of managing heightening levels of anxiety. He was still quite tentative about turning to his mother or to Dr. Bergman for help.

As Christina became less anxious, she expressed genuine pleasure in Bobby's extraordinary intelligence, his increasing ability to play, and his language development. In spite of these gains, there remained a feeling of instability about them, a sense that at any moment there might be a disruption. Bobby was easily distracted and was especially very sensitive to noise. His mother reported that at home he was still difficult to control, throwing things, even very big things, when angry. Christina always seemed very concerned about how to control, or to help him control, these feelings and behaviors. She was reluctant to see the connection between Bobby's dysregulation and his relationship with her because she was still carrying a burden of guilt and failure dating back to September 11, 2001.

Christina and Bobby's therapy sessions with Dr. Bergman were often cancelled because of Christina's illnesses and doctor visits. In spite of her health challenges and emotional stress with Bobby, Christina and John decided to try to have more children. In 2004, after several months of arduous fertility treatments, Christina became pregnant again. The pregnancy was extremely high risk, marked by numerous hospitalizations and bed rest at home. Through all of this, she insisted that Bobby was doing fine. She reported that during her hospital stays, Bobby communicated with her on the telephone and was well taken care of by relatives and grandparents. Dr. Bergman noted Christina's difficulty acknowledging any distress that her absence might have caused Bobby or herself.

The therapy with Dr. Bergman provided both mother and child a sense of continuity in the face of repeated threats of disruption. It served as an ongoing source of repair and helped to diminish the effect of the disruptions. In the sessions with Dr. Bergman, when Christina spoke of her pregnancy, Bobby acted out angry feelings in his play. Christina came to realize with Dr. Bergman's help that the things she said and did influenced Bobby's mood and play. Christina began to see how reactive they were to each other — how sensitive she was to him and he to her. Although she might at times disregard him (out of her fear of overwhelming him, and perhaps out of a fear of being overwhelmed herself by their relationship) or overdirect him, she was coming to realize that no matter what she did, it affected her child profoundly.

The therapy with Dr. Bergman also allowed Christina to feel safe with the understanding that she and Bobby were linked to one another, and that neither would, nor could, destroy the other. As this understanding deepened in Christina, Bobby's play consistently enacted the theme of rupture and repair. Given how exquisitely sensitive he was to his mother's state of mind, Bobby could recognize when his mother was able to realize that their bond to one another was a safe one. He became visibly more relaxed in his movements and in his facial affect.

With this lessening of anxiety in Christina's and Bobby's relationship, it was now possible to work more deeply in Bobby's s therapy. During a particularly significant session, Bobby played with a piggy that he depicted as quite naughty. Dr. Bergman spoke for the piggy, saying, "Piggy gets upset when things happen that piggy doesn't like, and piggy gets very angry. It isn't piggy's fault." Mother sat back and listened. Bobby calmed down considerably during this play. They both left in a happy mood. With the help of Dr. Bergman, Bobby had been able to connect with his own anger without shame, allowing him to reorganize and experience a sense of calm and control.

After the birth of the new baby, Bobby underwent a severe regression. Christina, quite concerned, asked Dr. Bergman to make a home visit. Bobby would not allow Dr. Bergman to see the baby. Christina invited Dr. Bergman to come to the home, but just for him, and only in his room. This visit was enormously helpful. Christina was demonstrating her trust in the therapy process. Dr. Bergman and Bobby played alone in his room during the whole visit. During this play, Bobby was listless and did not act his age. He was unable to show interest in his usual activities. Bobby finally went to the bookshelf and pulled out a book that was about an animal mother and baby. He sat very close, cuddled on Dr. Bergman's lap, and slowly looked at the book, page by page. He was helped to remember how he had once been a baby with his mother. He had turned to Dr. Bergman for help, and he trusted the relationship to contain and soothe him. He had clearly learned to use his therapist as someone who could genuinely understand him and share his feelings. This empathy could be enacted without explicitly interpreting his wishes to be a baby once again or his jealousy of his new sister. After reading the book, he jumped up. He seemed himself again.

It is interesting that these rather profound changes in Bobby could happen so quickly and without many words. Much can be accomplished with relatively little verbal input. The therapy functioned in the service of repairing the relationship between mother and child, and also tapping into the intrinsic reparative capacity that exists in all of us. This kind of child and mother-child treatment is different from a long-term individual child therapy, where the parent can often be very threatened by the therapist's relationship to the child.

Bobby and Christina were also responsive to the Project's therapeutic team approach. In addition to Christina's individual therapy with Dr. Remez, and Christina's and Bobby's mother-child work with Dr. Bergman, there was also a great deal of support and intervention from members of the Project's therapist team. Christina learned, through watching videotapes of her play with Bobby and discussing them with team members, how to be more receptive to some of Bobby's signals, especially his hypersensitivity to noise. She was helped to relax and to pause, in other words, to regulate her hyper-vigilance. Bobby's symptom of biting himself may have been his only recourse to the hyper-arousal he experienced in response to his mother's vigilance, her anxiety, and her fear that she could not protect him. This fear was based not only on her traumatic experience of September 11, 2001, but also in part on her own traumatic childhood where she was not protected. In the Project team video consultations and feedback sessions, Christina was helped to see the ways that she might have heightened Bobby's anxiety, which expressed itself in his hypersensitivity and his aggressive outbursts. She was helped to slow down and make more room for Bobby. The gains made in therapy proved to be quite enduring. Bobby has continued to grow and thrive in school and at home.

Christina's strategy of hiding her feelings from herself and others and presenting a normalized, cheerful, and confident façade grew out of an attempt to maintain some semblance of self-organization in her relationship with her mother. This strategy proved to be ineffective when applied to other relationships. The challenge she faced during this critical time with her son was to let others in and be able to know about and share her vulnerability. The video consultations and feedback sessions with Dr. Beebe and the Project team encouraged Christina to confront this core conflict involving communicating her distress openly. She noticed how unsafe and exposed she felt. She realized that she felt torn between trying to present herself in the best possible light and being open about her distress in order to receive help. Dr. Remez, her individual therapist, became an ally in this process. Dr. Remez helped her to prepare emotionally for the videotapings, and she accompanied Christina to the feedback sessions. Dr. Remez often explained to the Project team Christina's dilemma about being emotionally open and why it felt so unsafe. Christina was moved by the Project team's empathic response to information about Christina's difficult childhood that Dr. Remez disclosed in the feedback sessions. A profound process of internal reorganization was facilitated for Christina's. This feature of the treatment model is particularly mutative and unique.

Christina's reached a critical turning point after her fourth feedback session in 2007. Christina and Bobby went to a videotaping session at Dr. Beebe's lab, although there were multiple stressors at the time. Christina's should have canceled this session. She was suffering from a terrible migraine and was extremely worried about her father who had had a mild heart attack the day before. Bobby, who was most likely sensing his mother's anxious state, became sick in the car on the way to the lab. When Christina arrived, she did not divulge any of these details to the therapist team. Her extreme level of anxiety triggered in her a dissociated state. Later, upon reflection, she realized that she had feared the team would have felt let down and angry with her if she had cancelled. The function of her silence was to ward off imagined aggressive retaliation from the Project team. She also became aware of how unsafe she felt to be seen in such a distressed state. She went through the filming session feeling numb. Bobby, who was typically quite aware of his mother's feeling states and physical condition, felt very concerned about her. This proved to be a distraction for him. His interactions with members of the team were noticeably dampened. Christina left the filming session feeling empty and unsupported.

When Christina discussed the filming session with Dr. Remez, the question was explored as to why she did not share how she was feeling with Dr. Beebe and the team. Different strategies for achieving safety were discussed. Christina was beginning to recognize that sometimes she might feel safer by actually letting people know how she felt, and that this could feel empowering. It became clear to Christina that by using the same strategy she had used with her mother she was in fact contributing to her own lack of safety in this different context. She was beginning to unlink others (such as the team therapists) from her mother, and to consider a more flexible way of determining when it was safe to feel and show vulnerability, and when it was not.

A critical piece of Christina's therapy involved facilitating emotional separation from her mother and developing an authentic self-experience as an autonomous person. Christina experienced feelings of anger and loss over all the years spent accommodating a frightening and infantile parent. Christina became aware of her fears of her mother's retaliation. She had learned to feel her guilt for having wanted a life of joy and pleasure rather than a life of taking care of her mother's insatiable demands. As Christina now became more tolerant and accepting of her own distress, she was able to give Bobby more space to feel and deal with his distress. Her approach to parenting is now more joyful than anxious. She has achieved a more healthy separation not only from her but also from her children. She has gone back to work part-time and is becoming increasingly invested in spending time on her professional career.

As Christina learned to express her feelings and to trust that it is possible to be respected by others and responded to as a separate individual, her physical health improved dramatically. She weaned herself off all medications except for occasional pain medication for her less frequent migraines. She started to look healthier, vibrant, and beautiful. Her eyes, formerly dull and lifeless, became bright and shining. Christina regularly reported feeling a joyful connection to her husband and children. Her understanding of where she had been and what she had gone through stood in stark relief to her present circumstances. Christina had no illusions about the extent of her mother's difficulties. She said, "I learned to love my life, even though I had such a difficult mother." She also understood how closed off she had been from others. She took responsibility for her own communication difficulties. She said, "I played a part in not being easy to read."

Christina approached the most recent filming and feedback session with an entirely different attitude. She experienced the therapist team as supportive. She felt safe and trusting. She, along with others on the team, identified strengths, problem areas, and future challenges. When Christina and Dr. Remez spoke about the feedback session afterwards, Christina described it as a personal triumph for her, an important goal achieved. She no longer feared that she would be seen as crazy if she revealed her concerns. She expressed a genuine desire to continue her work within the Project and a feeling of heartfelt gratitude for the help she felt has been given.

Christina and Bobby demonstrate how the wellbeing of a mother and child was dramatically improved by the intervention of a coordinated and diversely skilled therapeutic team. Each aspect of the treatment, and the collaboration and communication among the therapists and with the mother, served as an important facilitator of therapeutic change in response to the trauma of September 11, 2001.

# The Team Approach to the Treatment of a Traumatized Mother and Child: Lydia and Ryan

Anni Bergman, Ph.D.

With sections by
K. Mark Sossin, Ph.D.
Suzi Tortora, Ed.D., BC–DMT, CMA
Lydia (Ryan's mother)
Phyllis Cohen, Ph.D.
Beatrice Beebe, Ph.D.

This article describes the tri-partite treatment of a mother and child, Lydia and Ryan, in the context of the Project for Mothers, Infants, and Young Children of September 11, 2001. Lydia and Ryan witnessed the attack on the World Trade Center from their home. Lydia, terrified, tried to protect her baby, who later developed atypical behaviors, which were originally suspected to reflect Pervasive Developmental Disorder. The treatment of the mother-child pair was of equal importance to both Ryan and Lydia, who both developed an important attachment to Dr. Bergman as well as the Project team. Visits to Dr. Beebe's lab became extremely meaningful to both mother and child. The presence of the Project team became a kind of family, providing security, support, and understanding for both mother and child.

## ANNI BERGMAN'S INTRODUCTION TO THE CASE

Ryan was referred to Anni Bergman for consultation by the psychoanalyst of his mother Lydia, when he was 2-and-a-half years old because he had been diagnosed with Pervasive Developmental Disorder (PDD) and had been referred for early intervention.

I (Anni Bergman) spoke to Ryan's parents who told me that they and their two children were living next door to the World Trade Center. On the morning of September 11, 2001, they had been awakened by 3-month-old Ryan, who had himself been awakened by the sound of the first airplane crashing into the World Trade Center building. The family was evacuated from their apartment. They first went to the home of friends where the television was constantly turned on. This was very upsetting to Ryan's parents and their older child, who was 4 years old. They quickly left to stay with the mother's family outside the city. They eventually returned to their home.

Subsequently, I saw Ryan with both parents, and then I began to see Ryan with his mother in joint play sessions once per week. I did not think Ryan had a Pervasive Developmental Disorder. He did not have much language for a child his age, but he had some. He showed no stereotyped or repetitive behavior. What language he had was communicative, but occasionally he would suddenly freeze in fright and demand that we leave the playroom. He was a sweet and friendly child, but at one point in one of the play sessions he unpredictably, without provocation, bit his mother on the breast. She was shocked and so was he. We never really quite understood what had evoked this attack, and it never happened again. He also never forgot it. During subsequent play sessions he often said, "Remember when I bit mommy?" We acknowledged it and tried to understand what had upset him so much.

Ryan also sometimes abruptly terminated our play sessions. In the middle of having a good time, he would decide that it was enough and that he had to go home. Once he made such a decision there was no way to change his mind, deter him, or distract him. It was never quite clear what brought on his need for an abrupt ending, just as it had not been clear what brought on his attack on his mother's breast.

Except for these abrupt endings of sessions and the biting of his mother, there was nothing that seemed abnormal in Ryan's play. He enjoyed songs, simple action games, and some symbolic play. He knew he was his mother's baby. He also went to a play group, which he seemed to like.

Because of the concerns that had been expressed about his diagnosis, I suggested further testing. The tester, Dr. Mark Sossin, agreed with my impression that Ryan did not have a Pervasive Developmental Disorder.

## COMMENTS FROM THE PSYCHOLOGICAL TESTING, BY DR. MARK SOSSIN

At 2 years, 8 months of age, Ryan was seen for a series of consultations. These included efforts to administer the Stanford-Binet-5th edition, the Hawaii Early Learning Profile Strands (HELP), which is a child-friendly curriculum-based developmental assessment, and parent self-report scales, including the Child Behavior Checklist (CBCL) for Ages 1.5–5. Other measures were envisioned, but developmental assessment across cognitive and perceptual-motor dimensions was not found to be valid, as Ryan did not obligingly engage with test materials. Nonetheless, observations of play with me, as well as of mother-child and father-child play in a large-playroom context, were highly informative. At that time, parental attributions described Ryan as a generally curious and engaged child. Mother noted Ryan's inclination toward jealous feelings and a vulnerability to having his feelings hurt. At home the parents experienced Ryan as demonstrating a high level of attention-seeking, and they noticed that Ryan did not seem to change his behavior after correctives. Notably, on the CBCL, there were no significant indicators of either internalizing or externalizing problems.

My observations of Ryan's nonverbal communication patterns found Ryan to show remarkable movement patterns of "freezing" behavior, in which he would hold his body in a nearly inanimate manner. This pattern is dubbed "neutral-bound flow" (involving a loss of elasticity in muscle tension) in one system of movement analysis, the Kestenberg Movement Profile (Kestenberg, Amighi, Loman, Lewis, & Sossin, 1999; Sossin & Birklein, 2006). This pattern underscored the obstacles to joining Ryan in affective play, or being joined by him. In fact, his management of the tension states and changes of his movement patterns were marked by a predilection for "even flow" (frequently holding muscle tension steady in intensity) alongside the neutral quality. When not neutral, he utilized "bound flow" (exercising a co-contraction of various muscles, akin to seeming "tense" rather than "relaxed"), holding such a state for long periods of time. For example, he would fix his gaze upon his mother, holding one hand within another, seeming ever-cautious but curiously attentive, and relatively nonadjusting to others. Sometimes the movements he made were then abrupt and characterized by an asymmetry, wherein one side would be especially disconnected from the mobility on the other side. Ryan was quite vigilant to all new sounds and sights.

During these consultation periods, it was difficult to discern Ryan's affective experience. Both father and mother, although concerned about distinctiveness in his behavioral repertoire, seemed confident that he could engage but was choosing not to do so. In fact, this bore out over the course of the consultations. Although he remained reluctant to engage in play with test materials, and he did not venture far into symbolic/representational play when offered the opportunity, Ryan "played" with glances and faces. He imitated, and he smiled in a characteristic way. His smile involved widening in his lower face, of course, but he would also pull his lips back while pinching them shut, creating an expression that combined his greeting with caution. With me, he especially shortened at his neck and shoulders, seeming on guard, along with the other features mentioned. He preferred "playing" in a manner of exchanging mimicry in gesture and posture with me, clearly appreciating the resonance attained. Ryan seemed to be communicating that he was enjoying the collaborative and synchronized behaviors, but that he was still managing discomfort and pulling back alongside his engagement.

In summary, the consultations found Ryan to demonstrate some insufficiencies in speech articulation, manifested by some substitutions and omissions, and indications that fine-motor coordination might be less developed than expectation. He showed moments of sophisticated thinking, but overall no predictive scores were derived directly from the testing efforts, and fuller and more clarifying testing of developing skills was deferred for a later time. However, his eye-to-eye gaze, his seeming awareness of the feelings of others, his interest in others, his overall curiosity, his manifestation of humor and his response to humor, were all reassuring, as were his communications with his parents.

From my observations, I was impressed with Ryan's capacity to know intention and emotion in another. I was generally reassuring to the parents regarding these skills and suggested that Ryan may not be manifesting the PDD that was suggested by others. I was concerned about his unusual efforts in managing his own affect and engagement, but I saw subjective experiences of stress as central. I supported Anni Bergman's treatment plan, and I foresaw future follow-up consultations. These would soon fold into the Project.

## DR. ANNI BERGMAN: REFERRAL TO DR. BEEBE FOR A CONSULTATION

To augment the psychological evaluation, I (Anni Bergman) suggested a videotaped consultation with Dr. Beatrice Beebe. Our group decided to include Ryan in the WTC Project because he had been 3 months old at the time of the September 11 attacks and seemed to have been affected by the crashing of the planes in the vicinity of his home. He first came to the lab when he was 2 years and 10 months old. During this consultation we observed Ryan with his mother in this new strange lab setting. His reaction to it was extremely interesting. As usual in our model, Ryan was in the waiting room as his mother signed a consent form with Dr. Beebe. Several therapists were available to talk or play with him. Confronted with this group of strangers, Ryan froze. He stood absolutely still without moving and without making a sound for several minutes. But his eyes darted around, vigilant. This "freeze" reaction may have led to what I considered the misdiagnosis of PDD. At the age of 3 months, Ryan had indeed endured his world standing still or falling apart. It is hard to know what he actually experienced as a baby, but his freezing reaction could have been an active repetition of the traumatic events that he had gone through as a young infant.

## DESCRIPTION OF FIRST FILMING LAB EVALUATION IN DR. BEEBE'S LAB, BY DR. SUZI TORTORA

Ryan stands motionless beside his mother in the small split-screen filming chamber. His hands are grasped midline below the belly. Dr. Beebe is setting the pair up in the room, and Ryan watches her without moving. He does not respond to any of Dr. Beebe's overtures, such as, "Would you like the stuffed monkey or bear?" Mother takes the bear, leans over to him and says, "Come on," as she touches his nose with the bear.

Dr. Beebe says, "This is your chair," to Ryan, and then turns to Mother and says, "If he takes the chair, he takes the chair. If he doesn't, don't worry." Ryan continues to stand motionless, with his hands center midline below his waist, watching his mother.

As soon as Dr. Beebe leaves the room, Ryan suddenly takes the chair without speaking. He then asks his mother, "Are we are going home?" His mother explains, "We'll play here for a little while and then we'll go home." Ryan sits motionless while his mother speaks. He then self-soothes as his left hand strokes his body. His bottom lip is pulled in, in an "uh oh" expression. He sits still, absolutely motionless.

Mother asks, "What did you do with the bird?" as she leaves the chair to pick up the toy bird from the floor. Ryan watches mother, motionless. Mother proceeds to try to engage Ryan verbally with the toys. But his response is often, "Why?" Ryan does not seem to know how to play. Or alternatively, he does not seem comfortable enough to play. Mother continues to encourage him. She says, "Hi birdie," and reaches into Ryan's "near-reach" space.

Ryan then asks questions about the room, such as, "Why is the door closed?" Now Ryan has a toy in each hand, and he watches mother intently with his lips compressed in a tight "line mouth" expression, indicating holding in distress.

Ryan points to the toy potty without speaking. Mother readily engages, asking him if a toy doll is going to the potty. He responds, "No," keeping his lips compressed tight in a line mouth expression. He starts to speak but his words are so garbled that Mother cannot understand him. He continues to sit, absolutely motionless, with wide eyes and a compressed lips expression.

## COMMENTS BY DR. SUZI TORTORA

Mother seemed uncomfortable. While she tried very hard to engage her son, she communicated mixed and confusing emotions — at the same time inviting, stern, and upset. Often her brow and lower face did not communicate the same thing. At first Ryan might seem not to be processing what was happening, but then an odd wry smile would emerge that was impish and knowing. We realized that Ryan did not miss anything that happened.

## DR. ANNI BERGMAN CONTINUES HER DESCRIPTION OF THE THERAPY

Recently, I asked Ryan's mother to be my co-author of this article in my attempt to describe his early symptoms and to understand the course of his treatment. She responded by giving me the following description of how, in her mind, the trauma of September 11, 2001, was connected to Ryan's birth and earliest development.

This is what she wrote:

### Description by Ryan's Mother, Lydia

Trauma One: For me it began in the hospital. Shortly after giving birth, the nurse took Ryan from me, just before midnight. I was not reunited with him until a few hours later because there wasn't a bed for me on the maternity floor and there was no one to bring him to me.

Trauma Two: It began with Ryan's first cry after hearing the crashing metal of the first plane going into the World Trade Center. On September 11, Ryan was the first in our family to react. He was napping in a bouncy seat by the window. At the sound of the crash of metal he woke up and cried out. I opened the window, stuck my head out looking south, and saw the glint of what I thought was paper falling from the very blue sky. From the small gathering across the street at the parking lot, I could tell something was going on. I went outside and saw the hole and the fire in the building. I soon heard that it was not an accident but that the plane had "banked" into the tower. I went back inside and asked my husband to take a look. He went outside and then began photographing what became the second plane crash. I was inside with my older son, age 3, denying that anything happened. The radio was on and it said, "The second building has been hit." I said, "No it hasn't," and I switched off the radio. I wanted to have my kids' world be normal. I could not accept this reality of planes attacking buildings blocks away. I was afraid of fire from the burning buildings spreading north. I wanted to leave. We had calls from friends and family coming in. I took a backpack with Similac samples that I had gotten in the mail, and I took diapers. I was afraid that my fear might cause me to not be able to produce milk, but in fact I was dripping. When we walked north with the two strollers, everyone was looking south at the buildings falling. I never looked south when we went outside because I figured that it might be too overwhelming. I wanted my kids not to be freaked out by seeing me freaked out. I thought, if I didn't look at the towers falling down, then perhaps I would be calmer than if I saw the disaster.

I tried to not have the kids watch the events on TV at my friend's house. Her children and my 3-year-old would look out the picture window and yell, "Fire!" Then they would look back to the large screen TV and point "Fire!" I stayed low with Ryan so he couldn't see the TV.

We then moved to a second friend's apartment in the East Village where their lives were carrying on as if everything were normal. I did not feel comfortable with the option of staying with friends. We moved for five days out of the city to Queens to my mother's house. Then we moved back to our apartment near the World Trade Center site just a week later. We stayed with the stench filtering through the windows throughout our loft. I was worried about this in particular for my baby.

I remember reading the *New York Times* as I breast fed, fearfully gaining information on Osama bin Laden. I feel badly now that I did this. I wonder how often I did that. I wonder if I was aware of this as a problem. It is difficult to imagine that I would not have thought it was a problem.

I noticed a few days later that children were back playing in our local park. I contacted the local Environmental Protection Agency in New York. Then with the help of my brother, who is a public health consultant in San Francisco, I arranged to have this local park, Washington Market Park, cleaned. It had opened once the police vehicles moved out, about a week after September 11. It was later vacuumed by men in hazmat suits while the park was shut down for three days.

I went back to work about two weeks after September 11, 2001, weeping as I walked down the street. Ryan was just over 3 months old. I was terrified for at least a year afterwards. I was extremely nervous about another attack on the city, particularly in the heavily guarded Telecom building across the street from where we live.

Ryan was slightly disengaged at times. He met all the markers of development, but there was a space between Ryan and me. Most of the time that space seemed to be part of his personality. But sometimes it was worrisome that he was not bonded fully. His interactions were a tiny bit removed. As he grew older his interactions with children his age highlighted this, but it was always subtle.

We went to Dr. Anni Bergman because we were concerned about Ryan's interactions, or lack of them, with other children in his playgroup. When he was with other children, he preferred to watch, not participate. Going to see Dr. Anni was a huge relief. She was patient with Ryan as he flitted around from toy to toy. He did not completely engage in any one activity for any length of time. He would often pick up a Barney trumpet and think it was funny as we cringed in hearing its repeated, grating, prerecorded music. He always wanted to be the director. We should sit, stand in line, and pay attention, as he moved from planning one activity to another. He would never get his play totally underway, and it would never advance. He would pick up the dolls, then he'd arrange all the cars, then he'd take out the Legos, then he'd put toys in the sandbox. He moved from one set-up to another until it was time to leave. Dr. Anni understood his need to be in control, his love of routine, and we followed his directions over and over, week after week. He was very affectionate and clearly delighted to be there, especially on his own terms. Dr. Anni was comfortable and accepting of Ryan. She seemed not to be concerned about his development. It helped us to relax and lighten up about his differences.

## PROGRESS AS SEEN THROUGH DESCRIPTIONS OF FILMING LAB EVALUATIONS – DR. MARK SOSSIN

To illustrate the progress that Ryan has made, Mark Sossin describes Ryan and his mother as they were in the early lab filming sessions, as compared to a recent one in spring 2011, as Ryan is approaching 10 years old.

When Ryan was first seen in the lab at age 3, he held his body stiffly, returning to periods of inertness that impeded the flow of play, communication and engagement. He was like this with his mother as well as the therapists. He was highly vigilant to new sounds and sights. With his mother, Ryan held his body even and still, and yet he contributed to the ongoing engagement with his characteristic smile that conveyed that he was enjoying her company. But simultaneously he conveyed a constriction and withdrawal. He was protective of himself and not fully participatory. Yet his mother was patient with him and responsive to his many "why?" questions.

Our concerns during early lab visits included not only Ryan's proclivity to constrict in expressivity but also in symbolic/representational play. Moreover, the process of play with his mother seemed especially marked by her signals of distress, her mixed emotional expressiveness, such as smiling and frowning at the same time, and by emotional discordance between them. Their affective changes did not seem to reflect a mutual adjustment to one another.

We saw steady progress over the years of lab visits and feedback consultations. These seemed to parallel Anni Bergman's work with the family. Ryan's parents were very astute and perceptive about him. They increasingly understood how he thought, felt, and processed experiences. They were reflective about how their own subjectivities interfaced with his.

The spring 2011 lab visit shows the continued progress made by Ryan and his mother. In this filmed play session, Ryan and Lydia showed an ease and comfort with each other. Lydia no long showed the mixed expressivity noted earlier. She was in harmony within her own expression of emotions, and this harmony was reflected in their interaction as well.

In this play session, Ryan's eyes were frequently focused down, toward the table. He still smiled with "hollowing," pulling his lips back while pinching them shut, creating an expression that combined his greeting with caution. His nonverbal gestures often had an abrupt/sudden quality to them. However, Ryan no longer showed the overuse of "neutral flow," holding his muscle tension steady in intensity, with a loss of variability and elasticity, which was perhaps the most salient feature of his earlier communication style. He was more available emotionally. Nonetheless, he often mobilized more with one side of his body, while overstabilizing with the other, often "locking" an arm and hand by his side or on his lap. Notably, he did this in the lab context with his mother and with me, even though he nicely engaged with each of us.

It was striking that with Anni Bergman in the filming context, he moved differently, using more whole-body organization and fluidity. Ryan still tended to be on the quiet side with his mother, preferring to trace her hand than to enter into more representational play or story narratives. The dialogue between him and Lydia, however, was characterized by more moments of affective concordance, which were appreciated by each, and served as building blocks for ongoing engagement. Lydia seemed receptive, patient, comfortable, and interested in what Ryan was thinking and feeling. Reciprocally, Ryan was more able to communicate to her what he was thinking and feeling.

## DESCRIPTION OF THE VIDEO FEEDBACK SESSION WITH RYAN'S PARENTS IN THE SPRING OF 2011, BY DRS. PHYLLIS COHEN AND BEATRICE BEEBE

Following the visit to the filming lab described above, Ryan's parents were invited to return for a video feedback session in Dr. Beebe's clinical office the next week. Here are excerpts from this feedback session with Ryan's parents. The session was attended by his mother Lydia, his father, and the therapist team, in this case, Drs. Beatrice Beebe, Anni Bergman, Phyllis Cohen and Mark Sossin.

*Dr. Beebe:* What would you like to talk about? How's it going in the family?

*Dad:* Not easy. Ryan teases his older brother. He is very good at getting into someone else's mind and twisting it. The irritation is constant.

*Dr. Beebe*: Do you have an example?

*Dad:* If you ask him to get something, like "Can you get me that cup?" He'll say, "Why?" Or "No;" or, "You never do that for me;" or, "What if I want a cup?"

*Dr. Beebe:* Why do you think he does that?

*Mom:* He's obstinate.

*Dad*: When Ryan was 3 years old, he would ask, and ask, and ask. It did actually build a knowledge base.

*Everyone laughs.*

*Dr. Bergman:* If you always ask "why," it means there is something else you want to know. He must want to know why he is a little different, why he goes to a different school. He senses he is different.

*Mom:* I don't tell him that he's going to this school because of learning disabilities. I say he's going because he needs to learn in smaller classrooms, in smaller pieces.

*Mom continues:* In school Ryan receives speech language therapy. They are working on his inferences, expressions and empathy, and what he thinks this means. They are also working on his social cues. He has trouble taking the other's perspective.

*Dr. Sossin:* If he does not easily see the other child's role, he answers the question in terms of what he himself sees, as opposed to taking the other child's perspective.

*Mom:* Ryan was recently reevaluated by the same person who tested him five years ago. We were in the waiting room, but it was cold, so we were able to sit in the room while Ryan was being evaluated. She considered that he may have a nonverbal learning disability or Asperger's, though she did not give that diagnosis.

*Dr. Beebe*: He does seem to have some Theory of Mind problems, but thankfully, he is getting therapy for this.

*Dad:* But he has a sense of humor. After the therapy, Ryan walks around saying, "The inferences of this could be . . .!"

*Dr. Sossin*: You've touched on a main issue. How do we turn this into an advantage? Are his friendships growing?

*Dad:* Yes. He does have friends, and we're happy about that. So, how do you think we're doing?

*Dr.Beebe*: Good. Though there are still some glitches with how he relates.

*Dad:* How does this relate to 9/11?

*Mom:* I was extremely traumatized and it affected him.

*Dr. Sossin:* I'm impressed with how comfortable you are with him now.

*Mom:* Sometimes it seems good. At other times it's hard. At the end of the summer, when school begins, it's around the same time as 9/11, so it gets hard.

*Dr. Beebe [to Dr. Bergman*]: What do you think Ryan has done with you, his Mom, and the team?

*Dr. Bergman*: He knows the group of therapists well. I've done little work with interpretation. I've been with him rather than question him about things.

*Dr. Beebe*: He's made an extraordinary attachment to Anni. This is because Mom gave him the space for this to happen

*Dr. Bergman*: I join him just where he is.

*Mom [to Dr. Bergman*]: You're the good mother – not a pushy mother.
[*This mother knows we respect her, admire her mothering, and see great progress in the dyad. We let this comment pass*].

*Dr. Cohen:* Ryan's privileged to be with Anni in therapy. Being with someone who lets him be who he is.

*Dr. Bergman:* Even during the "frozen part," underneath he observes everything.

*Mom:* He's o.k. if you give him enough time with someone who doesn't request him to do something. Being with Anni, she is totally sympathetic. He gets to set the stage, do what he wants. Most times they do nothing. He starts playing school but it never really happens. His play with Anni is comforting. I'm the one who's always telling him: "Do your math," "do your homework."

*Dr. Cohen*: Anni has the luxury of doing "nothing" with him. She doesn't have to get him to do his homework.

*Dr. Sossin*: addressing Mom, What do you do together?

Mom: I don't know. He likes to play by himself.

*Dr.Beebe* to Dad: How do you see Ryan's path?

*Dad:* Six years ago, I was so worried. I can't imagine what life would have been like if he hadn't been seeing Anni. One hour a week pulled out to play – like a time out in a good way. He derives a sense of calm from this. He is very scheduled at other times.

*Dr. Beebe:* Scheduling is not really the issue. The issue is what happened on 9/11 and how Ryan relates. The experience of 9/11 is about control and terror. Ryan is still involved with these issues, like when he is frozen.

*Dad*: I bat the baseball with him. He likes it. He doesn't freeze anymore, even with the fastball. There is less freezing, and he's less fixated.

*Dr. Beebe* to Dr. Sossin: What do you think he got and did not get from this treatment?

*Dr. Sossin:* In his first few months, like with all babies, there was a growing predictability of family life. Then, after 9/11 happened, it became unpredictable for many months afterward. The loss of control issues were the causal underbelly.

*Dad:* By now I should be able to predict when he will react. He shrieks. He doesn't like shampoo. He interrupts conversations. He doesn't like to be told what to do. Though he does a lot for himself and is well prepared.

*Dr. Sossin:* Everything he does is acceptable and meaningful and both of you convey this. He is valued. But when Ryan shrieks or is interrupted, his coping skills are overburdened at that moment.

*Dr. Cohen:* In some ways he's still like his old self. He's a very thoughtful, unique individual child. We accept him and we appreciate him. But in the outside world maybe people will not be as accepting of his uniqueness. We enjoy the way he thinks and you do too.

*Dad:* If he knows his way of being in the world has been strange, it's ok. It took me 40 years to realize I was considered strange. [Dad, who is an accomplished professor, comments tongue-in-cheek.]

*Mom:* What's the worst thing? That Ryan will turn out to be like us? *We all smile.*

## WATCHING THE VIDEO IN THE FEEDBACK SESSION – DR. PHYLLIS COHEN

At this point in the session, Dr. Cohen asks the parents if they would like to view the videotape. In this segment of the video that we turn to, we see remnants of Ryan's younger personality. Sometimes there is still some freezing. Sometimes he smiles, but he is still holding his hands and his chin down. He carries his eyes up to take it all in. In the past, this was his way of being, of communicating. Now he has these remnants, but he does not stay there. He comes out of it. While watching this video segment, we see Mom smiling at Ryan. We notice she is much more relaxed:

*Mom* [to Ryan]: How are you?
*On the video Mom's head and her eyes go down again. She gestures with her head as if to say, "Yes?" Then, "No?" Mom seems to wonder whether Ryan could be frozen at this moment.*

*Mom [on the video]:* I'm glad there are no baby toys here any more.
*In talking about the video Dr. Beebe says to the group*: This is what used to happen with Mom and Ryan. He'd be frozen and Mom didn't know what to do. It is so hard for him.

*Mom:* But I don't worry as much.

*Dr. Cohen:* Do you know you are an ice breaker for him. Do you see yourself as that?

*Mom:* No!

*Dr. Sossin:* Sometimes it requires extra effort to get him to engage.

*Dr. Cohen:* You mean when he goes into that frozen place?

*Dr. Sossin:* Yes. On the one hand it can be delicious when you get him to engage, but this behavior can be a hurdle.

*Dad:* But the videotaping is not a normal situation. It's odd. You have to "perform." There is a waiting time. Lydia manages him a bit. He thinks, "I have to perform. What will I do?

*We go back to watching the videotape:*

*{Mom, to Ryan, on video}:* Look, this is a funny box of crayons.

*Ryan puts the crayon in the sharpener.*

*{Mom}:* It doesn't need to be sharpened yet.

*Ryan continues sharpening.*

*{Mom}:* I'll choose a color too.

*There is a pause.*

*Ryan looks at mom.*

*{Mom [with raised eyebrows]}:* Let's get on with it.

*Ryan picks up another crayon.*

*The group pauses for a moment to discuss.*

*Dad:* He delays drawing by sharpening the crayons.

*Mom:* He's a tease.

*Dad:* It's a matter of how much will he be interested? He doles out his interest.

*Dr. Sossin:* Ryan activates and then holds back. Open and close.

*Dr. Beebe:* His "yes and no" has a complex meaning.

*Dad:* We both give yes and no. Mom is yes and Dad is no.

*We go back to watching the videotape. We see that Ryan is drawing while Mom watches and waits.*

*{Mom}:* Is it my turn?

*Ryan waits. He is dampened. There's a nonverbal negotiation of turn-taking.*

*{Mom}:* Is it your turn? No?

*Ryan begins to make a new drawing as Mom dabbles with the colors.*

*The group pauses for a moment to discuss.*

*Dr. Beebe:* Now he has both hands on the table, but with one hand he is stabilizing while with the other he is holding back.

*Dr. Sossin:* His body is saying, "How safe am I to put myself into the world? How secure am I? With only one hand I am only safe to put part of myself into the world."

---

*At the end of the session we typically do a "wrap-up."*

*Dr. Beebe:* What are you going to take home today?

*Mom:* I am thinking about Ryan's play with Anni and the spontaneity of it. I worry if this is what other kids would do, or is it Ryan being different? I wasn't worried about him this morning but now I'm feeling a bit more concerned.

*Dad:* I'm not as worried. I can see now that he has access to his play.

*Dr. Cohen:* Seeing Ryan have access to his play puts us in a more hopeful state.

*Dr. Sossin:* But it's contradictory. Mom is more worried and Dad is less worried.

*Dr. Beebe:* And we are less worried.

*Mom:* No, in general I actually feel really good about what's going on with him.

*Dr. Beebe:* So do we.

*Mom:* I felt good coming in here today.

*Dr. Beebe:* We are so moved by Ryan's journey. We adore him. It is so touching to watch him flower. And Anni's continued involvement has been key.

*Dr. Bergman:* He is so responsive. I don't have to do very much.

*Dr. Sossin:* If his partner is less active, then he can be more active.

*Mom:* He loves being followed by this group.

*Dad:* Yes, and I notice if I sit quietly with him, then he will do something on his own.

*Discussion among the therapists after the parents have left the video feedback session.*

*Dr. Bergman:* This was a slow-paced, good session. It gave the father a chance to reflect. He was much more active than usual. He is wonderful for Ryan. Ryan is so much like him.

*Dr. Beebe:* It was extraordinary to hear about how Ryan was able to play with Anni and to play with his yes/no.

*Dr. Sossin:* And there were no "shape/flow" contradictions. He is a whole integrated person with Anni. At the beginning of the treatment, mother had perplexing contradictions, such as furrowing her brow while smiling. Ryan had these contradictions as well. It was hard to read his emotions. Now he has much more harmony in his facial and bodily expressiveness and his emotions are much clearer.

*Dr. Bergman:* What's most amazing is his loyalty to me.

*Dr. Sossin:* You have that loyalty from both parents as well. Dad said he cannot imagine life without Ryan seeing Anni. Anni, your work is brilliant and Mom knows it too. She acknowledges that Anni does what she doesn't do. Mom says that Ryan needed it and he's gotten it from Anni.

We all observe that Ryan has shown us that he does have a good capacity for interpersonal relatedness. He can read Anni's needs and accommodate to her.

## DR. ANNI BERGMAN CONTINUES HER DESCRIPTION OF THE TREATMENT

As I write now in the spring of 2011, Ryan and his mother have been attending joint treatment sessions regularly, on a once-a-week basis, since spring 2004. They continue to attend, and Ryan and his whole family are loyal in their attachment to me.

Even though Ryan has grown up and is now nearly 10 years old, his mother remains present during the therapy sessions, partly because Ryan tends to be very silent and he relies on his mother to do the talking. Even though Ryan is silent, though, he is very present. What is remarkable is that he is always happy to come and be there, just as he loves to go to lab sessions with Dr. Beebe and the team. It seems that he loves all of us who have shared with him our desire to truly understand him, even if he says little.

The question is, what do we understand? I think we understand him as someone in his own right, which is not so easy to do because he tends to go along with others rather than to express his own self. I believe that both my work with Ryan and the presence and occasional meetings with the therapist group have given him a chance to express himself as a separate individual person in his family.

### *What Follows Is a Segment From a Recent Tripartite Session in Dr. Anni Bergman's Office*

As usual, Ryan and Lydia come to the session together. Lydia gets Ryan a pastry before arriving at my office, and she brings me coffee and a pastry as well. Lydia is consistently energetic and talkative, while Ryan is attentive, but reserved. In the beginning of the session, Lydia brings up that we had recently seen each other at Dr. Beebe's lab.

*Lydia:* I remember the last time we saw each other was at Beatrice's.
*Anni* [*to Ryan*]: Did you like it?
*Lydia:* He felt very proud of himself. He said, "I did good." He was very pleased when we left. Right, Ryan?
*Ryan:* Tell Anni what happened on the car ride home.
*Lydia:* What happened on the car ride home?
*Ryan:* On Thursday.
*Lydia:* On the car ride home from Beatrice's? Wasn't that the week before?
*Ryan:* No.
*Lydia:* Oh right. At the end of the day a car hit my car on 96th Street. And Ryan didn't like it so much.
*Anni:* Were you hurt?
*Lydia:* It's your story, Ryan. Tell her.
*Ryan:* No.
*Lydia:* It's Ryan's story. Tell it Ryan. I wasn't going to mention it. It wasn't so important to me.
*Ryan:* This is mine (talking about a scone).
*Lydia:* No, this is Anni's and mine. No, no you already had banana bread, you can't have it.

### Comments About the Session, by Dr. Anni Bergman

An important context of this session is that Ryan was eager to return to school for a special event, following the lab filming session. The car accident occurred just as Ryan was so eager to return to school.

Lydia begins the session by referring back to the previous time "when all three of us were together," and she tries to engage Ryan by asking him how he felt about the visit to Dr. Beebe's lab. Ryan ignores the question and instead directs the conversation to what he wants to talk about, which is "what happened in the car ride home." He does not want to say what happened, and he gives his mother an imperative to "tell Anni what happened." Lydia deflects for a moment but eventually concedes to Ryan and recalls what happened on the car ride home. "A car hit my car on 96th Street." She then tries to bring Ryan back into the conversation by repeating that the story is Ryan's and that he himself can tell me what happened. Ryan gives a clear one word response, "No." Lydia tries again, but instead of claiming the story, Ryan claims the scone or muffin, which Lydia does not allow him to have.

In this interaction Ryan is involved in and attentive to the conversation. He provides the prompt for the conversation, but he wants his mother to construct the narrative. From the beginning of the session, Lydia talks for Ryan. When I ask Ryan what he thought of the visit to Dr. Beebe's lab, Lydia eagerly responds that Ryan "felt very proud of himself." In this instance he does not have an opportunity to give a response except when Lydia proposes that Ryan agree with her. However, that is not what Ryan wants to talk about. In his request for his mother to tell me what happened, Ryan suggests that he wants to talk about how he felt in that situation. Somewhat reluctantly Lydia begins to describe what happened, but she also clearly wants Ryan to tell the story.

Lydia tries to be attentive and is willing to listen to Ryan, but she also attempts to help Ryan express his own self. She struggles with this balance and at times does speak for Ryan.

In our therapy sessions, in spite of Lydia's slightly overbearing presence, Ryan has become more and more someone in his own right. He has begun to express his own wishes more clearly and I think he has overcome anxieties that were very pronounced in the beginning of our work together. Some of those anxieties include Ryan's fear of something unexpected happening, as well as his inability to tolerate anything being imposed on him. At the beginning of our work together, these anxieties were so apparent that Ryan was often completely frozen and silent. Now, as seen in our most recent session together, although these anxieties are still a part of him, he has become much more vocal about what he wants. He is no longer frozen and withdrawn.

## CONCLUSION

The case of Ryan demonstrates how a massive trauma to a mother and a baby of less than 3 months old can have a significant effect on both. It also shows the way trauma can impair the development of the self of the baby. We can never know who Ryan would have been without the trauma of September 11, 2001.

Here it is of interest to recall Mahler and Furer's (1969) concept of the symbiotic phase of development. In the mother's heightened state of anxiety, the mother could not completely join her baby, nor could the baby join with her. We see in this case how there is a mutual influence between the mother's trauma and the baby's development, and between the trauma of the baby and the capacity of the mother to fully realize her maternal functioning. The devotion of Ryan's mother to her baby made it possible to have an effective treatment for both of them, using the tripartite model of therapy, as described by Mahler and Furer (1969). A mother and a child with a serious developmental trauma or delay should be seen together if the damage to the close interaction between the mother and baby caused by the trauma is to be repaired. Although Ryan made a profound attachment to me as his therapist, treatment of him alone without the mother would not have been sufficient or effective. I believe their ability to communicate and make use of their relationship was repaired and worked with over time. Ryan began to feel reassured about his mother's emotional availability, which necessarily had been disrupted by the trauma. Ryan's mother became able to trust me, to trust Ryan, and to trust herself. She trusted her instinct to get therapy for Ryan. She trusted Ryan's capacity to form a secure attachment to her and to me. She trusted herself to try to become a mother who could understand him. Tronick's (1989) work on disruption and repair is relevant here. He shows how profoundly small disruptions can affect a baby, but he also shows how quickly these disruptions can be repaired.

Ryan has developed into a boy who is able to function in school, make friends, and relate well to his parents and older brother. What is remarkable is the depth of his attachment to me and how important I continue to be to him and to the family. Over time he has even made friends with my dog, of whom he was quite terrified for a very long time. The fact that Ryan's family has been fully accepting of him and of me and his need for treatment has been a significant contributor to his development. Ryan's desire to continue his relationships with people who have been important to him is unusual. He asks to see Dr. Beebe and the other therapists in the lab, which means that he understands their importance to his development and their interest in understanding him. This, I believe, is connected to his parents' loyalty to him. They do not overprotect him, they encourage his independence, and they remain emotionally available.

A child who has suffered a severe disruption in attachment at a very early age may need help, possibly for quite a long time. In Ryan's case, he embraced the therapy and was available to form a deep attachment to his "Dr. Anni." But he needed his parents' consent, cooperation, and participation for the treatment to be fully effective. Often in work with children the therapy is ended prematurely, as soon as the worst symptoms disappear. I believe that the case of Ryan helps us to understand how important the involvement of parents in the treatment is for therapy of young children. They too need help because a child's difficulties are often related to the parents' own overlooked trauma, and they may feel guilty and disappointed in their child. Most importantly, both mother and child need to be involved in the repair of an early trauma.

Ryan, Lydia and I continue to work together. My goal in the therapy has been to help Ryan unfold as well as to help Lydia understand him, rather than impose on him. As a therapist, I am there to give both mother and child the opportunity to hear, and listen to, each other.

## REFERENCES


Kestenberg Amighi, J. Loman, S., Lewis, P., & Sossin, K. M. (1999). *The meaning of movement: Developmental and clinical perspectives of the Kestenberg Movement Profile*. New York: Brunner-Routledge.

Mahler, M., & Furer, M. (1969). *On human symbiosis and the vicissitudes of individuation*. New York, NY: International Universities Press.

Sossin, K. M., & Birklein, S. (2006). Nonverbal transmission of stress between parent and young child: Considerations and psychotherapeutic implications of a study of affective movement patterns. *Journal of Infant, Child, & Adolescent Psychotherapy*, *5*, 46–69.

Tronick, E. (1989). Emotions and emotional communication in infants. *American Psychologist*, *44*, 112–119.

# THE THERAPISTS' PROCESS

## The Therapist Group: A Transformational Process

Beatrice Beebe, Ph.D.
Phyllis Cohen, Ph.D.
Anni Bergman, Ph.D.
Sally Moskowitz, Ph.D.
K. Mark Sossin, Ph.D.
Rita Reiswig, M.S., L.P.
Suzi Tortora, Ed.D., BC–DMT, CMA
Donna Demetri Friedman, LCSW, Ph.D.

*"As long as we meet as a group, we will have a Project, whether the mothers are able to come to sessions or not."*
Anni Bergman

The therapists of the Project for Mothers, Infants, and Young Children of September 11, 2001 have continued to meet every other week in a mutually supportive two-hour peer-supervision group since the inception of the Project. The development of a trusting and nurturing therapist group forum has proven to be the most important factor in our ability to do this work with the mothers and children. As we grew to know and trust each other more, and to talk deeply about the experiences of the families we are working with, we became able to understand how our own histories influenced our investment in this Project. This article describes our credo and explores our histories in the context of the Project.

The events of September 11, 2001 evoked trauma, even for those individuals who were not directly affected. Because we were all practicing clinicians in New York City on September 11, 2001, we were particularly aware that we too had been affected by the catastrophic events. We were vulnerable to what has been described as "vicarious traumatization," the emotional residue of exposure to working with people suffering from a traumatic event. The therapist group provided a context in which this difficult work could be done.

Since the Project's inception, we have continued to meet every other week in a mutually supportive two-hour peer-supervision group. What has proven to be most important in our ability to do this work with the mothers and children has been the development of our trusting and nurturing therapist group forum. Our personal experiences of setting up the various parts of this Project and making connections with the mothers and children helped us to become aware of our need to become involved in our own group process. As we grew to know and trust each other more, and to talk deeply about the experiences of the families we were working with, we were able to understand how our own histories influenced our investment in this Project. To effectively work with victims of trauma, one must face traumatic themes evoked from one's own history. In this group we processed our own observations, feelings, clinical ideas, and evolving relationships with the families and with each other as a working team.

Our Project originally consisted of a group of 20 therapists with diverse backgrounds and areas of expertise, including analytically trained mother-infant researchers, mother-infant therapists, child therapists, a dance therapist, and adult clinicians. We felt we needed all these different areas of expertise to fully respond to the needs of these families. As the Project evolved over the first few years, a core group of eight therapists emerged. In retrospect, it is highly unusual that eight therapists would continue to meet unfailingly for nearly a decade.

We began with the task of understanding the effects of the events on the mothers and the children. Through our meetings we worked at combining our efforts to provide different kinds of support and feedback to mothers that could enhance their ability to reflect on their own experiences and those of their children. The mothers came to be known to the whole group of therapists, even though each mother might not know all the therapists. We found that some of us were involved with the same family in different roles.

A central core of our Project was that we would meet together as therapists, whether or not the mothers came. We held our biweekly peer-supervision group without fail. This supportive group helped us to tolerate our own anxieties, to contain disappointment when mothers did not come, and to process their grief when they did come. As the Project evolved, we came to understand how profoundly affected we ourselves were by these families and by the events. Each of us was affected in a different way, according to our own personal histories and styles of coping.

## OUR CREDO

Our credo was the following:

1. We were dedicated to something bigger than ourselves, one of the biggest tragedies of our lifetime.
2. We understood that there was something in our own histories and characters that allowed us to accept a tremendous amount of pain in these families. These families' experiences somehow resonated with our own experiences. We each had some personal experiences that allowed us to identify with the mothers and children we worked with—symbolically, either as the baby or as the mother, or both.

3. We held onto each other and felt comforted together when we were hearing so many searingly painful stories.
4. All of us wanted to be part of the Project and needed it ourselves. We were able to address our own feelings of helplessness by being able to do something. We felt lucky that we found a way to be active and to bond within our own therapist group, and with our mothers, in the face of the trauma. This work made us feel alive again, made us feel that things were meaningful in a time of such a profound loss of meaning for so many. How we connected to each other and to the families was remarkable. We all felt that we received from this experience as much as we gave.

## THE THERAPISTS' PERSONAL EXPERIENCES OF THE PROJECT BEATRICE BEEBE

I grew up exposed to the traumas of Hiroshima and Nagasaki. My father, Gilbert Beebe, was a radiation epidemiologist. He did research on the follow-up effects of these atomic bombs on the survivors. Later, he did the same kind of research on the effects of the Chernobyl disaster. I lived in Japan from the age of 12 until I was 14. Before my father died in 2003, we had many conversations about the Project. He told me something very powerful—that he admired that I was in a position to actually help the survivors of the trauma, while he had only been in a position to study what had happened. I am sure that my father's involvement with the disaster of the atomic bombs set the stage for my intense involvement in the World Trade Center disaster of September 11.

My mother was a school psychologist, and her influence was also very important. My mother was always available to help people as I was growing up. She did a lot of pro bono work. I combined their two different identities, my father as a researcher and my mother as a psychologist, in my intense wish to be able to be helpful, and also in my interest in studying the effects of this disaster on the families.

Both my parents lost their mothers to illness when they were young children. The idea of the death of a parent, and its devastating impact, was always in the background in my family. My mother talked about it openly; my father did not. But I always thought that this shared tragedy was a powerful bond between them. This aspect of my background was another key motivation for my involvement in this Project.

The opportunity to work with this extraordinary group of therapists has been deeply meaningful to me, both personally and professionally. They have become a kind of second family. The experience of working together with this gifted, nurturing and creative group continues to be one of the most important contexts of my life. I feel grateful for our Project, for the dedication of this remarkable group, and for the mothers and children who have so generously shared their lives with us.

## PHYLLIS COHEN

When I got a call from Beatrice Beebe shortly after the disaster of September 11th, I was volunteering at Pier 94 in New York City. Beatrice and I had already been talking about ways that we might, once again, join forces and work together following a number of years of collaborating on a mother-infant case, "Linda and Dan" (Cohen & Beebe, 2002). In this case we applied Beatrice's research methods to a clinical intervention. We wanted to expand our methods to help additional mothers and babies in need. In that call, Beatrice said that there were many women who were pregnant who had lost husbands in the Towers. Our mission was immediately clear. We began to search, first for the mothers, and then for therapists who might work with the mothers in their own towns, because many of the women lived too far away, or were too afraid to travel into the city. And so, the Project was launched.

A couple of months later, Beatrice and I were traveling to a distant New Jersey town to meet women who might join our Project. We were scheduled to speak with an ongoing church group, comprised of men and women who were grieving over their losses on 9/11. We had been told that a number of group members were pregnant or had just given birth. As we entered the church room, I suddenly remembered that I had met the group leader, Sister Pat, more than 20 years ago, while I was attending meetings at the Foundation of Thanatology. In the late 1970s I was thinking and writing about ways to help bereaved children who had lost a parent by death. After the meeting I was struck by the realization that my professional career path had come together, full circle.

More recently, during one of our therapist group meetings, I wondered what it was that had compelled me to do this painful work so long ago, and continuing into the present. I was then jolted back into remembering how, in 1968, I was a young woman raising two children under the age of 2, with an absent father. Although there was no death involved, still I knew how profoundly difficult it was to raise small children being a single mother. I felt instantly bonded with the women in our Project as single mothers called upon to raise their children alone. I shared their pain.

I have remained committed to the women and children of September 11, 2001, not only in helping them cope with life's challenges but also because of my ongoing interest in understanding how the loss of a parent affects children of all ages. I am grateful to the mothers who have shared their stories, their lives, and their children with us, enabling us to help them while we helped ourselves. I also feel privileged to have worked with such an incredible group of creative, capable therapists from whom I have learned a great deal. I have greatly enjoyed co-directing this Project with Beatrice. I am thankful for the many opportunities that my participation in the Project has offered me, and to the meaningful and enduring friendships that have developed over this past decade.

## SALLY MOSKOWITZ

In thinking about the months just after the terrorist attack, I am struck by the extraordinary nature of traumatic memory, how startling it is that almost 10 years later events can return so vividly. Processes that ordinarily cause memories to fade do not function in the same way on these sharply etched images and feeling states. I realize how far from that state of mind we have come, but also how easy it is for something to trigger a return to that state of mind, and how split from ordinary states of consciousness the states of emergency, terror, and trauma are. It was difficult for us as Project therapists to be part of the traumatized community, experiencing our own personal fears and disruptions, while also attempting to help these grieving mothers find some semblance of hope and normality in mothering their babies.

In retrospect, my deep and abiding interest in this Project stems from several sources. My interest in the effect of the mothers' trauma on their children and the ways in which they could talk to their children about what happened is rooted in remembering what it was like for me as a child trying to comprehend my own parents' histories. Several months into the support group work, I was surprised to realize I felt closely identified with the babies. It then struck me that I had also been born to a mother (and father) who had undergone massive trauma a few years before my birth, losing family and friends. Like many of the mothers in our Project, my mother clung to me as offering the possibility of hope and new life. Later in my very early childhood, I had an emergency hospitalization and a long separation from my mother. I remember how confusing and difficult it was to understand what was happening and why my parents were not there. I was aware of the reverberations of that experience throughout my life and the connections it had to the losses and separations my parents experienced before I was even born.

Then on September 11, 2001, one of my sons was downtown in school across the street from the World Trade Center. There are parts of that day I remember vividly and parts I do not. It is hard to piece together coherently and consistently the sequence of that day—my feelings and actions. I have realized since then that my memories of that day are typical of traumatic memories, that is, fragmented, alternating between intense and vivid, and vague.

I have been deeply and personally interested in the questions we have been looking at in this Project and in helping the mothers and children with the problems posed by traumatic loss. How were the babies going to form a mental image of the father who was lost; how would the trauma and loss the mothers experienced impact the children who never knew their fathers; how could we use what we knew as professionals to help? A strong colleagueship was created in our therapist group around these questions. During the early years of the Project, I think we were all in a somewhat altered frames of mind, feeling very raw and scared ourselves. Then, and continuing through the present, meeting as a group, feeling that we were tending to these babies and mothers, that we were tending to other people as well as to ourselves, has been extremely helpful and gratifying. I feel that the task of repair is staggering for these families. On the other hand, their resilience and capacity for growth is also stunning.

## ANNI BERGMAN

When I was 6 months old, my oldest sister, who was then 16, died. Throughout my childhood she was very present because she was always talked about. She became a model for me to follow as a way of replacing her for my parents. I lost another older sister when I was 5 and she was 10. She was somebody I had known. I knew that she was beautiful and gifted. I thought that I could, or should, replace her as well. From then on I understood what loss was because my older sister was someone I had loved and depended on in many ways, as my companion and role model.

When the events of September 11, 2001, happened, we all began to think about the problem of instant, unexpected loss, and especially for the infants not yet born and the mothers who carried them. When I lost my oldest sister, I was only 6 months old and there was hope in my parents and later in myself that I could replace her. Yet throughout my entire life, I knew I had never known her except through the tales told about her. With the events of September 11, my passion for understanding the mind of a baby, as I had been when I lost my oldest sister, was renewed. I knew that I could only imagine the loss, for the babies, of the fathers they would never have the opportunity to know. These babies would never have a father who could hold them or speak to them. For me, this evoked memories of my own experience of not knowing my sister.

The opportunity to become part of a group that would try to understand and help these mothers and babies whose lives had so suddenly been confronted with loss came when Beatrice Beebe and Phyllis Cohen asked me to join the Project, which I have been involved in ever since. I feel grateful that I could be a part of this group, wishing not only to help but also, more importantly, to understand what happens in the mind of a baby who loses his or her father and the mother who must try to help her baby grow up and become part of the world.

## RITA REISWIG

Many fathers, with children both born and not yet born, died in the collapse of the World Trade Center towers on September 11, 2001. The sudden loss of husbands and fathers has been a subject of compelling interest to me since the beginning of our work with the families of this Project. I am drawn to thinking about how these fathers are remembered by their wives and children, how wives mourn the loss of their spouses, and how memories and attributes of fathers are conveyed to and held in the minds of children, especially when these children never had any personal experience with their fathers.

My own father died suddenly of a heart attack one night after dinner. I was 19 — not a child but not a fully formed adult either. I was at home with my mother, older sister, and younger brother. I found out that evening that life can change in an instant. There was nothing to do to save him, no time to say goodbye. The suddenness of the World Trade Center losses resonates with me.

When I was a candidate in psychoanalytic training, I came across a letter of condolence that Sigmund Freud wrote to a friend, Ludwig Binswanger, in 1939. I have kept a copy of the letter, folded, tucked away in the back of my calendar. It is frayed and dog-eared. I read it from time to time and find it consoling because it captures something true about losing someone of great significance. As Freud said to his friend, "Although we know that after such a loss the acute state of mourning will subside, we also know we shall remain inconsolable and will never find a substitute. No matter what may fill the gap, even if it be filled completely, it nevertheless remains something else. And actually this is how it should be. It is the only way of perpetuating that love which we do not want to relinquish."

Loving feelings and a sense of premature loss are mixed in a complicated tangle. Like other aspects of development, mourning, for me, does not reach an end; on the contrary, the feelings for the lost person are there and are rethought, reawakened, reactivated, and reworked. I imagine something like this process is underway for the widows and children who are part of our Project.

## K. MARK SOSSIN

On September 11, 2001, I was at Pace University where I teach, a few blocks from the World Trade Center. I was in a consultative meeting with an adult, expecting to meet a new group of graduate students who would be joining my infant practicum a couple of hours later. I heard a loud, unusual blast. Within a minute, I was looking down from my fifth floor window seeing the firemen rushing to a call. I heard a radio blurb about a (conjectured small) plane flying into the World Trade Center. A minute later, another look out the window found gurneys from New York Downtown Hospital pushed out to the sidewalk in trauma-reception mode. A half hour later, another thunderous sound marked the moment the second plane hit.

My meeting over, I walked to Fulton and Broadway by myself, watching people streaming out and northward, watching rescuers stream in, looking up to, by then, two burning buildings: awesome buildings, utterly scathed and fragile. I saw the gaping holes, the black smoke, the falling debris, and then the people jumping/falling. It was horrifying. I was transfixed and consumed yet strangely detached, as if this was too horrifying to be real. I wanted to do something of use, but all I could think of was to go back to my "Nursery" setting a couple of blocks away to wait for the graduate students.

Within a couple of minutes of arriving there, the first World Trade Center building fell, leading us to be evacuated out into a thick ball of ash and debris. I exited, and with a Pace student and faculty member, tried walking outside, but the air was dense with ash, and breathing was hard. Walking in the blur on the streets near the World Trade Center site, it at once seemed deafening but strangely silent. When a person could be seen, usually a cell phone was pressed to an ear, but nobody was speaking. There were empty strollers abandoned on the street; they could not roll any longer in the streets covered in ruins and cinders. We entered a nearby lobby just to breathe. I tried to, but could not, convince the others to exit again into this ash, as they deemed leaving too risky.

But I left the lobby. Another block away, I found my car parked in the hospital lot, curiously freed from its usual place, in which it would have been boxed in. It was covered in two inches of residue. I decided I should head to my children. I drove onto the Brooklyn Bridge. The second building fell while I was on the bridge. I worried terribly about the people who I had left behind. It was a long drive home. I remember two men jumped out of their car while I was stopped on the expressway, due to congested traffic, to brush the ash on my car onto paper towels. They asked permission. Everything seemed so surreal. I was stuck on a crowded highway, with the radio chattering away, yet it seemed desolate. Sometime later I arrived at my daughter's school. Only the startled faces of the staff in the school office awakened me to my own ash-covered appearance, a fact of which I had remained wholly unaware.

The weeks that followed involved center-point focus on the tragedy. Pace students and staff had been shaken to the quick. Those of us in mental health talked and thought of what procedures would work to help people manage their stress and fear. We ran groups at Pace for staff and for students. After a delay, we started our semester, but the reminders so close to the site permeated all senses: the smell, the sights, the sounds. Pictures of "missing" people hung at every turn. It was as if our downtown-troposphere was infused with unresolved death. Highly equipped military personnel were all about, entry to most areas was blocked and screened, and a profound sense of loss flooded awareness. All the families participating in our Nursery setting, which I ran with Dr. Phyllis Ackman, had been deeply affected by the events of September 11th. We heard frightening stories of evacuation with babies, of feeling disconnected from loved ones at the height of uncertainty, and of homes that could not be returned to for many months. Fear led some to move away permanently. At some point, we started to function as a university and community again, but it remained otherworldly.

As most colleagues experienced, the residue of the events of September 11, 2001, filtered into all aspects of clinical and professional work as well as into our personal lives. A reasonably anticipated future seemed uncertain; prior losses seemed less resolved. So many people lost family members and dear friends. So many more knew others who did. We were riveted by the stories of lives cut short. Deeply wanting to find an entry point wherein I could bring a skill set that would be useful, I was eager to join the Project when it emerged. I had ideas about protecting babies from the transmission of stress and sorrow, and it was hope-engendering to meet with other people who were thinking similarly. Over time, we have learned enormously from the families who have allowed us to know them, and from each other. A terribly dark moment in our shared history gave birth to a collaboration that has been fruitful and enormously rewarding. In this way, our collective work parallels our Project goals for the children we deemed at risk, reflected in our efforts to spawn hope for their futures.

## DONNA DEMETRI FRIEDMAN

The week before September 11, 2001, I learned that my mother had a life-threatening illness. My beloved babysitter's brother had been killed in a bus accident in Africa that same week. Then September 11th happened. Life was not what it had been just days before.

On the morning of September 11, as my two-and-a-half year old daughter was watching Barney on the television, I spoke on the phone with a friend who had lost her father to cancer several years earlier. We hung up the phone, and she immediately called me back after seeing the news about the attack. A plane had struck one of the Twin Towers. At the same time our television went dead. My daughter asked, "Where's Barney?" I did not realize at the time that our television reception was connected to the towers. I stepped onto the balcony and could see from the 22nd floor the smoke billowing from the building.

By the late morning it was becoming clear what had happened. The armed guards in front of my building, which stood at the entrance into Manhattan from the Bronx, were proof that the situation was very bad. I went to work in the clinic that day, and people from the community started to come in with stories about loved ones who were missing. The reality was just beginning to sink in.

When Beatrice Beebe, with whom I had worked on my dissertation research, asked me to join her Project, I wanted to do something, and so I said yes. Like the mothers, I was also the mother of a young child at that time. In addition, I was a contemporary of the mothers in the Project. I identified with the mothers. I felt that if I could do something, life could go on. I involved myself with people I felt safe with. I felt some strength in that. Doing something made me feel hopeful.

## SUZI TORTORA

I was in New York City at my office in the Village on September 11, 2001. I was stunned and in shock. I remember stopping to notice how crystal clear and blue the sky was that early morning. What a beautiful early September day it was. Less than two hours later, I was on the street in the same spot and could only see dark black billows of smoke. I searched for hours for a dear friend with whom I had come to New York City that morning. I ended up at his office uptown, unaware that he, at the same time, was searching for me downtown at my office. We found each other by chance and got home safely.

I remember feeling that evening that the world had seemed to completely stop. It was a surreal feeling that was palpable all around me. At 11:00 PM, alone upstairs in my home, I heard the sound of taps floating across the Hudson River through my opened window. The air was still, the sky was dark. I thought I was hallucinating — it was haunting yet sincere at the same time. I realized it was real and coming from West Point, which is just across the river from where I live. I experienced those taps as a calling and knew at that moment that I would find a way to help, although I did not know how this would actually unfold. I had several friends who were volunteering at the Piers doing emergency relief work. I knew this was important work, but I felt it was not the best use of my expertise. My focus has always been on building relationships and supporting families through crisis and trauma. I remember sharing these thoughts with a good friend who advised me to wait—the right way to offer my skills would come, for support will be needed over time, not just in the shadow of the trauma, she said encouragingly.

Wait I did. When Beatrice began to develop her idea of reaching out to families to offer therapeutic support, I knew it was just what I was looking for. I would be able to provide consistent and caring support with a team of excellent therapists over a long period of time. This fit with the level of commitment I wanted to make and has proven to be a growing experience for all of us—the families and therapists alike.

Working together for so many years on such a delicate and intimate topic has naturally created a deep bond among us. These relationships have enabled us to reflect on our own experiences related to personal dramatic life-changing events of early childhood within our own personal family histories. The transgenerational transmission of psychological experience carried from family member to family member has been an especially intriguing focus of our Project because it has provoked us to explore this concept personally. It has enabled me to look with fresh eyes at the childhood experiences of my grandmother, who was separated from her mother and father as an infant in Italy for many years when her parents left for America. When my grandmother reunited with her family as an adolescent and was brought to America, she had to navigate yet another loss when she had to leave her grandmother whom she had experienced as her mother for all those years. My grandmother grew up to be a creative, complex person who was ahead of her time. She held a career as a fashion designer and seamstress while still being dedicated to her family. Her religious nature instilled a sense of service in all of us.

The Project led me to gain a new awareness of my own history. Here I am in the third generation, coming to this better understanding of the role of loss in my family, how my identity was shaped by loss, and how I have attempted to repair.

## REFERENCE

Cohen, P. M., & Beebe, B. (2003). Video feedback with a depressed mother and her infant: A collaborative individual psychoanalytic and mother-infant treatment. *Journal of Infant Child, and Adolescent Psychotherapy*, *2*(3), 1–55.

# PERSPECTIVES ON EARLY TRAUMA - NEUROPSYCHOLOGICAL AND CLINICAL LITERATURE

## Prenatal Maternal Stress and the Developing Fetus and Infant: A Review of Animal Models as Related to Human Research

Adrianne Lange, M.A.

Prenatal stress, a function of severe maternal psychological or physiological stress, including trauma and illness, can influence the development of the fetus in profound ways, extending into childhood and adulthood. Maternal trauma, acute and chronic, physiological and emotional, can create an environment for the fetus that may disrupt development in the womb, potentially setting the infant on a path of maladaptive reactivity to stressors in the world beyond. Prenatal stress influences psychological systems, including attachment, affect, and stress regulation; physiological systems, including endocrine and cardiovascular systems; and even neuroanatomical structure. This article reviews some of the findings from animal models associated with this important line of research and indicates the critical nature of early intervention for families such as those described in this issue on the Project for Mothers, Infants, and Young Children of September 11, 2001.

A growing number of researchers are focusing on the physiological and psychological effects of prenatal stress on the human infant. Prenatal stress, a function of severe maternal psychological or physiological stress, including trauma and illness, can influence the fetus in profound ways that we are only just beginning to understand (Wadhwa, 1998). We are learning that maternal trauma, acute and chronic, physiological and emotional, can create an environment for the fetus that may disrupt development in the womb, potentially setting the infant on a path of maladaptive reactivity to stressors in the world beyond. The impact of prenatal stress on psychological systems, including attachment, affect and stress regulation; and on physiological systems, including endocrine and cardiovascular systems, and even neuroanatomical structure, has been identified by numerous researchers (Sapolsky, Krey, & McEwen, 1986; McEwen, 1998; Sapolsky, 2000; Lupien & Lepage, 2001). This article reviews some of the findings from animal models associated with this important line of research (for reviews, see Kofman, 2002; Wadhwa, 1998; Weinstock, 2001a, 2001b) and indicates the critical nature of early intervention strategies for families who have undergone such trauma, such as the Project for Mothers, Infants, and Young Children of September 11, 2001, described in this issue.

## METHODS OF STRESS TRANSMISSION

Maternal stress reactivity and subsequent transmission to the child's brain can travel on one or more of several paths: environmental, genetic, and epigenetic. Environmental transmission can be *nongenomic*, passing through either the prenatal fetal environment or postnatal environment through behavior and relational processes, altering the developmental course of the child's brain through hormones and behavioral organization (Francis, Diorio, Liu, & Meaney, 1999; Ladd, Huot, Thrivikraman, Nemeroff, Meaney, & Plotsky, 2000; Ladd, Huot, Thrivikraman, Nemeroff, & Plotsky, 2004). Alternatively, environmental stress experienced by the mother when *she* was a fetus can be passed on to her own offspring through *transgenerational* processes. Such a process is a genetic memory of an environmental stress, demonstrating the combined power of environmental and genetic transmittal potential (Kapoor, Petropoulos, & Matthews, 2008; Santos, Mazzola, & Carvalho, 2005). This type of transmission is known as "epigenetic transmission," that is, a method of *dynamic* genetic transmission that is based on *nongenetic* input.

Understanding the neurobiological and physiological systems underlying the stress-response is a first step in contextualizing the impact that maternal stress has on the developing fetus. For example, hormones, the primary physiological messengers between the brain and the body, are shared between mothers and their developing babies. They are distributed by the maternal endocrine system and have a strong environmental effect on the developing brain of the fetus. As physiological-environmental conditions shape the fetal brain, they influence the cognitive, social, and emotional direction of development through the infant's first few years of life and beyond, through childhood and even into adulthood (Feldman & Eidelman, 2009).

## THE FETAL ORIGINS OF ADULT DISEASE

FOAD – The fetal origins of adult disease is a well-documented concept most commonly associated with purely physical conditions such as heart disease and diabetes. More recently, researchers are finding that prenatal stress contributes to the manifestation of psychopathology, bringing neurobiological research to the forefront of strategies for the prevention of mental health disease.

Recent epidemiological work with human data and animal laboratory studies confirm that stress in the fetal and postnatal environment can disrupt normal development and create a lifelong vulnerability to metabolic and cardiovascular disease (for reviews, see Kapoor, Dunn, Kostaki, Andrews, & Matthews, 2006; Kapoor et al., 2008; Sapolsky, 2004; Nathanielsz & Padmanabhan,

2006). The brain is exposed to powerful organizational processes during key points of early development with demonstrable effects into adulthood and reproductive life. Dramatic examples of the "fetal origins of adult disease" (FOAD) model are seen in studies on the Dutch Hunger Winter of September 1944–May 1945, when Nazis severely restricted the food supply in Holland during World War II. The average caloric intake dropped from 1,500 calories a day to 450–750. The stress of food deprivation was combined with an extremely harsh winter and the acute psychological strain of the last months of the war. Children born during this winter have shown increased incidence of cardiovascular and metabolic disease, notably diabetes and obesity (Barker, 1998; Lumey, Ravelli, Wiessing, Koppe, Treffers, & Stein, 1993; Roseboom, Rooij, & Painter, 2006).

The implications of FOAD are strong. But human epidemiological studies lack precise controls and are difficult to replicate. For obvious ethical reasons, human studies on this topic cannot be manipulated. As such, animal models are critical in the study of prenatal stress effects on human development. Animal models allow for the precise control of most variables, including environmental factors. They allow for the detailed collection of data using invasive measurement techniques, impossible in human research. Despite the rich evidence from animal research on prenatal stress outcomes, the generalizability of animal models to humans is subject to important limitations, notably differences in the physiology and normal developmental courses between species (Wadhwa, 2005). Recent human research using the "fetal challenge paradigm" helps to bridge the gap between human clinical studies and animal models of prenatal stress. Wadhwa and colleagues have articulated a neurobiological model of prenatal stress in humans "that proposes maternal psychosocial stress exerts a significant and independent negative influence on fetal developmental outcomes" (Wadhwa, 2005, p. 726). Their work suggests that these effects are mediated by maternal-fetal placental mechanisms and are moderated by the nature, timing and duration of stress (Wadhwa, 1998; Wadhwa, 2005, 2008). These limitations and models for generalizability are important to consider when evaluating both animal and human models of research and their clinical implications.

## FETAL DEVELOPMENT AND EARLY RISK

The cerebral cortex, or simply "cortex," is the folded outer layer of neural tissue that covers the entire brain. Often referred to as "gray matter," the cortex is made up of neurons and unmylinated neuronal fibers. In the human fetus, the initial formation of the neural plate, the foundation of the cortex, occurs during the third week of gestation. Fetal brain development proceeds with the development of the brainstem at six to seven weeks. Thereafter, the brain follows carefully choreographed sequelae of cell birth and proliferation, resulting in up to six thin, precise layers of cortex (Harding & Bocking, 2001). Myelination, the process of sheathing neurons to increase the speed and efficiency of communication among cells, begins during gestation and continues through adolescence and adulthood. Cell birth (synaptogenesis) and controlled cell death continue throughout life, as the brain grows, adapts, and reacts to genetic maps and environmental influences.

The brain is particularly vulnerable to developmental disruptions while the cortex is being formed and later when the fetus is near term, when the forebrain, the most evolutionarily advanced structure of the human brain, begins to mature. Acute and mild stressors can have varied impact, depending on when in development they occur. During certain stages, the brain protects itself against hormonal fluctuations from the mother; in others, these fluctuations serve to prepare the brain for the physiological circumstances of the emotional environment to come.

In nonhuman primates, vulnerability to developmental disruption in response to prenatal stress follows an inverted bell curve across the pregnancy, with the greatest risk appearing in early gestation and decreasing throughout the pregnancy as the endocrine, immune, and neurobehavioral systems mature (Coe & Lubach, 2000; Schneider, Moore, Roberts, & Dejesus, 2001). This makes sense from a developmental standpoint: disruptions occurring while the essential foundations are constructed pose risks for more profound alterations. Research on late-stage prenatal stress administered in rat dams during the last week of pregnancy resulted in the rat pups showing abnormally increased fearful behavior that increased with age (Dickerson, Lally, Gunnel, Birkle, & Salm, 2005). Thus, it is important to consider the timing of the stressor during gestation, as well as its chronicity, when evaluating findings and applying them to experimental and treatment models.

## EPIGENETIC INHERITANCE

In animal models, parental phenotypic responses to the environment can transfer to offspring and even grand-offspring through epigenetic changes in gene expression, even when the DNA itself is not altered (Santos et al., 2005; Suomi & Levine, 1998). A "phenotype"[1] is the term used to describe the collection of observable traits in a group of like organisms, as defined by their same behavior, environment, and physiology. There is even a strong argument that temperamental variation may be transmitted similarly through epigenetic processes (Harper, 2005). Kostaki, Owen, Li, and Matthews (2005) demonstrated that antenatal glucocorticoid exposure alters the Hypothalamic Pituitary Adrenal Axis (HPA; the system that regulates stress hormones in mammals) function and behavior in the offspring of mothers (guinea pig dams) who were themselves exposed to synthetic glucocorticoid stressors prenatally. Those mothers showed reduced reproductive capacity (Dunn, Owen, Kostaki, & Matthews, 2005), and their offspring showed a reduction in basal and stressed state salivary cortisol levels. Transgenerational effects have also been identified in liver enzyme function (Drake, Tang, & Nyirenda, 2007).

When the mother experiences severe stress or trauma, the fetus may suffer developmental disruption that can create vulnerabilities, or diatheses, for a number of adult syndromes and diseases. In the diathesis-stress model,[2] a genetic vulnerability or predisposition interacts with the environment and life events to trigger behavioral or metabolic disorders. The greater the underlying vulnerability, the less stress needed to trigger the behavior or disorder. Conversely, where there is a smaller genetic contribution, greater life stress is required to produce the particular result. Even so, someone with a diathesis toward a disorder does not necessarily develop the disorder; genetic expression is also a product of probabilities. Much of the current stress research focuses on the isolation and development of protective factors that may mitigate stress or its impact, thus reducing the intensity or likelihood of diathesis expression.

## NEUROBIOLOGY/ENDOCRINOLOGY OF ATTACHMENT

Considerable research examines the long-term developmental role of attachment. Researchers are increasingly examining the neurobiological correlates of attachment from early in development, focusing on the key pathways of the HPA and the limbic system (Swain, Thomas, Leckman, & Mayes, 2008; Hofer, 2006). Hofer's work (1994, 2006) on animal models of the psychobiological origins of early attachment documents that the metaphorical "bond" of attachment is actually based on a system of "hidden regulators." These hidden regulators serve the thermoregulation, sensory integration, physiological and affect regulation needs of the infant.

In an excellent review of 30 years of work, Winberg (2005) details the complexities of human mother-infant mutual regulation systems in the period just after birth. Close physical contact between the infant and mother regulates the newborn's temperature, energy conservation, acid-base balance, respiration, distress, and nursing behaviors. Through this early physiological intimacy, in a reciprocal fashion, the human infant regulates the mother's energy efficiency through vagal activation. The vagus nerve is responsible for regulating the efficiency of physiological functions such as heart rate, gastrointestinal processes, temperature regulation, and some motor movements. The infant thus contributes to an adaptive hormonal response in the mother's gastrointestinal tract, which aids in offsetting the extreme physical challenge posed by lactation (Uvnas-Moberg & Winberg, 1989).

In optimal pregnancy and postpartum, mammalian mothers and infants maintain a symbiotic physiological relationship. Among other critical systems, mothers share their endocrine systems with the fetus through the placenta during pregnancy. Later, mothers and infants facilitate each other's recovery from the stress of birth, stimulating growth and ensuring physiological efficiency through the pathways described above. The now famous "love" hormone, oxytocin, circulates to reinforce bonding, which facilitates emotional security and lays down the foundation for attachment behaviors later in development (Keverne & Kendrick, 1994; Christiensson, Nilsson, Stock, Matthiesen, & Uvnas-Moberg, 1989; Feldman, Weller, Zagoory-Sharon, & Levine, 2007). The frequency and duration of breastfeeding may contribute to the attachment process via opioid systems as well (Winberg, 2005; Uvnas-Moberg, 1996, 1997).

The hypothalamic-pituitary-adrenal axis (HPA),[3] part of the body's endocrine system, not only regulates stress hormones but also participates in the regulation of immune function, reproduction, growth, metabolism, and the breakdown and disposal of tissue on a cellular level. When one element becomes deregulated, the entire system is affected. This system is part of the neurobiological basis of attachment. Its development is significantly influenced by variations in maternal stress levels. A range of mild to moderate prenatal stressors in rodent studies has demonstrated significant effects on the fetus and offspring from infancy through adulthood. After rat dams were treated with restraint stress or saline injection stress in a novel environment, levels of cortisol and acetyl-corticotropin hormones (primary stress hormones) were elevated in the hypothalmi of the fetuses during gestation (Lephard, Watson, Jacobson, Rhees, & Ladel, 1997; Skinner, White, & Birkle, 1999; Kofman, 2002), demonstrating the sensitivity of the fetus to maternal stress. Altered baseline levels of stress hormones influence the offspring's patterns of stress reactivity later in life. Much as the children of the Dutch Hunger Winter "learned a lesson" about their environment while in the womb (specifically about the limited availability of food), these rat offspring established an elevated baseline for these hormones and a hypo-responsivity to stress itself.

The rat fetus monitors the signals of stress from the mother, as glucocorticoids readily pass through the placenta into fetal circulation. An overabundance of glucocorticoids from the stressed mother tells the fetus that the world is a stressful place: Be vigilant and secrete this amount of hormone to cope with the challenges of your environment. If stressful conditions dominate the pregnancy, the fetus may carry this "lesson" into infancy and beyond, even if those taxing conditions no longer dominate the environment. Prenatally stressed rats can grow into adults with a larger stress-response and/or slowed recovery time from a stress-response. This programming appears to be due to the permanent establishment of an atypical number of receptors for glucocorticoids in the part of the brain responsible for "turning off" the stress response. Fewer glucocorticoid receptors in this area cause decreased sensitivity to the "off" signal, which means a less effective modulation of glucocorticoid secretion and absorption. Studies with rats indicate that variations in maternal glucocorticoid circulation have a strong impact on infant stress response programming, especially during early developmental windows during which the fetal brain is laying down critical foundations. If these results translate to human patterns, the result could be a lifelong tendency towards elevated level of stress and maladaptive stress responses (Sapolsky, 2004; Viltart & Vanvesien-Mailliot, 2007).

A chronic maternal stress paradigm in guinea pigs has shown significant changes to offspring in several areas, including sex-dependent differences (Emack, Kostaki, Walker, & Matthews, 2008). Chronic maternal stress, in the form of variable stressors through the second half of gestation to the time of weaning, leads to changes in fetal growth trajectory, levels of locomotor activity and HPA axis stress responses in offspring. Male offspring appeared more vulnerable to these effects than female offspring, specifically in the areas of body weight and locomotor activation.

## NEUROBIOLOGY OF PRENATAL STRESS

Stress and trauma in humans, as noted clinically in PTSD and trauma patients, can reroute standard fear and anxiety responses, causing a normally adaptive system to become maladaptive, stuck in either hyper- or hypo-sensitive patterns of response to even normal levels of stress (Ogden, Minton, & Pain, 2006). In prenatally stressed animal offspring, the maternal experience of stress effectively programs the child *in utero* for maladaptive neurobiological response patterns. Also, prenatal stress models with animals have been shown to alter the even the physical structure of the stress regulation system itself, cited below. This may result in cognitive deficits in learning and memory in the offspring, deepening maladaptive response patterns and impairing emotional development. An examination of the effects of prenatal stress in animal models on the infant systems responsible for emotion, learning and memory follows.

### Amygdala

The amygdala is a collection of nuclei located in the limbic system. It is responsible for rapid emotional processing such as the recognition of basic facial expressions such as fear, surprise and aggression, and it is implicated in emotion and anxiety disorders in humans. The amygdala serves a critical function as the first line of defense in threat situations. It reacts in milliseconds to generate hormonal changes long before the rational, logical prefrontal cortex kicks in, which could be seconds or minutes later. Dysfunctional processing at this split-second level can present as disturbances in physiological stress responses and emotion regulation. Research in rodents demonstrates prenatal stress-induced differences in the developmental trajectories of the basolateral (BL), central (Ce), and lateral (La) amygdalar nuclei, seen primarily through stereological analyses of Nissl stains at postnatal days 7–45 (Kraszpulski, Dickerson, & Salm, 2006). Building on previous research demonstrating anatomical and biochemical alterations in the adult amygdalae of prenatally stressed rat offspring, Dickerson and colleagues (Dickerson, Lally, Gunnel, Birkle, & Salm, 2005) modeled the behavioral correlates of these amygdalar changes in young prenatally stressed rats. Fearful behaviors in these young rats emerge prior to sexual maturation and increase through adulthood. This work validates the model as analogous to human data, which shows that anxiety disorders often appear first in childhood.

### Hippocampus

The hippocampus (from the Greek word meaning "seahorse") is an oddly shaped structure near the amygdala associated with learning, working memory, and the formation of short-term memories. Short-term memories spend some time here before coalescing and graduating to long-term memory, which resides in the frontal lobe. Working memory allows us to hold several items of any sequence in mind while processing the next few items, facilitating fluid understanding (e.g., reading).

On a molecular level, prenatal stress affects the hippocampal development of the offspring (Cai, Zhu, Fan, Jia, Bai, Song, & Li, 2006; Yaka, Salomon, Matzner, & Weinstock, 2007; Yang, Han, Cao, Li, & Xu, 2006). Data from electrophysiological sampling of calcium (Ca2+) and potassium (K+) channels suggest that prenatal stress, characterized by restraint stress to the pregnant dam, causes enduring changes in the CA3 region of the hippocampus of the offspring (Cai et al., 2006).

Yang et al. (2006) found that prenatal stress to the rat dam (unpredictable foot shocks during gestational days 13–19) increased the effects of acute stress on hippocampal long-term potentiation (LTP), long-term depression (LTD), and impaired spatial learning and memory on a maze task. Results were supported in a histological examination of the hippocampi of these five-week-old offspring. Similarly, prenatally stressed offspring, reared in identical environments as their nonstressed counterparts, showed significantly impaired spatial learning and memory in adulthood (Son, Geum, Chung, Kim, Jo, Kikm, Lee, Kim, Choi, Kim, Lee, & Kim, 2006).

### Neurotransmitters

Researchers speculate that altered synaptic plasticity in the CA1 region of the hippocampus, caused by a reduction in glutamate (NMDA – an excitatory neurotransmitter) receptor-mediated long-term potentiation (LTP), is the mechanism for the impaired spatial learning and memory found in these prenatally stressed rats (Son et al., 2006). Synaptic plasticity is a feature which allows synapses to grow and change as needed. LTP is a process essential to the formation of strong synaptic connections, which facilitates many types of learning, from simple classic conditioning to the complex cognitive process known as long-term memory. Yaka et al. (2007) elaborate on this hypothesis by implicating very high levels of "scaffolding" proteins in the offspring in response to maternal stress. High levels of these proteins disrupt NMDA receptors in the CA1 synapses of the hippocampus and cause the impairment in spatial learning and memory observed in prenatally stressed rat offspring.

A prospective, longitudinal, and comparative study examined the serotonergic activity (5-HT1A) in human infants who suffer from intrauterine growth restriction (IUGR). Epigenetic factors were found to alter cerebral sensory cortex development and may be associated with serotonin disorders later in life, including Diabetes Types 1 and 2 (Manjarrez, Cisneros, Herrera,

Vazquez, Robles, & Hernandez, 2005). IUGR, the fetal diagnosis analogous to "failure to thrive" in infants, can be caused by maternal stressors during pregnancy, for example, chronic maternal disease, abnormal or insufficient placentation, genetic disorder, substance abuse, low socioeconomic status, or emotional trauma (Peleg, Kennedy, & Hunter, 1998). Other serotonin-related disorders in the mother, such as depression and sleep disturbances, may affect fetal development and maternal-child relations (Vashadze, 2007).

### Synaptic Growth and Gene Expression

Research also shows that prenatal stress alters the expression of brain-derived neurotrophic factor (BDNF). BDNF is a key protein found in the central nervous system (CNS) and peripheral nervous system (PNS) that supports cell survival and synaptic plasticity, particularly in structures associated with learning and memory, including the hippocampus and key areas of the cortex. Rat pups exposed to prenatal stress showed reduced BDNF expression in the prefrontal cortex, striatum (Fumagalli, Bedogni, Perez, Racagni, & Riva, 2004) and in the olfactory bulbs and hippocampus (Van den Hove, Steinbusch, Scheepens, Van de Berg, Kooiman, Boosten, Prickaerts, & Blanco, 2006). As adults, rats exposed to prenatal stress showed dysregulation of BDNF expression in the same structures, demonstrating that prenatal stress causes neurotrophic disruption in fetal life through adulthood (Fumagalli et al., 2004). Neurotrophins are critical for normal neural growth and development; they are essential components of synaptogenesis, or synaptic growth. Disturbances in neurotrophic activity may have serious developmental consequences in the limbic system, which may limit the brain's capacity for neural plasticity and synaptic growth in adulthood, and impair the brain's ability to heal and learn throughout adulthood.

## NEONATOLOGY

Alder and colleagues (Alder, Fink, Bitzer, Hosli, & Holzgreve, 2007) conducted a comprehensive review of the human literature of the past 15 years on maternal depression and anxiety during pregnancy and resulting birth outcomes. They found that maternal depression and anxiety were associated with obstetric complications, preterm labor, and decreased capacity for pain relief during labor.

Interestingly, prenatal stress induces sex-specific changes on the offspring, notably in the maternal behavior of prenatally stressed daughters. Maternal stress induced even in the final week of gestation causes neuroanatomical and hormonal changes in female offspring. Prenatally stressed female rat pups in maturity showed severe decreases in the quality of induced maternal behavior (foster-rearing behavior), including an increase in the incidence of cannibalism of foster pups (Perez-Laso, Segovia, Martin, Ortega, Gomez, & Del Cerro, 2007), increased plasma levels of stress hormones (ACTH and corticosterone) and increased number of mitral cells in the accessory olfactory bulb, showing a "male-like pattern" of maternal behavior.

However, prenatal stress in the last weeks of gestation has also been interpreted as facilitating adaptive, progressive behavioral responses to environmental challenges (Palleres, Scacchi Bernasconi, Feleder, & Cutrera, 2007). In a rodent study assessing anxiety and motor performance (using tight-rope and t-maze tests), prenatally stressed mice showed gender and age dependent results. In addition, males exposed to prenatal stress demonstrated an increase in spontaneous exploratory behavior (a persistent effect) and better performance on the tightrope test in the first month of life. Females showed reduced anxiety compared to the control group in the t-maze test. The authors suggest the possibility of an adaptive response to prenatal stress.

## ADULT PATHOPHYSIOLOGY AND DISEASE

There is considerable evidence from animal models and epidemiological (disease incidence and distribution data collection) studies in humans associating prenatal stress with cardiovascular, metabolic, neuroendocrine, psychiatric, and emotional disorders across the lifespan (see Drake, Tang, & Nyirenda, 2007; Seckl & Holmes, 2007, Wadhwa, 2005). "Fetal programming" and "imprinting" are terms that describe the process by which maternal physiological and psychological stress during pregnancy affects the developmental course of the offspring's stress response, which can lead to disordered physiological and behavioral responses to stress through adult life, in both animal models and human data.

In humans, fetal exposure to an overabundance of maternal glucocorticoids (acute or chronic) can result in reduced birth weight and hypertension, hyperglycemia, abnormal behavior, and increased HPA-axis activity through adulthood. Reduced birth weight is directly associated with higher plasma cortisol levels through the life cycle supporting the "programming" hypothesis (Sapolsky, 2004; Viltart & Vanvesien-Mailliot, 2007). Further, prenatal stress has been implicated as a risk factor for postpartum mood disorders with changes in HPA-axis reactivity as a potential factor (Bosch, Müsch, Bredewold, Slattery, & Neumann, 2007).

## ADULT PSYCHOPATHOLOGY AND EMOTIONAL DISORDERS

Huizink, Mulder, and Buitelaar (2004) reviewed the data documenting that prenatal stress results in disruptions in HPA-axis reactivity, specifically overactivity and impaired negative feedback regulation. As noted above, neurotransmitter functioning is also disrupted; in particular, neurotransmitters GABA, serotonin, and dopamine, which are involved in the regulation and maintenance of mood and anxiety. Neurotransmitters are complex, endogenous chemical compounds that affect the entire brain. Because they are linked to a variety of mood and anxiety disorders, it is difficult to link specific animal results with any one diagnostic category. Huizink and colleagues conclude that prenatal stress effects may result in an increased *generalized* susceptibility to psychopathology in humans, which is theoretically consistent with the contemporary view of psychological diagnosis as fluid and on a spectrum (as per current developments in the publication of the DSM-V, in progress).

## PROTECTIVE/MEDIATING FACTORS

The nature of early life experiences, specifically early caregiving relationships, has been shown to affect infant and child development in profound ways. Research in the area of early relationships and environment (the "nurture" of "nature versus nurture") opens up the possibility of important avenues that can moderate the consequences of prenatal stress on the neurological and behavioral systems of the infant. Beginning with Bowlby (1969), the critical nature of the relationship between the primary caregiver and infant has been increasingly emphasized as essential to healthy social and emotional development (Cassidy & Shaver, 1999). Significant disruptions in the primary relationship (most notably trauma, abuse, or neglect) contribute to the development of disorders of psychological and behavioral nature over the entire life course and are associated with the formation of insecure attachment (Sroufe, 2005; Sroufe, Carlson, Levy, & Egeland, 1999). Supporting or facilitating the early attachment relationship through early clinical intervention may operate as a protective factor for development.

Systematic research on early intervention using rodent models has uncovered a number of useful insights relating animal models to human research. In rodent models, maternal behavior in the days just following birth can effectively program HPA-axis stress reactivity and even the future parenting behaviors of the offspring. Maternal behavior even influences gene expression in areas associated with learning and memory in offspring (Pryce, Bettschen, & Feldon, 2001; Francis, Diorio, Liu, & Meaney, 1999). Francis and colleagues (1999) have established that maternal caregiving behaviors (MCBs) of archbacked nursing and licking and grooming behaviors, seen as highly engaged behavioral patterns, influence the development of phenotypic behavioral and endocrine stress reactivity in offspring (Caldji, Tannenbaum, Sharma, Francis, Plotsky, & Meaney, 1998; Francis & Diorio, 1999; Liu et al., 1997). It has been suggested that these variations are reflected in the levels of oxytocin receptors in the brain, in both rodents and non-human primates (Francis, Champagne, & Meaney, 2000; Winslow, 2005). Hofer's body of work (e.g., 1994, 2006) details the developmental psychobiology of attachment and separation using rat models, demonstrating the potential that attachment quality between rat dam and pup, represented by the quality of maternal caregiving behaviors, can mediate the stress reactivity of offspring.

In humans, Hane and Fox (2006) have shown that ordinary variations in maternal caregiving behaviors influence the infant's response to stress. Coupled with a body of research indicating that early environment shapes the behavioral development of both animals and humans, they provide compelling support for early intervention models that emphasize relational skill-building including parenting, coping and caregiving behaviors.

A growing number of successful early intervention treatment protocols are expanding our knowledge of the ways that effective and sensitive caregiving behaviors can offset many of the effects of prenatal stress, curtailing the damage and potential for vulnerabilities later in life (please see all articles by Beebe and colleagues in this special issue; see also Gwynne, Blick, & Duffy, 2009; Baradon, Fonagy, Bland, Lénárd, & Sleed, 2008; Bakermans-Kranenburg, van IJzendoorn, Mesman, Alink, & Juffer, 2008; Cicchetti & Gunnar, 2008; Dozier, Peloso, Lewis, Laurenceau, & Levine, 2008; Juffer, Bakermans-Kranenberg, & van IJzendoorn, 2008; Mayers, Hager-Budny, & Buckner, 2008; Toth, Rogosch, & Cicchetti, 2008; Oppenheim & Goldsmith, 2007; Sadler, Slade, & Mayes, 2006; Slade, Sadler, de Dios-Kenn, Webb, Ezepchick, & Mayes, 2005). These interventions aim to improve attachment behaviors and encourage a secure attachment relationship, thus improving the infant's social and emotional prognosis. Such interventions also seek to moderate the effects of trauma on the primary caregiver, helping to reduce the transmission of stress from caregiver to infant via relational pathways, and even to improve relational ties within the family as a whole.

## CONCLUSION

The body of research reviewed here is directly relevant to the women who were pregnant when they lost their husbands on September 11, 2001. The tragic significance of this type of stressor has many implications for the developing fetus. The specific effects of the stressor may vary with the exact month of fetal development. However, the research reviewed also provides evidence, based on both animal models and human clinical intervention techniques, that stress-induced changes in the fetal brain can be modulated by secure attachment and positive emotional development in early childhood. The clinical intervention Project described in this issue was informed by the research reviewed above, and it has attempted to modulate the effects of the heartrending losses of September 11, 2001, on the mothers and children, and their families, who lost their husbands and fathers on that day. It is hoped that with an improved understanding of the potential effects of maternal stress on the developing fetus, that clinicians, researchers and funders will appreciate the critical nature of early clinical interventions tailored not only to ameliorate those effects, but to strengthen the foundation of important early relationships and of families, as a whole.

## NOTES

1. A phenotype of a particular animal is made up of both gene expression and the influence of environmental factors, as well as any possible interactions. By contrast, an animal's genotype is comprised of inherited genetic information. Animals with the same genotype can appear very different from one another because both behavior and appearance are altered by environmental and developmental influences.
2. The "diathesis-stress" model explains the appearance of certain diseases and behaviors as the combined result of genetic factors or pre-existing vulnerable conditions (diathesis), and environmental influences (stress); that is, nature and nurture. The model is particularly useful in treatment models that incorporate stress-reduction and environmental controls as a way to mitigate genetic predisposition to illness and disease. It has been expanded to include a discussion of protective factors, which allows for a more nuanced understanding of when and why disease manifests itself (Mrazek & Haggert, 1994).
3. The hypothalamic-pituitary-adrenal axis (HPA axis) consists of the hypothalamus, the pituitary gland and the adrenal gland, all part of the body's endocrine system which regulates hormone levels. Using a negative feedback loop, the HPA axis releases and regulates the steroid hormones known as glucocorticoids (cortisol in humans; corticosterone in rodents). Glucocorticoids, together with the epinephrine and norepinephrine secreted by the sympathetic nervous system, generate the majority of the physiological changes induced by stress throughout the body. Unlike epinephrine and norepinephrine, which act on a rapid, split-second basis in the bloodstream generating a "fight or flight" response, glucocorticoids cross the blood-brain barrier and manage the stress response on a slower, minute-by-minute to hourly basis, causing sustained behavioral responses.

## REFERENCES

Alder, J., Fink, N., Bitzer, J., Hosli, I., & Holzgreve, W. (2007). Depression and anxiety during pregnancy: A risk factor for obstetric, fetal and neonatal outcome? A critical review of the literature. *Journal of Maternal-Fetal and Neonatal Medicine*, *20*(3), 189–209.

Bakermans-Kranenburg, M., van IJzendoorn, M., Mesman, J., Alink, L., & Juffer, F. (2008). Effects of an attachment-based intervention on daily cortisol moderated by dopamine receptor D4: A randomized control trial on 1- to 3-year-olds screened for externalizing behavior. *Development and Psychopathology*, *20*(3), 805–820.

Baradon, T., Fonagy, P., Bland, K., Lénárd, K., & Sleed, M. (2008). New beginnings—an experience-based program addressing the attachment relationship between mothers and their babies in prisons. *Journal of Child Psychotherapy, 34*(2), 240–258.

Barker, D. (1998). *In utero* programming of chronic disease. *Clinical Science, 95*, 115–128.

Bosch, O., Müsch, W., Bredewold, R., Slattery, D., & Neumann, I. (2007). Prenatal stress increases HPA axis activity and impairs maternal care in lactating female offspring: Implications for postpartum mood disorder. *Psychoneuroendocrinology, 32*(3), 267–278.

Bowlby, J. (1969). *Attachment and Loss, Vol. 1*. New York, NY: Basic Books.

Cai, Q., Zhu, Z., Fan, X., Jia, N., Bai, Z., Song, L., & Li, X. (2006). The effects of prenatal stress on Ca2+ channel and K+ channel of hippocampal CA3 pyramidal neurons in rat offspring. *Fen Zi Xi Bao SHeng Wu Xue Bao, 39*(3), 223–228. (Chinese: English abstract available)

Caldji, C., Tannenbaum, B., Sharma, S., Francis, D., Plotsky, P., & Meaney, M. (1998). Maternal care during infancy regulates the development of neural systems mediating the expression of fearfulness in the rat. *Proceedings of the National Academy of Sciences of the United States of America, 95*, 5335–5340.

Cassidy, J., & Shaver, P. (Eds.). (1999). *Handbook of attachment: Theory, research and clinical applications*. New York, NY: Guilford.

Christiensson, K., Nilsson, B., Stock, S., Matthiesen, A., & Uvnas-Moberg, K. (1989). Effect of nipple stimulation on uterine activity and on plasma levels of oxytocin in full term, healthy, pregnant women. *Acta Obstetricia et Gynecologica Scandinavica, 68*(3), 205–210.

Cicchetti, D., & Gunnar, M. (2008). Editorial: Integrating biological measures into the design and evaluation of preventive interventions. *Development and Psychopathology, 20*(3), 737–743.

Coe, C., & Lubach, G. (2000). Prenatal influences on neuroimmune set points in infancy. *Annals of the New York Academy of Sciences, 917*, 468–477.

Dickerson, P., Lally, B., Gunnel, E., Birkle, D., & Salm, A. (2005). Early emergence of increased fearful behavior in prenatally stressed rats. *Physiology & Behavior, 86*(4), 586–593.

Dozier, M., Peloso, E., Lewis, E., Laurenceau, J., & Levine, S. (2008). Effects of an attachment-based intervention of the cortisol production of infants and toddlers in foster care. *Development and Psychopathology, 20*(3), 845–859.

Drake, A., Tang, J., & Nyirenda, M. (2007). Mechanisms underlying the role of glucocorticoids in the early life programming of adult disease. *Clinical Science (Lond), 113*(5), 219–232.

Dunn, E., Owen, D., Kostaki, A., & Matthews, S. (2005). Prenatal glucocorticoid exposure affects reproductive capacity and adrenocortical function in mature female guinea pig offspring. *Pediatric Research 58*, 0–008 (Abstract).

Emack, J., Kostaki, A., Walker, C., & Matthews, S. (2008). Chronic maternal stress affects growth, behaviour and hypothalamo-pituitary-adrenal function in juvenile offspring. *Hormones and Behavior, 54*(4), 514–520.

Feldman, R., & Eidelman, A. (2009). Biological and environmental initial conditions shape the trajectories of cognitive and social-emotional development across the first years of life. *Developmental Science, 12*(1), 194–200.

Feldman, R., Weller, A., Zagoory-Sharon, O., & Levine, A. (2007). Evidence for a neuroendocrinological foundation of human affiliation: Plasma oxytocin levels across pregnancy and the postpartum period predict mother-infant bonding. *Psychological Science, 18*(11), 965–970.

Francis, D., Champagne, F., Liu, D., & Meaney, M. (1999). Maternal care, gene expression, and the development of individual differences in stress reactivity. In N. Adler, M. Marmot, B. McEwen, & J. Stewart (Eds.), *Socioeconomic status and health in industrial nations: Social, psychological, and biological pathways* (pp. 66–84). New York, NY: New York Academy of Sciences.

Francis, D., Champagne, F., & Meaney, M. (2000). Variations in maternal behavior are associated with differences in oxytocin receptor levels in the rat. *Journal of Neuroendocrinology, 12*(12), 1145–1148.

Francis, D., Diorio, J., Liu, D., & Meaney, M. (1999). Nongenomic transmission across generations of maternal behavior and stress responses in the rat. *Science, 286*(5442), 1155–1158.

Fumagalli, F., Bedogni, F., Perez, J., Racagni, G., & Riva, M. (2004). Corticostriatal brain-derived neurotrophic factor dysregulation in adult rats following prenatal stress. *European Journal of Neuroscience, 20*(5), 1348–1354.

Gwynne, K., Blick, B., & Duffy, G. (2009). Pilot evaluation of an early intervention programme for children at risk. *Journal of Paediatrics and Child Health, 45*(3), 118–124.

Hane, A., & Fox, N. (2006). Ordinary variations in maternal caregiving influence human infants' stress reactivity. *Psychological Science, 17*(6), 550–556.

Harding, R., & Bocking, A. (2001). *Fetal growth and development*. Cambridge, MA: Cambridge University Press.

Harper, L. (2005). Epigenetic inheritance and the intergenerational transfer of experience. *Psychological Bulletin, 131*(3), 340–360.

Hofer, M. (2006). Psychobiological roots of early attachment. *Current Directions in Psychological Science, 15*(2), 84–88.

Hofer, M. (1994). Early relationships as regulators of infant physiology and behavior. *Acta Paediatrica, 397*(Suppl.), 9–18.

Huizink, A., Mulder, E., & Buitelaar, J. (2004). Prenatal stress and risk for psychopathology: Specific effects or induction of general susceptibility? *Psychological Bulletin, 130*(1), 115–142.

Juffer, F., Bakermans-Kranenburg, M., & van IJzendoorn, M. (2008). *Promoting positive parenting: An attachment-based intervention*. New York, NY: Taylor & Francis.

Kapoor, A., Dunn, E., Kostaki, A., Andrews, M., & Matthews, S. (2006). Fetal programming of hypothalamo-pituitary-adrenal function: Prenatal stress and glucocorticoids. *Journal of Physiology, 572*(1), 31–44.

Kapoor, A., Petropoulos, S., & Matthews, S. (2008). Fetal programming of hypothalamic-pituitary-adrenal (HPA) axis function and behavior by synthetic glucocorticoids. *Brain Research Reviews, 57*(2), 586–595.

Keverne, E., & Kendrick, K. (1994). Maternal behaviour in sheep and its neuroendocrine regulation. *Acta Paediatric Supplement, 397*, 47–56.

Kofman, O. (2002). The role of prenatal stress in the etiology of developmental behavioral disorders. *Neuroscience & Biobehavioral Reviews, 26*(4), 457–470.

Kostaki, A., Owen, D., Li, D., & Matthews, S. (2005). Transgenerational effects of prenatal glucocorticoid exposure on growth, endocrine function and behaviour in the guinea pig. *Pediatric Research, 58,* P1–P052 (Abstract).

Kraszpulski, M., Dickerson, P., & Salm, A. (2006). Prenatal stress affects the developmental trajectory of the rat amygdala. *Stress: The International Journal on the Biology of Stress, 9*(2), 85–95.

Ladd, C., Huot, R., Thrivikraman, K., Nemeroff, C., Meaney, M., & Plotsky, P. (2000). Long-term behavioral and neuroendocrine adaptations to adverse early experience. *Progress in Brain Research, 122*, 81–103.

Ladd, C., Huot, R., Thrivikraman, K., Nemeroff, C., & Plotsky, P. (2004). Long-term adaptations in glucocorticoid receptor and mineralocorticoid receptor MRNA and negative feedback on the hypothalamo-pituitary-adrenal axis following neonatal maternal separation. *Biological Psychiatry, 55*(4), 367–375.

Lephard, E., Watson, M., Jacobson, N., Rhees, R., & Ladel, D. (1997). Calbindin-D28K is regulated by adrenal steroids in the hypothalamic tissue during prenatal development. *Developmental Brain Research, 100*, 117–120.

Liu, D., Diorio, J., Tannenbaum, B., Caldji, C., Francis, D., Freedman, A., . . . Meaney, M. J. (1997). Maternal care, hippocampal glucocorticoid receptors, and hypothalamic–pituitary–adrenal responses to stress. *Science, 277*, 1659–1662.

Lumey, L., Ravelli, A., Wiessing, L., Koppe, J., Treffers, P., & Stein, Z. (1993). The Dutch famine birth cohort study: Design, validation of exposure, and selected characteristics of subjects after 43 years follow-up. *Paediatric and Perinatal Epidemiology, 7*(4), 354–367.

Lupien, S., & Lepage, M. (2001). Stress, memory, and the hippocampus: Can't live with it, can't live without it. *Behavioral Brain Research, 127*, 137–158.

Mayers, H., Hager-Budny, M., & Buckner, E. (2008). The chances for children teen parent-infant project: Results of a pilot intervention for teen mothers and their infants in inner city high schools. *Infant Mental Health Journal, 29*(4), 320–342.

Manjarrez, G., Cisneros, I., Herrera, R., Vazquez, F., Robles, A., & Hernandez, J. (2005). Prenatal impairment of brain serotonergic transmission in infants. *Journal of Pediatrics, 147*(5), 592–596.

McEwen, B. (1998). Stress, adaptation, and disease: Allostasis and allostatic load. *Annals of the New York Academy of Science, 840*, 33–44.

Mrazek, P., & Haggert, R. (1994). *Reducing risks for mental disorders: Frontiers for prevention research*. Washington, DC: National Academy Press.

Nathanielsz, P., & Padmanabhan, V. (2006). Developmental origins of health and disease. *Journal of Physiology, 572*(1), 3–4.

Ogden, P., Minton, K., & Pain, C. (2006). *Trauma and the body: A sensorimotor approach to psychotherapy*. New York, NY: Norton.

Oppenheim, D., & Goldsmith, D. (2007). *Attachment theory in clinical work with children: Bridging the gap between research and practice*. New York, NY: Guilford Press.

Palleres, M., Scacchi Bernasconi, P., Feleder, C., & Cutrera, R. (2007). Effects of prenatal stress on motor performance and anxiety behavior in Swiss mice. *Physiology & Behavior, 92*(5), 951–956.

Peleg, D., Kennedy, C., & Hunter, S. (1998). Intrauterine growth restriction: Identification and management. *American Family Physician, 58*, 453–460.

Perez-Laso, C., Segovia, S., Martin, J., Ortega, E., Gomez, F., & Del Cerro, M. (2007). Environmental prenatal stress alters sexual dimorphism of maternal behavior in rats. *Behavioral Brain Research, 187*(2), 284–288.

Pryce, C., Bettschen, D., & Feldon, J. (2001). Comparison of the effects of early handling and early deprivation on maternal care in the rat. *Developmental Psychobiology, 38*(4), 239–251.

Roseboom, T., Rooij, S., & Painter, R. (2006). The Dutch famine and its long-term consequences for adult health. *Early Human Development, 82*, 485–491.

Sadler, L., Slade, A., & Mayes, L. (2006). Minding the baby: A mentalization-based parenting program. In J. G. Allen & P. Fonagy (Eds.), *Handbook of Mentalization-Based Treatment* (pp. 271–288). Chichester, UK: Wiley.

Sapolsky, R. (2000). Glucocorticoids and hippocampal atrophy in neuropsychiatric disorders.*Archives of General Psychiatry, 57*(10), 925–935.

Sapolsky, R. (2004). *Why zebras don't get ulcers: A guide to stress, stress-related diseases and coping*. New York, NY: Holt.

Sapolsky, R., Krey, L., & McEwen, B. (1986). The neuroendocrinology of stress and aging: The glucocorticoid cascade hypothesis. *Endocrinology Review, 7*(3), 284–301.

Santos, K., Mazzola, T., & Carvalho, H. (2005). The prima donna of epigenetics: The regulation of gene expression by DNA methylation. *Brazilian Journal of Medical and Biological Research, 38*(10), 1531–1541.

Schneider, M., Moore, C., Roberts, A., & Dejesus, O. (2001). Prenatal stress alters early neurobehavior, stress reactivity and learning in non-human primates: A brief review. *Stress, 4*, 183–193.

Seckl, J., & Holmes, M. (2007). Mechanisms of disease: Glucocorticoids, their placental metabolism and fetal 'programming' of adult pathophysiology. *Nature Clinical Practice Endocrinology & Metabolism, 3*(6), 479–488.

Skinner, H., White, D., & Birkle, D. (1999). The effects of maternal stress on plasma corticosterone and ACTH levels in rats. *Social Neuroscience Abstracts, 857*.

Slade, A., Sadler, L., de Dios-Kenn, C., Webb, D., Ezepchick, J., & Mayes, L. (2005). Minding the baby: A reflective parenting program. *Psychoanalytic Study of the Child, 60*, 74–100.

Son, G., Geum, D., Chung, S., Kim, E., Jo, J., Kikm, C., . . . Kim, K. (2006). Maternal stress produces learning deficits associated with impairment of NMDA receptor-mediated synaptic plasticity. *Journal of Neuroscience, 26*(12), 3309–3318.

Sroufe, L. (2005). Attachment and development: A prospective, longitudinal study from birth to adulthood. *Attachment & Human Development, 7*(4), 349–367.

Sroufe, L., Carlson, E., Levy, A., & Egeland, B. (1999). Implications of attachment theory for developmental psychopathology. *Development and Psychopathology, 11*(1), 1–13.

Suomi, S. J., & Levine, S. (1998). Psychobiology of intergenerational effects of trauma. Evidence from animal studies In Y. Danieli (Ed.), *International handbook of multigenerational legacies of trauma* (pp. 623–637). New York, NY: Plenum Press.

Swain, J., Thomas, P., Leckman, J., & Mayes, L. (2008). Parent-infant attachment systems: Neural circuits and early-life programming. In E. Jurist, A. Slade, & S. Bergner (Eds.), *Mind to mind: Infant research, neuroscience and psychoanalysis* (pp. 264–303). New York, NY: Other Press.

Toth, S., Rogosch, F., & Cicchetti, D. (2008). Attachment-theory-informed intervention and reflective functioning in depressed mothers. In *Clinical applications of the adult attachment interview* (pp. 154–172). New York, NY: Guilford Press.

Uvnas-Moberg, K. (1996). Neuroendocrinology of the mother-child interaction. *Trends in Endocrinology and Metabolism, 7*(4), 126–131.

Uvnas-Moberg, K. (1997). Physological and endocrine effects of social contact. *Annals of the New York Academy of Science, 807*, 146–163.

Uvnas-Moberg, K., & Winberg, J. (1989). Role of sensory stimulation in the energy economy in mother and infant with particular regard to the gastrointestinal endocrine system. In E. Lebenthal (Ed.), *Textbook of gastroenterology and nutrition in infancy* (2nd ed., pp. 53–62). New York, NY: Raven Press.

Van den Hove, D., Steinbusch, H., Scheepens, A., Van de Berg, W., Kooiman, L., Boosten, B., Prickaerts, J., & Blanco, C. (2006). Prenatal stress and neonatal rat brain development. *Neuroscience, 137*(1), 145–155.

Vashadze, S. (2007). Insomnia, serotonin and depression. *Georgian Medical News, 150*, 22–24.

Viltart, O. & Vanbesien-Mailliot, C. (2007). Impact of prenatal stress on neuroendocrine programming. *Scientific World Journal, 7*, 1493–1537.

Wadhwa, P. (1998). Prenatal stress and life-span development. In: H. Friedman (Ed.), *Encyclopedia of Mental Health*, (*Vol. 3*, pp. 265–280). San Diego: Academic Press.

Wadhwa, P. (2005). Psychoneuroendocrine processes in human pregnancy influence fetal development and health. *Psychoneuroendocrinology*, *30*(8), 724–743.

Weinstock, M. (2001a). Alterations induced by gestational stress in brain morphology and behaviour of the offspring. *Progress in Neurobiology*, *65*(5), 427–451.

Weinstock, M., (2001b). Alterations induced by gestational stress in brain morphology and behaviour of the offspring. *Progress in Neurobiology*, *63*, 427–452.

Winberg, J. (2005). Mother and newborn baby: Mutual regulation of physiology and behavior–a selective review. *Developmental Psychobiology*, *47*(3), 217–229.

Winslow, J. (2005). Neuropeptides and non-human primate social deficits associated with pathogenic rearing experience. *International Journal of Developmental Neuroscience*, *23*(2–3), 245–251.

Yaka, R., Salomon, S., Matzner, H., & Weinstock, M. (2007). Effect of varied gestational stress on acquisition of spatial memory, hippocampal LTP and synaptic proteins in juvenile male rats. *Behavioral Brain Research*, *179*(1), 126–132.

Yang, J., Han, H., Cao, J., Li, L., & Xu, L. (2006). Prenatal stress modifies hippocampal synaptic plasticity and spatial learning in young rat offspring. *Hippocampus*, *16*(5), 431–436.

# Dyadic Trauma in Infancy and Early Childhood: Review of the Literature

Sara Markese, Ph.D.

The clinical and empirical literature on trauma and loss in infancy and early childhood largely focuses on children's exposure to traumatic events, direct "event trauma." This article seeks to expand the definition of trauma in infancy to include "indirect trauma," implicit emotional and relational events, such as infant exposure to traumatized parents, which occurred in the Project for Mothers, Infants, and Young Children of September 11, 2001, described in this issue. Four empirical literatures are reviewed to develop an understanding of the cognitive, behavioral, and social sequelae of early trauma and parental loss: (1) research on childhood trauma symptoms in the verbal period; (2) research on child and parent attachment security and the parent-child relationship; (3) research on the preverbal period of infant development, specifically addressing nonverbal parent-child communication patterns; and (4) research on the impact of maternal trauma prenatally, on the infant's capacity to remember and represent trauma occurring preverbally, and on the effect of early trauma on neurological development. The article argues that trauma and treatment in infancy and early childhood should be construed as dyadic, occurring between parent and child.

In response to traumatic events of the last decade, researchers and clinicians have struggled to define and treat exposure to trauma and loss in early childhood (Osofsky, 2004; Osofsky, Osofsky, & Harris, 2007; Chemtob, Nomura, & Abramovitz, 2008; Chemtob et al., 2010; Lieberman, Compton, Van Horn, & Ippen, 2003; Klein, DeVoe, Miranda-Julian, & Linas, 2009; DeVoe, Klein, Bannon, & Miranda-Julian, 2011; Yehuda et al., 2005; Hoven et al., 2005; Scheeringa, Zeanah, Myers, & Putnam, 2005; Scheeringa & Zeanah, 2008; Laor, Wolmer, & Cohen, 2001). Children are the most vulnerable to the effects of trauma, particularly catastrophic community disaster (Kitzmann, Gaylord, & Aber, 2003), which impacts the parent and the parent-child dyad in both acute and long-term ways. However, until recently the effects of trauma on infants and young children have been relatively neglected in the research and treatment literatures. Young children are underrepresented in populations generating research aimed at clarifying specific reactions to trauma (Osofsky, Osofsky, & Harris, 2007). Young children are also underrepresented in the planning of comprehensive postdisaster treatment (Covell, Allen, & Essock, 2006). The reasons for this underrepresentation of children may include the lack of development of outreach models and service delivery pathways as well as difficulties in defining young children's responses to trauma (Osofsky, Osofsky, & Harris, 2007; Chemtob et al., 2008).

In the wake of the events of the terrorist attacks of September 11, 2001, the need for a better understanding of the ways that young children experience and express trauma symptoms became abundantly clear. In addition to the large numbers of young children who were "directly" exposed to the trauma, by living or going to school near the World Trade Center site, children across the nation were affected through exposure to their parents' trauma and post-trauma symptoms and through loss of a parent or family member. It has been estimated that 10,000 children lost a parent on September 11, 2001, and hundreds of these children were in their first two years of life (Covell et al., 2006; Hoven et al., 2005). This issue, the "September 11, 2001, Mothers, Infants and Young Children Project," describes efforts to treat those women who were pregnant when their husbands were killed in the World Trade Center attacks, and the infants and young children of these women. This project both builds on and extends the growing body of literature describing the sequelae of direct and indirect trauma on infants and young children.

The past decade has also seen a surge in theoretical and empirical literature on infant trauma. This literature has generated more refined conceptualizations of both infant trauma and dyadic trauma, through disaster research, and through extensive reviews of what is known about trauma in the preverbal period (see Coates & Gaenbauer, 2009, and Scheeringa & Gaensbauer, 2000, for reviews). This article will review the literature with the infants of the "September 11, 2001 Mothers, Infants and Young Children Project" in mind. The introduction will consider some of the difficulties in defining the effects of trauma in infancy and early childhood, addressing the fact that most theory and research has focused on infants who have actually been exposed to traumatic circumstances, termed "event trauma" (see Coates & Gaensbauer, 2009). In addition to direct exposure, this article will specifically focus on the "dyadic trauma" experienced by the infants and children in this Project, including exposure to pre-natal maternal stress hormones and exposure to maternal trauma symptoms in infancy. This review will also briefly set the stage by reviewing some of the important recent research on the effects of the World Trade Center attacks of September 11 on infants and young children.

While there is much important recent trauma research, this article contends that all the diverse developmental research currently available to conceptualize infant and early childhood trauma has not been brought together to understand forms of infant trauma beyond direct exposure. Four areas of relevant literature will be reviewed: (1) research on childhood trauma symptoms in the verbal period; (2) research utilizing child and parent attachment security to understand infant and early childhood trauma, and research on the transmission of maternal trauma to the child; (3) research on the preverbal period of infant development, specifically addressing nonverbal communication patterns between parent and child; and (4) research on the impact of maternal trauma prenatally, on the infant's capacity to remember and represent trauma occurring preverbally, and on the effect of early trauma on neurological development. Consideration of these areas of research will enrich the conceptualization of infant trauma in general, and specifically the trauma of the infants of September 11, 2001, discussed in this issue.

## INTRODUCTION

The infants in this Project were born to mothers traumatized by the death of their husbands in the disaster of September 11 and by their exposure to the terrorist threat. These mothers were traumatized acutely when the infant was in utero, and continuously over the course of the infant's early development. Although ongoing efforts are underway, conceptualizing the assessment and treatment of infants at risk has posed difficulties for two central reasons. First, how exactly are infants affected in a trauma? In our case, how exactly were these infants born after September 11, 2001, affected? Second, how can we understand how preverbal infants and young children in general process, experience, and react to trauma?

To address the first question, there are several pathways by which to understand the nature of the World Trade Center disaster trauma for both unborn and infant children. For the children of our Project, there are actually two separate traumas that impact their development. The first trauma is a relational one, the death of a parent in the attacks. For unborn and very young infants, this traumatic loss will have a physical effect on them through the fetal environment and a relational effect through their early interactions with a bereaved mother who will experience severe emotional distress, including heightened anxiety, hypervigilance to danger, depression, and periods of dissociative withdrawal as a result of the loss of her spouse. Because these mothers were doubly affected, by their exposure as New Yorkers under threat and by the exposure to graphic details of the attacks in connection with the death of their husbands, they are likely to experience significant, if not clinical, levels of posttraumatic stress symptoms. The second trauma is a physical one, the mother's exposure to the acute and ongoing threat of terrorist attacks after September 11, 2001. For unborn infants, this trauma will have a physical effect on them through the fetal environment (Feldman & Eidelman, 2009). Similar to the trauma of loss, this trauma will then be continued through the relational trauma of early interactions with a traumatized mother.

To address the second question, how preverbal infants and young children process, experience and react to trauma in general, specialized assessment tools and an understanding of the empirical literature in early developmental research are essential. This article will review the related research, as described above. To assess trauma in young children, research spurred by recent disasters has defined both trauma and posttraumatic stress disorder (PTSD) for young children in increasingly more specific ways (Scheeringa, Peebles, Cook, & Zeanah, 2001). Scales used to assess life-long trauma history in adults have been adapted for research on infants and young children, such as the Traumatic Events Screening Inventory (TESI; Ford & Rogers, 1997; adapted by Ghosh-Ippen et al. (2002), and the Post-Traumatic Stress Disorder Checklist-Terror (PCL: Weathers, 1993; adapted by Norris, 2001). In addition, scales used to quantify a child's level of exposure have been created and refined (DeVoe et al., 2011; Chemtob et al., 2008, 2010). These scales allow the nature of the trauma to be specified and quantified.

Researchers in the past decade have used modified adult trauma exposure scales and have created new scales to assess the youngest trauma victims. However, the unborn infants later assessed and treated with the parent-infant dyad in the "September 11, 2001 Mothers, Infants and Young Children Project" pose particular questions about the nature of trauma over the course of development and bring to light the risk of "dyadic trauma" (see Wolmer, Laor, Gershon, Mayes, & Cohen, 2000; Scheeringa & Zeanah, 2001; Sossin & Birklein, 2006; Birklein & Sossin, 2006; Yehuda & Bierer, 2008).

In fact, it is increasingly believed that for infants and very young children, the degree of threat to the parent, the parent's reactions to the trauma, and the impact of the parent's posttraumatic stress symptoms on the parent-child relationship, may be more important in the child's functioning and mental health outcomes than the actual direct trauma exposure (DeVoe et al., 2011; Chemtob et al., 2008, 2010; Scheeringa, Zeanah, Myers, & Putnam, 2003; Laor et al., 2001). In this sense, PTSD in infancy and early childhood may be conceptualized as relational or dyadic in that parents may transmit their own symptoms to infants via nonverbal stress responses and parent-infant interactions (Scheeringa & Zeanah, 2001; Yehuda & Bierer, 2008; see Tortora, *Beyond The Face and Words,* this issue).

Infants in our Project were first exposed to the trauma in utero via their mother's physiological reactions to the threat of attack and to their grief reactions in learning of their husband's death. They were then exposed to the trauma via their mothers' posttrauma symptoms in their infant and early childhood years. Although they were not directly exposed to physical "event" trauma, or to the acute experience of loss, being born into the "dysregulated psychological environment" (Chemtob et al., 2008) of post-September 11, 2001 put them at significant risk.

Once these infants are defined as having been traumatized themselves, in addition to thinking about their trauma as dyadically constructed between mother and infant, it is possible to look for other trauma sequelae that can be directly observed in early infancy. Although much research in infancy begins at about 12 months, the earliest that attachment can be assessed, it is important to conceptualize the effects of trauma on the infants of September 11 well before this point. The literature offers such well-researched developmental concepts as early infant "temperament," microanalytic self- and interactive regulation patterns, neurological, and cognitive development before measures of attachment security can be assessed. By considering these measures of infant development following infant exposure to direct or dyadic trauma, specific risk factors for the later development of insecure attachment and possible subsequent child psychopathology may be discerned. If so, they can enrich research and primary prevention/intervention programs for infants and preverbal toddlers coping with all forms of trauma.

The impact of traumatic events and early loss, with lasting effects on the infant and young toddler's psychosocial development, has historically inspired psychoanalytic theory but little empirical research. This area has been difficult to investigate because of inherent difficulties in studying infants and young children. First, symbolic enactment and verbal representation of loss and distress are generally conceptualized as central to the experience of trauma, but preverbal infants preclude this type of assessment. Second, trauma in early childhood has generally been thought to involve direct exposure to events, or actual physical impingement or harm, rather than "indirect" implicit emotional and relational events. The symptoms and behaviors associated with indirect trauma may be less overt and therefore less detectable by conventional measures.

The area of developmental research that has been most utilized in conceptualizing the effects of very early trauma in infants and preverbal toddlers is Attachment Theory. The two most widely researched methods involve assessing the nature of a young toddler's relationship to a primary attachment figure with the Ainsworth Strange Situation (Ainsworth, Blehar, Waters, & Wall, 1978), and assessing the parents' attachment representations with the Adult Attachment Inventory (AAI: Main & Goldwyn, 1988; Main, Goldwyn, & Hesse, 2008) to understand the intergenerational transmission of trauma from parent to child (Steele, Steele, & Murphy, 2010). These methods have provided developmental researchers and therapists with ways of understanding the processes by which infants and young children respond to and internalize their parents' own traumatic experiences and representations of unresolved loss, and the pathological developmental trajectories that can be set in motion and observed in the preverbal and early verbal stages of childhood.

Attachment research has proven to be an extremely valuable method of assessing the effect of unresolved parental mourning and traumatic loss on the attachment bond. However, this research does not directly examine the effect on infant development in the preverbal period, prior to the 12-month point, when attachment can first be assessed. Infants may begin to represent trauma and loss in presymbolic, implicit/procedural modes, through the expression of maladaptive forms of self- or interactive-regulatory behaviors. Problematic dyadic interactions, both with primary attachment figures and with strangers, may be evident (see Beebe et al., 2010; Jaffe, Beebe, Feldstein, Crown, & Jasnow, 2001). The direct measurement of early infant physiological, neuropsychological and cognitive development and memory following a traumatic loss may result in empirical outcome measures that provide measures of risk prior to 12 months. In the second year of life, early nonverbal symbolic play may also be a valuable way of assessing very early representations of loss and distress. Such direct measurement holds the promise of enriching research and treatment in the transmission of parental trauma and loss, and the effects of parental depression, anxiety and posttraumatic stress, on parent-infant interaction and attachment in the wake of traumatic loss.

In the past decade, researchers have made great strides in documenting, identifying, and working to amend the previous lack of research on the effects of trauma on young children. For example, the impact of violence on infants and young children has been studied in children's exposure to family and community violence (Osofsky, 2004; Levendosky, Huth-Bocks, Shapiro, & Semel, 2003; McClosky & Walker, 2000; Lieberman & Van Horn, 2005). Researchers in Israel have contributed extensively to the empirical literature through the study of the impact of war and terrorism on parents and their parenting, and on children themselves (see Fremont, 2004, for a review; Laor et al., 1996, 1997, 2001). In the United States, much valuable immediate and long-term follow-up research has been done on the effects of the September 11 attacks on infants (Yehuda et al., 2005), preschool children (Klein et al., 2009; Chemtob et al., 2008, 2010; DeVoe et al., 2011), school-age children (Hoven et al., 2005; DeVoe et al., 2011; Gershoff, Aber, Ware, & Kotler, 2010; Kitzmann et al., 2004; Klein et al., 2009; Pfefferbaum, 2005; Covell et al., 2006), and their parents (Wilson, Lengua, Meltzoff, & Smith, 2010; Mowder, Guttman, Rubinson, & Sossin, 2007; Pfefferbaum, 2005; Kitzmann et al., 2004; Gershoff et al., 2010).

Other trauma research includes large-scale efforts to document posttraumatic stress symptoms particular to young children exposed to natural disasters, such as Hurricanes Andrew and Katrina (LaGreca, Silverman, Vernberg, & Prinstein, 1996; Osofsky, Osofsky, & Harris, 2007; Scheeringa & Zeanah, 2008), and to the global violence of the past decade, such as war exposure in Israel, Bosnia, and Afghanistan (Laor et al., 1996, 1997, 2001; Pine, Costello, & Masten, 2005). Recent efforts to document childhood symptoms of posttraumatic stress, and long-term effects of exposure to acute trauma and loss, have led to the reorganization of the description of childhood PTSD using developmentally specific diagnostic criteria (Zero to Three, 2005; Scheeringa et al., 2001, 2003).

Despite the emergence of a body of research on the impact of trauma and loss on young children, the concept of measuring and defining preverbal infant and early toddler trauma is relatively recent and is currently emerging (see Scheeringa et al., 2003). To add to assessment difficulties, young children seem to be less likely to show specific symptoms of posttraumatic stress and instead demonstrate their distress in more global disturbances of emotion and behavior, including separation difficulties, aggression and regressive behaviors (Laor et al., 1996; Scheeringa & Zeanah, 1994; Scheeringa, Zeanah, Drell, & Larrieu, 1995). In addition, trauma assessment in infancy and young childhood often depends on parental report, and the detection of these more global disturbances may be particularly difficult for parents who may expect their children's trauma reactions to mirror their own (Koplewicz et al., 2002). Klein and colleagues (2009) have provided an important descriptive study of young children exposed to the attacks of September 11. They describe toddlers' reactions, expected and unexpected, to the disaster in powerful clinical detail, providing a more alive picture of toddlers undergoing acute trauma and their stress reactions over time.

In addition to the important work of the past decade noted above, several related bodies of empirical literature are reviewed in this article. This research can be used to enhance our understanding of the cognitive, behavioral, and social sequelae of dyadic trauma in the preverbal infant period as well as early childhood. The available empirical literature of the past three decades that will be reviewed is divided into four areas.

The first area reviewed is research on childhood trauma symptoms in the verbal period, including recent terror, disaster, and war exposure research, as well as research on the effects of the relational trauma of early loss of a parent on young children's later psychosocial development. The second area includes research utilizing the child's attachment security at 12–18 months (a) as a means of understanding early internalization and representation of parents' unresolved trauma (including parental depression, anxiety, dissociation, and emotional withdrawal) and (b) as a predictor of later maladaptive psychosocial functioning. The third area reviewed is research on the preverbal period of infant development, which attempts to understand the infants' representations of relational, dyadic parent-child distress through nonverbal communication. The fourth area reviewed is research on the infant's capacity to remember and represent trauma occurring preverbally and includes research on the effect of early trauma on neurological development.

## CONTRIBUTIONS OF TRAUMA RESEARCH: THE VERBAL CHILD

In this section the following are reviewed: (a) the effects of trauma and loss in the early verbal period, (b) the symptom picture of childhood trauma and its similarities to and differences from adult bereavement, (c) trauma in childhood as a risk factor for psychopathology over the course of development into adulthood, (d) mediating factors in the outcome of trauma and loss in early childhood, and (e) conceptualizing dyadic trauma.

### Effects of Trauma and Loss in the Early Verbal Period on Psychosocial Development

Research on the effects of trauma and loss in early childhood remains relatively sparse (but see Lieberman, Compton, Van Horn, & Ippen, 2003). Trauma occurring following the onset of language has been given far more attention than that occurring prior to the development of language (Coates & Gaensbauer, 2009; Perry, 1996). The central problem that compromises empirical research on the effects of trauma and loss in childhood is the lack of useable research tools that can directly measure a child's actual experience and states of mind following the trauma. Two such tools, the Pre-School Affective Interview (Kranzler, Schaffer, Wasserman, & Davies, 1990) and the Affect Task (Steele, Steele, Croft, & Fonagy, 2001), use visual imagery to elicit children's response to a wide range of emotions in relation to different experiences. Until more empirical tools of this sort are created and empirically validated, research on trauma in early childhood will continue to be centered around parents' and teachers' accounts of the child's experience and resulting psychological and behavioral symptoms, to the exclusion of children's own behavioral, verbal or symbolic means of representing the effects of the trauma.

Several studies have addressed the use of parental interview as a means of understanding childhood trauma, and have repeatedly demonstrated the discordance between adults' accounts (including parents, relatives, and teachers) of the degree and nature of the child's distress, and the child's directly reported experience (Koplewicz et al., 2002; Schecter, Coates, & First, 2002; Weller, Weller, Fristad, Cain, & Bowes, 1988; Weissman et al., 1987). Clinical accounts of interactions between parents and their toddlers following the events of September 11 support this research. For example, children in the presence of a therapist were observed to repeatedly surprise their parents both with their understanding of the traumatic events, and with the extent of their emotional responses to the trauma (Schecter, Coates, & First, 2002). The therapists of this issue report a similar picture (see Cohen, *The Evolution of the Project,* and Sossin & Cohen, *Children's Play in the Wake of Trauma,* this issue). Even when parents have been subjected to the trauma themselves, they still tend to underestimate the psychological effects of the experience, reporting mostly behavioral symptoms, whereas children tend to report more subjective psychological and somatic feelings (Ronen, 2002; Weissman et al., 1987). In the words of Perry (1996, p. 271), "It is an ultimate irony that at the time when the human is most vulnerable to the effects of trauma, during infancy and childhood, adults generally presume the most resilience."

## Childhood Symptoms: Similarities to and Differences From Adult Bereavement and PTSD

In attempting to characterize the symptom picture following trauma in early childhood, researchers have started from knowledge of adults' traumatic symptoms and bereavement processes. Children's stress reactions to threat, grief, and loss have been demonstrated to have both important similarities and dissimilarities to those of adults (see Coates & Gaensbauer, 2009 for a review; Klein et al., 2009).

### Childhood Bereavement

Children have been found to respond to loss similarly to adults in both the nature and frequency of their grief reactions and have been found to demonstrate a chronological pattern of bereavement similar to that of adults (Pynoos, Nader, Frederick, Gonda, & Stuber, 1987; Parkes, 1967). While these similarities provide researchers with a model of grief within which to understand children's bereavement, there are important differences in childhood symptoms which distinguish bereaved children from bereaved adults, and from nonbereaved children with disorders of mood and behavior. Loss in the preverbal stages of development has many characteristics unique to infancy (Lieberman et al., 2003).

Children have been reported to exhibit depressive symptoms following the loss of a parent. However, despite significant mood disturbance and diminished interest and pleasure, these children were distinguishable from a group of nonbereaved, depressed controls by the absence of feelings of guilt and worthlessness (Clayton, Desmarais, & Winokur, 1968). An additional symptom unique to bereaved children was the high prevalence (37 percent) of children exhibiting suicidal ideation following their loss, without any corresponding suicidal behavior (Pynoos, 1992; Clayton et al., 1968).

Another symptom of bereaved children is a high incidence of separation anxiety, co-mingled with depressive symptoms. Following bereavement, children have been observed to exhibit significantly more anxiety at imagined separations than controls; they also manifested more overt, anxious attachment behaviors in response to normal separations (Kranzler et al., 1990). This regressive attachment behavior, in combination with the prevalence of conduct-disordered behaviors following loss, may contribute to adults' focus on reporting behavior disturbances and regressive patterns of interaction, when in fact these behaviors serve as ways for children to enact their feelings of anger and emptiness following their loss (Kranzler et al., 1990; Pynoos, 1992).

## Childhood Posttraumatic Stress Disorder

Beginning with an adult model of Post-Traumatic Stress Disorder, children have been shown to display a range of symptoms similar to those of adults, including behavioral disorders, anxiety, phobia, and depressive disorders (Scheeringa & Gaensbauer, 2000; Schwartz & Perry, 1994). In this way, children's reactions to grief and trauma may be measured on a continuum of symptoms related to the PTSD symptoms reported in adults. Similar to adults with PTSD symptoms, children who have experienced a loss or trauma have intrusive thoughts and memories, and have been shown to either obsessively re-enact the trauma or loss or inhibit symbolic play and affective expressions of grief (Coates & Gaensbauer, 2009; Scheeringa & Gaensbauer, 2000; Pynoos, 1992). Similarly, following trauma or loss, children may exhibit aggressive behaviors and emotional displays, or they may appear dissociated or numb to the trauma, inhibiting emotional reactions and symbolic enactment (Coates & Gaensbauer, 2009; Scheeringa & Gaensbauer, 2000; Pynoos et al., 1987). However, different from adults, children's reactions to trauma often reflect specific developmental challenges that may be derailed or accentuated by posttraumatic stress symptoms (Deering, 2000; McDermott & Palmer, 2002; Ronen, 2002; Klein et al., 2009).

Basic trauma reactions in childhood have been characterized as the reflection of two distinct neuronal response patterns: the hyperarousal continuum and the dissociative continuum (Perry, 1996, 2006). In states of acute trauma, or even when re-experiencing traumatic thoughts, children demonstrate a "freezing" mechanism in response to their anxiety. Depending on the pattern of hyperarousal or dissociation, this freezing may appear aggressive and oppositional or as a lack of feeling about the traumatic events (Perry, 1996). These neurobiological reactions to trauma are often misconstrued as defiant behavior, or alternatively as a lack of emotion on the part of the child, when in fact these behaviors signal a high level of distress and anxiety. These behavioral differences from adult bereavement contribute to enduring misconceptions about the nature of bereavement and distress in children.

## Trauma Symptoms Specific to Childhood

Differences in the ways that young children react to and express distress during trauma have been increasingly described in the past decade (see Fremont, 2004; Coates & Gaensbauer, 2009; Scheeringa et al., 2001, for reviews), as studies have focused more on the specific trauma reactions of preschool children (Chemtob et al., 2008, 2010; Klein et al., 2009). Both biological differences, such as heart rate lability (Scheeringa et al., 2004), and behavioral differences have been observed. Quantitative and qualitative research methods have contributed to an improved understanding of children's reactions to trauma, and thus to a differentiated diagnostic outline for childhood PTSD (Scheeringa et al., 2001; Zero to Three, 2005). Researchers in the past have used the diagnostic criteria for adult PTSD, modifying the criteria to fit young children's expression of trauma symptoms in terms of quantity of symptoms needed for diagnosis of PTSD.

In research on the exposure of preschool children to the World Trade Center attacks of September 11, 2001, both quantitative and qualitative data have been reported. Quantitative research has examined the extent of children's behavioral difficulties following trauma exposure, and the child's life-time exposure to trauma, using such measures as the Child Behavior Checklist and the "Life Events" scale of the Infant-Toddler Social and Emotional Assessment (ITSEA), respectively. In examining both the effects of increased maternal trauma symptoms, and the child's past history of exposure to trauma, an "allostatic load" model of trauma, suggesting that trauma is cumulative in its effects, has been supported for traumatized preschoolers (McEwan, 1998; Chemtob et al., 2008, 2010). Particular areas of child behavioral difficulties following trauma exposure have been described, including emotional reactivity, sleep difficulties, and symptoms of anxiety and depression (Chemtob et al., 2010).

Rich qualitative research on pre-school children's behavioral reactions to trauma uses parents' descriptive accounts of their children's reactions to the events of September 11 (Klein et al., 2009). This research provides a differentiated, descriptive view of trauma symptoms in young children. During the actual disaster, parents were surprised to observe children reacting in a quiet, calm and cooperative manner, listening to parent direction without difficulty, and playing calmly by themselves while parents developed escape plans (Klein et al., 2009). A symptom of acute trauma exposure specific to very young children was observed as some children actually fell asleep during the chaos, demonstrating withdrawn, catatonic reactions to traumatic stress (Klein et al., 2009). In the aftermath of the attacks, children were particularly sensitive to separations from caregivers and important other attachment figures and to changes in their daily routines (Klein et al., 2009). Taken together, qualitative and quantitative trauma research specific to traumatized young children has provided the new information necessary for an increasingly specific and well-defined criteria for assessing childhood PTSD (Scheeringa et al., 2001; Zero to Three, 2005).

## Trauma and Parental Loss in Childhood as a Risk Factor for Psychopathology

Studies that have assessed children following parental loss and have retrospectively interviewed adults who lost a parent in their childhood have documented an increase in overall psychopathology. These studies document an increase in a wide range of affective disorders, compared to controls, and specifically document an increase in suicidality, depression, and anxiety disorders, including agoraphobia, panic disorder, and phobic avoidance; an increased incidence in substance abuse; and greater incidence of Borderline Personality Disorder and PTSD in adulthood (Yehuda et al., 2005; Kendler, Sheth, Gardner, & Prescott, 2002; Dowdney, 2005; Garber, 1997; Kranzler et al., 1990; Weller et al., 1988; Harris, Brown, & Bifulco, 1986; Clayton et al., 1968).

Studies also have shown that adults who themselves experienced trauma or the early loss of a parent are at significant risk of transmitting this "unresolved" loss and attachment insecurity to their children. As parents, these adults have an increased likelihood of evidencing "unresolved" attachment representations as measured by the AAI (Lyons-Ruth, Repacholi, McCleod, & Silva, 1991). Due to their distress, these parents may behave in atypical ways, evidencing conflicting "hostile/helpless" states of mind (Lyons-Ruth, Bronfman, & Atwood, 1999a), evidencing "helpless/fearful" parenting (Lyons-Ruth & Spielman, 2004), and in these ways "transmitting" their own trauma to their infants (Madigan et al., 2006; Lyons-Ruth & Spielman, 2004; Lyons-Ruth, 2003; Goldberg, Benoit, Blokland, & Madigan, 2003; Kelly, Ueng-McHale, Grienenberger, & Slade, 2003; Lyons-Ruth, Bronfman, & Parsons, 1999b). These infants then have an increased risk of "disorganized" attachment (Lyons-Ruth & Jacobvitz, 2008; Lyons-Ruth, 2008; Lyons-Ruth & Spielman, 2004; Main & Hesse, 1990; Lyons-Ruth, Repacholi, McCleod, & Silva, 1991).

Several large epidemiological, community-based studies have confirmed the greater incidence of psychopathology in adults with early parental loss in the general population (Kendler et al., 2002; Wheaton, Roszell, & Hall, 1997; Tweed, Schoenbach, George, & Blazer, 1989). In attempting to understand studies that document an increase in adult psychopathology over the normal population (as much as a fourfold increase in psychiatric diagnosis: Wheaton et al., 1997), as well as to understand those that do not show such an increase in psychopathology following early loss, it becomes important to consider possible neurobiological models of the processing of early trauma and loss, as well as to consider mediating environmental factors.

The neurobiological model of trauma is useful in understanding the risk factors associated with childhood trauma for later development. According to the hyperarousal/dissociative model of posttraumatic stress and bereavement, children are particularly susceptible to the lasting effects of trauma on personality and psychosocial development. Perry (1996, 2006) stresses the fact that while internalization of the fear response can be incorporated into the mature brain structure and personality of the adult, these neurological reactions to trauma organize the child's developing neural systems, and thus become a filter through which subsequent experience is organized. In this way, the experience of early trauma can become a template through which later experiences are processed, turning "state" experiences of trauma and loss into later "traits." Specifically, these states of either neural hyperarousal or dissociation become sensitized and reinforced as a result of their continued activation each time a child is exposed to environmental reminders, or even thoughts, of a traumatic event.

The brain regions involved in processing traumatic experience are also responsible for a variety of developing cognitive and affective capacities in the child. Therefore, early trauma may sensitize these neuronal pathways of hyperarousal or dissociation, leading to an increasing reliance on maladaptive coping strategies, and additionally compromising the development of other brain structures. The system associated with hyperarousal may interfere with the child's ability to regulate affect, physiological arousal, locomotion, attention, and stress (Andrade & Aghajanian, 1984; Bhaskaran & Freed, 1988). Children who exhibit dissociative coping mechanisms may have later difficulty with affect regulation, ability to form attachment relationships, and may be prone to later depressive episodes and PTSD as adults (Schore, 2002; Perry, 1996, 2006). Early experience of trauma and loss have been shown to result in neurobiological brain abnormalities, including dysfunction in the regulation of the pituitary-adrenal axis, the locus coeruleus, and the ventral tegmental nucleus, and subsequently impoverished regulation of the stress response (Schore, 2002; Perry, 1996, 2006; Weller et al., 1990). As the initially adaptive response to trauma becomes sensitized through re-experiencing the trauma in intrusive thoughts and memories, this reaction becomes maladaptive, resulting in a priming of states of either hyperarousal or dissociation, and leaving the child vulnerable to future disorders of mood, attention, and dissociation.

## Mediating Factors in the Psychosocial Outcome of Loss in Early Childhood

Parental care is powerful in mediating a child's grief or traumatic stress reaction. This important finding emerges from research documenting that the quality of the attachment bond predicts childhood psychopathology (Wilson et al., 2010; Gershoff et al., 2010; Chemtob et al., 2008,

2010; DeVoe et al., 2011; Mowder et al., 2006). Several studies examining the psychosocial outcomes of early loss have repeatedly documented the importance of parental availability and psychological stability as predictors of nonpathological early childhood grief reactions. The relationship between the surviving parent and the child following the death of one of the parents can be highly complicated and fraught with difficulty. In a simple measure of the amount of attention and care children receive following the death of a parent, Kranzler et al. (1990) estimated that when children lose a parent, they experience a 30 percent reduction in caretaking and time spent with the surviving parent.

This decrease in parental care has been incorporated into the "Life Trajectory Model" which posits that the higher incidence of depression in children who experienced the early loss of a parent is a result of the combined effect of loss and the reduction of attuned, empathic caretaking by the surviving, bereaved parent (Harris et al., 1986). In another study, the likelihood of depression in adults who had experienced early parental loss was almost completely determined by the nature of the relationship with the surviving parent (Brier, 1988). Similarly, a literature review of parental loss in childhood concluded that compromised parenting following the loss was the major risk factor for later depression, rather than the loss itself (Tennant, 1988).

Another factor that may mediate a child's subsequent psychosocial development following parental loss is the level of distress and the coping ability of the surviving parent (Chemtob et al., 2008, 2010; Wilson et al., 2010; Gershoff et al., 2010). In several studies assessing children's pathology following the early loss of a parent and other trauma, the degree of distress and the level of coping skills in the surviving parent were the most significant mediators of the child's later psychological and behavioral symptoms (Chemtob et al., 2010; Wilson et al., 2010; Kranzler et al., 1990; Elizur & Kaffman, 1983). Maternal depression and other acute or chronic forms of distress have also been shown to affect the child's grieving and recovery process and have been associated with negative child outcomes (Chemtob et al., 2010; Weller et al., 1988; Kranzler et al., 1990; Hoffman, 1979).

Following the loss of a parent, children show an increase in empathic attunement to the mental well-being of the surviving parent, as well as a heightened need to monitor the parent's recovery. In response to extreme grief reactions in the surviving parent, children tend to inhibit their own grief reactions so as not to increase their parent's distress and anxiety (Pynoos, 1992). Conversely, the inhibition of parental affect may be equally derailing to the child's bereavement process. In response to parental withdrawal and denial of the influence of the trauma, children tend to exhibit an increase in aggressive, externalizing behavior (Schecter et al., 2002). Bereaved children who expressed their own sadness were less likely to exhibit emotional and behavioral disturbances (Kranzler et al., 1990). Therefore, the child's externalization or inhibition of affect in relation to the exaggerated or inhibited distress responses of a grieving parent may impede the child's own grieving process.

## Conceptualizing Dyadic Trauma: Mutual Effects of Trauma on Parents and Children

In this section, the concept of dyadic distress in understanding trauma in young children is explored. This concept has been advanced in current research examining the impact of trauma on young children within the context of the parent-child dyad (Wolmer et al., 2000). Because young children rely on their parents for cognitive, emotional and behavioral regulation, traumatic stress and distress are best understood within the parent-child system (Yehuda & Bierer, 2008). Thus, trauma is dyadic in a biological, environmental, and relational sense. Much of the research on the impact of terror and war on children has focused on clarifying children's responses to traumatic stress, on the parents' role in helping children process trauma and loss, and on the role that protective and risk factors in specific parenting and parental distress states may play in children's acute and long-term mental health (see Wolmer et al., 2000).

While it has been documented that parental distress and subsequent parenting practices affect children's processing of trauma, social-emotional functioning, and recovery (Ronen, 2002), it is also important to consider the impact of distressed children on their parents. Mothers who have lost their husbands and parenting partners are vulnerable to post-trauma symptoms. In our sample of families who lost a parent in the attacks of September 11, many mothers have older children who have been traumatized by the loss of the father in the attacks. Infants born to these mothers will have both direct and indirect exposure to the trauma. In conceptualizing dyadic systems, it is important to consider the bi-directional effects that the traumatized child and parent have on one another. An additional stress to these mothers lies in the fact that exposure to children's distress affects parents through the "evocative influence" of child stress reactions on parents' functioning (Philips, Prince & Schiebelhut, 2004). Adults exposed to distressed children during the World Trade Center disaster were twice as likely to feel threatened and unsafe themselves as those who were not exposed to children's distressed reactions, furthering evidence that parents are more vulnerable following trauma than nonparents (Philips et al., 2004; Norris et al., 2002). Thus, parents have the dual pressure of their own increased vulnerability following trauma, and their increased responsibility to regulate their own and their child's distress. This reciprocal process places parent-infant and parent-child dyads under increased strain during traumatic events (Chemtob et al., 2010).

## CONTRIBUTIONS OF ATTACHMENT RESEARCH TO CONCEPTUALIZING CHILDHOOD TRAUMA

This section reviews research on (1) the effect of trauma on development through assessments of infant and child attachment; (2) the intergenerational transmission of maternal trauma and infant attachment; (3) the impact of maternal depression and emotional unavailability on infant development; (4) the impact of maternal PTSD, anxiety, and hypervigilance on infant development; (5) early insecure attachment and psychopathology in childhood; and (6) early insecure attachment and psychopathology outcomes in adulthood.

### Conceptualizing the Effect of Trauma on Infant Development by Way of Attachment

In evaluating the mediating factors that affect the course of a child's grieving process and later psychosocial development, the child's relationship to the surviving parent and the parent's mental health have emerged as central to developmental outcomes, as noted above (Appleyard & Osofsky, 2003; Banyard, Rozelle, & Eglund, 2001; Levendosky et al., 2003). Another useful way of conceptualizing early trauma comes from the attachment literature. This research considers the intergenerational transmission of trauma, the association between maternal psychopathology and child attachment, and the predictive power of insecure child attachment for later maladaptive psychosocial and cognitive development.

The attachment literature provides a detailed infant behavioral (Ainsworth Strange Situation) assessment, and an AAI as methods of understanding the importance of early relationships to the developing symbolic and representational world of the child, and the ways in which the relationship to the primary attachment figure may set the trajectory for later development (Ainsworth, Blehar, Waters, & Wall, 1978; Main & Hesse, 1990; Main, Hesse, & Goldwyn, 2008). Recent research has also identified early patterns of nonverbal facial-visual and vocal rhythm communication in parent-infant interactions, patterns of vigilant as well as withdrawn interactive contingency, as well as maternal behavioral patterns such as maternal emotional unavailability and lack of sensitivity to infant cues, that underlie developing attachment insecurity (Beebe et al., 2010; Jaffe, Beebe, Feldstein, Crown, & Jasnow, 2001; Lyons-Ruth, 2003, 2008; Leyendecker, Lamb, Fracasso, Scholmerich, & Larson, 1997; Markese, Beebe, Feldstein, & Jaffe, 2008).

## Intergenerational Transmission of Maternal Trauma and Infant Attachment

An important approach to the effect of loss on early development can be found in research which has linked a maternal history of trauma or unresolved mourning to compromised infant cognitive, neurological, and social development, insecure attachment outcomes, and later childhood psychopathology (see Lyons-Ruth & Jacobvitz, 2008, for a review; Lyons-Ruth, 2008; Lyons-Ruth & Spielman, 2004; Main & Hesse, 1990). Maternal representations of attachment assessed through the AAI have been linked to patterns of infant attachment at 1 year (Lyons-Ruth & Jacobvitz, 2008; Fonagy, Steele, & Steele, 1991b; Main, Kaplan, & Cassidy, 1985). Research over the past two decades has provided evidence that unresolved trauma, loss, or abuse in the mother's history predicts insecure-disorganized attachment in the infant and young child. The mechanism for this "intergenerational transmission of trauma" is conceptualized by attachment theorists as the mother's continuing state of fear, conveyed through atypical "frightened/frightening" behavior in response to the child during painful separation and reunion episodes (Lyons-Ruth 2003, 2008; Madigan et al., 2006; Lyons-Ruth & Spielman, 2004; Goldberg et al., 2003; Kelly et al., 2003; Lyons-Ruth et al., 1999b; Osofsky, 1995; Yehuda, 1990; Cramer, 1998; Gunnar, 1995; Zeanah & Barton, 1989; Lebovici, 1983; Fraiberg, 1980).

The "unresolved" category of adult attachment describes an adult who becomes dissociated or incoherent when discussing primary attachment figures or, for example, who expresses disbelief that the person has died. This category of attachment is particularly relevant to the study of the intergenerational transmission of trauma and loss, and it has been shown to be related to the presence of "disorganized" attachment behaviors in the infant (Lyons-Ruth & Jacobvitz, 2000, 2008; Lyons-Ruth, 1998). In a pioneering study by Main and Hesse (1990), only 8 percent of the mothers of avoidant, resistant, or secure infants had experienced early loss, whereas nearly four times as many parents of disorganized infants had experienced early loss. Although mothers who have recently been widowed may not have shown these "unresolved" patterns of attachment prior to their loss, the effect of the recent trauma may comprise the mother's attachment state. This topic deserves more research.

Another alternative is that the immediacy of the loss may head to a maternal preoccupation with the loss, resulting in a "preoccupied" attachment classification in the surviving parent, with a corresponding likelihood of "anxious/resistant" infant attachment. Or the surviving parent may become "dismissing" as a result of their unprocessed anger or denial of the importance of the loss, with a corresponding likelihood of "avoidant" infant attachment. Adult attachment classification, as measured by the AAI, has been tied to infant attachment status at one year, both when assessed before the infant's birth (Fonagy, Steele, & Steele, 1991; van Ijzendoorn, 1995), and during the mother's pregnancy (Slade et al., 1995). Therefore the loss of a spouse at the time of the infant's birth may have a powerful effect on the surviving parent's representations of the loss, the infant, and their own security. A sudden shift in the surviving parent's "internal working model of attachment relationships" (Bowlby, 1969), with a possible shift to insecurity, might result in potentially insecure early mother-infant bonding and subsequently compromised infant development.

The Adult Attachment Interview has been used to demonstrate that early loss and unresolved mourning in the mother's history predicts her infant's disorganized attachment. However, further research is needed to assess the effect of the simultaneous loss of a spouse, or other primary attachment figure, and the birth of a child. Such research would provide us with a better sense of how sudden, traumatic loss affects a mother's internal working model of attachment, which adult attachment outcomes are likely, and what subsequent, potentially maladaptive infant attachment patterns may ensue. This is an important area of investigation.

## Maternal Depression and Emotional Unavailability

Another body of empirical literature important for the conceptualization of infant trauma is the study of maternal distress, especially depression, and maternal emotional unavailability or dissociation, as it predicts infant social and cognitive development, infant attachment, and later child psychopathology. Mothers in the early stages of mourning the loss of their husbands are likely to experience fatigue, preoccupation, distraction, and sadness, either acutely or chronically, over the course of their bereavement. In addition, they may exhibit either withdrawn or intrusive types of depression. Although these states of mind are part of an adaptive process of bereavement and mourning, the parent's emotional availability for the infant may be severely compromised in the first year of development, and possibly over the course of the child's early years.

Several studies have shown that the security of the infant's attachment to the parent is dependent on the parent's emotional availability (Field et al., 2006; van Ijzendorn, 1995). A longitudinal study of attachment found a composite measure of maternal sensitivity from infancy to 16 years to be one of the two strongest predictors of the offspring's adult attachment at age 22. This finding demonstrates the importance of maternal emotional availability to developing attachment representations over the entire course of the child's development into adulthood (Grossman, Grossman, Winter, & Zimmermann, 2002).

Other studies focusing on early childhood social and cognitive development and behavior disorders have demonstrated the detrimental effect of maternal depression and unavailability on child outcomes. At 1 year, infants of depressed mothers show significant delays in physical growth, social and cognitive development, and social referencing (Field, 1995, 2011; Murray & Cooper, 1997). At 18 months, impairments in cognitive development as measured by the Bayley Scales of Infant Development (Bayley, 1993) have been observed in connection with lack of maternal involvement/availability, as observed in interactions between mothers and their infant in home visits (Lyons-Ruth, 1993, 2008). Maternal depression, and the components of maternal fatigue, negativity and hostility predict increased parent-child dyadic conflict in toddlerhood; childhood behavioral problems, conduct disorders, and difficulties with peer relationships during the school years; and externalizing behavior problems into adolescence (White & King, 2011;

O'Brien Caughy, Huang, & Lima, 2009; Foster, Garber, & Durlak, 2008; Foster, Huang, & Lima, 2008; Hammen, Burge, Burney, & Adrian, 1990).

In a series of studies by Beebe and colleagues, maternal depression (as measured by the CESD at infant ages 6 weeks and 4 months) did not directly predict infant attachment outcomes at 1 year. However, early maternal depression at 6 weeks predicted patterns of mother-infant face-to-face interaction at 4 months; the 4-month interaction in turn predicted infant attachment at 12 months (Beebe et al., 2008, 2010). The 4-month dyadic communication patterns interaction already tap the early emerging attachment climate (Beebe et al., 2010; Jaffe et al., 2001). However, looking at the joint effects of six-week postpartum maternal depression and 12-month infant attachment status, Beebe and colleagues found that 6-week maternal depression affected the 4-month mother-infant interaction in different ways for infants who would be classified secure versus insecure at 12-months (Beebe et al., 2011). Depressed mothers who nevertheless remained highly emotionally responsive to their infants at 4 months had infants who were securely attached at 1 year, whereas depressed mothers who emotionally withdrew from their infants had infants who were insecurely attached at 1 year. This study highlights the complexity of early mother-infant communication patterns and the role of maternal distress in the effect of these early dyadic interactions on developing infant attachment representations. The findings provide a further critical rationale for supporting the quality of the mother-infant face-to-face interaction in bereaved mothers and infants in order to ensure optimal infant social and cognitive development, and optimal attachment representations. The findings also emphasize the importance of early parent-infant face-to-face interaction, and the process of mutual regulation between parents and infants, as the "common final pathway" in which disturbances play out (Weinberg & Tronick, 1998).

## Maternal Posttrauma Symptoms and Hypervigilance to Threat

Just as the mothers widowed in the World Trade Center attacks of September 11, 2001, are likely to experience acute symptoms of depression in their infants' first years, they are likely to have symptoms of posttraumatic stress, if not clinically significant PTSD. These mothers endured the trauma of their personal losses, as well as being exposed to the traumatic climate in New York City during the terrorist threat. Increased rates of PTSD were reported overall in New York City following September 11 (Hoven et al., 2005; Galea et al., 2002). While symptoms of depression predispose mothers to interact in particular ways with their infants, symptoms of PTSD have their own set of specific difficulties (Chemtob et al., 2010).

Symptoms PTSD might create distance and withdrawal in mothers due to the dissociative aspects of the disorder. In addition, PTSD carries with it the added risk that mothers may become highly anxious and hypervigilant to threat, setting up a dyadic context of heightened fear, and leading to mother-child emotional regulation difficulties (Chemtob et al., 2010; Michael & Ehlers, 2007). Maternal anxiety has been linked to specific maladaptive patterns of parent-child interaction in other literature as well (Beebe et al., 2011; Britton, 2005; Mertsacker, Bade, Haverkock, & Pauli-Pott, 2004; Nicol-Harper, Harvey, & Stein, 2007).

## Early Insecure Attachment and Psychpathology in Childhood

A growing body of literature documents the psychosocial outcomes of children and adolescents who manifested early disorganized attachment patterns at 12 months (DeKlyen &

Greenberg, 2008; Kobak, Cassidy, Lyons-Ruth, & Ziv, 2006; Lyons-Ruth, 1996, 1998, 2003, 2008). Specifically, disorganized attachment at 1year has been associated with disorders of conduct, cognition, and social relatedness. These children show an increase in oppositional, hostile-aggressive, fearful and disorganized behavior, lower self-esteem, cognitive difficulties in childhood (see Lyons-Ruth & Jacobvitz, 2008, for a review; Lyons-Ruth, Bronfman, & Parsons, 1999; Jacobson, Edelstein, & Hofmann, 1994), and psychopathology and peer difficulties in adolescence (Carlson, 1998; Jacobvitz & Hazen, 1998).

Disorganized infant and toddler attachment has been shown to be a strong predictor of later hostile-aggressive behavior in children in both the home and in the preschool environment (Lyons-Ruth & Jacobvitz, 2008; Lyons-Ruth, 2008, 1993). Particularly, children with deviant levels of hostile-aggressive behavior have been shown to have up to a 71 percent rate of disorganized attachment classification at age 18 months compared to only 33 percent of nondeviant children (Lyons-Ruth, Alpern, & Repacholi, 1993). Children classified as having disorganized attachment also show increased levels of both "controlling-punitive" and "controlling-caregiving" behaviors in comparison to their peers (Lyons-Ruth et al., 1993; Main, Kaplan, & Cassidy, 1985). Attachment classifications of both disorganized and anxious-resistant predict childhood difficulty and are specifically implicated in the development of dissociative and mood disorders, with an emphasis on disorders of anxiety (Lyons-Ruth & Jacobvitz, 2008; Lyons-Ruth, 2003, 2008; Carlson, 1998; Warren, Huston, Egeland, & Sroufe, 1997; Liotti, 1992).

In a longitudinal study of 172 children, anxious/resistant attachment at 12 months predicted the presence of anxiety disorders, including separation anxiety disorder, overanxious disorder, panic disorder, agoraphobia, social phobia, avoidant disorder, and obsessive-compulsive disorder in adolescence. The connection between early "anxious/resistant" attachment in infancy and the presence of anxiety disorders in adolescence was found independent of both maternal anxiety and infant temperament (Warren et al., 1997). This connection was found specifically for the anxiety disorders, while more adolescents with dissociative and affective disorders were likely to have been classified as having "avoidant" attachment at 1 year (Warren et al., 1997). These findings speak to the specificity of the maladaptive attachment patterns assessed in infancy through the Ainsworth Strange Situation, as well as to the unique risks to later child and adolescent development that underlie each category of insecure infant attachment.

## Early Insecure Attachment and Long-Term Child Outcomes

Research on the effect of maternal states of mind and unresolved mourning on infant social/cognitive development and attachment demonstrate the contemporary empirical emphasis on assessing insecure attachment outcomes as a way of understanding and predicting later psychopathology (Lyons-Ruth, 2008; Sroufe, 2005; Waters, Merrick, Treboux, Crowell, & Albershein, 2000; Grossman, Grossman, Winter, & Zimmerman, 2002; Carlson, 1998; Lewis, Feiring, & Rosenthal, 2000). Important longitudinal studies of infant attachment that have shown the stability of insecure attachment patterns from infancy through young adulthood have emerged (Waters, Merrick, Treboux, Crowell, & Albershein, 2000; Grossman, Grossman, Winter, & Zimmerman, 2002; Carlson, 1998).

These studies have documented that infant attachment security/insecurity assessed at 1 year in the Ainsworth Strange Situation test may be retained by up to almost 80 percent of adults assessed 20 years later using the AAI (Waters et al., 2000). When attachment status changes, it is likely because the child experienced a traumatic event. Securely attached infants whose mothers reported one or more traumatic event (e.g., loss of a parent, parental divorce, life-threatening illness of child or parent, parental psychiatric disorder) were four times more likely to change to an insecure attachment classification than secure infants whose mothers reported no traumatic life events. Other longitudinal studies have shown that the loss of a parent predicts disturbances in school adjustment and attachment security suffer (Howard, 2000; Tremblay & Israel, 1998; Worden & Silverman, 1996). More importantly, loss of a parent is a predictor of the transformation of a child's early attachment from secure to insecure (Waters et al., 2000; Vondra, Shaw, Swearingen, Cohen, & Owens, 1999). These studies demonstrate both the stability of attachment classification under relatively stable developmental circumstances and the transformational nature of attachment under the stress of traumatic events across development.

Additional support for the stability of "internal working models of attachment" relationships from infancy to young adulthood comes from the work of Grossman et al. (2002). In a longitudinal study following families from infancy through young adulthood, including both mothers and fathers with their infants, one of the two strongest predictors of young adult attachment was a composite measure of maternal sensitivity from infancy through adolescence (Grossman et al., 2002). This study not only included many measures of parental states of mind and sensitivity but also examined dyadic interaction patterns and parent-child play, child and mother attachment, and child discourse quality in relation to attachment outcomes across infancy, childhood (2, 3, 6, and 10 years), and adolescence (age 16). Another dimension of attachment was assessed in adolescence, the flexibility of response to social rejection by a "romantic" partner via projective stories. In young adulthood (age 22), these same subjects were assessed for security of their romantic attachments, another dimension of attachment essential to optimal development in adulthood (Grossman et al., 2002; Owens, Crowell, Pan, & Treboux, 1995).

One of the two strongest predictors of young adult attachment was a composite measure of maternal sensitivity from infancy to adolescence. This measure defined maternal sensitivity as attentiveness to her child's communications, "correct" interpretation of her infant/child's cues, "appropriate" responses, acknowledgement of her child's feelings, the ability to help her child know his/her own motives and put them into words, and the ability to explain her own motives (Grossman et al., 2002). In addition, infant attachment status predicted childhood attachment status (at age 6), and child attachment status predicted security of attachment representations with a romantic partner in young adulthood. This latter finding suggests that infant attachment affects adult romantic attachment representations in a transformational way via its link to attachment representations in early childhood (Beebe & McCrorie, 2010).

## CONTRIBUTIONS OF RESEARCH ON PARENT-INFANT NONVERBAL COMMUNICATION

In this section the following are reviewed: (a) parent-infant nonverbal communication as a way of assessing the effect of trauma on infant development, (b) parent-infant facial-visual communication as a predictor of attachment, (c) parent-infant vocal rhythm communication as a predictor of attachment, and (d) maternal depression, anxiety, and PTSD and early infant regulatory behavior.

## Parent-Infant Nonverbal Communication as a Way of Assessing the Effect of Trauma on Infant Development: 0–12 Months

To assess the effect of early trauma and loss in infancy and to design effective early interventions, studies of infants prior to 12 months must become a priority in trauma research. Before attachment can be assessed at 12 months, studies of nonverbal behavior in infants and facial-visual dyadic communication between infants and bereaved or traumatized mothers are extremely useful tools of risk assessment (see Cassidy et al., 2005; Reck Hunt et al., 2004; Tronick & Reck, 2009; Birklein & Sossin, 2006). Disturbed patterns of nonverbal communication in traumatized mother-infant dyads may provide valuable information and allow for improved designs of primary prevention and intervention programs addressing trauma in infancy and early childhood.

Studies of infant memory and neurobiological models of infant development provide important clues as to the ways in which infants process early loss and trauma (see above). Also, limited clinical evidence suggests that trauma is in fact remembered and represented preverbally, through an implicit, procedural action-sequence format (Gaensbauer, 2002, 2004). These studies suggest that specific treatment methods are needed in the early presymbolic, preverbal period of infancy.

### Mother-Infant Facial-Visual Communication in Infancy as a Predictor of Attachment

Another way in which attachment research may contribute to the understanding of infant trauma is through research demonstrating that early dyadic patterns of face-to-face interaction at 4 months are later predictors of infant attachment at 1 year (Cassidy et al., 2005; Beebe et al., 2010). Moreover, even without considering the mother's interaction patterns, the 4-month infant's own patterns of interacting face-to-face with the mother predicts attachment in infancy (Koulomzin, Beebe, Anderson, Jaffe, Feldstein, & Crown, 2002; Sarro, 1993). In the Koulomzin et al. (2002) study, the interactive behavior of 4-month infants later classified as "avoidant" attachment at 12 months differed from that of the infants later classified as "secure." At 4 months, infants later classified as avoidant showed more self-touch and the necessity to self-touch in order to look at mother for durations comparable to those of secure infants. These infants displayed a decreased range of positive/negative facial affect, constricting toward a predominance of neutral, thus showing a dampening of facial affect. In addition, these "future" avoidant infants showed a disruption of the capacity to coordinate gaze and head orientation into a stable posture while smiling so that infant gaze at mother occurred while the infant's head was averted. These infants also showed a difficulty in affective regulation, manifesting "labile" affective states compared to more "stable" states seen in "secure" infants. These difficulties can be conceptualized as a self-regulatory disturbance in the infant (Beebe & Lachmann, 2002). However, because the mother was not included in the analyses, it was not possible to determine her possible contribution to the effects.

Other research has shown connections between 4-month-old infant facial-visual behavior in interaction with the mothers and toddler behavior during interactions with the mother. When infants whose facial-visual behavior with mother was assessed at 4 months were videotaped in a face-to-face play situation with their mothers at 2 years, further behavioral differences emerged (Sarro, 1993). While avoidant and secure toddlers and their mothers showed similar patterns of mutual responsivity to gaze at 2 years, differences emerged in these toddlers in their responsivity to their mothers' vocalizations. Whereas secure toddlers were responsive to a mother's vocalization in all modalities (gaze, orientation, and touch), avoidant toddlers showed no responsivity in any modality to their mother's vocal behavior. The insecure/avoidant toddler is thus unresponsive to the mother's vocal focus, thus markedly altering the context for language acquisition (Beebe & Lachmann, 2002). As a consequence, the insecure toddler developing language will not experience mother-child communications in the same way as a secure infant, thus language will not be imbued with the same level of dyadically shared meaning (Adrienne Harris, personal communication to Beatrice Beebe, April 10, 1993; Beebe & Lachmann, 2002).

The link between self-regulatory disturbances in "avoidant" infants at 4 months and later behavioral and affective differences between insecure and secure toddlers in relation to their mothers may lie in the development of insecure/avoidant attachment, which can only be assessed at 1 year. A 4-month-old infant's need for increased self-touch in order to sustain gaze with mother predicts insecure/avoidant attachment at 1 year (Koulomzin et al., 2002), which is then linked to a disturbance in the toddler's responsivity to the mother's language at 2 years (Sarro, 1993). In this way, early disturbances in self-regulation can be seen as the underpinnings of a maladaptive developmental trajectory which may lead to insecure attachment outcomes, and later difficulties in self-and interactive regulation (see Beebe & Lachman, 2002).

### Mother-Infant Vocal Rhythm Communication in Infancy as a Predictor of Attachment

The expression of affect preverbally can be observed in mother-infant facial and visual communication and mother-infant vocalizations. Infants actively express both positive and negative states through vocal quality. As early as 4 months, infants of depressed mothers are more "vocally activated" in expressing both positive and negative affect, and they are more "vocally variable" in moving in and out of different affect states, particularly fuss/whimper (Demetri Friedman, Beebe, Jaffe, Ross, & Triggs, 2010).

Patterns of mother-infant vocal rhythm coordination as early as 4 months predict attachment outcomes at 12 months (Jaffe et al., 2001) and at 4 years (Markese, Beebe, Feldstein, & Jaffe, 2008). Vocal rhythm coordination is a measure of the degree to which each partner's durations of sounds and silences is contingent on that of the other. Midrange degrees of vocal rhythm coordination predicted 12-month secure attachment; both high and low degrees of coordination predicted insecure attachment (Jaffe et al., 2001). Vocal rhythm has been interpreted as an early form of preverbal attunement in which the caregiver conveys a sense of "being with" the infant through the coordination of pauses, the frequency of vocalization, and the length of the vocal "turn" (Beebe et al., 2000).

To understand these findings, Jaffe et al. (2001), Beebe et al. (2000), and Beebe and McCrorie (2010) proposed the "optimal midrange model of self- and interactive-regulation." This model uses the research on interactive regulation, and proposes that self-regulation operates similarly, with midrange optimal. The optimal midrange model of vocal rhythm suggests that nonverbal communication systems that are either skewed toward self-regulation (avoidance of partner), or those that are too dependent on interactive regulation (hypervigilance to partner), can be detrimental to the infant's ability to form a secure attachment. In such skews, the infant (or mother) is unable to balance self- and interactive regulation. This optimal midrange model suggests that partners who sense that the other is optimally coordinated and predictable while still having the flexibility to move between self- and interactive regulation will have more optimal levels of attention, affect, and arousal (Beebe et al., 2000). The study of mother-infant vocal rhythm interaction generated the important idea that interactive regulation can be too high (vigilant or preoccupied with the partner), as well as too low (sacrificing engagement) (Jaffe et al., 2001).

A related study explored the association between vocal rhythm coordination at 4 and 12 months with attachment outcomes at 4 years (Markese, 2008; Markese et al., 2008). Vocal rhythm "dialogues" of infants at 4- and 12 months with their mothers and novel partners ("strangers") predicted 4-year representations of attachment security in childhood, assessed through children's representations of attachment relationships as measured by the ASCT narrative story stem task (Markese, 2008; Markese et al., 2008). This study explored continuities in relational patterns spanning the child's first four years in order to identify early nonverbal patterns of relating as early as age 4 months for those children who evidence insecure attachment representations and relational difficulties at 4 years. Prior longitudinal studies have largely failed to document correlations between 12-month attachment and symbolic, narrative measures of attachment at four years. The Markese et al. (2008) study took a different approach to investigating the origins of developing attachment representations by using vocal rhythm coordination in infancy rather than 12-month infant attachment. Thus early vocal rhythm coordination served as the early measure of developing internal working models of attachment relationships assessed in childhood.

Building on the research of Jaffe et al. (2001), the Markese et al. (2008) study showed that particularly the 4-month vocal rhythm coordination patterns, in the novel context of the stranger-infant interaction, predicted security of child attachment at 4 years. Specifically 4-year-old children who avoided the emotional content of attachment-themed stories on the ASCT measure (both those who evidenced chaotic disorganized "D" narrative strategies and those who evidenced rigid avoidant "A" narrative strategies) shared similar communication patterns in infancy. Strangers interacting with 4-month infants later identified as having avoidant and disorganized attachment narratives at 4 years lowered their degree of vocal rhythm coordination. This pattern is one of interactive withdrawal. It suggests that these infants who are in the process of developing insecure attachment representations at 4 months evoke a withdrawal response in the novel partner. Thus these infant seem to be limited in their ability to engage in positive, supportive interpersonal exchanges with novel partners (Markese et al., 2008). Despite its distance in time from both attachment measures, the 4-month preverbal face-to-face exchange is remarkably sensitive as a predictor of future outcomes from 1 to 4 years (Beebe et al., 2010; Jaffe et al., 2001; Markese et al., 2008).

## Maternal Depression, Anxiety and PTSD and Early Infant Regulatory Behavior

The impact of maternal distress, including depression, anxiety, and PTSD, on the infant's early emotional regulation has been increasingly documented in the past decade (see Field, Diego, & Hernandez-Reif, 2006, for a review; Field et al., 2005; Beebe et al., 2008, 2011; Beeghly, Weinberg, Olson, Keman, Riley, & Tronick, 2001; Tronick & Reck, 2009; Warren et al., 2003; Weinberg, Tronick, Beeghly, Olson, Kernan, & Riley, 2001). From 4 months of age, infants of depressed mothers utilize different patterns of self- and interactive-regulation than infants of nondepressed mothers (Field, 1995, 2011; Beebe et al., 2008; Feldman, Granat, Pariente, Kanety, Kuint, & Gilboa-Schechtman, 2009). This work documents the detrimental effect that maternal emotional unavailability has on early nonverbal interaction between mothers and infants. In particular, in the still-face procedure, which mimics maternal depression, infants exhibit more protest/despair and are more difficult to soothe than in an actual separation episode (Tronick & Reck, 2009). Thus maternal withdrawal and insensitivity to infant cues are actually more difficult for infants and young children than actual physical separation from the parent.

Infants of depressed mothers also show more avoidance than do controls, with higher rates of looking away, little mutual visual regard, fewer positive bouts, a greater frequency of negative expressions, little matching of positive affect, and more matching of negative affect. When these infants do become positive, their mothers tend to become more sober-faced instead of responding with matched positive affect as control mothers do (Field, 1995, 2011; Tronick & Reck, 2009; Warren et al., 2003; Weinberg et al., 2001; Tronick & Weinberg, 1997). Researchers hypothesize that because depressed mother do not respond sufficiently to the infants' cues, these infants develop defensive regulatory mechanisms in the absence of co-regulation, a "disengaged and self-directed" regulatory style that becomes automatic over time (Tronick & Reck, 2009; Warren et al., 2003; Weinberg et al., 2001; Tronick & Weinberg, 1997). This leads to the finding that by 6 months, when infants of depressed mothers interact with a nondepressed stranger, they generalize their more negative style of relating to the stranger (Field 2011; Field et al., 1988).

Infants of depressed mothers are also physiologically overaroused, based on elevated heart-rate and cortisol (Field, 2011, 1995). Perhaps to manage this overarousal, infants of depressed mothers have more avoidant interactive patterns and appear less alert than infants of nondepressed mothers. These infants show more turning away from the dyadic partner and often a loss of postural control. They are preoccupied with various forms of self-regulation, such as oral self-comfort and self-touch, at the expense of interactive regulation (Tronick & Reck, 2009; Warren et al., 2003; Weinberg et al., 2001; Tronick, 1989). When depressed mothers are separated into two types of depression, withdrawn and intrusive, infants exhibit different relational patterns (Field, 2011, 1996; Tronick & Reck, 2009; Warren et al., 2003; Weinberg et al., 2001; Tronick & Weinberg, 1997). When mothers are withdrawn (i.e., flat affect, looking away, slouching back, passively watching without responding), infants show more vocal protest. When mothers are intrusive (i.e., more angry faces or poking), infants look away more.

## INFANT DEVELOPMENT AND CAPACITY TO PROCESS TRAUMA

In this section the following are reviewed: (a) infant memory in the preverbal period, (b) neurological development and affective processing, (c) fetal development and early risk of trauma transmission, and (d) and traumatic symptomatology specific to infancy.

The exploration of the ways in which infants process and represent traumatic experiences is a new area of research that has burgeoned in the past decade (see Zeanah, Stafford, Boris, & Scheeringa, 2003; Scheeringa & Gaensbauer, 2000; Coates & Gaensbauer, 2009, for reviews). Much of what is known about infant experiences of distress and trauma is based on dyadic observation, in that the mother's experience and behavior is central to understanding that of the infant. However, research on infant memory and affective processing can lead to more specific understanding of the infant's experience of trauma. In addition to reviewing infant developmental research, this section will also explore another dyadic measure of distress—that of the earliest transmission of maternal distress states to the infant in utero.

## Infant Memory in the Preverbal Period

Studies of infant memory in the experimental setting have demonstrated the infant's astounding capacity to remember and represent events occurring as early as 6 months of age (Scheeringa & Gaensbauer, 2000; Gaensbauer, 2002; Coates & Gaensbauer, 2009). Toddlers can recall events which occurred at 6 months, tested through behavioral recognition at the point of re-exposure in later development (Perris, Myers, & Clifton, 1990; Rovee-Collier & Hayne, 1987; Daehler & Greco, 1985). Infant memory studies contribute to an increasingly specific understanding of the ways in which early infant traumatic experiences may be represented nonverbally (Terr, 1988) and later verbally (Gaensbauer, 2002, 2004), as well as the ways in which early memories contribute to the organization of the infant's developing cognitive and social schema.

Not only do these studies show how infant memory functions, they also provide evidence that early memories mediate the ways that developing infants and toddlers respond to new challenges. Perris et al. (1990) exposed 6-month-old infants with a single trial of rattles presented in lit and dark rooms. These infants were then examined as toddlers at age 2.5 years. The toddlers demonstrated that their early experience modified their behavior in toddlerhood. Specifically, the "experienced" toddlers reached and grasped for rattles in the dark room condition significantly more than the control group children (Perris et al., 1990). These results suggest that early memory of the situation at 6 months allowed these children to endure the "scary" dark condition and thus apply an "action memory" learned at 6 months to the task presented at 2.5 years (Furman, 1974). This experiment demonstrates that the infant long-term memory system is functional as early as 6 months and that these early memory traces can mediate long-term memory, despite years of cognitive, social, neurological, and physiological development (Perris et al., 1990).

In more recent research, neurological models have been posited which may explain the results obtained by earlier infant memory studies (Schore, 2002). Particular neurological models offer an explanation for the early encoding of traumatic memory in the infant brain, as well as a way of understanding how these early memories influence the parallel development of infant systems of cognitive and social development. Schore's (2002) model hypothesizes that early infant experiences and memories are imprinted into the infant's right brain, specifically the amygdala, and are stored as early behavioral, autobiographical memories. These early memories in the right brain are largely unregulated by the orbitofrontal area, which is responsible for correcting and adjusting memories. According to this and other models of infant memory, these early "action memories" can be understood as "the literal mirroring of traumatic events by behavioral memory" (Terr, 1988) and may be re-experienced in later stages of development as sudden and uncontrollable experiences of bodily dysregulation (Schore, 2002).

A limited but developing body of clinical literature addresses the infant and preverbal child's ability to remember traumatic events, and to later represent these preverbal events with the advent of language (Coates & Gaensbauer, 2009). This clinical literature addresses the transformation of the infant's implicit behavioral, emotional, and sensory memories into the declarative, autobiographical memories reported by young children entering the verbal period. In a study of children traumatized prior to age 5, children were unable to produce coherent verbal accounts of their traumatic experiences, but they were able to enact and represent these traumas behaviorally (Terr, 1988). Similarly, children whose verbal abilities were developed at the time of the trauma (ages 16 and 24 months) were able to provide rather detailed, verbal reports of the traumatic occurrence, whereas an 18-month old without verbal skills at the time of the trauma was able to convey only an incoherent visual memory of the traumatic events (Sugar, 1992). These clinical case studies suggest that representation of traumatic events prior to the development of language skills exists in the child's behavioral or visual memory. However, there is other compelling clinical evidence that preverbal trauma is not only represented behaviorally and visually but also that these early memories may later be verbally represented as children develop language (Gaensbauer, 1995, 2002, 2004).

In Gaensbauer's work, small numbers of children who have experienced different degrees of trauma in the preverbal period (between ages 6 and 15 months) have been interviewed in a play therapy session to assess their memories of infantile trauma (Gaensbauer, 1995, 2002, 2004). When provided with the means to represent and reenact the trauma, these children are able to convey accurate sensory and somatic details of the trauma, both behaviorally and verbally, despite not having been told any of the details by parents and caretakers. In these cases, it is posited that behavioral re-enactment, and the representation and enactment of the trauma through symbolic play, allowed the children to verbalize their experience of the trauma (Gaensbauer, 1995, 2002, 2004; Coates & Gaensbauer, 2009; Scheeringa & Gaensbauer, 2000).

Particularly compelling is the case of a child who at 12 months witnessed the violent death of her mother. Although the child had not been told anything about the circumstances of her mother's death, when prompted with a dollhouse and a female figure, she was able to describe in detail what she had been doing at the time, the details of the crime scene, and her mother's appearance (Gaensbauer, 1995). Another child who had been sexually abused by his father at 6 months showed a pattern of dissociative episodes in which he appeared to relive the trauma from an infantile perspective. He reenacted the trauma behaviorally in the position of an infant, conveying a chaotic sense of bodily dysregulation, and screamed, "Don't hurt me, I'm just a baby," conveying his immature understanding of the bodily invasion caused by the sexual abuse (Gaensbauer, 1995). Although limited in scope, these important case presentations shed light on the connection between infantile behavioral, sensory, and emotional memories, and their more symbolically enacted and verbal represented forms in later childhood.

## Infant Neurological Development: Stress Reactivity and Affective Processing

Another area of research relevant to an understanding of the infant's processing of trauma concerns the infant's affective processing capacities and cerebral activation patterns (Hane & Fox, 2006; Fox, Russo, & Dutton, 2002). Delayed infant disengagement from negative emotional faces may indicate an "attentional bias for threat" (Fox, Russo, & Dutton, 2002).

In normal development, similar to adults, infants as young as 10 months process positive and negative affective stimuli in different cerebral frontal lobes, showing the specificity of infant's affect processing capabilities (Fox, Russo, & Dutton, 2002; Davidson & Fox, 1982). Infants show activation in the left frontal lobe in response to seeing a woman laughing; activation in the right frontal love while watching a woman crying (Davidson & Fox, 1982). Building on this research, other studies have shown that infants of depressed and non-depressed mothers begin to demonstrate different cerebral activation patterns in response to affect at 10 months of age (Dawson et al., 2003; Dawson, 1992). This work demonstrates that the responsivity of infants of depressed mothers is already organized differently from that of infants with non-depressed parents; these infants have already begun to perceive and react to emotional stimuli differently than controls. In this study, the same positive event (mother playing peek-a-boo, or returning following separation) that resulted in a positive affective behavior and EEG pattern in infants of nondepressed parents resulted in negative behavior and a negative pattern of EEG activation in infants of depressed parents.

Similar to the neuronal activation of the hyperarousal/dissociative pathways model characterizing trauma in early childhood (Perry, 1996, 2006), a model of right brain dysregulation in infancy in response to traumatic attachment relationships has been proposed (Schore, 2002). According to this model, the developing relationship between an infant and primary caretaker mediates the infant's early ability to regulate emotion, and thus, the mother is instrumental in co-regulating the infant's developing autonomic nervous system (Schore, 2002). The right hemisphere of the infant's brain stores this dyadic relationship neuronally as an internal working model of the attachment relationship. Thus, this working model is encoded in the infant's implicit, nonconscious memory (Schore, 1994; Valent, 1998; Siegel, 1999). The early attachment relationship is conceptualized as organizing the regulation of interactive states. As this early attachment relationship sets the course for neurological development, dyadic co-regulation by both mother and infant in the infant's first year plays an essential role in determining the infant's later ability to regulate internal physiological states, as well as to experience and express emotion (Schore, 2002; Lyons-Ruth, 2003). One pathway by which parents may help regulate infants' experiences of trauma may be through the parent's ongoing initiation of interactive repair to help modulate negative arousal (Schore, 2002; Lyons-Ruth, 2003).

According to this model, relational trauma, which may include maternal withdrawal or intrusion, has an effect most immediately on the infant's developing right hemisphere. This area of the developing brain is tied to other neuronal systems, such as the autonomic, limbic, and arousal systems, which are essential in the development of the infant's ability to process social, emotional, and physiological information (Schore, 1994). The developing right hemisphere is dominant for the reception, expression, and communication of emotion, as well as the regulation of spontaneous emotional reaction, and the regulation of affect (Schore, 1994, 2002). Self-recognition and the ability to construct a coherent and unified sense of self are also the domain of right brain function (Devinsky, 2000; Schore, 2002). As a result, early relational trauma directly affects the infant's developing capacity to process, interpret, and regulate his emotions and developing sense of self. Thus, disturbances in early relationships can set in motion developmental trajectories that show differences in both infant stress reactivity and distress regulation (Feldman et al., 2009). These differences not only compromise an infant's ability to self-regulate affect, attention, and arousal but also sensitize the system to later interpersonal and environmental stressors, increasing the infant's predisposition to pathological outcomes over the course of development.

## Fetal Development and Early Risk of Trauma Transmission

In addition to exploring the transmission of trauma from mother to infant within early dyadic interactions and the developing attachment relationship, recent research has offered another truly dyadic and powerful way of understanding the impact of maternal trauma on the child prenatally (see Field, Diego, & Hernandez-Reif, 2006, for a review; Feldman & Eidelman, 2009; see Lange, *Prenatal Maternal Stress,* this issue). This new research conceptualizes both maternal distress and trauma transmission as "transmission of increased cortisol" (Yehuda & Bierer, 2008). It is a transmission of an underlying vulnerability for the development of posttraumatic stress symptoms through the developing fetus' exposure to increased cortisol in vitro as "transmission of PTSD risk" (Yehuda et al., 2005; Yehuda & Bierer, 2008). Through exposure to elevated cortisol levels during midgestation (Field et al., 2006; Monk, Myers, Sloan, Ellman, & Fifer, 2003; Yehuda et al., 2005), children of distressed and traumatized mothers are subject to distress transmission, and thus to an array of "fetal symptoms," including lower fetal weight (Diego et al., 2006; Field, 2011; Field et al., 2006; Yehuda et al., 2005; Yehuda & Bierer, 2008), delayed fetal growth (Field et al., 2006), elevated fetal activity (Field et al., 2006), and dysregulated fetal heart rate (Monk et al., 2003).

In fact, these same developmental differences have been observed not only in the fetuses of women exposed to trauma, but also in fetuses of women with moderate levels of distress, including heightened anxiety and depression (Field et al., 2006; Monk et al., 2003). Extensive research has been done to investigate the impact of maternal depression on the child in vitro, as well as to examine the lasting impact of pre-natal maternal depression.

With elevated maternal prenatal cortisol, the fetus and newborn experience prenatal, perinatal and postnatal complications (Field et al., 2006). These early effects continue to impact the child in infancy. Amazingly, researchers have shown that the actual biochemistry and physiology of a distressed mother is transmitted to the infant, and that newborns of depressed mothers have similarly altered physiology and brain chemistry as their mothers (Field et al., 2006). These newborns, like their depressed mothers, show such altered characteristics as elevated cortisol, lower levels of dopamine and serotonin, greater relative right frontal EEG activation and lower vagal tone (Field et al., 2006).

Thus the mother's experience of psychological distress, at moderate levels of depression and anxiety and especially under severe stress or trauma, leads to developmental disruption in the fetus that can alter the course of the child's biochemical and physiological development. This disruption can create vulnerabilities for a number of adult syndromes and diseases, especially posttraumatic stress disorder (Alder, Fink, Bitzer, Hosli, & Holzgreve, 2007; see Lange, *Prenatal Maternal Stress,* this issue).

This neurological and biochemical research, exploring the earliest impact of the relational trauma of maternal distress on the developing fetus, also has implications for clinical theory, assessment and treatment. Researchers and theorists have used evidence from animal and human research to expand the concept of attachment. This evidence suggests that attachment can be thought to begin with the mother's patterning of the infant's biochemical system in vitro, which contributes to a physiological and behavioral regulation of the infant's stress response system (Lyons-Ruth, 2003; Hane & Fox, 2006). Novel methods from this developing area of research use biological markers and substrates for assessment of risk (Ciccheti & Gunnar, 2008), and measures of treatment success (Bakermans-Kranenburg, van IJzendoorn, Mesman, Alink, & Juffer, 2008).

## Traumatic Symptomatology in Infancy

The clinical literature on infant trauma draws the symptom picture of a traumatized infant. Similar to children and adults, infants also have PTSD-like symptoms following exposure to traumatic events, lasting years after the initial traumatic experience (Scheeringa & Gaensbauer, 2000; Coates & Gaensbauer, 2009). Physical and kinesthetic experiences linked to the trauma, such as vomiting and convulsive episodes, have been observed as acute reactions to stress, especially separation distress occurring later in development (Gaensbauer, 1995). As in childhood, stress responses to separation are especially pronounced following trauma in infancy. Re-experiencing of the trauma, and intrusive thoughts, are also seen in young children following trauma in infancy. These experiences are behaviorally enacted in early symbolic play, and in the development of phobias specifically connected to the experience of the traumatic incident (Gaensbauer, 1995, 2002, 2004; Terr, 1988; Markese, 2007).

Other physiological symptoms similar to adult PTSD are present in infants (Drell, Siegel, & Gaensbauer, 1993). They take the form of difficulties in eating and sleeping, and an increased preoccupation with self-regulatory behaviors such as rocking and self-touch (Gaensbauer, 2002, 2004). In addition, infant behavioral problems similar to those seen in older children experiencing loss or trauma have been observed, including mood swings, problems with attention, and episodes of agitation and uncontrollable crying (Gaensbauer, 1995). While these PTSD-like symptoms have been described in infants and young children following discrete trauma, more research is needed to understand the effect of loss and relational trauma on development in the preverbal period.

### Applying Infant and Toddler Trauma Research to Dyadic Mother-Child Treatment

The bodies of research discussed above are important for primary prevention methods for infants and toddlers affected by traumatic events. Studies of infant memory of traumatic experiences and clinical cases illustrating the effects of trauma provide compelling evidence that early traumatic experiences may jeopardize early infant relational development, and set the course for maladaptive patterns of relatedness as children mature.

The attachment literature provides a compelling rationale for early intervention with traumatized infants (see, e.g., Lyons-Ruth & Spielman, 2004; Oppenheim & Goldsmith, 2007; Dozier, Peloso, Lewis, Laurenceau, & Levine, 2008; Bakermans-Kranenburg et al., 2008; Baradon, Fonagy, Bland, Lénárd, & Sleed, 2008; Juffer, Bakermans-Kranenburg, & van IJzendoorn, 2008; Lieberman, Ghosh Ippen, & Van Horn, 2006; Toth, Rogosch, & Cicchetti, 2008). Interventions aimed at strengthening the dyadic parent-child relationship, the parent's reflective functioning, and positive parenting are all influenced by attachment theory and research (Grienenberger, Kelly, & Slade, 2005; Slade, Grienenberger, Bernbach, Levy, & Locker, 2005; Toth, Rogosch, & Cicchetti, 2008; Klapper & Markese, 2007). Parents suffering from trauma or loss are at psychological risk for developing depressive and dissociative symptoms. These parental experiences negatively affect early parent-infant face-to-face interactions and place infants at risk for the insecure attachment outcomes. Additionally, trauma and loss may result in "unresolved," "preoccupied," or "dismissive" parental attachment representations, which may in turn compromise infant attachment strategies. On the other hand, parental involvement and sensitivity are critically important positive mediating factors in a child's recovery following trauma and loss.

## CONCLUSION

This final section considers (a) the application of infant trauma research to dyadic parent-infant trauma treatment and (b) the need for further research on acute trauma and loss in the preverbal period of infancy.

## Parent-infant Treatment in the Acute Stages of Bereavement

The research reviewed on adult and child trauma; links among unresolved mourning, infant insecure attachment, and childhood psychopathology; and maternal distress and disturbances of mother-infant face-to-face communication intersect. They all point to the importance of strengthening mother-child attachment bonds over the course of development to ensure optimal social and cognitive child outcomes. Several methods of primary prevention which are informed by psychoanalytic theory, attachment theory, and systems models of mother-infant mutual regulation have been described, and are currently being utilized to treat at-risk mother-infant dyads (Lieberman, Ghosh Ippen, & Van Horn, 2006; Slade, Sadler, Dios-Kenn, Webb, Currier-Ezepchick, & Mayes, 2005; Baradan et al., 2008; Marvin, Cooper, Hoffman, & Powell, 2002; Beebe, 2003, 2005; Cohen & Beebe, 2002; Hoffman, 2001; Malphurs & Field, 1996; Lieberman, 1992; Lieberman & Pawl, 1993; Fraiberg, 1975).

The literature on the effects of maternal unresolved attachment and distress on mother-infant face-to-face communication documents observable interactional patterns that mothers can learn to observe through therapeutic intervention. These methods of early intervention combine psychoanalytic exploration of the mother's experience of loss and its relation to her experience of her infant with behavioral and educational methods to assist mothers in becoming more aware of patterns of communication between her and her infant or young child (see Sossin & Cohen, *Children's Play in the Wake of Trauma;* Cohen, *The Evolution of the Project*; and Bergman, *Lydia and Ryan,* this issue).

One such early intervention program implemented specifically in response to the needs of new mothers who were widowed as a result of the World Trade Center disaster is described in this issue. This approach to primary prevention rests on the hypothesis that the early face-to-face interaction between mothers and their 4 month-olds can be valuable clinically. The mother-infant face-to-face interaction facilitates the assessment of risk and is a powerful tool enabling clinicians to help grieving mothers attune to the signals and needs of their infants. The dyadic conceptualization of trauma and its treatment outlined in this issue is in accordance with the recent findings of September 11 research on the mutual impact of child and parent trauma, and the importance of parental mental health and adaptive parenting post-trauma, particularly for the youngest children (Chemtob et al., 2008, 2010; Yehuda et al., 2005; Yehuda & Bierer, 2008).

The mother-infant and mother-child video feedback treatment methods described in this issue are similar to other models for at-risk mother-child dyads (see, e.g., Schecter, Myers, Brunelli, Coates, Zeanah, & Davies, 2006; Hoffman, 2001; Marvin et al., 2002; Malphurs, Field, & Larrain, 1996; Schechter et al., 2006; Cohen & Beebe, 2002; Beebe, 2003). In the Project described in this issue, treating women who were pregnant, lost their husbands in the WTC attacks, and were exposed to the ongoing threat of terror in New York City with video feedback therapy helped mothers to be more attuned to their own, and their child's, nonverbal communication.

Mothers in the acute stages of trauma and grief have the additional risk of transmitting unstable attachment representations to their infants and young children (Lyons-Ruth, 2008). As such, this primary prevention/intervention Project described in this issue also facilitated mothers' mourning and development of representations of their lost spouse.

Interactional approaches to treating early mother-child dyadic difficulty, in combination with individual psychodynamic, representational treatment of bereaved mothers, strike a balance between focusing on short-term and long-term treatment models. These multidisciplinary primary prevention models are likely to provide more complex, lasting treatment outcomes by promoting optimal regulation of dyadic parent-child distress through facilitating infant and child mourning, strengthening the relational and cognitive development of young children, and simultaneously providing mothers with the capacity to form strong attachment bonds with their children in the face of the loss of a primary attachment figure.

The research reviewed in this article provides extensive support for the importance of early intervention models that emphasize dyadic parent-child treatment for infants and young children exposed to trauma. To take a strength-based perspective, even ordinary variations in parental caregiving and emotional interactions with infants can significantly influence the infant's regulation of distress. Therefore, change in parent-infant interactions translates directly into improvements in young children's mental health (Hane & Fox, 2006). The past decade has seen a huge leap in research on trauma exposure in young children. In parallel, there is a burgeoning of reports of successful dyadic early intervention protocols (Beebe, 2003, 2005; Gwynne, Blick, & Duffy, 2009; Baradon et al., 2008; Bakermans-Kranenburg et al., 2008; Cicchetti & Gunnar, 2008; Dozier et al., 2008; Juffer, Bakermans-Kranenberg, & van IJzendoorn, 2008; Mayers, 2008; Toth, Rogosch, & Cicchetti, 2008; Oppenheim & Goldsmith, 2007). Our understanding of the effects of trauma on infants and young children is rapidly expanding.

## Need for Further Research on "Event" and "Relational" Trauma in the Preverbal Period

Despite compelling evidence that infants in the preverbal period experience and remember trauma, and evidence that parental trauma affects infants relational development from as early as four months through the course of childhood, more research must be conducted. More sensitive ways of assessing infant trauma before measures of attachment become relevant at one year are urgently needed. The World Trade Center attacks of September 11, 2001, have highlighted the need for new models of therapy (Seeley, 2008) and for further research on the effect of trauma on the surviving parent, the developing infant and toddler, and the dyadic system. The microanalytic study of early face-to-face interactions of these affected mother-child dyads may provide clues to the ways in which acute trauma and unresolved loss are communicated within the parent-child relationship. Taken together with research on direct infant trauma exposure, such studies may serve as an early method of risk assessment, and a pathway to the dyadic treatment of trauma in infancy and early childhood.

## REFERENCES

Ainsworth, M., & Wittig, B. (1969). Attachment and exploratory behavior of one year olds in a strange situation. In B. M. Foss (Ed.), *Determinants of infant behavior* (Vol. 4). London, England: Methuen.

Ainsworth, M. (1982). Attachment: Retrospect and prospect. In C. M. Parkes & J. Stevenson-Hinde (Eds.), *The place of attachment in human behavior*. New York, NY: Basic Books.

Ainsworth, M., Blehar, M., Waters, E., & Wall, S. (1978). *Patterns of attachment: A psychological study of the strange situation*. Hillsdale, NJ: Lawrence Erlbaum Associates.

Alder, J., Fink, N., Bitzer, J., Hosli, I., & Holzgreve, W. (2007). Depression and anxiety during pregnancy: A risk factor for obstetric, fetal and neonatal outcome? A critical review of the literature. *Journal of Maternal-Fetal and Neonatal Medicine*, *20*(3), 189–209.

Andrade, R., & Aghajanian, G. (1984). Locus coeruleus activity in vitro: Intrinsic regulation by a calcium-dependent potassium conductance but not alpha-2 adrenoreceptors. *Journal of Neuroscience*, *4*, 161–170.

Appleyard, K., & Osofsky, J. D. (2003). Parenting after trauma: Supporting parents and caregivers in the treatment of children impacted by violence. *Infant Mental Health Journal*, *24*, 111–125.

Bakermans-Kranenburg, M., van IJzendoorn, M., Mesman, J., Alink, L., & Juffer, F. (2008). Effects of an attachment-based intervention on daily cortisol moderated by dopamine receptor D4: A randomized control trial on 1- to 3-year-olds screened for externalizing behavior. *Development and Psychopathology*, *20*(3), 805–820.

Banyard, V., Rozelle, D., & Englund, D. (2001). Parenting the traumatized child: Attending to the needs of nonoffending caregivers of traumatized children. *Psychotherapy: Theory, Research, Practice and Training*, *38*, 74–87.

Baradon, T., Fonagy, P., Bland, K., Lénárd, K., & Sleed, M. (2008). New beginnings—an experience-based programme addressing the attachment relationship between mothers and their babies in prisons. *Journal of Child Psychotherapy*, *34*(2), 240–258.

Bayley, N. (1993). *Bayley scales of infant development* (2nd ed.). San Antonio, TX: Psychological Corporation.

Beebe, B. (2000). Co-constructing mother-infant distress: The micro-synchrony of maternal impingement and infant avoidance in the face-to-face encounter. *Psychoanalytic Inquiry*, *20*(3), 421–440.

Beebe, B. (2003). Brief mother-infant treatment using psychoanalytically informed video microanalysis. *Infant Mental Health Journal*, *24*(1), 24–52.

Beebe, B. (2005). Mother-infant research informs mother-infant treatment. *Psychoanalytic Study of the Child*, *60*, 7–46.

Beebe, B., & Lachmann, F. (2002). *Infant research and adult treatment: Co-constructing interactions*. Hillsdale, NJ: The Analytic Press.

Beebe, B., & Jaffe, J. (2002). *Support groups, parent-infant video bonding consultation, and 2-year infant follow-up for mothers pregnant and widowed on 9/11*. Grant request, New York State Psychiatric Institute, unpublished manuscript.

Beebe, B., Jaffe, J., Buck, K., Chen, H., Cohen, P., Feldstein, S., & Andrews, H. (2008). Six-week postpartum maternal depressive symptoms and 4-month mother-infant self- and interactive contingency. *Infant Mental Health Journal*, *29*(5), 442–471.

Beebe, B., Jaffe, J., Lachmann, F., Feldstein, S., Crown, C., & Jasnow, J. (2000). Systems models in development and psychoanalysis: The case of vocal rhythm coordination and attachment. *Infant Mental Health Journal*, *21*, 99–122.

Beebe, B., Jaffe, J., Markese, S., Buck, K., Chen, H., Cohen, P., . . . Andrews, H. (2010). The origins of 12-month attachment: A microanalysis of 4-month mother-infant interaction. *Attachment & Human Development*, *12*(1–2), 3–141.

Beebe, B., & McCrorie, E. (2010). The optimum midrange: Infant research, literature, and romantic attachment. *Attachment: New Directions in Psychotherapy and Relational Psychoanalysis*, *4*, 39–58.

Beebe, B., Steele, M., Jaffe, J., Buck, K., Chen, H., Cohen, P., . . . Feldstein, S. (2011). Maternal anxiety and 4-month mother-infant self- and interactive contingency. *Infant Mental Health Journal*, *32*(2), 174–206.

Beebe, B., Markese, S., Steele, M., Buck, K., Cohen, P., Reuben, J., . . . Jaffe, J. (2011, in preparation). Paths of risk and resilience in 4-month mother-infant interaction: From 6-week maternal depression to 12-month insecure and secure attachment. Manuscript in preparation, New York State Psychiatric Institute.

Beeghly, M., Weinberg, K., Olson, K., Keman, H., Riley, J., & Tronick, E. (2001). Stability and change in level of maternal depressive symptomatology during the first postpartum year. *Journal of Affective Disorders*, *71*(1), 169–180.

Bergman, A. (2011, this issue). The team approach to the treatment of a traumatized mother and child: Lydia and Ryan. *Journal of Infant, Child and Adolescent Psychology*, *10*, 301–315.

Bretherton, I., Ridgeway, D., & Cassidy, J. (1990). Assessing internal working models of the attachment relationship: An attachment story completion task for 3-year-olds. In M. Greenberg, D. Cicchetti, & M. Cummings (Eds.), *Attachment in the preschool years: Theory, research and intervention* (pp. 273–308). Chicago: University of Chicago Press.

Bhaskaran, D., & Freed, C. (1988). Changes in neurotransmitter turnover in locus coruleus by changes in arterial blood pressure. *Brain Research Bulletin*, *21*, 191–199.

Birklein, S. B., & Sossin, K. M., (2006). Nonverbal indices of stress in parent-child dyads: Implications for individual and interpersonal affect regulation and intergenerational transmission. In S. Koch & I. Bruninger (Eds.), *Advances in DMT research*. Berlin, Germany: Logos.

Bowlby, J. (1969). *Attachment and loss, vol.1: Attachment*. London, England: Hogarth Press.

Brier, A., Kelsoe, J., Kirwin, P., Beller, S., Wolkowitz, O., & Pickar, D. (1988). Early parental loss and development of adult psychopathology. *Archives of General Psychiatry*, *45*, 987–993.

Britton, J. (2005). Pre-discharge anxiety among mothers of well newborns: Prevalence and correlates. *Acta Paediatrica, 94*, 1771–1776.

Carlson, E. (1998). A prospective longitudinal study of attachment disorganization/disorientation. *Child Development, 69*(4), 1107–1128.

Cassidy, J., Woodhouse, S., Cooper, G., Hoffman, K., Powell, B., & Rodenberg, M. (2005). Examinations of the precursors of infant attachment security: Implications for early intervention and intervention research. In L. J. Berlin, Y. Ziv, L. M. Amaya-Jackson, & M. T. Greenberg (Eds.), *Enhancing early attachments: Theory, research, intervention, and policy*. New York, NY: Guilford Press.

Chemtob, C., Nomura, Y., & Abramovitz, R. (2008). Impact of conjoined exposure to the World Trade Center Attacks and to other traumatic events on the behavioral problems of preschool children. *Archives of Pediatric and Adolescent Medicine, 162*(2), 126–133.

Chemtob, C., Nomura, Y., Rajendran, K., Yehuda, R., Schwartz, D., & Abramovitz, R. (2010). Impact of maternal posttraumatic stress disorder and depression following exposure to the September 11 attacks on preschool children's behavior. *Child Development, 81*(4), 1129–1141.

Cicchetti, D., & Gunnar, M. (2008). Editorial: Integrating biological measures into the design and evaluation of preventive interventions. *Development and Psychopathology, 20*(3), 737–743.

Clayton, P., Desmarais, L., & Winokur, G. (1968). A study of normal bereavement. *American Journal of Psychiatry, 125*(2), 168–178.

Coates, S., & Gaensbauer, T. J. (2009). Event trauma in early childhood: Symptoms, assessment, intervention. *Child & Adolescent Psychiatry Clinics of North America, 18*(3), 611–626.

Cohen, P. M. (2011, this issue). The evolution of the project: Helping the mothers, infants and young children of September 11, 2001. *Journal of Infant, Child and Adolescent Psychology, 10*, 186–200.

Cohen, P. M., & Beebe, B. (2002). Video feedback with a depressed mother and her infant: A collaborative individual psychoanalytic and mother-infant treatment. *Journal of Infant Child, and Adolescent Psychotherapy, 2*(3), 1–55.

Covell, N., Allen, G., Essock, S., Pease, E., Felton, C., Lanzara, C., & Donahue, S. (2006). Service utilization and event reaction patterns among children who received Project Liberty counseling services. *Psychiatric Services, 57*(9), 1277–1282.

Cramer, B. (1998). Mother-infant psychotherapies: A widening scope in technique. *Infant Mental Health Journal, 19*(2), 151–167.

Daehler, M., & Greco, C. (1985). Memory in very young children. In M. Pressley & C. Brainerd (Eds.), *Cognitive learning and memory in children* (pp. 49–79). New York, NY: Springer-Verlag.

Davidson, R., & Fox, N. (1982). Assymetrical brain activity discriminates between positive versus negative affective stimuli in human infants. *Science, 218*, 1235–1237.

Dawson, G. (1992). Frontal lobe activity and affective behavior of infants of mothers with depressive symptoms. *Child Development, 63*, 725–737.

Dawson, G., Ashman, S., Panagiotides, H., Hessl, D., Self, J., Yamada, E., & Embry, L. (2003). Preschool outcomes of children of depressed mothers: Role of maternal behavior, contextual risk, and children's brain activity. *Child Development, 74*(4), 1158–1175.

Deering, C. (2000). A cognitive developmental approach to understanding how children cope with disasters. *Journal of Child and Adolescent Psychiatric Nursing, 13*, 7–16.

DeKlyen, M., & Greenberg, M. T. (2008). Attachment and psychopathology in childhood. In J. Cassidy & P. Shaver (Eds.), *Handbook of attachment: Theory, research and clinical applications* (2nd ed., pp. 637–665). New York, NY: Guilford Press.

Demetri Friedman, D., Beebe, B., Jaffe, J., Ross, D., & Triggs, S. (2010). Microanalysis of 4-month infant vocal affect qualities and maternal postpartum depression. *Clinical Social Work Journal, 38*(1), 8–16.

Devinsky, O. (2000). Right cerebral hemisphere dominance for a sense of corporeal and emotional self. *Epilepsy & Behavior, 1*, 60–73.

DeVoe, E. E., Klein, T., Bannon, W., & Miranda-Julian, C. (2011). Young children in the aftermath of the World Trade Center attacks. *Psychological Trauma: Theory, Research, Practice, and Policy, 3*(1), 1–7.

Diego, M., Jones, N., Field, T., Hernandez-Reif, M., Schanberg, S., Kuhn, C., & Gonzalez-Garcia, A. (2006). Maternal psychological distress, prenatal cortisol, and fetal weight. *Psychosomatic Medicine, 68*, 747–753.

Dowdney, L. (2005). Children bereaved by parent or sibling death. *Psychiatry, 4*(9), 118–122.

Dozier, M., Peloso, E., Lewis, E., Laurenceau, J., & Levine, S. (2008). Effects of an attachment-based intervention of the cortisol production of infants and toddlers in foster care. *Development and Psychopathology, 20*(3), 845–859.

Drell, M., Siegel, C., & Gaensbauer, T. (1993). Post-traumatic stress disorder. In C. Zeanah (Ed.), *Handbook of infant mental health* (pp. 291–304). New York, NY: Guilford Press.

Elgar, F. J., McGrath, P. J., Waschbusch, D. A., Stewart, S. H., & Curtis, K. J. (2004). Mutual influences on maternal depression and child adjustment problems. *Clinical Psychology Review, 24*(4), 441–459.

Elizur, E., & Kaffman, M. (1983). Factors influencing the severity of childhood bereavement reactions. *American Journal of Orthopsychiatry, 53*, 668–676.

Feldman, R., & Eidelman, A. (2009). Biological and environmental initial conditions shape the trajectories of cognitive and social-emotional development across the first years of life. *Developmental Science, 12*(1), 194–200.

Feldman, R., Granat, A., Pariente, C., Kanety, H., Kuint, J., & Gilboa-Schechtman, E. (2009). Maternal depression and anxiety across the postpartum year and infant social engagement, fear regulation, and stress reactivity. *Journal of the American Academy of Child and Adolescent Psychiatry, 48*(9), 919–927.

Field, T. (1977). Effects of early separation, interactive deficits and experimental manipulations of infant-mother face-to-face interaction. *Child Development, 48*, 763–771.

Field, T. (1989). Matching and synchrony of behavior states and heart rate in mother-infant interactions of nondepressed versus "depressed" dyads. *Developmental Psychology, 26*, 7–14.

Field, T. (1994). The effects of mother's physical and emotional unavailability on emotion regulation. In N. Fox (Ed.), *The development of emotion regulation* (pp. 208–227). *Monographs of the Society for Research in Child Development*, 59 (22-3, Serial No. 240).

Field, T. (1995). Infants of depressed mothers. *Infant Behavior and Development, 18*, 1–13.

Field, T., Diego, M., & Hernandez-Reif, M. (2006). Prenatal depression effects on the fetus and newborn: A review. *Infant Behavior & Development, 29*, 445–455.

Field, T., Healy, B., Goldstein, S., & Guthertz, M. (1990). Behavior state matching and synchrony in mother-infant interactions of nondepressed versus depressed dyads. *Developmental Psychology, 26*(1), 7–14.

Field, T., Healy, B., Goldstein, S., Perry, D., Bendell, D., Schanberg, S., . . . Kuhn, O. (1988). Infants of depressed mothers show "depressed" behavior even with non-depressed adults. *Child Development, 59*, 1596–1579.

Field, T., Hernandez-Reif, M., Vera, Y., Gil, K., Diego, M., Bendell, D., & Yando, R. (2005). Anxiety and anger effects on depressed mother–infant spontaneous and imitative interaction. *Infant Behavior & Development, 28*, 1–9.

Fogel, A. (1993). Two principles of Field, T. (2011). Prenatal depression effects on early development: A review. *Infant Behavior and Development, 34*, 1–14.

Fonagy, P., Steele, H., & Steele, M. (1991b). Maternal representations of attachment during pregnancy predict the organization of infant-mother attachment at one year of age. *Child Development, 62*, 891–905.

Foster, C., Garber, J., & Durlak, J. (2008). Current and past maternal depression, maternal interaction behaviors, and children's externalizing and internalizing symptoms. *Journal of Abnormal Child Psychology: International Society for Research in Child and Adolescent Psychopathology, 36*(4), 527–537.

Foster, C., Webster, M., Weissman, M., Pilowsky, D., Wickramaratne, P., Rush, J., . . . Cerda, G. (2008). Course and severity of maternal depression: Associations with family functioning and child adjustment. *Journal of Youth and Adolescence, 37(8)*, 906–916.

Fox, E., Russo, R., & Dutton, K. (2002). Attentional bias for threat: Evidence for delayed disengagement from emotional faces. *Cognition and Emotion, 16*(3), 355–379.

Fraiberg, S. (1980). *Clinical studies in infant mental health: The first year of life*. New York, NY: Basic Books.

Fraiberg, S., Adelson, E., & Shapiro, V. (1975). Ghosts in the nursery: A psychoanalytic approach to the problems of impaired infant-mother relationships. *Journal of the American Academy of Child and Adolescent Psychiatry, 14*, 387–421.

Fremont, W. P. (2004). Childhood reactions to terrorism induced trauma: A review of the past 10 years. *Journal of the American Academy of Child and Adolescent Psychiatry, 43*, 381–392.

Furman, E. (1974). *A child's parent dies: Studies in childhood bereavement*. New Haven, CT: Yale University Press.

Gaensbauer, T. (1995). Trauma in the preverbal period: Symptoms, memories, and developmental impact. *The Psychoanalytic Study of the Child, 16*, 122–149.

Gaensbauer, T. (2002). Representations of trauma in infancy: Clinical and theoretical implications for the understanding of early memory. *Infant Mental Health Journal, 23*(3), 259–277.

Gaensbauer, T. (2004). Telling their stories: Representation and reenactment of traumatic experiences occurring in the first year of life. *Journal of Zero to Three: National Center for Infants, Toddlers and Families, 24*, 25–31.

Galea, S., Ahern, J., Resnick, H., Kilpatrick, D., Bucuvalas, M., Gold, J., & Vlahov, D. (2002). Psychological sequelae of the September 11 terrorist attacks in New York City. *New England Journal of Medicine, 346*, 982–987.

Garber, B. (1997). Parent loss in childhood and adult psychopathology. In L. Flaherty & H. Horowitz (Eds.), *Adolescent psychiatry, vol. 21: Developmental and clinical studies. Annals of the American Society for Adolescent Psychiatry* (pp. 101–118). Hillsdale, NJ: The Analytic Press.

Gershoff, E., Aber, J., Ware, A., & Kotler, J. (2010). Exposure to 9/11 among youth and their mothers in New York City: Enduring associations with mental health and sociopolitical attitudes. *Child Development, 81*(4), 1142–1160.

Goldberg, S., Benoit, D., Blokland, K., & Madigan, S. (2003). Atypical maternal behavior, maternal representations and infant disorganized attachment. *Development and Psychopathology, 15*(2), 239–257.

Ghosh-Ippen, C., Ford, J., Racusin, R., Acker, M., Bosquet, K., Rogers, C., . . . Edwards, J. (2002). Trauma events screening inventory-parent report revised. The Child Trauma Research Project of the Early Trauma Network and The National Center for PTSD. Dartmouth Child Trauma Research Group, San Francisco, CA.

Grienenberger, J., Kelly, K., & Slade, A. (2005). Maternal reflective functioning, mother–infant affective communication, and infant attachment: Exploring the link between mental states and observed caregiving behavior in the intergenerational transmission of attachment. *Attachment & Human Development, 7*(3), 299–311.

Grossman, K. E., Grossman, K., Winter, M., & Zimmermann, P. (2002). Attachment relationships and appraisal of partnership: From early experience of sensitive support of later relationship representation. In L. Pulkkinen & A. Caspi (Eds.), *Paths to successful development* (pp. 73–105). Cambridge, England: Cambridge University Press.

Gunnar, M., Porter, F., Wolf, C., & Rigatuso, J. (1995). Neonatal stress reactivity: Predictions to later emotional temperament. *Child Development, 66*, 1–13.

Gwynne, K., Blick, B., & Duffy, G. (2009). Pilot evaluation of an early intervention programme for children at risk. *Journal of Paediatrics and Child Health, 45*(3), 118–124.

Halligan, S., Murray, L., Martins, C., & Cooper, P. (2007). Maternal depression and psychiatric outcomes in adolescent offspring: A 13-year longitudinal study. *Journal of Affective Disorders, 97*(1), 145–154.

Hammen, C., Burge, D., Burney, E., & Adrian, C. (1990). Longitudinal study of diagnoses in children of women with unipolar and bipolar affective disorder. *Archives of General Psychiatry, 47*(12), 1112–1117.

Hane, A., & Fox, N. (2006). Ordinary variations in maternal caregiving influence human infants' stress reactivity. *Psychological Science, 17*(6), 550–556.

Harris, T., Brown, G., & Bifulco, A. (1986). Loss of parent in childhood and adult psychiatric disorder: The role of lack of adequate parental care. *Psychological Medicine, 16*, 641–659.

Hennighausen, K., & Lyons-Ruth, K. (2010). Disorganization of attachment strategies in infancy and childhood. In R. E. Tremblay, R. G. Barr, R. V. Peters, & M. Boivin (Eds.), *Encyclopedia on early childhood development* (pp. 1–7). Montreal, Quebec: Centre of Excellence for Early Childhood Development.

Hoffman, K. (2001). *Circle of security project, Marycliff Institute and the University of Virginia*. Unpublished manuscript.

Hoffman, I. (1979). Death anxiety and adaptation to mortality in psychoanalytic theory. *Annual of Psychoanalysis, 7*, 233–267.

Hopkins, J. (1992). Infant and parent psychotherapy. *Journal of Child Psychotherapy, 18*(1), 5–19.

Hoven, C. W., Duarte, C. S., Lucas, C. P., Wu, P., Mandell, D. J., Goodwin, R. D., . . . Susser, E. (2005). Psychopathology among New York City public school children 6 months after September 11. *Archives of General Psychiatry, 62*, 545–552.

Howard, D. (2000). An exploratory study of attachment and coping for bereaved elementary school children. *Dissertations Abstracts International, A (Humanities and Social Sciences), 61*(5-A), 1752.

Jacobson, E. (1964). *Self and object world*. New York, NY: International Universities Press.

Jacobsen, T., Edelstein, W., & Hofmann, V. (1994). A longitudinal study of the relation between representations of attachment in childhood and cognitive functioning in childhood and adolescence. *Developmental Psychology, 30*, 112–124.

Jacobvitz, D., & Hazen, N. (1998). *Developmental pathways from infant disorganization to childhood peer relationship*. Manuscript submitted for publication.

Jaffe, J., Beebe, B., Feldstein, S., Crown, C., & Jasnow, M. (2001). Rhythms of dialogue in early infancy. *Monographs of the Society for Research in Child Development, 66*(2 Serial No. 264).

Juffer, F., Bakermans-Kranenburg, M., & van IJzendoorn, M. (2008). *Promoting positive parenting: An attachment-based intervention*. New York, NY: Taylor & Francis.

Kelly, K., Ueng-McHale, J., Grienenberger, J., & Slade, A. (2003, April). *Atypical maternal behaviors and their relation to infant attachment disorganization*. Poster session presented at the meeting of the Society for Research in Child Development, Tampa, FL.

Kendler, K., Sheth, C., Gardner, O., & Prescott, C. (2002). Childhood parental loss and risk for first-onset of major depression and alcohol dependence: The time-decay of risk and sex differences. *Psychological Medicine, 32*, 1187–1194.

Kitzmann, K. M., Gaylord, N. K., & Aber, J. L. (2004). Child, youth, and parent responses to the terrorism of September 11, 2001: Implications for applied developmental science and practice. *Applied Developmental Science, 8*, 221–225.

Klapper, W., & Markese, S. (2008, June). *Evolution of a parent-infant group of highly traumatized families in long-term treatment*. Presentation at the Fordham University School of Social Work, Early Childhood Mental Health Conference, New York, NY.

Klein, T., DeVoe, E., Miranda-Julian, C., & Linas, K. (2009). Young children's responses to September 11th: The New York City experience. *Infant Mental Health Journal, 30*(1), 1–22.

Kobak, R., Cassidy, J., Lyons-Ruth, K., & Ziv, Y. (2006). Attachment, stress, and psychopathology: A developmental pathways model. In D. Cicchetti & D. J. Cohen (Eds.), *Developmental psychopathology: Vol. 1. Theory and method* (2nd ed., pp. 333–369). Hoboken, NJ: Wiley.

Koplewicz, H., Vogel, J., Solanto, M., Morrissey, R., Alonso, C., Abikoff, H., . . . Novick, R. (2002). Child and parent response to the 1993 World Trade Center bombing. *Journal of Traumatic Stress, 15*(1), 77–85.

Koulomzin, M., Beebe, B., Anderson, S., Jaffe, J., Feldstein, S., & Crown, C. (2002). Infant gaze, head, face, and self-touch at four months differentiate secure vs. avoidant attachment at one year: A microanalytic approach. *Attachment and Human Development, 4*, 3–24.

Kranzler, E., Schaffer, D., Wasserman, G., & Davies, M. (1990). Early childhood bereavement. *Journal of the American Academy of Child and Adolescent Psychiatry, 29*, 413–520.

La Greca, A., Silverman, W. K., Vernberg, E. M., & Prinstein, M. J. (1996). Symptoms of posttraumatic stress in children after Hurricane Andrew: A prospective study. *Journal of Consulting and Clinical Psychology, 64*, 712–723.

Lange, A. (2011). Prenatal maternal stress and the developing fetus and infant: A review of animal models as related to human research. *Journal of Infant, Child and Adolescent Psychology*, this issue.

Laor, N., Wolmer, L., & Cohen, D. J. (2001). Mothers' functioning and children's symptoms 5 years after a SCUD missile attack. *American Journal of Psychiatry, 158*, 1020–1026.

Laor, N., Wolmer, L., Mayes, L. C., Gershon, A., Weizman, R., & Cohen, D. J. (1997). Israeli preschool children under Scuds: A 30-month follow-up. *Journal of the American Academy of Child & Adolescent Psychiatry, 36*, 349–356.

Laor, N., Wolmer, L., Mayes, L. C., Golomb, A., Silverberg, D. S., Weizman, R., & Cohen, D. (1996). Israeli preschoolers under Scud missile attacks: A developmental perspective on risk-modifying factors. *Archives of General Psychiatry, 53*, 416–423.

Lebovici, S. (1983). *Le nourrison, la mere, et le psychoanalyste: Les interventions precoces*. Paris, France: Le Centurion.

Levendosky, A., Huth-Bocks, A., Shapiro, D., & Semel, M. (2003). The impact of domestic violence on the maternal-child relationship and pre-school age children's functioning. *Journal of Family Psychology, 17*, 275–287.

Lewis, M., Feiring, C., & Rosenthal, S. (2000). Attachment over time. *Child Development, 71*(3), 707–720.

Lieberman, A. (1992). Infant-parent psychotherapy with toddlers. *Development and Psychopathology, 4*, 559–574.

Lieberman, A., Compton, N., Van Horn, P., & Ippen, C. (2003). *Losing a parent to death in the early years: Guidelines for the treatment of traumatic bereavement in infancy and early childhood*. Washington, DC: Zero to Three Press/National Center for Infants, Toddlers and Families.

Lieberman, A., & Pawl, J. (1993). Infant-parent psychotherapy. In C. Zeanah (Ed.), *Handbook of infant mental health* (pp. 427–442). New York, NY: Guilford Press.

Lieberman, A., & Van Horn, P. (2005). *Don't hit my mommy*. Washington, DC: Zero to Three Press.

Lieberman, A., Ghosh Ippen, C., & Van Horn, P. (2006). Child-parent psychotherapy: 6-month follow-up of a randomized controlled trial. *Journal of the American Academy of Child & Adolescent Psychiatry, 45*, 913–918.

Linares, L. O., Heeren, T., Bronfman, E., Zuckerman, B., Augustyn, M., & Tronick, E. (2001). A mediational model for the impact of exposure to community violence on early child behavior problems. *Child Development, 72*, 639–652.

Liotti G. (1992). Disorganized/disoriented attachment in the etiology of the dissociative disorders. *Dissociation, IV*, 196–204.

Lojkasek, M., Cohen, D., & Muir, E. (1994). Where is the infant in infant intervention? A review of the literature on changing troubled mother-infant relationships. *Psychotherapy, 31*, 208–220.

Leyendecker, B., Lamb, M., Fracasso, M., Scholmerich, A., & Larson, D. (1997). Playful interaction and the antecedents of attachment: A longitudinal study of Central American and Euro-American mothers and infants. *Merrill Palmer Quarterly, 43*, 24–47.

Lyons-Ruth, K. (1996). Attachment relationships among children with aggressive behavior problems: The role of disorganized early attachment patterns. *Journal of Consulting and Clinical Psychology, 64*, 32–40.

Lyons-Ruth, K. (1998). Attachment disorganisation: Unresolved loss, relational violence, and lapses in behavioral and attentional strategies. In J. Cassidy & P. Shaver (Eds.), *Handbook of attachment theory and research* (pp. 520–554). New York, NY: Guilford Press.

Lyons-Ruth, K. (2003). Dissociation and the parent-infant dialogue: A longitudinal perspective from attachment research. *Journal of the American Psychoanalytic Association, 51*, 883–911.

Lyons-Ruth, K. (2003). The two-person construction of defenses: Disorganized attachment strategies, unintegrated mental states, and hostile/helpless relational processes. *Journal of Infant Child and Adolescent Psychotherapy, 2*, 105–114.

Lyons-Ruth, K. (2008). Contributions of the mother-infant relationship to dissociative, borderline, and conduct symptoms in young adulthood. *Infant Mental Health Journal, 29(3)*, 203–218.

Lyons-Ruth, K., Alpern, L., & Repacholi, B. (1993). Disorganized infant attachment classification and maternal psychosocial problems as predictors of hostile-aggressive behavior in the preschool classroom. *Child Development, 64*, 572–585.

Lyons-Ruth, K., Bronfman, E., & Atwood, G. (1999a). A relational diathesis model of hostile-helpless states of mind: Expressions in mother-infant interaction. In J. Solomon & C. George (Eds.), *Attachment disorganization* (pp. 33–70). New York, NY: Guilford Press.

Lyons-Ruth, K., Bronfman, E., & Parsons, E. (1999b). Maternal frightened, frightening or atypical behavior and disorganized infant attachment patterns. In J. Vondra & D. Barnett (Eds.), *Monographs of the Society for Research in Child Development, 64(3)*, Serial No. 258, 67–96,

Lyons-Ruth, K., & Jacobvitz, D. (2008). Attachment disorganization: Genetic factors, parenting contexts, and developmental transformation from infancy to adulthood. In J. Cassidy & P. R. Shaver (Eds.), *Handbook of attachment: Theory, research, and clinical applications* (2nd ed., pp. 666–697). New York, NY: Guilford Press,

Lyons-Ruth, K., Repacholi, B., McCleod, S., & Silva, E. (1991). Disorganized attachment behavior in infancy: Short-term stability and maternal and infant correlates and risk-related subtypes. *Development and Psychopathology, 3*, 377–396.

Lyons-Ruth, K., & Spielman, E. (2004). Disorganized infant attachment strategies and helpless-fearful profiles of parenting: Integrating attachment research with clinical intervention. *Infant Mental Health Journal, 25*(4), 318–335.

Madigan, S., Bakermans-Kranenburg, M., van IJzendoorrn, M., Moran, G., Pederson, D., & Benoit, D. (2006). Unresolved states of mind, anomalous parental behavior, and disorganized attachment: A review and meta-analysis of a transmission gap. *Attachment and Human Development, 8*, 89–111.

Main, M., & Goldwyn, R. (1988/1993). *Adult attachment classification system.* Unpublished manuscript, University of California at Berkeley.

Main, M., Goldwyn, R., & Hesse, E. (2003). *Adult attachment classification system version 7.2*. Unpublished manuscript, University of California, Berkeley.

Main, M., & Hesse, E. (1990). Parents' unresolved traumatic experiences are related to infant disorganized attachment status: Is frightened and/or frightening parental behavior the linking mechanism? In M. Greenberg, D. Cicchetti, & E. Cummings (Eds.), *Attachment in the preschool years: Theory, research, and intervention* (pp. 161–182). Chicago, IL: University of Chicago Press.

Main, M., & Hesse, E. (1992). Disorganized/disoriented infant behavior in the strange situation, lapses in the monitoring of reasoning and discourse during the parent's Adult Attachment Interview, and dissociative states. In M. Ammaniti & D. Stern (Eds.), *Attachment and psychoanalysis* (pp. 80–140). Rome, Italy: Guis, Laterza & Figli.

Main, M., Hesse, E., & Goldwyn, R. (2008). Studying differences in language usage in recounting attachment history: An introduction to the AAI. In H. Steele & M. Steele (Eds.), *Clinical application of the adult attachment interview* (pp. 31–68). New York, NY: The Guilford Press.

Main, M., Kaplan, N., & Cassidy, J. (1985). Security in infancy, childhood, and adulthood: A move to the level of representation. In I. Bretherton & E. Waters (Eds.), *Monographs of the Society for Research in Child Development, 50*(1–2), 66–104.

Main, M., & Solomon, J. (1990). Procedures for identifying infants as disorganized/disoriented during the Ainsworth Strange Situation. In M. Greenberg, D. Cicchetti, E. Cummings (Eds.), *Attachment in the preschool years* (pp. 121–160). Chicago, IL: University of Chicago Press.

Malphurs, J., Field, T., & Larrain, C. (1996). Altering withdrawn and intrusive interaction behaviors of depressed mothers. *Infant Mental Health Journal, 17*(2), 152–160.

Markese, S. (2007). Taping together broken bones: Treatment of the trauma of infant abuse. *Journal of Infant, Child and Adolescent Psychotherapy, 6*(4), 309–326.

Markese, S. (2008). Rhythms of dialogue in infancy and attachment narratives in childhood. *Dissertation Abstracts International, 68*(11).

Markese, S., Beebe, B., Feldstein, S., & Jaffe, J. (2008). *Rhythms of dialogue in infancy and attachment narratives in childhood*. Paper presented at the International Conference for Infant Studies, Vancouver, Canada.

Marvin, R., Cooper, G., Hoffman, K., & Powell, B. (2002). The circle of security project: Attachment-based intervention with caregiver-preschool child dyads. *Attachment and Human Development*, 4(1).

McClosky, L., & Walker, M. (2000). Posttraumatic stress in children exposed to family violence and single-event trauma. *Journal of the American Academy of Child and Adolescent Psychiatry, 39*, 108–115.

McDermott, B., & Palmer, L. (2002). Postdisaster emotional distress, depression and event-related variables: Findings across child and adolescent developmental stages. *Australian and New Zealand Journal of Psychiatry, 36*, 754–761.

McEwan, B. (1998). Protective and damaging effects of stress mediators. *New England Journal of Medicine, 338*, 171–179.

Mertesacker, B., Bade, U., Haverkock, A., & Pauli-Pott, U. (2004). Predicting maternal reactivity/sensitivity: The role of infant emotionality, maternal depressiveness/anxiety, and social support. *Infant Mental Health Journal, 25*, 47–61.

Michael, T., & Ehlers, A. (2007). Enhanced perceptual priming for neutral stimuli occurring in a traumatic context: Two experimental investigations. *Behaviour Research and Therapy, 45*, 341–358.

Miller, J. (2010). Anomalous maternal behavior at 4 months and infant attachment disorganization at one year. (Unpublished doctoral dissertation). City University of New York.

Monk, C., Myers, M., Sloan, R., Ellman, L., & Fifer, W. (2003). Effects of women's stress elicited physiological activity and chronic anxiety on fetal heart rate. *Journal of Developmental & Behavioral Pediatrics, 24*, 32–38.

Mowder, B. A., Guttman, M., Rubinson, F., & Sossin, K. M. (2007). Parents, children, and trauma: Parent role perceptions and behaviors related to the 9/11 tragedy. *Journal of Child and Family Studies, 15*(6), 733–743.

Murray, L., & Cooper, P. (1997). *Postpartum depression and child development*. New York, NY: Guilford.

Nicol-Harper, R., Harvey, A., & Stein, A. (2007). Interactions between mothers and infants: Impact of maternal anxiety. *Infant Behavior & Development, 30*, 161–167.

Norris, F. (2001). *PCL adapted for 9/11/01 research*. Unpublished checklist.

Norris, F., Friedman, M., Watson, P., Byrne, C., Diaz, E., & Kaniasty, K. (2002). 60,000 disaster victims speak: Part I: An empirical review of the empirical literature, 1981–2001. *Psychiatry, 65*, 207–239.

O'Brien Caughy, M., Huang, K. Y., & Lima, J. (2009). Patterns of conflict interaction in mother–toddler dyads: Differences between depressed and non-depressed mothers. *Journal of Child and Family Studies, 18*(1), 10–20.

Oppenheim, D., & Goldsmith, D. (2007). *Attachment theory in clinical work with children: Bridging the gap between research and practice*. New York, NY: Guilford Press.

Osofsky, J. (1995). Perspectives on attachment and psychoanalysis. *Psychoanalytic Psychology, 12*, 347–363.

Osofsky, J. (2004). *Young children and trauma: Intervention and treatment*. New York, NY: Guilford Press.

Osofsky, J., Osofsky, H., & Harris, W. (2007). Katrina's children: Social policy considerations for children in disasters. *SRCD Social Policy Report, 21*(1), 3–18.

Owens, G., Crowell, J. A., Pan, H., & Treboux, D. (1995). The prototype hypothesis and the origins of attachment working models: Adult relationships with parents and romantic partners. *Monographs of the Society for Research in Child Development, 60*(2–3), 216–233.

Parkes, C. (1967). *Bereavement: Studies of grief in adult life*. Madison, CT: International University Press.

Perris, E., Myers, N., & Clifton, R. (1990). Long-term memory for a single infancy experience. *Child Development, 61*, 1796–1807.

Perry, B. (1994a). Neurobiological sequelae of childhood trauma: Post-traumatic stress disorders in children. In M. Murberg (Ed.), *Catecholamines in post-traumatic stress disorder: Emerging concepts* (pp. 253–276). Washington, DC: American Psychiatric Press.

Perry, B. (1996). Childhood trauma, the neurobiology of adaptation, and "use-dependent" development of the brain: How "states" become "traits." *Infant Mental Health Journal, 16*(4), 271–291.

Perry, B. (2006a). Applying principles of neurodevelopment to clinical work with maltreated and traumatized children. In N. Boyd Webb (Ed.), *Working with traumatized youth in child welfare* (pp. 27–52). New York, NY: The Guilford Press.

Perry, B. (2007). *The boy who was raised as a dog and other stories from a child psychiatrist's notebook: What traumatized children can teach us about loss, love and healing*. New York, NY: Basic Books.

Pfefferbaum, B. J. (2005). Psychological impact of terrorism on children and families in the United States. *Journal of Aggression, Maltreatment and Trauma, 9*, 305–317.

Philips, D., Prince, S., & Schiebelhut, L. (2004). Elementary school children's responses 3 months after the September 11 terrorist attacks: A study in Washington, DC. *American Journal of Orthopsychiatry, 74*, 509–528.

Pine, D., Costello, J., & Masten, A. (2005). Trauma, proximity, and developmental psychopathology: The effects of war and terrorism on children. *Neuropsychopharmacology, 30*, 1781–1792.

Porter, C. L., & Hsu, H. (2003). First-time mothers' perceptions of efficacy during the transition to motherhood: Links to infant temperament. *Journal of Family Psychology, 17*, 54–64.

Pynoos, R. (1991). Grief and trauma in children and adolescents. *Disasters: Planning for a caring response*. London, England: The Disasters Working Party.

Pynoos, R., Nader, K., Frederick, C., Gonda, L., & Stuber, M. (1987). Grief reactions in school-age children after a sniper attack at school. *Israel Journal of Psychiatry and Related Sciences, 24*(1–2), 53–63.

Reck, C., Hunt, A., Fuchs, T., Weiss, R., Noon, A., Moehler, E., . . . Mundt, C. (2004). Interactive regulation of affect in postpartum depressed mothers and their infants: An overview. *Psychopathology, 37*(6), 272–280.

Ronen, T. (2002). Difficulties in assessing traumatic reactions in children. *Journal of Loss and Trauma, 7*, 87–106.

Rovee-Collier, C., & Fagan, J. (1981). The retrieval of memory in early infancy. In L. Lipsett (Ed.), *Advances in infancy research* (Vol. 1, pp. 225–254). Norwood, NJ: Ablex.

Rovee-Collier, C., & Hayne, H. (1987). The reactivation of infant memory: Implications for cognitive development. In H. Reese (Ed.), *Advances in child development and behavior* (pp. 185–238). New York, NY: Academic Press.

Sarro, S. (1993). The mutual regulation of mother-toddler attention. (Unpublished doctoral dissertation). Yeshiva University, New York.

Schecter, D., Coates, S., & First, E. (2002). Observations of acute stress reactions of young children and their families to the World Trade Center attacks. *Zero to Three, 22*(3), 9–13.

Schecter, D., Myers, M., Brunelli, S., Coates, S., Zeanah, C., Davies, M., . . . Liebowitz, M. (2006). Traumatized mothers can change their minds about their toddlers: Understanding how a novel use of video feedback supports positive change in maternal attributions. *Infant Mental Health Journal, 27*, 429–447.

Scheeringa, M. S., & Zeanah, C. H. (1994). *PTSD semi-structured interview and observational record for infants and young children*. New Orleans, LA: Department of Psychiatry and Neurology, Tulane University Health Sciences Center.

Scheeringa, M., Zeanah, C., Drell, M., & Larrieu, J. (1995). Two approaches to the diagnosis of posttraumatic-stress-disorder in infancy and early-childhood. *Journal of the American Academy of Child and Adolescent Psychiatry, 34*, 191–200.

Scheeringa, M. S., & Gaensbauer, T. J. (2000). Posttraumatic stress disorder. In C. H. Zeanah (Ed.), *Handbook of infant mental health* (2nd ed., pp. 360–381). New York, NY: Guilford Press.

Scheeringa, M., Peebles, C., Cook, C., & Zeanah, C. (2001). Toward establishing procedural, criterion and discriminant validity for PTSD in early childhood. *Journal of the American Academy of Child and Adolescent Psychiatry, 40*, 52–60.

Scheeringa, M., & Zeanah, C. (2001). A relational perspective on PTSD in early childhood. *Journal of Traumatic Stress, 14*, 799–815.

Scheeringa, M., & Zeanah, C. (2008). Reconsideration of harm's way: Onsets and comorbidity patterns in preschool children and their caregivers following Hurricane Katrina. *Journal of Clinical Child and Adolescent Psychology, 37*, 508–518.

Scheeringa, M., Zeanah, C., Myers, L., & Putnam, F. (2003). New findings on alternative criteria for PTSD in preschool children. *Journal of the American Academy of Child and Adolescent Psychiatry, 42*, 561–570.

Scheeringa, M., Zeanah, C., Myers, L., & Putnam, F. (2004). Heart period and variability findings in preschool children with posttraumatic stress symptoms. *Biological Psychiatry, 55*, 685–691.

Scheeringa, M., Zeanah, C., Myers, L., & Putnam, F. (2005). Predictive validity in a prospective follow-up of PTSD in preschool children. *Journal of the American Academy of Child and Adolescent Psychiatry*, *44*, 899–906.

Schore, A. (1994). *Affect regulation and the origin of the self: The neurobiology of emotional development*. Hillsdale, NJ: Lawrence Erlbaum Associates.

Schore, A. (1996). The experience-dependent maturation of a regulatory system in the orbital prefrontal corex and the origin of developmental psychopathology. *Development and Psychopathology*, *8*, 59–87.

Schore, A. (2002). Dysregulation of the right brain: A fundamental mechanism of traumatic attachment and the psychopathogenesis of posttraumatic stress disorder. *Australian and New Zealand Journal of Psychiatry*, *36*, 9–30.

Seeley, K. (2008). *Therapy after terror: 9/11, psychotherapists, and mental health*. New York, NY: Cambridge University Press.

Siegel, D. J. (1999). *The developing mind: Toward a neurobiology of interpersonal experience*. New York, NY: Guilford Press.

Slade, A., Dermer, M., Gerber, J., Gibson, L., Graf, F., Siegel, N., & Tobias, K. (1995). *Prenatal representation, dyadic interaction and quality of attachment*. Paper presented at the Society for Research in Child Development Conference, Indianapolis, IN.

Slade, A., Grienenberger, J., Bernbach, E., Levy, D., & Locker, A. (2005). Maternal reflective functioning, attachment, and the transmission gap: A preliminary study. *Attachment and Human Development*, *7*(3), 283–298.

Slade, A., Sadler, L., Dios-Kenn, C., Webb, D., Currier-Ezepchick, J., & Mayes, L. (2005). Minding the baby: A reflective parenting program. *Psychoanalytic Study of the Child*, *60*, 74–100.

Sossin, K. M., & Birklein, S. (2006). Nonverbal transmission of stress between parent and young child: Considerations and psychotherapeutic implications of a study of affective movement patterns. *Journal of Infant, Child, & Adolescent Psychotherapy*, *5*, 46–69.

Sossin, K. M., & Cohen, P. (2011, this issue). Children's play in the wake of loss and trauma. *Journal of Infant, Child and Adolescent Psychology*, *10*, 255–272.

Sroufe, A. (1983). Infant-caregiver attachment and patterns of adaptation in the preschool: The roots of maladaptation and competence. In M. Permutter (Ed.), *Minnesota symposia on child psychology* (Vol. 16, pp. 41–79). Hillsdale, NJ: Erlbaum Associates.

Sroufe, L. (2005). Attachment and development: A prospective, longitudinal study from birth to adulthood. *Attachment & Human Development*, *7*(4), 349–367.

Steele, M., Steele, H., & Murphy, A. (2010). The adult attachment interview and relational trauma: Implications for parent-infant psychotherapy. In T. Baradon (Ed.), *Relational trauma in infancy: Psychoanalytic, attachment and neuropsychological contributions to parent-infant psychotherapy* (pp. 180–194). London, England: Routledge.

Steele, H., Steele, M., Croft, C., & Fonagy, P. (2001). Infant-mother attachment at one year predicts children's understanding of mixed emotions at six years. *Social Development*, *8*(2), 161–178.

Sugar, M. (1992). Toddler's traumatic memories. *Infant Mental Health Journal*, *13*, 245–251.

Tennant, C. (1988). Parental loss in childhood: Its effects on adult life. *Archives of General Psychiatry*, *45*, 1045–1050.

Terr, L. (1988). What happens to early memories of trauma: A study of twenty children under age five at the time of documented traumatic events. *Journal of the American Academy of Child and Adolescent Psychiatry*, *27*, 96–104.

Tomlinson, M., Cooper, P., & Murray, L. (2005). The mother-infant relationship and infant attachment in a South African peri-urban settlement. *Child Development*, *76*, 1044–1054.

Tortora, S. (2006). *The dancing dialogue: Using the communicative power of movement with young children*. Baltimore, MD: Paul H. Brookes Publishing Co., Inc.

Tortora, S. (2011, this issue). Beyond the face and words: How the body speaks. *Journal of Infant, Child and Adolescent Psychology*, *10*, 242–254.

Toth, S., Rogosch, F., & Cicchetti, D. (2008). Attachment-theory-informed intervention and reflective functioning in depressed mothers. In *Clinical applications of the adult attachment interview* (pp. 154–172). New York, NY: Guilford Press.

Tremblay, G., & Israel, A. (1998). Children's adjustment to parental death. *Clinical Psychology-Science and Practice*, *5*(4), 424–438.

Tronick, E., Ricks, M., & Cohn, J. (1982). Maternal and infant affective exchanges: Patterns of adaptation. In T. Field & N. Fox (Eds.), *Emotion and interaction: Normal and high-risk infants* (pp. 83–100). Hillsdale, NJ: Erlbaum.

Tronick, E. (1989). Emotions and emotional communication in infants. *American Psychologist*, *44*, 112–119.

Tronick, E., & Reck, C. (2009). Infants of depressed mothers. *Harvard Review of Psychiatry*, *17*(2), 47–56.

Tweed, J., Schoenbach, V., George, L., & Blazer, D. (1989). The effects of childhood parental death and divorce on six-month history of anxiety disorders. *British Journal of Psychiatry, 154*, 823–828.

van Ijzendoorn, M., Juffer, F., & Duyvesteyn, M. (1995). Breaking the intergenerational cycle of insecure attachment: A review of the effects of attachment-based interventions on maternal sensitivity and infant security. *Journal of Child Psychology and Psychiatry, 36*(2), 225–248.

Valent, P. (1998). *From survival to fulfillment. A framework for the life-trauma dialectic*. Philadelphia, PA: Brunner/Mazel.

Vondra, J., Shaw, D., Swearingen, L., Cohen, M., & Owens, B. (1999). Early relationship quality from home to school: A longitudinal study. *Early Education & Development, 10*(2), 163–190.

Warren, S., Gunnar, M., Kagan, J., Anders, T., Simmens, S., Rones, M., . . . Sroufe, L. (2003). Maternal panic disorder: Infant temperament, neurophysiology, and parenting behavior. *Journal of the American Academy of Child and Adolescent Psychiatry, 42*, 814–825.

Warren, S., Huston, L., Egeland, B., & Sroufe, A. (1997). Child and adolescent anxiety disorders and early attachment. *Journal of the American Academy of Child and Adolescent Psychiatry, 36*(5), *637–644*.

Waters, E., Merrick, S., Treboux, D., Crowell, J., & Albersheim, L. (2000). Attachment security in infancy and early adulthood: A twenty-year longitudinal study. *Child Development, 71*(3), 684–689.

Weathers, F. W. (1993). *Rational and empirical scoring rules for the clinician-administered PTSD scale*. Unpublished manuscript.

Weinberg, K., & Tronick, E. (1998). The impact of maternal psychiatric illness on infant development. *Journal of Clinical Psychology, 59*, 53–61.

Weinberg, K., Tronick, E., Beeghly, M., Olson, K., Kernan, H., & Riley, J. (2001). Subsyndromal depressive symptoms and major depression in postpartum women. *American Journal of Orthopsychiatry, 71*(1), 87–97.

Weissman, M., Wickramaratne, P., Warner, J., John, K., Prusoff, B., Merikangas, K., & Gammon, D. (1987). Assessing psychiatric disorders in children. *Archives of General Psychiatry, 44*, 747–753.

Weissman, M., Pilowsky, D., Wickramaratne, P., Talati, A., Wisniewski, S., Fava, M., . . . Rush, J. (2006). Remissions in maternal depression and child psychopathology – A STAR*D-child report. *Journal of the American Medical Association, 295*, 1389–1393.

Weller, E., Weller, R., Fristad, M., Cain, S., & Bowes, J. (1988). Should children attend their parent's funeral? *Journal of the American Academy of Child and Adolescent Psychiatry, 27*, 559–562.

Wheaton, B., Roszell, P., & Hall, K. (1997). The impact of twenty childhood and adult traumatic stresses on the risk of psychiatric disorder. In I. Gotlieb & B. Wheaton (Eds.), *Stress and adversity over the life-course: Trajectories and turning point*. New York, NY: Cambridge University Press.

White, C. P., & King, K. (2011). Is maternal fatigue mediating the relationship between maternal depression and child outcomes? *Journal of Child and Family Studies*. doi: 10.1007/s10826-011-9452-5

Wilson, A., Lengua, L., Meltzoff, A., & Smith, K. (2010). Parenting and temperament prior to 9-11 and parenting specific to 9-11. *Journal of Clinical Child and Adolescent Psychology, 39*(4), 445–459.

Wolmer, L., Laor, N., Gershon, A., Mayes, L., & Cohen, D. J. (2000). The mother-child dyad facing trauma – a developmental outlook. *Journal of Nervous and Mental Disease, 188*, 409–415.

Worden, J., & Silverman, P. (1996). Parental death and the adjustment of school age children. *Omega, 33*, 91–102.

Yehuda, R., & Bierer, L. M. (2008). Transgenerational transmission of cortisol and PTSD risk. *Progress in Brain Research, 167*, 121–135.

Yehuda, R., Mulherin Engel, S., Brand, S. R., Seckl, J., Marcus, S. M., & Berkowitz, G. S. (2005). Transgenerational effects of posttraumatic stress disorder in babies of mothers exposed to the World Trade Center attacks during pregnancy. *The Journal of Clinical Endocrinology & Metabolism, 90*(7), 4115–4118.

Yehuda, R., Sertus, I., & Goler, J. (2001). Relationship between childhood traumatic experiences and PTSD in adults. In E. Spencer (Ed.), *PTSD in children and adolescents*. Washington, DC: American Psychiatric.

Yehuda, R., Southwick, S., Nussbaum, G., Wahlby, V., Giller, E., & Mason, J. (1990). Low urinary cortisol excretion in patients with post-traumatic stress disorder. *Journal of Nervous and Mental Disease, 178*, 366–369.

Zeanah, C., & Barton, M. (1989). Internal representations and parent-infant relationships. *Infant Mental Health Journal, 10*, 135–141.

Zeanah, C., Stafford, B., Boris, N., & Scheeringa, M. (2003). Infant development: The first 3 years of life. In A. Tasman, J. Kay, & J. Lieberman (Eds.), *Psychiatry* (2nd ed., Vol. 1, pp. 91–117). West Sussex, England: Wiley.

Zero to Three. (2005). Diagnostic classification: 0-3. *Diagnostic classification of mental health and developmental disorders of infancy and early childhood*. Arlington, VA: National Center for Clinical Infant Programs.

# COMMENTARY

# The Strength of Relationships in the Face of Trauma From Terror

Marsha Kaitz, Ph.D.

The Project for Mothers, Infants, and Young Children was established for bereaved families. Looking from afar (Jerusalem, Israel), I hold in mind a vivid representation of the Project as concentric circles in which the bereaved mothers and children are positioned at the center, encircled by the support of the therapists in the Project, who are standing (figuratively) shoulder-to-shoulder and hand-in-hand for mutual and reciprocal support. At each level, interpersonal support is generated, diffuses, and permeates to others on the same rung and also across rungs. This commentary focuses primarily on the outer rung, the one that can be envisioned as therapists holding each other, encircling the families. I discuss the therapists' mutual support through linkage of emotions, common goals, and brain-to-brain connections. The therapists' reciprocal support is the foundation, essential character, and the strength of the Project, and it is passed to and reinforced by the trust of the families that are served.

## PREFACE

I have read this manuscript from afar, both in physical distance (I live in Israel) and in perspective, as I was not part of the World Trade Center Intervention Project described here by founding members, Dr. Beebe and her colleagues. At the same time, the Project is most relevant to me. As an Israeli and one who has raised a family in Jerusalem (a city with a history of terror attacks), I am sorrowfully aware of the effects that terror can have on individuals and families. Professionally, I have worked with mothers who were directly exposed to terror in the course of research studies (e.g., Kaitz, Devor, & Stecklov, 2008; Kaitz, Levy, Ebstein, Faraone, & Mankuta, 2009) and in field work. I might add that I have spent half my life living in the United States (East Coast) and half in Jerusalem.

With this background, I approached the writing of this commentary with modesty, and with some ideas about culture and trauma, challenges in treating trauma victims, and possibilities for future expansion of the intervention Project described in this special issue of the *Journal of Infant, Child, and Adolescent Psychotherapy*. I felt more comfortable with this kind of multipoint format then what seemed to me the (audacious) goal of summarizing the content of the articles, which were written on the basis of first-hand knowledge of the Project, heart-felt familiarity with the families that it served, and because the Project is not mine. However, the multipoint essay that I had envisioned evolved "organically" into a semi-unified whole, with overriding themes of attachment, affiliation, social support, and relationships, which seem absolutely fitting to the spirit of the intervention Project described in other articles in this issue. Although these constructs have frequently been tied to trauma (e.g., Connor, 2006; Schwarzer & Knoll, 2007), the efficacy of a WTC relation-based intervention project, as described in every article, demonstrates the healing power of social connections in the context of one of the most dastardly acts in human history.

## INTRODUCTION

The articles in this special issue describe a primary prevention project for mothers, infants, and young children of September 11, 2001, which was initiated by a group of therapists in the wake of the terror attacks on the twin towers in New York on September 11, 2001. The Project aims to help families who had suffered the loss of spouse/father as a result of the attacks and, in particular, families in which the wife/mother was pregnant at the time that their husbands were killed. The focus on these families was motivated by evidence that the trauma experienced by mothers can affect their children, even if they had not been born at the time of the traumatic events (Danieli, 1998). Also, one route of intergenerational transmission is insensitive mothering, which has been related to trauma and its correlates, including posttraumatic stress disorder (PTSD) and depression (Kaitz et al., 2009). On this basis, the aim of the intervention Project was to offer emotional support, guidance, and a secure base to the mothers in hopes that they would be better able to provide the same to their infants, once born, and to their older children, if they had them. Methods of intervention include psychotherapy and support groups for treating mothers, age-appropriate methods (e.g., play therapy) for treating children, and video feedback for observing fine details of mother-infant and mother-child interactions. This manuscript marks the tenth year anniversary of the Project.

## STAGE I: LAYING THE FOUNDATION

### Therapists Joining Together

For Dr. Beebe and her colleagues, the motives for considering a project aimed at supporting the grieving families were complex, and the candidness with which the therapists describe their feelings during the early stages of the Project are important for understanding the bases of their initiative. The therapists mention a felt need to secure humanity, to do something, to regulate their own inner states, as well as to care for and soothe others. Perhaps above all, the Project was motivated by the therapists' knowledge that help and support for the grieving families was needed *now* in an effort to prevent the traumatic experiences from being "etched" (perhaps, permanently) into mothers' and children's brains (and hearts) and to thwart the risk that the trauma suffered by the parents would affect their children (Pine, Costello, & Masten, 2005; Yehuda, 2002; Yehuda & Hyman, 2005). The importance of treating trauma victims has been described in many studies (e.g., Foa, Cahill, Boscarino, Hobfoll, Lahad, McNally, & Solomon, 2005; Ritchie, Watson, & Friedman, 2006). For families that had endured sudden, traumatic loss on September 11, 2001, the WTC intervention Project offered the highest standard of professional care and support, without charge.

The therapists' description of their feelings at the start of the Project also provides insight into the minds of thoughtful professionals who were struggling with realizing events that were almost incomprehensible and suffering from some degree of trauma themselves. I believe that it is a mark of their professionalism, strength, and commitment that, under these circumstances, the therapists were able to plan and design the intervention Project and reach out to grieving families. The initiative of the therapists also serves as an example of the now recognized response to stress called "tend and befriend," which refers to the management of stress by caring for others, seeking or giving social support, and forming groups (Taylor & Master, 2011). Important research is now uncovering the neuro-circuit that prompts such stress-related affiliative efforts, and it seems that this system regulates social approach behavior, much as hunger and thirst regulate approach to food and drink. Evolutionarily, tending and befriending in the face of challenge is adaptive because it promotes safety for self and the social group.

The affiliation of like-minded professionals for mutual emotional and professional support in the early stages of the Project was critical to its "health" and solidity during its development. Without doubt, partnering with others who are committed, have similar visions, and are there for the long haul is one sure way that a project will be given a fighting chance at its fragile beginning. As in the early days after childbirth, "caregivers" (of new projects) need support because it regulates internal state, cognitions, and behavior (Cohen & Willis, 1985); promotes sensitivity to others; and provides a "push" when needed and reminders of the importance of the job at hand. Further, support that is mutual builds relationships and affords the opportunity for organizers to merge different perspectives so that solutions rest on a broad and stable base. More importantly, mutual support knits persons into a cooperative team. Here I am reminded of our Jerusalem-based home-visiting program for distressed mothers of infants ("Mom-to-Mom," funded by the Harris Foundation, Chicago, IL), which is "co-parented" by me and my friends and colleagues Miriam Chriki and Naomi Tessler. I knew from the beginning of the project and am reminded every day (for the past 11 years) that our trust and commitment to one another are essential to our efforts to support families. Our deeply-felt interpersonal connection, quite simply, makes the home-visiting project possible. Without it I am quite sure that, years ago, the home-visiting project would have gotten lost in the piles of work on the desk, despite our good intentions. In more general terms, partnerships that "work" serve to strengthen not only personal resolve but also the very foundation on which projects are built, so that future development and expansion can be grounded in a solid, secure, and strong foundation.

## Outreach to Families

The challenge of reaching families is discussed repeatedly in the articles of this special issue, and the therapists' disappointment and distress at not reaching as many as they would have liked is clearly transmitted. With this, it is not surprising that some families refused help. As noted in the other articles in this issue, some parents shied away from exposing their feelings to strangers, were certain that nothing would help, were very busy with the practical considerations related to the death of their spouse, or were so pained by their own grief that it was difficult to plan or make meetings. Again, I am reminded of our own challenges in reaching parents who are in need of support, because here, too, some mothers, including those with histories of trauma and mental health issues, choose not to participate because they are embarrassed that they need help or are so overwhelmed that they do not know what to do with our offer. Indeed, many mothers who joined our home-visiting project months after childbirth have told us that they were sorry they did not join our project earlier, but explained that that their energy was devoted in full to getting through the day — or in the words of some, just surviving.

Given the difficult circumstances surrounding the aftermath of September 11, 2001, and in reaching the families, it is a testimony to the New York team's efforts that 40 joined the Project. It also is a testimony to the strength of the mothers who were willing to expose their feelings to strangers in the hopes that it would help them and their families. In this regard, much could be learned from a discussion of specific outreach techniques that worked (or did not work) and the kinds of families who were willing to participate and those who were not in order to tune and improve the efficacy of outreach efforts. These issues are important because outreach is crucial for most intervention projects, and many rise or fall on the ability to bring clients to their doors. Once there, the processes of affiliation and attachment between client and therapist can take hold, strengthen relations between them, and increase the likelihood that they will coalesce into an effective therapeutic team.

## STAGE II: WORKING TOGETHER AND BUILDING RELATIONSHIPS

### The Therapists

Deep-seated trust and affectional bonds between the professionals are clearly expressed throughout this issue. Although some of the therapists knew each other prior to the Project, once they embarked on the Project together their shared goals, the shared responsibility of caring/treating families, and the dependable, supportive backup that they provided for one another clearly had an important role in strengthening relationships and drawing the professionals into a joint (intersubjective) space that was and is fostered by shared subjective and real experiences (Beebe, Knoblauch, Rustin, & Sorter, 2005). Although the composition of the group changed over time, the respect that the group members have for each other, their shared and deep concern for the families who were victims of the September 11 attacks, and their common goals seems to be what held and continues to hold the Project together.

Of special note is the co-therapy (several therapists for each family) and the evolution of a "peer group forum," which served as a place for the Project team to manage rejections and disruptions and to contain anxiety and disappointment (see Cohen, *The Evolution of the Project,* this issue). I also am sure that, at times, the peer forum served as a safe place to let off steam, provided opportunities for relief from stress, and curtailed the risk of burnout. Scholars in the field of development and interpersonal relations have explicitly discussed the importance of sharing goals, attentional focus, emotions, and physiology as a basis for interpersonal connectedness.

Although often described in the context of mother-infant interactions (e.g., Trevarthen & Hubley, 1978), these same processes foster and strengthen personal ties, trust, and the potential for secure attachment between persons of all ages (Stern, 2004).

In the words of Trevarthen (2001, p. 98), "It is also becoming very clear that the human central nervous system, with the human body, is designed for an exceptionally elaborate brain-to-brain linking so that . . . the brain [of one person] can powerfully interact with the brain of another person." For adults, brain-to-brain linking often comes from and promotes the sharing of intersubjective space. It requires trust but also encourages it and expands creative energy and informational sources. Interpersonal brain (or mind) connections promote the mutual regulation of emotions, meaning that emotions are reciprocally kept balanced and maintained within comfortable and appropriate bounds. The deep, visceral connections among the therapists are clearly part of the foundation, the support structure, and the essential character of the Project, and these connections apparently continue to benefit the therapists and the families that they serve.

## Therapists and Families

The interventions offered to families by the Project were aimed at providing the families with a secure base and for promoting parents' mindfulness and sensitivity, with regard to themselves and their children. In keeping with this, listening, caring, and perspicuity were among the therapists' primary tools for gaining the families' trust, establishing and maintaining relationships with the parents and children, and competently tuning the therapeutic process to their needs. The effectiveness with which the therapists were able to follow the families, to move on (with them) from the place of acute stress and turmoil to grieving, and then through the recuperative and healing process, is an amazing achievement. It is especially so given that some of the children were young infants at the start of the Project and are almost 10 years old today. In addition, the success and longevity of the Project also speak to the willingness of the families to depend on professionals and to allow themselves not only to grieve but also to heal, in front of others, without guilt, knowing that their feelings would be appreciated and understood.

The strong feelings that the therapists developed toward the families and their work together is a common thread woven throughout this collection of articles. According to the expressed emotions of the some of the mothers who participated in the Project, feelings of the participants were mutual (see "The Mothers' Experiences of the Project," this issue). In part, this was made possible by the stated goal of the therapists not to act as the "experts" but rather to serve as a source of dependable support and to foster connections between parents and children and among mothers in the Project so that they could support each other. Dr. Sally Moskowitz describes this beautifully when she writes, "We tried to hold the mothers so that they could hold the babies" (see Moskowitz, this issue). It is difficult to think of a better gift for the mothers and their children than that.

## Promoting and Sustaining a Secure Bond Between Mothers and Infants

One aim of the intervention Project was to provide mothers with the emotional strength and availability to hear and respond sensitivity to their infants, thus promoting a secure bond between them. Both the use of video feedback in conjunction with group support, together with the support of an empathetic and knowledgeable professional, has been shown to be highly effective in these respects (Beebe, 2005; Jones, 2006). Within the Project, these methods and tools were effective in directing mothers' attention toward their children, seeing their needs, and being mindful of the effect they (the mothers) have on their children. The gentle guidance of the professionals in helping mother to see the fine details, of not being scared, of recognizing and accepting who they are and who their children are *now* was, in the mothers' own words, an essential part of the healing process.

### Supportive Alliances: Circles of Support Within Circles of Support

From the first articles of this special issue, I have imagined the therapists involved in the Project as standing arm-in-arm or hand-in-hand, encircling the mothers and their children. The hug that was constructed by the mutual support of professionals encircling the families seems to have been core strength of the Project. It seems to have provided the therapists with a sense of security and, at the same time, enabled the families to feel well taken care of, to lower their stress levels, and to open their minds and hearts to the feelings of their children, without fear, and with the sensitivity that can foster and maintain good relations between professionals and the families and between the parents and their children. Further, as years passed, the borders of "the hug" seemed to fuse so that families' strengths and experiences merged with those of the therapists—producing a "family" with mutual interests and interpersonal appreciation, respect, and trust that seemed to benefit all concerned and will likely remain part of their lives forever.

## FUTURE DIRECTIONS: EXPANDING THE CIRCLE OF SUPPORT

Efforts to describe the aims, history, challenges, and successes of the Project on its tenth anniversary are important because there is so much to learn from the Project. Of special note is the use of multiple therapists for one family, the marriage of video microanalysis and video feedback with more traditional psychotherapy, and the focus on mothers who were traumatized during pregnancy and on the intergenerational transmission of trauma. Getting the word out about such a creative and novel project is essential for teaching, guiding, and supporting similar efforts by other teams of professionals who treat victims of trauma, whether it be of terror or other kinds of violence.

In this regard, it would be important to complement information provided in this issue with evaluation data in the form of group comparisons (controls vs. treatment groups), clinical assessment, and observation of children in the cohort who were born before versus after September 11, 2001, or perhaps feedback from mothers and children who participated in the Project, in order to learn about their retrospective feelings about different aspects of the Project. This kind of information can provide insight into what worked well or did not work and how to improve and tune the Project for future use with families who suffer trauma from terror or other pathogens.

In addition, it would be wonderful if different projects aimed at supporting families that had endured sudden traumatic loss could be compared in order to learn how to merge them for optimal effectiveness. Extending this further, it would be beneficial if additional sources of support and guidance (e.g., lawyers, financial advisors, medical specialists, occupational therapy, professional enrichment) could be knit into the intervention project (from the beginning) so that a package of services could be offered to families in need. The addition of services and the integration of professionals from different projects and different areas/domains would essentially widen and strengthen the "hug" around families and would serve as a reminder that, along with our fragility as humans and the terrible things that can happen to us and our society, there is a community of men and women who care and who can help us pick up the pieces and go on. As repeatedly described in this issue, timely and effective support can go far in helping victims, combating negative world views, pessimism, and despair that can be elicited by terror and can continue for years afterwards if not resolved. Equally important, our efforts to affiliate, treat, and help in the aftermath of terror can counter the intimidation and widespread fear which are among the major goals of terrorists. Effective efforts in this direction, exemplified by the Project for Mothers, Infants and Young Children of September 11, 2001, need to be supported, emulated, and applauded.

## BIBLIOGRAPHY

Anonymous. (2011, this issue). The mothers' experiences of the project. *Journal of Infant, Child, and Adolescent Psychotherapy*, *10*, 202–204.

Beebe, B. (2005). Mother-infant research informs mother-infant treatment. *Psychoanalytic Study of the Child*, *60*, 7–46.

Beebe, B., Knoblauch, S., Rustin, J., & Sorter, J. (2005). *Forms of intersubjectivity in infant research and adult treatment*. New York, NY: Other Press.

Cohen, S., & Willis, T. A. (1985). Stress, social support, and the buffering hypothesis. *Psychological Bulletin*, *98*, 310–357.

Connor, K. M. (2006). Assessment of resilience in the aftermath of trauma. *Journal of Clinical Psychiatry*, *67*, 46–69.

Danieli, Y. (1998). *Intergenerational handbook of multigenerational legacies of trauma*. New York, NY: Plenum Press.

Foa, E. B., Cahill, S. P., Boscarino, J. A., Hobfoll, S. E., Lahad, M., McNally, R. J., & Solomon, Z. (2005). Social, psychological, and psychiatric interventions following terrorist attacks: Recommendations for practice and research. *Neuropsychopharmacology*, *30*, 1806–1817.

Jones, A. (2006). How video can bring to view pathological defensive processes and facilitate the creation of triangular space in perinatal parent-infant psychotherapy. *Infant Observation*, *9*, 109–123.

Kaitz, M., Devor, N., & Stecklov, G. (2008). Anxiety symptoms of new mothers during a period of recurrent, local terror. *Journal of Affective Disorders*, *107*, 211–215.

Kaitz, M., Levy, M., Ebstein, R., Faraone, S., & Mankuta, D. (2009). The intergenerational effects of trauma from terror: A real possibility. *Infant Mental Health Journal*, *30*, 158–179.

Moskowitz, S. (2011, this issue). Primary maternal preoccupation disrupted by trauma and loss: Early years of the project. *Journal of Infant, Child, and Adolescent Psychotherapy*, *10*, 229–237.

Pine, D., Costello, J., & Masten, A. (2005). Trauma, proximity, and developmental psycholopathology: The effects of war and terrorism on children. *Neuropsychopharmacology*, *30*, 1781–1792.

Ritchie, E., Watson, P., & Friedman, M. (Eds.). (2006). *Interventions following mass violence and disasters: Strategies for mental health practice*. New York, NY: Guilford Press.

Schwarzer, R., & Knoll, N. (2007). Functional roles of social support within the stress and coping process: A theoretical and empirical overview. *International Journal of Psychology*, *42*, 243–252.

Stern, D. (2004). *The present moment in psychotherapy and everyday life*. New York, NY: WW Norton & Company.

Taylor, S. (2006). Tend and befriend: Biobehavioral bases of affiliation under stress. *Current Directions in Psychological Science*, *15*, 273–277.

Taylor, S., & Master, S. (2011). Social responses to stress: The tend-and-befriend model. R. J. Contrada & A. Baum (Eds.), *The handbook of stress science: Biology, psychology, and health* (pp. 101–109). New York, NY: Springer Publishing Co.

Trevarthen, C. (2001). Intrinsic motives for companionship in understanding: Their origin, development, and significance for infant mental health. *Infant Mental Health Journal*, *22*, 95–131.

Trevarthen, C., & Hubley, P. (1978). Secondary intersubjectivity: Confidence, confiding and acts of meaning in the first year. In A. Lock (Ed.), *Action, gesture and symbol: The emergence of language* (pp. 183–229). London, England: Academic Press.

Yehuda, R. (2002). Post-traumatic stress disorder. *New England Journal of Medicine*, *346*, 108–114.

Yehuda, R., & Hyman, S. (2005). The impact of terrorism on brain, and behavior: What we know and what we need to know. *Neuropsychopharmacology*, *30*, 1773–1780.

# Conclusion

## Phyllis Cohen, Ph.D.

This book has addressed the early years of our primary prevention Project for mothers pregnant and widowed on September 11, 2001, and their infants and young children. We have described the intensely difficult time following the traumatic loss of the husband and father in these families. We also have described some of the struggles and accomplishments leading up to the present time. We found these mothers and children to be distraught and vulnerable when we first met them, nearly 10 years ago. Now, with time and support, families have grown, parent-child relationships have flourished, and some of the children have amazed us with their capacity to talk about their fathers and their loss. On the other hand, we are aware of the sorrows and voids that still remain.

While the mothers experienced the immediate depression, dissociation, and disorganization that were inevitable consequences of trauma and loss, they have been, from the beginning, dedicated to their children and to the well-being of their families. Over time their understanding has deepened with an added sensitivity to their children's internal worlds and emotional needs.

The mothers and their children who have remained in our Project have made significant gains. As life's transitions have evolved, including, for some, new marriages, new siblings, and new homes, many of the mothers have utilized Project support to help them navigate these changes. As the children have developed cognitively and emotionally, mothers have sought help in explaining the loss of the father to their children and have found ways to represent him. In turn, these efforts have aided the children in experiencing enduring connections with their lost fathers.

In this primary prevention Project we have offered mother-infant groups, videotaped sessions of mother-child and therapist-child interactions, and video feedback consultations with mothers in a clinical intervention. The families have shared many of their joys and disappointments with us, and in turn, we have helped them to construct more coherent narratives of their lives and family histories. As the children enter adolescence, new identity challenges will inevitably emerge and new experiences will bring new challenges. We plan to continue following these families. We also plan to use some of the data that we have collected for research in the future. In the wake of such devastating loss, we have witnessed remarkable resilience, growth, and the re-emergence of hope.

# Index

Page numbers followed by n represent endnotes.